MW00477639

# Records of
# North American
# Elk and Mule Deer

# RECORDS OF NORTH AMERICAN ELK AND MULE DEER

A book of the Boone and Crockett Club containing tabulations of elk and mule deer of North America as compiled from data in the Club's Big Game Records Archives.

Edited by Wm. H. Nesbitt and Jack Reneau

First Edition
1991
The Boone and Crockett Club
Dumfries, Virginia

Records of North American Elk and Mule Deer

First Edition - 1991

Library of Congress Catalog Card Number: 91-073121
ISBN Number: 0-940864-18-5
Published August 1991


Published in the United States of America
by the
Boone and Crockett Club
P.O. Box 547
Dumfries, VA  22026

# Contents

# Illustrations

# INTRODUCTION

*The Story of This Book*

The Boone and Crockett Club has universal recognition as the source for "the" records book for native North American big game. The Club has published its all-time records books at roughly six-year intervals since adoption of the current scoring system in 1950, with nine such editions to date. (*Records of North American Big Game*, 9th Ed., 1988 is the latest issue of the all-time records book.) The first "Awards period" records book, (*Boone and Crockett Club's 18th Big Game Awards*) published in 1984, summarized only the years of the 18th Awards entry period, 1980-1982. The 19th (1983-1985) and 20th (1986-1988) Awards records books then followed, using the same basic pattern of data presentation and book design as that of the 18th Awards.

The two books differ significantly in content. The huge number of trophies in the all-time records (nearly 10,000 in the 9th Edition, 1988), allows little room for much beyond the trophy listings and a dozen short chapters on subjects pertaining to the records and other Boone and Crockett Club interest areas. The fewer trophies of an Awards records book (just over 2,100 in the 20th Awards records), permits featuring the photo and hunting story, in the hunter's own words, for each of the award-winning trophies. This results in nearly 100 "armchair hunts," providing unique and enjoyable reading about big-game hunting today.

But, even with these two fine book series, there existed a void. North America's favorite big game animal, the whitetail deer, easily merited a separate records book. That book, *Records of North American Whitetail Deer*, became reality in 1986 and it proved popular from the start. It established state and provincial records and ranked lists, for both typical and non-typical categories. For the first time, interested parties could consult a single volume to determine state records, how many made the "book" from a particular state or province, and other useful data. This book no doubt settled some long-standing arguments, while starting some others.

The first edition of the whitetail records featured two data items not found in the traditional records books, but of strong interest to deer hunters: greatest spread and the total of lengths of abnormal points for both typical and non-typical categories. Greatest spread does not figure into the Final Score, but it is a widely-used assessment of trophy character. The total of lengths of abnormal points is useful in forming an image of the rack and conformation, and the total does affect the final score. Both features proved popular. The 2nd Ed. (1991) had another new feature, the inclusion of *all-time rank* in addition to state or provincial rank. With this information, the reader has a very complete picture of where a trophy stands, in both the locality taken and in terms of the continuing all-time records. (State rank, by the way, does *not* appear in the data of the all-time and Awards records.)

The success of the whitetail records book suggested this approach should be considered for other categories. Naturally, the mule deer came to mind first, since it is the western equivalent of the whitetail and eagerly sought by hunters where it occurs. Combining elk with mule deer in a single volume made sense as they often exist on the same areas and are sought by the same segment of the hunting population. The successful features of the whitetail records book are included in this 1st Ed. of *Records of North American Elk and Mule Deer* and those who buy both books will notice many similarities.

The trophy listings presentation in this book, by state and province, makes comparison by state or province very easy but does pose a problem in easy location of the all-time top few trophies. For that reason, an index to the top 10 trophies is printed opposite the opening page of each major category section. This index provides a quick and easy to use reference to the largest trophies ever recorded for the category, and the reader can refer to the regular listing if detailed information is needed.

With this volume in hand, the reader can readily identify the areas that have historically produced larger specimens of elk and mule deer and make some general assessments of the better areas to plan a hunt for a "big-un." Just as importantly, areas of little promise are quickly eliminated from the short list of good prospects. Of course, going to an area that likely has large specimens is only one of the necessary factors that must be considered in hunt planning. Just as important are personal condition, desire, and perhaps a few prayers to, and hopefully a resultant smile from, Diana, the Goddess of the Hunt.

*Scoring of Trophies*

The current scoring system dates from its adoption date of 1950. It has been in continuing usage, without major change, which underscores its sound base. Its great strength lies in the repeatability of the measurements. Should someone question an individual measurement (or the entire scoring, for that matter), the measurements and scoring can be repeated to demonstrate correctness, even years after the original measurement. This is, of course, possible only because the enduring characters of skull (for cat and bear only), horns, and antlers are the measured characters. Had body length or weight (or some combination of such factors) been chosen, there could be no such repeating of the measurements. By relying on objective measurements of enduring characters, the system can be applied by almost anyone, and few folks would argue with the basic premise. That sense of understanding has greatly aided its universal acceptance as the system for native North American big game trophies.

*Typical or Non-Typical?*

Non-typical categories are described for both American elk and mule deer. There are no non-typical Roosevelt's elk or Columbia and Sitka blacktail deer. The non-typical category differs from the typical in the recording of the abnormal points (points beyond the "usual" pattern for a typical specimen). Such points are subtracted as a penalty from the final score for typical trophies, while in the non-typical category they add into the final score. Thus, the higher minimum entry score for the non-typical category. There is no set definition for how much non-typical material must be present to call a trophy "non-typical." In fact, that decision can be made by the trophy owner, with some preferring to call trophies with any abnormal points "non-typical."

With the non-typical designations, this book deals with seven separate records keeping categories: typical and non-typical American elk; Roosevelt's elk; typical and non-typical mule deer; Columbia blacktail deer; and Sitka blacktail deer. Although measuring technique is relatively the same for all, non-typicals and Roosevelt's elk require separate score charts. Keep in mind that the only basic difference in measuring typical and non-typical is the manner in which the abnormal points affect the final score.

## Geographic Boundaries

Geographically defined boundaries for trophy entry limit entries of Roosevelt's elk, Columbia blacktail deer, and Sitka blacktail deer. These boundaries are a reflection of the fact that these are smaller subspecies and the boundaries are necessary to prevent their larger cousins from being erroneously entered. For example, a small mule deer could be a large "Columbia blacktail" if there were no such boundaries. The general boundary descriptions appear in information given at the start of the data sections.

## Scoring of Trophies

Scoring of a trophy begins with careful reading of the Official Score Chart, then following its instructions to record the measurements. All five of the elk and mule deer charts (including typical and non-typical) are reproduced so you can fill them in to see how your favorite trophy stacks up. For detailed instructions and discussion of scoring *all* categories of acceptable big game, see the Club's book, *Measuring and Scoring North American Big Game Trophies*. Extensively illustrated, this book gives a step-by-step approach to measuring and scoring and is the basic reference for Official Measurers, as well as interested hunters.

## Entry of Trophies

Only an Official Measurer (specially trained and appointed by the Club) can measure a trophy for official entry into the records keeping. An official measurement cannot be made until the trophy has dried for at least 60 days, under normal atmospheric conditions, after kill. This is necessary to allow for the normal shrinkage that occurs in all trophies. This standard drying period ensures shrinkage will be relatively the same for all trophies, an impossible condition if green scores were allowed. Trophies in velvet must have it removed and dry for 60 days prior to an official measurement. This drying period also allows all trophies to be measured at roughly the same interval after kill. The sportsman on an extended hunting trip is not disadvantaged, as he or she would be by a "green score" system.

Official Measurers have all necessary materials for trophy entry, including the score charts for recording the entry measurements. Official Measurers donate their time to measure trophies as a public service, and there is no charge for a measurement. But, the trophy must be taken to them, and it must be at their convenience, since they donate their time. Sportsmen should premeasure their trophies to determine that an official measurement is necessary. This helps avoid wasting the measurer's time, as well as that of the trophy owner.

*The Awards Programs*

For the top-ranking trophies in each three-year program of trophy entry, there is special recognition available. The top few trophy entries of each category receive invitation to the triennial Awards program. There, a select panel of Official Measurers remeasure and certify the invited trophies for possible awards of the Boone and Crockett Club Medal and/or Certificate. Should an invited trophy not appear before the Judges Panel, its records book(s) listing will be with an asterisk and without rank, pending submission of additional verifying measurements. In the case of a potential World's Record, the trophy *must* come before a Judges Panel in order to be certified as a World's Record. There is *no* alternate path.

Trophies invited to an Awards program are on public display for an extended period that precedes the Awards banquet. These displays draw tens of thousands of people. Awards, as determined by the Judges Panel, are the highlight of the Awards Banquet.

The Awards entry periods are on a three-year basis, with the Awards events held during the following mid-year. Thus the 21st Awards will be held in 1992, with the three years of the 21st Awards entry period ending on 31 December 1991. Trophies acknowledged with an award at an Awards program will be profiled in the records book for that period, with a photo and the hunting story, in addition to the ranking of the trophy in its rightful place in the trophy rankings of that book.

Records of North American
Big Game

BOONE AND CROCKETT CLUB

P.O. Box 547
Dumfries, VA 22026

Minimum Score: Awards  All-time
360       375

TYPICAL
AMERICAN ELK (WAPITI)

DETAIL OF POINT
MEASUREMENT

| | Abnormal Points | |
|---|---|---|
| | Right Antler | Left Antler |
| | | |
| | | |
| | | |
| | | |

E. Total of Lengths
of Abnormal Points

| SEE OTHER SIDE FOR INSTRUCTIONS | | | Column 1 | Column 2 | Column 3 | Column 4 |
|---|---|---|---|---|---|---|
| A. No. Points on Right Antler | No. Points on Left Antler | | Spread Credit | Right Antler | Left Antler | Difference |
| B. Tip to Tip Spread | C. Greatest Spread | | | | | |
| D. Inside Spread of Main Beams | (Credit May Equal But Not Exceed Longer Antler) | | | | | |
| F. Length of Main Beam | | | | | | |
| G-1. Length of First Point | | | | | | |
| G-2. Length of Second Point | | | | | | |
| G-3. Length of Third Point | | | | | | |
| G-4. Length of Fourth (Royal) Point | | | | | | |
| G-5. Length of Fifth Point | | | | | | |
| G-6. Length of Sixth Point, If Present | | | | | | |
| G-7. Length of Seventh Point, If Present | | | | | | |
| H-1. Circumference at Smallest Place Between First and Second Points | | | | | | |
| H-2. Circumference at Smallest Place Between Second and Third Points | | | | | | |
| H-3. Circumference at Smallest Place Between Third and Fourth Points | | | | | | |
| H-4. Circumference at Smallest Place Between Fourth and Fifth Points | | | | | | |
| TOTALS | | | | | | |

| Enter Total of Columns 1, 2, and 3 | | Exact Locality Where Killed: | |
|---|---|---|---|
| Subtract Column 4 | | Date Killed: | By Whom Killed: |
| Subtotal | | Present Owner: | |
| Subtract (E) Total of Lengths of Abn. Points | | Guide Name and Address: | |
| FINAL SCORE | | Remarks: | |

6

I certify that I have measured the above trophy on _____ 19 _____

at (address) _____ City _____ State _____
and that these measurements and data are, to the best of my knowledge and belief, made in accordance with the instructions given.

Witness: _____ Signature _____

B&C OFFICIAL MEASURER

I.D. Number

## INSTRUCTIONS FOR MEASURING TYPICAL AMERICAN ELK (WAPITI)

All measurements must be made with a 1/4-inch flexible steel tape to the nearest one-eighth of an inch. Wherever it is necessary to change direction of measurement, mark a control point and swing tape at this point. (Note: a flexible steel cable can be used to measure points and main beams only.) Enter fractional figures in eighths, without reduction. Official measurements cannot be taken until the antlers have dried for at least 60 days after the animal was killed.

A. Number of Points on Each Antler: to be counted a point, the projection must be at least one inch long, with length exceeding width at one inch or more of length. All points are measured from tip of point to nearest edge of beam as illustrated. Beam tip is counted as a point but not measured as a point.

B. Tip to Tip Spread is measured between tips of main beams.

C. Greatest Spread is measured between perpendiculars at a right angle to the center line of the skull at widest part, whether across main beams or points.

D. Inside Spread of Main Beams is measured at a right angle to the center line of the skull at widest point between main beams. Enter this measurement again as Spread Credit if it is less than or equal to the length of longer antler; if longer, enter longer antler length for Spread Credit.

E. Total of Lengths of all Abnormal Points: Abnormal Points are those non-typical in location (such as points originating from a point or from bottom or sides of main beam) or pattern (extra points, not generally paired). Measure in usual manner and record in appropriate blanks.

F. Length of Main Beam is measured from lowest outside edge of burr over outer curve to the most distant point of what is, or appears to be, the main beam. The point of beginning is that point on the burr where the center line along the outer curve of the beam intersects the burr, then following generally the line of the illustration.

G. 1-2-3-4-5-6-7 Length of Normal Points: Normal points project from the top or front of the main beam in the general pattern illustrated. They are measured from nearest edge of main beam over outer curve to tip. Lay the tape along the outer curve of the beam so that the top edge of the tape coincides with the top edge of the beam on both sides of point to determine the baseline for point measurement. Record point length in appropriate blanks.

H. 1-2-3-4 Circumferences are taken as detailed for each measurement.

* * * * * * * * * * * * * * * * *

### FAIR CHASE STATEMENT FOR ALL HUNTER-TAKEN TROPHIES

To make use of the following methods shall be deemed as UNFAIR CHASE and unsportsmanlike, and any trophy obtained by use of such means is disqualified from entry.

    I.   Spotting or herding game from the air, followed by landing in its vicinity for pursuit;

    II.  Herding or pursuing game with motor-powered vehicles;

    III. Use of electronic communications for attracting, locating or observing game, or guiding the hunter to such game;

    IV.  Hunting game confined by artificial barriers, including escape-proof fencing; or hunting game transplanted solely for the purpose of commercial shooting.

* * * * * * * * * * * * * * * * *

I certify that the trophy scored on this chart was not taken in UNFAIR CHASE as defined above by the Boone and Crockett Club. I further certify that it was taken in full compliance with local game laws of the state, province, or territory.

Date _____ Signature of Hunter _____

(Have signature notarized by a Notary Public)

Records of North American
Big Game

BOONE AND CROCKETT CLUB

P.O. Box 547
Dumfries, VA 22026

Minimum Score: Awards  All-time
385         385

NON-TYPICAL
AMERICAN ELK (WAPITI)

| | Abnormal Points | |
|---|---|---|
| | Right Antler | Left Antler |
| | | |
| | | |
| | | |
| | | |
| | | |
| | | |
| | | |
| | | |
| | | |
| | | |
| | | |
| | | |

E. Total of Lengths
of Abnormal Points

| SEE OTHER SIDE FOR INSTRUCTIONS | | | Column 1 | Column 2 | Column 3 | Column 4 |
|---|---|---|---|---|---|---|
| A. No. Points on Right Antler | No. Points on Left Antler | | Spread Credit | Right Antler | Left Antler | Difference |
| B. Tip to Tip Spread | C. Greatest Spread | | | | | |
| D. Inside Spread of Main Beams | (Credit May Equal But Not Exceed Longer Antler) | | | | | |
| F. Length of Main Beam | | | | | | |
| G-1. Length of First Point | | | | | | |
| G-2. Length of Second Point | | | | | | |
| G-3. Length of Third Point | | | | | | |
| G-4. Length of Fourth (Royal) Point | | | | | | |
| G-5. Length of Fifth Point | | | | | | |
| G-6. Length of Sixth Point, If Present | | | | | | |
| G-7. Length of Seventh Point, If Present | | | | | | |
| H-1. Circumference at Smallest Place Between First and Second Points | | | | | | |
| H-2. Circumference at Smallest Place Between Second and Third Points | | | | | | |
| H-3. Circumference at Smallest Place Between Third and Fourth Points | | | | | | |
| H-4. Circumference at Smallest Place Between Fourth and Fifth Points | | | | | | |
| TOTALS | | | | | | |

| Enter Total of Columns 1, 2, and 3 | | Exact Locality Where Killed: | |
|---|---|---|---|
| | | Date Killed: | By Whom Killed: |
| Subtract Column 4 | | Present Owner: | |
| Subtotal | | Guide Name and Address: | |
| Add (E) Total of Lengths of Abnormal Points | | Remarks: | |
| FINAL SCORE | | | |

8

I certify that I have measured the above trophy on _____ 19 _____

at (address) _____ City _____ State _____
and that these measurements and data are, to the best of my knowledge and belief, made in accordance with the
instructions given.

Witness: _____ Signature _____

B&C OFFICIAL MEASURER

I.D. Number

## INSTRUCTIONS FOR MEASURING NON-TYPICAL AMERICAN ELK (WAPITI)

All measurements must be made with a 1/4-inch flexible steel tape to the nearest one-eighth of an inch. Wherever
it is necessary to change direction of measurement, mark a control point and swing tape at this point. (Note: a
flexible steel cable can be used to measure points and main beams only.) Enter fractional figures in eighths,
without reduction. Official measurements cannot be taken until the antlers have dried for at least 60 days after
the animal was killed.

A. Number of Points on Each Antler: to be counted as a point, the projection must be at least one inch long, with
length exceeding width at one inch or more of length. All points are measured from tip of point to nearest edge
of beam as illustrated. Beam tip is counted as a point but not measured as a point.

B. Tip to Tip Spread is measured between tips of main beams.

C. Greatest Spread is measured between perpendiculars at a right angle to the center line of the skull at widest
part, whether across main beams or points.

D. Inside Spread of Main Beams is measured at a right angle to the center line of the skull at widest point
between main beams. Enter this measurement again as the Spread Credit if it is less than or equal to the length
of longer antler; if longer, enter longer antler length for Spread Credit.

E. Total of Lengths of all Abnormal Points: Abnormal Points are those non-typical in location (such as points
originating from a point or from bottom or sides of main beam) or pattern (extra points, not generally paired).
Measure in usual manner and record in appropriate blanks.

F. Length of Main Beam is measured from lowest outside edge of burr over outer curve to the most distant point of
what is, or appears to be, the main beam. The point of beginning is that point on the burr where the center line
along the outer curve of the beam intersects the burr, then following generally the line of the illustration.

G. 1-2-3-4-5-6-7 Length of Normal Points: Normal points project from the top or front of the main beam in the
general pattern illustrated. They are measured from nearest edge of main beam over outer curve to tip. Lay the
tape along the outer curve of the beam so that the top edge of the tape coincides with the top edge of the beam
on both sides of point to determine the baseline for point measurement. Record point length in appropriate
blanks.

H. 1-2-3-4 Circumferences are taken as detailed for each measurement.

* * * * * * * * * * * * * * * * *

### FAIR CHASE STATEMENT FOR ALL HUNTER-TAKEN TROPHIES

To make use of the following methods shall be deemed as UNFAIR CHASE and unsportsmanlike, and any trophy
obtained by use of such means is disqualified from entry.

    I. Spotting or herding game from the air, followed by landing in its vicinity for pursuit;
    II. Herding or pursuing game with motor-powered vehicles;
    III. Use of electronic communications for attracting, locating or observing game, or guiding the
       hunter to such game;
    IV. Hunting game confined by artificial barriers, including escape-proof fencing; or hunting game
       transplanted solely for the purpose of commercial shooting.

* * * * * * * * * * * * * * * * *

I certify that the trophy scored on this chart was not taken in UNFAIR CHASE as defined above by the Boone
and Crockett Club. I further certify that it was taken in full compliance with local game laws of the
state, province, or territory.

Date _____ Signature of Hunter _____

(Have signature notarized by a Notary Public)

**Records of North American**
**Big Game**

BOONE AND CROCKETT CLUB

P.O. Box 547
Dumfries, VA 22026

Minimum Score: Awards All-time
                275       290

ROOSEVELT'S ELK

| Crown Points | |
|---|---|
| Right Antler | Left Antler |
| | |
| | |
| | |
| | |

I. Add to Total

| Abnormal Points | |
|---|---|
| Right Antler | Left Antler |
| | |
| | |
| | |
| | |

DETAIL OF POINT
MEASUREMENT

E. Total of Lengths
of Abnormal Points

SEE OTHER SIDE FOR INSTRUCTIONS

| | | | | Column 1 | Column 2 | Column 3 | Column 4 |
|---|---|---|---|---|---|---|---|
| A. No. Points on Right Antler | | No. Points on Left Antler | | Spread Credit | Right Antler | Left Antler | Difference |
| B. Tip to Tip Spread | | C. Greatest Spread | | | | | |
| D. Inside Spread of Main Beams | | (Credit May Equal But Not Exceed Longer Antler) | | | | | |
| F. Length of Main Beam | | | | | | | |
| G-1. Length of First Point | | | | | | | |
| G-2. Length of Second Point | | | | | | | |
| G-3. Length of Third Point | | | | | | | |
| G-4. Length of Fourth (Royal) Point | | | | | | | |
| G-5. Length of Fifth Point | | | | | | | |
| G-6. Length of Sixth Point, If Present | | | | | | | |
| G-7. Length of Seventh Point, If Present | | | | | | | |
| H-1. Circumference at Smallest Place Between First and Second Points | | | | | | | |
| H-2. Circumference at Smallest Place Between Second and Third Points | | | | | | | |
| H-3. Circumference at Smallest Place Between Third and Fourth Points | | | | | | | |
| H-4. Circumference at Smallest Place Between Fourth and Fifth Points | | | | | | | |
| | | TOTALS | | | | | |

| | | | |
|---|---|---|---|
| Enter Total of Columns 1, 2, 3 and (I) | | Exact Locality Where Killed: | |
| SUBTRACT Column 4 | | Date Killed: | By Whom Killed: |
| Subtotal | | Present Owner: | |
| SUBTRACT (E) Abn. Pts. | | Guide Name and Address: | |
| FINAL SCORE | | Remarks: | |

I certify that I have measured the above trophy on _____ 19 _____

at (address) _____ City _____ State _____
and that these measurements and data are, to the best of my knowledge and belief, made in accordance with the
instructions given.

Witness: _____ Signature _____

## INSTRUCTIONS FOR MEASURING ROOSEVELT'S ELK

All measurements must be made with a 1/4-inch flexible steel tape to the nearest one-eighth of an inch. Wherever it is necessary to change direction of measurement, mark a control point and swing tape at this point. (Note: a flexible steel cable can be used to measure points and main beams only.) Enter fractional figures in eighths, without reduction. Official measurements cannot be taken until the antlers have dried for at least 60 days after the animal was killed.

A. Number of Points on Each Antler: to be counted a point, the projection must be at least one inch long, with length exceeding width at one inch or more of length. All points are measured from tip of point to nearest edge of beam as illustrated. Beam tip is counted as a point but not measured as a point.

B. Tip to Tip Spread is measured between tips of main beams.

C. Greatest Spread is measured between perpendiculars at a right angle to the center line of the skull at widest part, whether across main beams or points.

D. Inside Spread of Main Beams is measured at a right angle to the center line of the skull at widest point between main beams. Enter this measurement again as the Spread Credit if it is less than or equal to the length of longer antler; if longer, enter longer antler length for Spread Credit.

E. Total of Lengths of all Abnormal Points: Abnormal Points are those non-typical in location (such as points originating from a point or from bottom or sides of main beam) or pattern (extra points, not generally paired). Measure in usual manner and record in appropriate blanks. **Note: do not confuse with Crown Point that may occur at base of Royal.**

F. Length of Main Beam is measured from lowest outside edge of burr over outer curve to the most distant point of what is, or appears to be, the main beam. The point of beginning is that point on the burr where the center line along the outer curve of the beam intersects the burr, then following generally the line of the illustration.

G. 1-2-3-4-5-6-7 Length of Normal Points: Normal points project from the top or front of the main beam in the general pattern illustrated. They are measured from nearest edge of main beam over outer curve to tip. Lay the tape along the outer curve of the beam so that the top edge of the tape coincides with the top edge of the beam on both sides of point to determine the baseline for point measurement. Record point length in appropriate blanks.

H. 1-2-3-4 Circumferences are taken as detailed for each measurement.

I. Crown Points: From the well-defined Royal on out to end of beam, all points other than the normal points in their typical locations are Crown Points. This includes points occurring on the Royal, on other normal points, and on Crown Points. Measure and record in appropriate blanks provided and add to score below.

* * * * * * * * * * * * * * * * *

## FAIR CHASE STATEMENT FOR ALL HUNTER-TAKEN TROPHIES

To make use of the following methods shall be deemed as UNFAIR CHASE and unsportsmanlike, and any trophy obtained by use of such means is disqualified from entry.

I. Spotting or herding game from the air, followed by landing in its vicinity for pursuit;

II. Herding or pursuing game with motor-powered vehicles;

III. Use of electronic communications for attracting, locating or observing game, or guiding the hunter to such game;

IV. Hunting game confined by artificial barriers, including escape-proof fencing; or hunting game transplanted solely for the purpose of commercial shooting.

* * * * * * * * * * * * * * * * * *

I certify that the trophy scored on this chart was not taken in UNFAIR CHASE as defined above by the Boone and Crockett Club. I further certify that it was taken in full compliance with local game laws of the state, province, or territory.

Date _____ Signature of Hunter _____

(Have signature notarized by a Notary Public)

| Records of North American Big Game | BOONE AND CROCKETT CLUB | P.O. Box 547 Dumfries, VA 22026 |
|---|---|---|

| Minimum Score: | Awards | All-time |
|---|---|---|
| mule | 185 | 195 |
| Columbia | 120 | 130 |
| Sitka | 100 | 108 |

TYPICAL
MULE AND BLACKTAIL DEER

Kind of Deer _____

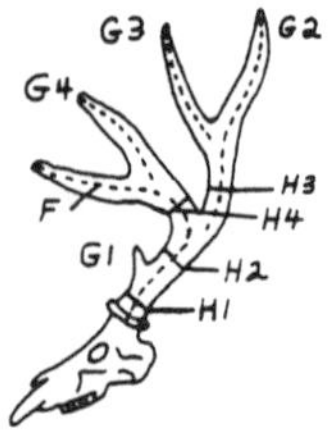

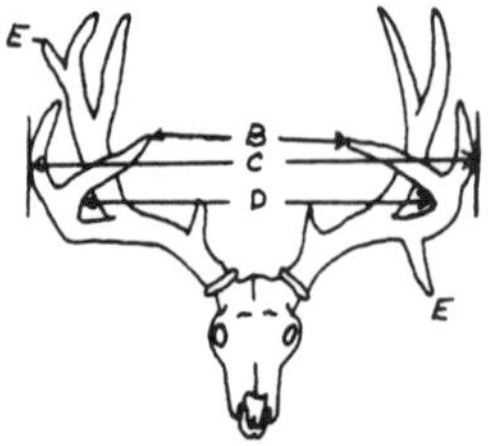

DETAIL OF POINT MEASUREMENT

|  | Abnormal Points | |
|---|---|---|
|  | Right Antler | Left Antler |
|  |  |  |
|  |  |  |
|  |  |  |
|  |  |  |
| E. Total of Lengths of Abnormal Points |  |  |

| SEE OTHER SIDE FOR INSTRUCTIONS | | Column 1 | Column 2 | Column 3 | Column 4 |
|---|---|---|---|---|---|
| | | Spread Credit | Right Antler | Left Antler | Difference |
| A. No. Points on Right Antler | No. Points on Left Antler | | | | |
| B. Tip to Tip Spread | C. Greatest Spread | | | | |
| D. Inside Spread of Main Beams | (Credit May Equal But Not Exceed Longer Antler) | | | | |
| F. Length of Main Beam | | | | | |
| G-1. Length of First Point, if Present | | | | | |
| G-2. Length of Second Point | | | | | |
| G-3. Length of Third Point, if Present | | | | | |
| G-4. Length of Fourth Point, if Present | | | | | |
| H-1. Circumference at Smallest Place Between Burr and First Point | | | | | |
| H-2. Circumference at Smallest Place Between First and Second Points | | | | | |
| H-3. Circumference at Smallest Place Between Main Beam and Third Point | | | | | |
| H-4. Circumference at Smallest Place Between Second and Fourth Points | | | | | |
| TOTALS | | | | | |

| Enter Total of Columns 1, 2, and 3 | | Exact Locality Where Killed: | |
|---|---|---|---|
| Subtract Column 4 | | Date Killed: | By Whom Killed: |
| Subtotal | | Present Owner: | |
| Subtract (E) Total of Lengths of Abn. Points | | Guide Name and Address: | |
| FINAL SCORE | | Remarks: | |

I certify that I have measured the above trophy on _____ 19 _____

at (address) _____ City _____ State _____
and that these measurements and data are, to the best of my knowledge and belief, made in accordance with the
instructions given.

Witness: _____ Signature: _____

## INSTRUCTIONS FOR MEASURING TYPICAL MULE AND BLACKTAIL DEER

All measurements must be made with a 1/4-inch flexible steel tape to the nearest one-eighth of an inch. Wherever it is necessary to change direction of measurement, mark a control point and swing tape at this point. (Note: a flexible steel cable can be used to take point and beam length measurements only.) Enter fractional figures in eighths, without reduction. Official measurements cannot be taken until antlers have dried for at least 60 days after the animal was killed.

A. Number of Points on Each Antler: to be counted a point, the projection must be at least one inch long, with length exceeding width at one inch or more of length. All points are measured from tip of point to nearest edge of beam as illustrated. Beam tip is counted as a point but not measured as a point.

B. Tip to Tip Spread is measured between tips of main beams.

C. Greatest Spread is measured between perpendiculars at a right angle to the center line of the skull at widest part, whether across main beams or points.

D. Inside Spread of Main Beams is measured at a right angle to the center line of the skull at widest point between main beams. Enter this measurement again as Spread Credit if it is less than or equal to the length of longer antler; if longer, enter longer antler length for Spread Credit.

E. Total of Lengths of all Abnormal Points: Abnormal Points are those non-typical in location such as points originating from a point (exception: G-3 originates from G-2 in perfectly normal fashion) or from bottom or sides of main beam, or any points beyond the normal pattern of five (including beam tip) per antler. Measure each abnormal point in usual manner and enter in appropriate blanks.

F. Length of Main Beam is measured from lowest outside edge of burr over outer curve to the most distant point of what is, or appears to be, the Main Beam. The point of beginning is that point on the burr where the center line along the outer curve of the beam intersects the burr, then following generally the line of the illustration.

G. 1-2-3-4 Length of Normal Points: Normal points are the brow and the upper and lower forks as shown in the illustration. They are measured from nearest edge of beam over outer curve to tip. Lay the tape along the outer curve of the beam so that the top edge of the tape coincides with the top edge of the beam on both sides of point to determine the baseline for point measurement. Record point lengths in appropriate blanks.

H. 1-2-3-4 Circumferences are taken as detailed for each measurement. If brow point is missing, take H-1 and H-2 at smallest place between burr and G-2. If G-3 is missing, take H-3 halfway between the base and tip of second point. If G-4 is missing, take H-4 halfway between second point and tip of main beam.

* * * * * * * * * * * * * * * * * *

### FAIR CHASE STATEMENT FOR ALL HUNTER-TAKEN TROPHIES

To make use of the following methods shall be deemed as UNFAIR CHASE and unsportsmanlike, and any trophy obtained by use of such means is disqualified from entry.

I. Spotting or herding game from the air, followed by landing in its vicinity for pursuit;

II. Herding or pursuing game with motor-powered vehicles;

III. Use of electronic communications for attracting, locating or observing game, or guiding the hunter to such game;

IV. Hunting game confined by artificial barriers, including escape-proof fencing; or hunting game transplanted solely for the purpose of commercial shooting.

* * * * * * * * * * * * * * * * * *

I certify that the trophy scored on this chart was not taken in UNFAIR CHASE as defined above by the Boone and Crockett Club. I further certify that it was taken in full compliance with local game laws of the state, province, or territory.

Date: _____ Signature of Hunter: _____

(Have signature notarized by a Notary Public)

13

Records of North American
Big Game

BOONE AND CROCKETT CLUB

P.O. Box 547
Dumfries, VA 22026

Minimum Score: Awards  All-time
225      240

NON-TYPICAL
MULE DEER

DETAIL OF POINT MEASUREMENT

| | Abnormal Points | |
|---|---|---|
| | Right Antler | Left Antler |
| | | |
| | | |
| | | |
| | | |
| | | |
| | | |
| | | |
| | | |
| | | |
| | | |
| | | |
| E. Total of Lengths of Abnormal Points | | |

| SEE OTHER SIDE FOR INSTRUCTIONS | | Column 1 | Column 2 | Column 3 | Column 4 |
|---|---|---|---|---|---|
| | | Spread Credit | Right Antler | Left Antler | Difference |
| A. No. Points on Right Antler | No. Points on Left Antler | | | | |
| B. Tip to Tip Spread | C. Greatest Spread | | | | |
| D. Inside Spread of Main Beams | (Credit May Equal But Not Exceed Longer Antler) | | | | |
| F. Length of Main Beam | | | | | |
| G-1. Length of First Point, if Present | | | | | |
| G-2. Length of Second Point | | | | | |
| G-3. Length of Third Point, if Present | | | | | |
| G-4. Length of Fourth Point, if Present | | | | | |
| H-1. Circumference at Smallest Place Between Burr and First Point | | | | | |
| H-2. Circumference at Smallest Place Between First and Second Points | | | | | |
| H-3. Circumference at Smallest Place Between Main Beam and Third Point | | | | | |
| H-4. Circumference at Smallest Place Between Second and Fourth Points | | | | | |
| TOTALS | | | | | |

| Enter Total of Columns 1, 2, and 3 | | Exact Locality Where Killed: | |
|---|---|---|---|
| Subtract Column 4 | | Date Killed: | By Whom Killed: |
| Subtotal | | Present Owner: | |
| Add (E) Total of Lengths of Abnormal Points | | Guide Name and Address: | |
| FINAL SCORE | | Remarks: | |

I certify that I have measured the above trophy on _____ 19 _____

at (address) _____
                                               City             State
and that these measurements and data are, to the best of my knowledge and belief, made in accordance with the
instructions given.

Witness: _____ Signature: _____

B&C OFFICIAL MEASURER        I.D. Number

## INSTRUCTIONS FOR MEASURING NON-TYPICAL MULE DEER

All measurements must be made with a 1/4-inch flexible steel tape to the nearest one-eighth of an inch. Wherever
it is necessary to change direction of measurement, mark a control point and swing tape at this point. (Note: a
flexible steel cable can be used to measure points and main beams only.) Enter fractional figures in eighths,
without reduction. Official measurements cannot be taken until antlers have dried for at least 60 days after the
animal was killed.

A. Number of Points on Each Antler: to be counted a point, the projection must be at least one inch long, with
the length exceeding width at one inch or more of length. All points are measured from tip of point to nearest
edge of beam as illustrated. Beam tip is counted as a point but is not measured as a point.

B. Tip to Tip Spread is measured between tips of main beams.

C. Greatest Spread is measured between perpendiculars at a right angle to the center line of the skull at widest
part, whether across main beams or points.

D. Inside Spread of Main Beams is measured at a right angle to the center line of the skull at widest point
between main beams. Enter this measurement again as the Spread Credit if it is less than or equal to the length
of longer antler; if longer, enter longer antler length for Spread Credit.

E. Total of Lengths of all Abnormal Points: Abnormal Points are those non-typical in location such as points
originating from a point (exception: G-3 originates from G-2 in perfectly normal fashion) or from bottom or sides
of main beam, or any points beyond the normal pattern of five (including beam tip) per antler. Measure each
abnormal point in usual manner and enter in appropriate blanks.

F. Length of Main Beam is measured from lowest outside edge of burr over outer curve to the most distant point of
what is, or appears to be, the main beam. The point of beginning is that point on the burr where the center line
along the outer curve of the beam intersects the burr, then following generally the line of the illustration.

G. 1-2-3-4 Length of Normal Points: Normal points are the brow and the upper and lower forks, as shown in the
illustration. They are measured from nearest edge of main beam over outer curve to tip. Lay the tape along the
outer curve of the beam so that the top edge of the tape coincides with the top edge of the beam on both sides of
point to determine the baseline for point measurement. Record point lengths in appropriate blanks.

H. 1-2-3-4 Circumferences are taken as detailed for each measurement. If brow point is missing, take H-1 and
H-2 at smallest place between burr and G-2. If G-3 is missing, take H-3 halfway between the base and tip of
second point. If G-4 is missing, take H-4 halfway between second point and tip of main beam.

\* \* \* \* \* \* \* \* \* \* \* \* \* \* \* \* \* \* \*

### FAIR CHASE STATEMENT FOR ALL HUNTER-TAKEN TROPHIES

To make use of the following methods shall be deemed as UNFAIR CHASE and unsportsmanlike, and any trophy obtained
by use of such means is disqualified from entry.

    I.   Spotting or herding game from the air, followed by landing in its vicinity for pursuit;

   II.  Herding or pursuing game with motor-powered vehicles;

  III.  Use of electronic communications for attracting, locating or observing game, or guiding the
       hunter to such game;

  IV.  Hunting game confined by artificial barriers, including escape-proof fencing; or hunting game
       transplanted solely for the purpose of commercial shooting.

\* \* \* \* \* \* \* \* \* \* \* \* \* \* \* \* \* \* \*

I certify that the trophy scored on this chart was not taken in UNFAIR CHASE as defined above by the Boone and
Crockett Club. I further certify that it was taken in full compliance with local game laws of the state,
province, or territory.

Date: _____ Signature of Hunter: _____

(Have signature notarized by a Notary Public)

TOP 10 AMERICAN ELK LISTINGS INDEX

# Tabulations of Recorded American Elk

The trophy data shown on the following pages is taken from score charts in the Records Archives of the Boone and Crockett Club. A comparison of all-time rankings of this book with those of the last all-time records book (*Records of North American Big Game*, 9th Ed., 1988) will show some significant differences. This is generally caused by two factors: the addition of trophies accepted during the 20th Awards entry period (1986-1988) and elimination of the "double penalty" for excessive inside spread. The rankings shown in this book are official and supercede those of the all-time records and other publications.

American elk (wapiti) are found in many western states and are a favored trophy species by hunters. Geographic boundaries are not described, as elk racks can be easily distinguished from the other deer categories. Geographic boundaries are described for the smaller antlered Roosevelt's elk, to prevent entry of American elk.

The scores and rank shown are final, except for trophies shown with an asterisk. The asterisk identifies entry scores subject to final certification by an Awards Panel of Judges. The asterisk can be removed (except in the case of a potential World's Record) by the submission of two additional, independent scorings by Official Measurers of the Boone and Crockett Club. The Records Committee of the Club will review the three scorings available (original plus two additional) and determine which, if any, will be accepted in lieu of the Judges Panel measurement. When the score has been accepted as final by the Records Committee, the asterisk will be removed in future editions of the all-time records book and other publications. In the case of a potential World's Record, the trophy *must* come before a Judges Panel at the end of an entry period. Only a Judges Panel can certify a World's Record and finalize its score. Asterisked trophies are shown at the end of their category, without rank.

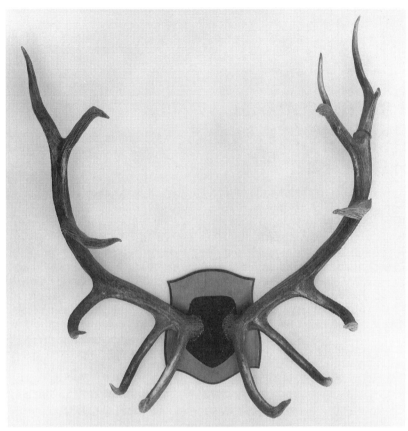

**ARIZONA STATE RECORD**
**TYPICAL AMERICAN ELK**
**SCORE: 405-7/8**
Locality: Ft. Apache Indian Reservation    Date: September 1970
Hunter: Roy R. Blythe

# ARIZONA

## TYPICAL AMERICAN ELK

| Score | Length of Main Beam R | Length of Main Beam L | Inside Spread | Greatest Spread | Circumference at Smallest Place Between Burr and First Point R | Circumference at Smallest Place Between Burr and First Point L | Number of Points R | Number of Points L | Total of Lengths Abnormal Points | All-Time Rank | State Rank |
|---|---|---|---|---|---|---|---|---|---|---|---|
| ♦ *Locality Killed / By Whom Killed / Owner / Date Killed* | | | | | | | | | | | |
| 405 7/8 | 53 4/8 | 55 5/8 | 44 6/8 | 48 7/8 | 8 5/8 | 8 5/8 | 6 | 8 | 7 5/8 | 10 | 1 |
| ♦ *Ft. Apache Res. / Roy R. Blythe / Roy R. Blythe / 1970* | | | | | | | | | | | |
| 401 7/8 | 57 4/8 | 58 4/8 | 42 4/8 | 48 4/8 | 9 4/8 | 9 2/8 | 6 | 7 | 2 7/8 | 15 | 2 |
| ♦ *Apache County / Bruce R. Keller / Bruce R. Keller / 1987* | | | | | | | | | | | |
| 399 3/8 | 58 3/8 | 58 | 49 3/8 | 55 6/8 | 9 2/8 | 9 1/8 | 6 | 6 | | 25 | 3 |
| ♦ *Coconino County / Terry J. Rice / Terry J. Rice / 1979* | | | | | | | | | | | |
| 396 6/8 | 56 1/8 | 56 3/8 | 43 4/8 | 47 3/8 | 9 7/8 | 10 6/8 | 6 | 6 | | 33 | 4 |
| ♦ *Volunteer Canyon / Lamar Haines / Lamar Haines / 1960* | | | | | | | | | | | |
| 393 7/8 | 57 1/8 | 58 | 43 7/8 | 48 7/8 | 8 | 8 | 6 | 6 | | 47 | 5 |
| ♦ *Apache County / T.R. Tidwell / T.R. Tidwell / 1983* | | | | | | | | | | | |
| 388 3/8 | 53 5/8 | 55 | 47 1/8 | 50 2/8 | 9 | 9 3/8 | 7 | 6 | | 77 | 6 |
| ♦ *Coconino County / Picked Up / Tim Cotten / PR 1982* | | | | | | | | | | | |
| 388 2/8 | 52 5/8 | 51 3/8 | 39 | 48 7/8 | 10 1/8 | 10 1/8 | 6 | 6 | | 78 | 7 |
| ♦ *Gila County / Fred B. Dickey / Fred B. Dickey / 1984* | | | | | | | | | | | |
| 386 4/8 | 56 2/8 | 54 6/8 | 44 | 50 1/8 | 8 5/8 | 8 6/8 | 6 | 6 | | 100 | 8 |
| ♦ *Coconino County / Lee Clemson / Lee Clemson / 1974* | | | | | | | | | | | |
| 385 5/8 | 59 6/8 | 56 6/8 | 41 2/8 | 45 3/8 | 8 7/8 | 9 3/8 | 7 | 8 | 2 7/8 | 110 | 9 |
| ♦ *Ft. Apache Res. / Glen Daly / Glen Daly / 1957* | | | | | | | | | | | |
| 384 6/8 | 54 | 54 | 50 | 62 7/8 | 10 1/8 | 10 | 7 | 6 | 9 6/8 | 121 | 10 |
| ♦ *Hualapai Indian Res. / Tod Reichert / Tod Reichert / 1975* | | | | | | | | | | | |
| 384 6/8 | 56 2/8 | 58 4/8 | 44 | 49 | 9 4/8 | 9 6/8 | 6 | 6 | | 121 | 10 |
| ♦ *Ft. Apache Res. / Jim P. Caires / Jim P. Caires / 1978* | | | | | | | | | | | |
| 384 6/8 | 60 | 60 2/8 | 44 3/8 | 47 1/8 | 9 5/8 | 10 | 7 | 7 | 4 1/8 | 121 | 10 |
| ♦ *Apache County / H.C. Meyer & J.T. Caid / Herman C. Meyer / 1982* | | | | | | | | | | | |
| 384 5/8 | 57 6/8 | 56 6/8 | 40 5/8 | 43 7/8 | 8 7/8 | 8 7/8 | 6 | 6 | | 125 | 13 |
| ♦ *Graham County / Laura R. Williams / Laura R. Williams / 1986* | | | | | | | | | | | |

| Score | Length of Main Beam R | L | Inside Spread | Greatest Spread | Circumference at Smallest Place Between Burr and First Point R | L | Number of Points R | L | Total of Lengths Abnormal Points | All-Time Rank | State Rank |
|---|---|---|---|---|---|---|---|---|---|---|---|
| ◆ | Locality Killed / By Whom Killed / Owner / Date Killed | | | | | | | | | | |
| 384 2/8 | 61 7/8 | 64 6/8 | 40 6/8 | 45 | 11 | 10 4/8 | 6 | 8 | 2 | 132 | 14 |
| ◆ Ft. Apache Res. / Ralph C. Winkler, Jr. / Ralph C. Winkler, Jr. / 1977 | | | | | | | | | | | |
| 384 2/8 | 58 1/8 | 60 6/8 | 49 3/8 | 52 7/8 | 10 | 8 3/8 | 6 | 7 | 1 1/8 | 132 | 14 |
| ◆ Apache County / Roy W. Baker / Roy W. Baker / 1980 | | | | | | | | | | | |
| 383 5/8 | 54 6/8 | 55 3/8 | 54 4/8 | 58 5/8 | 8 2/8 | 8 | 6 | 7 | 6 5/8 | 138 | 16 |
| ◆ Apache County / Randall S. Ulmer / Randall S. Ulmer / 1987 | | | | | | | | | | | |
| 383 2/8 | 55 5/8 | 53 1/8 | 45 | 50 2/8 | 10 3/8 | 10 5/8 | 6 | 7 | | 141 | 17 |
| ◆ Coconino County / Jay E. Elmer / Jay E. Elmer / 1979 | | | | | | | | | | | |
| 383 | 55 | 55 | 52 2/8 | 55 3/8 | 9 3/8 | 8 6/8 | 6 | 8 | | 144 | 18 |
| ◆ Coconino County / Gene Bird / Gene Bird / 1972 | | | | | | | | | | | |
| 382 6/8 | 56 7/8 | 55 4/8 | 48 | 50 6/8 | 9 3/8 | 10 5/8 | 6 | 6 | | 148 | 19 |
| ◆ Apache County / William E. Moss / William E. Moss / 1985 | | | | | | | | | | | |
| 382 3/8 | 49 6/8 | 52 1/8 | 35 5/8 | 42 1/8 | 11 | 10 1/8 | 6 | 6 | | 155 | 20 |
| ◆ Morman Lake / Wayne A. Barry / John E. Rhea / 1965 | | | | | | | | | | | |
| 382 2/8 | 58 4/8 | 62 6/8 | 48 | 53 | 8 | 7 4/8 | 6 | 6 | | 157 | 21 |
| ◆ Williams / Oscar B. Skaggs / Oscar B. Skaggs / 1954 | | | | | | | | | | | |
| 381 5/8 | 59 6/8 | 58 | 39 7/8 | 48 5/8 | 9 5/8 | 9 2/8 | 6 | 6 | | 168 | 22 |
| ◆ Coconino County / George E. Long / George E. Long / 1985 | | | | | | | | | | | |
| 380 5/8 | 54 3/8 | 53 4/8 | 42 3/8 | 53 3/8 | 10 2/8 | 9 3/8 | 6 | 6 | | 182 | 23 |
| ◆ Apache County / Don L. Corley / Don L. Corley / 1984 | | | | | | | | | | | |
| 380 4/8 | 52 4/8 | 52 6/8 | 41 | 49 | 9 | 8 6/8 | 6 | 6 | | 185 | 24 |
| ◆ Payson / Harold Foard / Harold Foard / 1947 | | | | | | | | | | | |
| 380 2/8 | 56 2/8 | 54 1/8 | 45 | 51 5/8 | 8 5/8 | 8 7/8 | 7 | 6 | | 188 | 25 |
| ◆ Coconino County / Doug Kittredge / Doug Kittredge / 1975 | | | | | | | | | | | |
| 380 | 53 2/8 | 56 2/8 | 50 3/8 | 55 1/8 | 10 3/8 | 9 7/8 | 7 | 6 | 1 7/8 | 193 | 26 |
| ◆ Ft. Apache Res. / George E. Crosby / George E. Crosby / 1957 | | | | | | | | | | | |
| 379 7/8 | 56 1/8 | 56 2/8 | 42 | 48 2/8 | 8 1/8 | 8 4/8 | 8 | 6 | 3 7/8 | 196 | 27 |
| ◆ Graham County / Gerald Williams / Gerald Williams / 1985 | | | | | | | | | | | |
| 379 3/8 | 60 1/8 | 61 1/8 | 45 5/8 | 49 | 8 7/8 | 8 3/8 | 6 | 6 | | 206 | 28 |
| ◆ Coconino County / Tammy J. Otero / Tammy J. Otero / 1984 | | | | | | | | | | | |
| 379 2/8 | 58 3/8 | 57 2/8 | 41 6/8 | 45 3/8 | 9 | 9 4/8 | 6 | 6 | | 210 | 29 |
| ◆ Sierra Blanca Lake / Joseph A. Rozum / Joseph A. Rozum / 1965 | | | | | | | | | | | |
| 378 1/8 | 53 4/8 | 54 7/8 | 52 5/8 | 54 3/8 | 7 5/8 | 7 5/8 | 7 | 6 | | 228 | 30 |
| ◆ Navajo County / Stanford H. Atwood, Jr. / Stanford H. Atwood, Jr. / 1987 | | | | | | | | | | | |

| Score | Length of Main Beam R | L | Inside Spread | Greatest Spread | Circumference at Smallest Place Between Burr and First Point R | L | Number of Points R | L | Total of Lengths Abnormal Points | All-Time Rank | State Rank |
|---|---|---|---|---|---|---|---|---|---|---|---|
| | *Locality Killed / By Whom Killed / Owner / Date Killed* | | | | | | | | | | |
| 377 5/8 | 54 2/8 | 54 5/8 | 40 6/8 | 45 6/8 | 8 6/8 | 8 1/8 | 6 | 7 | 12 1/8 | 234 | 31 |
| ♦ *Apache County / A.C. Goodell / A.C. Goodell / 1963* | | | | | | | | | | | |
| 377 1/8 | 52 1/8 | 53 1/8 | 42 2/8 | 48 2/8 | 8 1/8 | 8 6/8 | 6 | 6 | | 236 | 32 |
| ♦ *Ft. Apache Res. / Picked Up / Gary Marsh / 1971* | | | | | | | | | | | |
| 377 2/8 | 55 4/8 | 60 1/8 | 50 6/8 | 52 1/8 | 9 7/8 | 10 3/8 | 6 | 6 | | 243 | 33 |
| ♦ *Show Low / Michael Pew / Michael Pew / 1964* | | | | | | | | | | | |
| 377 2/8 | 54 2/8 | 54 2/8 | 44 2/8 | 50 7/8 | 8 2/8 | 8 1/8 | 7 | 7 | | 243 | 33 |
| ♦ *Apache County / Donald E. Franklin / Donald E. Franklin / 1981* | | | | | | | | | | | |
| 377 | 45 6/8 | 46 4/8 | 42 2/8 | 53 2/8 | 7 4/8 | 7 2/8 | 7 | 7 | | 248 | 35 |
| ♦ *Navajo County / Melvin Nolte, Jr. / Melvin Nolte, Jr. / 1983* | | | | | | | | | | | |
| 375 1/8 | 58 4/8 | 58 5/8 | 37 3/8 | 51 | 10 2/8 | 9 7/8 | 7 | 7 | | 292 | 36 |
| ♦ *Tonto Lake / Louise F. Campbell / Louise F. Campbell / 1967* | | | | | | | | | | | |
| 365 2/8 | 50 4/8 | 53 6/8 | 39 6/8 | 43 2/8 | 10 | 9 6/8 | 7 | 7 | | 303 | 37 |
| ♦ *Navajo County / Joe B. Reynolds / Joe B. Reynolds / 1987* | | | | | | | | | | | |
| 389 6/8 | 56 3/8 | 55 7/8 | 39 1/8 | 53 | 8 5/8 | 8 5/8 | 6 | 7 | | * | * |
| ♦ *Navajo County / Fred Fortier / Fred Fortier / 1985* | | | | | | | | | | | |

Photograph by Wm. H. Nesbitt

**ARIZONA STATE RECORD**
**WORLD'S RECORD**
**NON-TYPICAL AMERICAN ELK**
**SCORE: 445-5/8**
Locality: Apache Co.    Date: October 1984
Hunter: Jerry J. Davis

# ARIZONA

## NON-TYPICAL AMERICAN ELK

| Score | Length of Main Beam R | Length of Main Beam L | Inside Spread | Greatest Spread | Circumference at Smallest Place Between Burr and First Point R | Circumference at Smallest Place Between Burr and First Point L | Number of Points R | Number of Points L | Total of Lengths Abnormal Points | All-Time Rank | State Rank |
|---|---|---|---|---|---|---|---|---|---|---|---|
| \* Locality Killed / By Whom Killed / Owner / Date Killed | | | | | | | | | | | |
| 445 ⅝ | 58 | 57 ⅞ | 41 ⁶⁄₈ | 60 ³⁄₈ | 9 ²⁄₈ | 10 | 8 | 8 | 49 ⅝ | 1 | 1 |
| ♦ Apache County / Jerry J. Davis / Jerry J. Davis / 1984 | | | | | | | | | | | |
| 423 | 53 ⁴⁄₈ | 52 ³⁄₈ | 40 | 57 ⁴⁄₈ | 8 ²⁄₈ | 8 ⁶⁄₈ | 8 | 10 | 47 ⁴⁄₈ | 2 | 2 |
| ♦ Coconino County / James L. Ludvigson / James L. Ludvigson / 1985 | | | | | | | | | | | |
| 406 ⅞ | 48 ⅛ | 47 ²⁄₈ | 34 ⅞ | 45 ⅞ | 8 ²⁄₈ | 7 ⁴⁄₈ | 7 | 8 | 47 | 4 | 3 |
| ♦ Apache County / Joe W. Carroll / Joe W. Carroll / 1982 | | | | | | | | | | | |
| 408 | 53 ⅝ | 53 | 40 ⁶⁄₈ | 50 ⁶⁄₈ | 9 | 9 ⅛ | 7 | 8 | 30 ⁴⁄₈ | \* | \* |
| ♦ Apache County / J.G. Brittingham & W. Dale / Jack G. Brittingham / 1987 | | | | | | | | | | | |

**COLORADO STATE RECORD**
**WORLD'S RECORD**
**TYPICAL AMERICAN ELK**
**SCORE: 442-3/8**
Locality: Dark Canyon    Date: 1899
Hunter: John Plute
Owner: Ed Rozman

24

# COLORADO

## TYPICAL AMERICAN ELK

| Score | Length of Main Beam R | L | Inside Spread | Greatest Spread | Circumference at Smallest Place Between Burr and First Point R | L | Number of Points R | L | Total of Lengths Abnormal Points | All-Time Rank | State Rank |
|---|---|---|---|---|---|---|---|---|---|---|---|
| | *Locality Killed / By Whom Killed / Owner / Date Killed* | | | | | | | | | | |
| 442 3/8 | 55 5/8 | 59 5/8 | 45 4/8 | 51 6/8 | 12 1/8 | 11 2/8 | 8 | 7 | 2 5/8 | 1 | 1 |
| ◆ *Dark Canyon / John Plute / Ed Rozman / 1899* | | | | | | | | | | | |
| 407 | 56 7/8 | 56 6/8 | 43 4/8 | 53 4/8 | 9 4/8 | 8 4/8 | 8 | 7 | | 9 | 2 |
| ◆ *Summit County / Robert G. Young / Robert G. Young / 1967* | | | | | | | | | | | |
| 402 3/8 | 59 4/8 | 62 1/8 | 47 1/8 | 60 1/8 | 8 2/8 | 8 6/8 | 8 | 7 | 2 4/8 | 14 | 3 |
| ◆ *San Miguel County / Lewis Fredrickson / Jay Scott / 1954* | | | | | | | | | | | |
| 400 4/8 | 59 4/8 | 61 | 48 4/8 | 61 1/8 | 8 2/8 | 8 5/8 | 8 | 7 | 2 | 21 | 4 |
| ◆ *Routt County / Lewis Frederickson / Lewis Frederickson / 1953* | | | | | | | | | | | |
| 397 2/8 | 50 2/8 | 50 6/8 | 45 2/8 | 49 3/8 | 9 6/8 | 9 5/8 | 8 | 7 | 6 | 32 | 5 |
| ◆ *Gunnison County / John R. Burritt / John R. Burritt / 1970* | | | | | | | | | | | |
| 392 4/8 | 51 3/8 | 51 1/8 | 42 3/8 | 58 5/8 | 7 1/8 | 7 1/8 | 7 | 7 | 10 5/8 | 54 | 6 |
| ◆ *Buford / Picked Up / Robert T. Fulton / PR 1967* | | | | | | | | | | | |
| 392 | 54 6/8 | 56 6/8 | 45 2/8 | 51 4/8 | 10 | 10 | 6 | 6 | | 56 | 7 |
| ◆ *Jackson County / James A. Baller / North Park State Bank / 1969* | | | | | | | | | | | |
| 391 6/8 | 52 6/8 | 53 6/8 | 35 6/8 | 43 4/8 | 7 1/8 | 7 1/8 | 6 | 6 | | 57 | 8 |
| ◆ *Slater / W.J. Bracken / W.J. Bracken / 1963* | | | | | | | | | | | |
| 391 4/8 | 54 5/8 | 56 3/8 | 43 2/8 | 55 3/8 | 9 1/8 | 9 | 6 | 6 | | 59 | 9 |
| ◆ *Mt. Evans / Unknown / Frank Brady / 1874* | | | | | | | | | | | |
| 391 3/8 | 55 7/8 | 50 3/8 | 39 3/8 | 54 4/8 | 7 2/8 | 8 2/8 | 7 | 6 | | 61 | 10 |
| ◆ *Grand Lake / John Holzwarth / John Holzwarth / 1949* | | | | | | | | | | | |
| 388 6/8 | 50 6/8 | 47 1/8 | 45 6/8 | 49 2/8 | 10 | 9 4/8 | 7 | 6 | | 76 | 11 |
| ◆ *Larimer County / John Zimmerman / Ft. Collins Mus. / PR 1890* | | | | | | | | | | | |
| 386 2/8 | 52 4/8 | 54 1/8 | 48 | 50 1/8 | 8 7/8 | 9 1/8 | 6 | 6 | | 103 | 12 |
| ◆ *Delta County / Bert Johnson / Bert Johnson / 1974* | | | | | | | | | | | |
| 385 1/8 | 48 5/8 | 49 3/8 | 34 7/8 | 49 3/8 | 8 3/8 | 8 6/8 | 6 | 6 | | 117 | 13 |
| ◆ *Trappers Lake / Byron W. Kneff / Byron W. Kneff / 1954* | | | | | | | | | | | |

| Score | Length of Main Beam R | L | Inside Spread | Greatest Spread | Circumference at Smallest Place Between Burr and First Point R | L | Number of Points R | L | Total of Lengths Abnormal Points | All-Time Rank | State Rank |
|---|---|---|---|---|---|---|---|---|---|---|---|
| 384 3/8 | 54 5/8 | 54 5/8 | 50 7/8 | 53 3/8 | 9 7/8 | 9 2/8 | 6 | 6 | | 129 | 14 |
| ♦ Clear Creek County / John Wallace / John Wallace / 1973 | | | | | | | | | | | |
| 384 | 56 4/8 | 54 | 47 | 53 2/8 | 7 6/8 | 8 1/8 | 7 | 7 | | 134 | 15 |
| ♦ Costilla County / William E. Carl / William E. Carl / 1967 | | | | | | | | | | | |
| 382 4/8 | 56 6/8 | 56 7/8 | 41 6/8 | 46 3/8 | 8 7/8 | 9 2/8 | 6 | 7 | | 151 | 16 |
| ♦ Summit County / Marshall Sherman / Marshall Sherman / 1966 | | | | | | | | | | | |
| 382 | 53 2/8 | 51 1/8 | 48 | 50 6/8 | 8 7/8 | 9 1/8 | 6 | 6 | | 162 | 17 |
| ♦ Little Cimmaron / Newell Beauchamp / Bud Lovato / 1957 | | | | | | | | | | | |
| 381 3/8 | 55 4/8 | 54 5/8 | 37 4/8 | 47 5/8 | 9 6/8 | 9 1/8 | 7 | 7 | 2 5/8 | 171 | 18 |
| ♦ Larimer County / Earl L. Erbes / Earl L. Erbes / 1972 | | | | | | | | | | | |
| 380 5/8 | 50 6/8 | 54 6/8 | 47 5/8 | 54 6/8 | 9 4/8 | 9 7/8 | 6 | 6 | | 182 | 19 |
| ♦ Medicine Bow Range / Mike Holliday / Mike Holliday / 1966 | | | | | | | | | | | |
| 380 5/8 | 54 2/8 | 55 | 51 3/8 | 56 2/8 | 7 1/8 | 7 4/8 | 6 | 7 | 2 2/8 | 182 | 19 |
| ♦ Chaffee County / Anton Purkat / Anton Purkat / 1972 | | | | | | | | | | | |
| 380 2/8 | 53 2/8 | 55 6/8 | 55 6/8 | 57 | 9 6/8 | 9 7/8 | 7 | 7 | | 188 | 21 |
| ♦ Las Animas County / Picked Up / Crawford Ranch / 1987 | | | | | | | | | | | |
| 378 2/8 | 51 4/8 | 52 6/8 | 50 | 58 4/8 | 9 2/8 | 10 | 6 | 7 | 4 2/8 | 226 | 22 |
| ♦ White River / Art Wright / Art Wright / 1953 | | | | | | | | | | | |
| 378 | 56 1/8 | 56 7/8 | 44 2/8 | 48 6/8 | 7 6/8 | 7 6/8 | 7 | 6 | 9 | 229 | 23 |
| ♦ Gunnison / Ed Lattimore, Jr. / Ed Lattimore, Jr. / 1966 | | | | | | | | | | | |
| 377 6/8 | 51 3/8 | 52 3/8 | 45 | 49 6/8 | 8 | 8 3/8 | 7 | 7 | | 231 | 24 |
| ♦ Routt County / Tom Nidey / Tom Nidey / 1959 | | | | | | | | | | | |
| 377 4/8 | 47 5/8 | 47 2/8 | 45 | 48 6/8 | 8 4/8 | 8 5/8 | 6 | 6 | | 236 | 25 |
| ♦ Gunnison County / Leo Welch / Leo Welch / 1972 | | | | | | | | | | | |
| 376 5/8 | 58 6/8 | 56 3/8 | 48 1/8 | 53 | 7 6/8 | 7 6/8 | 6 | 6 | | 258 | 26 |
| ♦ Granby / Melvin Van Lewen / Colo. Div. of Wildl. / 1961 | | | | | | | | | | | |
| 376 3/8 | 48 4/8 | 49 2/8 | 40 3/8 | 51 2/8 | 8 | 8 1/8 | 7 | 7 | | 262 | 27 |
| ♦ White River / Ron Vance / Ronald Crawford / 1957 | | | | | | | | | | | |
| 376 3/8 | 49 3/8 | 49 7/8 | 41 5/8 | 55 6/8 | 7 1/8 | 7 4/8 | 6 | 6 | | 262 | 27 |
| ♦ Radium / Bill Mercer / Bill Mercer / 1964 | | | | | | | | | | | |
| 376 3/8 | 55 4/8 | 55 5/8 | 39 1/8 | 44 5/8 | 9 | 9 | 6 | 6 | | 262 | 27 |
| ♦ Gunnison County / Gerald J. Obertino / Gerald J. Obertino / 1986 | | | | | | | | | | | |

| Score | Length of Main Beam R | Length of Main Beam L | Inside Spread | Greatest Spread | Circumference at Smallest Place Between Burr and First Point R | Circumference at Smallest Place Between Burr and First Point L | Number of Points R | Number of Points L | Total of Lengths Abnormal Points | All-Time Rank | State Rank |
|---|---|---|---|---|---|---|---|---|---|---|---|
| ♦ *Locality Killed / By Whom Killed / Owner / Date Killed* | | | | | | | | | | | |
| 376 | 60 4/8 | 59 | 44 4/8 | 50 1/8 | 7 5/8 | 8 | 6 | 6 | | 267 | 30 |
| ♦ *Almont / John Schwartz / John Schwartz / 1961* | | | | | | | | | | | |
| 375 6/8 | 50 3/8 | 50 6/8 | 40 4/8 | 45 7/8 | 9 4/8 | 10 4/8 | 6 | 6 | | 270 | 31 |
| ♦ *Crow Valley / Dale R. Leonard / Dale R. Leonard / 1961* | | | | | | | | | | | |
| 375 2/8 | 55 2/8 | 52 3/8 | 47 2/8 | 51 3/8 | 8 7/8 | 8 7/8 | 8 | 8 | 2 6/8 | 286 | 32 |
| ♦ *Craig / Kenneth W. Cramer / Kenneth W. Cramer / 1960* | | | | | | | | | | | |
| 414 6/8 | 55 3/8 | 58 3/8 | 53 3/8 | 56 4/8 | 13 5/8 | 13 | 9 | 7 | 9 5/8 | * | * |
| ♦ *Gunnison County / J.J. Carpenter / Hugh Carpenter / 1900* | | | | | | | | | | | |
| 391 4/8 | 57 5/8 | 57 3/8 | 42 4/8 | 49 1/8 | 10 3/8 | 10 3/8 | 6 | 7 | | * | * |
| ♦ *Ouray County / Eugene D. Guilaroff / Eugene D. Guilaroff / 1973* | | | | | | | | | | | |

**IDAHO STATE RECORD**
**TYPICAL AMERICAN ELK**
**SCORE: 412-5/8**
Locality: Wieser River    Date: October 1954
Hunter: Elmer Bacus

# IDAHO

## TYPICAL AMERICAN ELK

| Score | Length of Main Beam R | Length of Main Beam L | Inside Spread | Greatest Spread | Circumference at Smallest Place Between Burr and First Point R | Circumference at Smallest Place Between Burr and First Point L | Number of Points R | Number of Points L | Total of Lengths Abnormal Points | All-Time Rank | State Rank |
|---|---|---|---|---|---|---|---|---|---|---|---|
| ♦ *Locality Killed / By Whom Killed / Owner / Date Killed* | | | | | | | | | | | |
| 412 5/8 | 51 6/8 | 51 1/8 | 42 5/8 | 47 4/8 | 10 | 9 1/8 | 9 | 8 | 2 2/8 | 7 | 1 |
| ♦ *Wieser River / Elmer Bacus / Elmer Bacus / 1954* | | | | | | | | | | | |
| 400 4/8 | 59 1/8 | 60 1/8 | 42 6/8 | 49 | 9 3/8 | 10 | 7 | 7 | | 21 | 2 |
| ♦ *Owyhee County / Cecil R. Coonts / Cecil R. Coonts / 1965* | | | | | | | | | | | |
| 395 | 56 2/8 | 56 2/8 | 48 7/8 | 53 4/8 | 8 7/8 | 9 | 7 | 7 | 1 7/8 | 39 | 3 |
| ♦ *Salmon Natl. For. / Fred W. Thomson / Fred W. Thomson / 1964* | | | | | | | | | | | |
| 394 4/8 | 53 4/8 | 53 2/8 | 46 4/8 | 54 | 8 7/8 | 8 7/8 | 6 | 6 | | 41 | 4 |
| ♦ *Idaho County / L.M. White / L.M. White / 1977* | | | | | | | | | | | |
| 393 2/8 | 58 6/8 | 52 1/8 | 45 2/8 | 49 | 9 6/8 | 9 4/8 | 6 | 6 | | 48 | 5 |
| ♦ *Winchester / Doyle Shriver / Doyle Shriver / 1954* | | | | | | | | | | | |
| 390 6/8 | 59 6/8 | 58 | 42 | 46 2/8 | 8 7/8 | 9 | 7 | 7 | | 62 | 6 |
| ♦ *Caribou County / Ken Homer / Ken Homer / 1963* | | | | | | | | | | | |
| 389 3/8 | 56 5/8 | 60 5/8 | 43 7/8 | 57 | 8 3/8 | 8 2/8 | 6 | 6 | | 71 | 7 |
| ♦ *Salmon River / Unknown / John M. Anderson / 1915* | | | | | | | | | | | |
| 389 2/8 | 49 4/8 | 51 1/8 | 42 6/8 | 48 5/8 | 12 2/8 | 12 3/8 | 6 | 7 | | 72 | 8 |
| ♦ *Nez Perce County / Picked Up / Michael Throckmorton / 1949* | | | | | | | | | | | |
| 388 | 57 1/8 | 55 1/8 | 55 | 59 | 8 6/8 | 8 1/8 | 7 | 6 | | 82 | 9 |
| ♦ *Medicine Lodge Creek / D.W. Marshall & E.J. Stacy / D.W. Marshall & E.J.Stacy / 1961* | | | | | | | | | | | |
| 387 6/8 | 50 2/8 | 51 7/8 | 43 2/8 | 45 6/8 | 9 5/8 | 10 2/8 | 6 | 6 | | 88 | 10 |
| ♦ *Fremont / Charles A. Preston / Charles A. Preston / 1963* | | | | | | | | | | | |
| 386 4/8 | 49 2/8 | 50 3/8 | 39 6/8 | 46 4/8 | 8 6/8 | 9 | 7 | 7 | | 100 | 11 |
| ♦ *Nez Perce County / H.H. Schnettler / H.H. Schnettler / 1957* | | | | | | | | | | | |
| 386 | 53 7/8 | 55 4/8 | 51 | 57 7/8 | 9 6/8 | 9 6/8 | 6 | 6 | | 106 | 12 |
| ♦ *Valley County / Denny Young / Kenny Poe / 1957* | | | | | | | | | | | |

| Score | Length of Main Beam R | L | Inside Spread | Greatest Spread | Circumference at Smallest Place Between Burr and First Point R | L | Number of Points R | L | Total of Lengths Abnormal Points | All-Time Rank | State Rank |
|---|---|---|---|---|---|---|---|---|---|---|---|
| | *Locality Killed  /  By Whom Killed  /  Owner  /  Date Killed* | | | | | | | | | | |
| 385 7/8 | 49 1/8 | 51 7/8 | 44 3/8 | 49 3/8 | 7 7/8 | 7 7/8 | 6 | 6 | | 108 | 13 |
| | *Shoshone County  /  Jerry Nearing  /  Jerry Nearing  /  1976* | | | | | | | | | | |
| 385 5/8 | 53 2/8 | 53 | 40 3/8 | 47 4/8 | 8 4/8 | 8 1/8 | 6 | 6 | | 110 | 14 |
| | *Kootenai County  /  Arth Day  /  Arth Day  /  1971* | | | | | | | | | | |
| 384 4/8 | 57 | 56 4/8 | 43 4/8 | 45 | 9 5/8 | 9 3/8 | 7 | 7 | | 127 | 15 |
| | *Bonneville County  /  David W. Anderson  /  David W. Anderson  /  1967* | | | | | | | | | | |
| 384 4/8 | 53 2/8 | 53 7/8 | 43 | 46 7/8 | 8 5/8 | 8 2/8 | 7 | 7 | | 127 | 15 |
| | *Bonneville County  /  Keith W. Hadley  /  Keith W. Hadley  /  1972* | | | | | | | | | | |
| 383 2/8 | 52 2/8 | 52 | 41 6/8 | 55 2/8 | 9 4/8 | 9 2/8 | 7 | 7 | | 141 | 17 |
| | *Nez Perce County  /  Thenton L. Todd  /  Thenton L. Todd  /  1956* | | | | | | | | | | |
| 382 5/8 | 52 3/8 | 52 3/8 | 36 5/8 | 45 2/8 | 9 2/8 | 9 | 7 | 7 | | 150 | 18 |
| | *Kootenai County  /  Terry Cozad  /  Terry Cozad  /  1968* | | | | | | | | | | |
| 381 | 48 | 54 4/8 | 40 4/8 | 47 | 8 5/8 | 8 7/8 | 7 | 8 | | 177 | 19 |
| | *Bonneville County  /  Mrs. E. LaRene Smith  /  Mrs. E. LaRene Smith  /  1966* | | | | | | | | | | |
| 379 6/8 | 52 | 51 6/8 | 36 2/8 | 47 5/8 | 10 | 10 | 9 | 8 | 1 | 197 | 20 |
| | *Adams County  /  William V. Baker  /  William V. Baker  /  1976* | | | | | | | | | | |
| 379 5/8 | 53 7/8 | 48 2/8 | 55 | 56 | 8 2/8 | 8 4/8 | 7 | 7 | | 203 | 21 |
| | *Valley County  /  Joe Gisler  /  Joe Gisler  /  1961* | | | | | | | | | | |
| 379 | 50 4/8 | 51 1/8 | 40 6/8 | 44 3/8 | 9 | 8 6/8 | 6 | 6 | | 215 | 22 |
| | *Big Creek  /  Picked Up  /  George Dovel  /  1963* | | | | | | | | | | |
| 378 4/8 | 54 3/8 | 55 3/8 | 45 2/8 | 48 7/8 | 8 6/8 | 8 6/8 | 6 | 6 | | 223 | 23 |
| | *Shoshone County  /  Edward L. Bradford  /  Edward L. Bradford  /  1963* | | | | | | | | | | |
| 376 5/8 | 48 | 50 1/8 | 39 3/8 | 50 2/8 | 8 5/8 | 8 7/8 | 7 | 7 | | 258 | 24 |
| | *Teton County  /  Edwin E. Schiess  /  Tim Schiess  /  1966* | | | | | | | | | | |
| 375 6/8 | 52 1/8 | 50 4/8 | 37 2/8 | 42 2/8 | 8 4/8 | 7 7/8 | 7 | 7 | | 270 | 25 |
| | *Shoshone County  /  Ralph H. Brandvold, Jr.  /  Ralph H. Brandvold, Jr.  /  1983* | | | | | | | | | | |
| 375 | 52 6/8 | 52 5/8 | 47 4/8 | 54 2/8 | 8 6/8 | 9 | 6 | 6 | | 294 | 26 |
| | *Fremont County  /  Eva Calonge  /  Eva Calonge  /  1960* | | | | | | | | | | |

The late Slim Pickens, veteran cowboy actor and entertainer, with the 46-inch wide typical American elk he took in Colfax County, New Mexico, in 1981. Pickens' bull scores 375-2/8 points final score.

Photograph by Wm. H. Nesbitt

**IDAHO STATE RECORD**
**NON-TYPICAL AMERICAN ELK**
**SCORE: 403-7/8**
Locality: Shoshone Co.    Date: October 1964
Hunter: Fred S. Scott
Owner: Mannie Moore

# IDAHO

## NON-TYPICAL AMERICAN ELK

| Score | Length of Main Beam R | Length of Main Beam L | Inside Spread | Greatest Spread | Circumference at Smallest Place Between Burr and First Point R | Circumference at Smallest Place Between Burr and First Point L | Number of Points R | Number of Points L | Total of Lengths Abnormal Points | All-Time Rank | State Rank |
|---|---|---|---|---|---|---|---|---|---|---|---|
| \[diamond] Locality Killed / By Whom Killed / Owner / Date Killed ||||||||||||
| 403 7/8 | 46 5/8 | 52 | 32 4/8 | 43 5/8 | 10 3/8 | 10 6/8 | 8 | 9 | 49 5/8 | 6 | 1 |
| \[diamond] Shoshone County / Fred S. Scott / Mannie Moore / 1964 ||||||||||||
| 385 1/8 | 50 5/8 | 48 6/8 | 40 4/8 | 51 2/8 | 7 5/8 | 7 4/8 | 9 | 8 | 24 5/8 | 14 | 2 |
| \[diamond] Latah County / James A. Carpenter / James A. Carpenter / 1985 ||||||||||||

Photograph by Wm. H. Nesbitt

**KANSAS STATE RECORD**
**NON-TYPICAL AMERICAN ELK**
**SCORE: 398-4/8**
Locality: Morton Co.    Date: September 1987
Hunter: Camron Paxton

# KANSAS

## NON-TYPICAL AMERICAN ELK

| | Length of Main Beam | | Inside | Great-est | Circumference at Smallest Place Between Burr and First Point | | Number of Points | | Total of Lengths Abnor-mal | All-Time | State |
|---|---|---|---|---|---|---|---|---|---|---|---|
| Score | R | L | Spread | Spread | R | L | R | L | Points | Rank | Rank |

♦ *Locality Killed / By Whom Killed / Owner / Date Killed*

| | | | | | | | | | | | |
|---|---|---|---|---|---|---|---|---|---|---|---|
| 398 4/8 | 52 7/8 | 51 4/8 | 42 3/8 | 46 3/8 | 10 1/8 | 10 1/8 | 7 | 9 | 19 3/8 | 10 | 1 |

♦ *Morton County / Camron Paxton / Camron Paxton / 1987*

**MONTANA STATE RECORD**
**TYPICAL AMERICAN ELK**
**SCORE: 419-4/8**
Locality: Madison Co.    Date: October 1958
Hunter: Fred C. Mercer

# MONTANA
## TYPICAL AMERICAN ELK

| Score | Length of Main Beam R | L | Inside Spread | Greatest Spread | Circumference at Smallest Place Between Burr and First Point R | L | Number of Points R | L | Total of Lengths Abnormal Points | All-Time Rank | State Rank |
|---|---|---|---|---|---|---|---|---|---|---|---|
| 419 4/8 | 59 7/8 | 60 1/8 | 53 | 55 3/8 | 9 2/8 | 9 3/8 | 7 | 7 | | 4 | 1 |
| ♦ Madison County / Fred C. Mercer / Fred C. Mercer / 1958 | | | | | | | | | | | |
| 404 6/8 | 58 6/8 | 57 | 47 2/8 | 54 | 9 5/8 | 9 1/8 | 8 | 7 | | 11 | 2 |
| ♦ Mineral County / Carl B. Snyder / Warren G. Stone / 1959 | | | | | | | | | | | |
| 403 2/8 | 54 4/8 | 55 | 61 1/8 | 64 | 9 6/8 | 10 3/8 | 7 | 7 | | 12 | 3 |
| ♦ Montana / Robert Swan / B&C National Collection / 1912 | | | | | | | | | | | |
| 401 4/8 | 53 1/8 | 55 1/8 | 44 4/8 | 47 4/8 | 7 1/8 | 8 1/8 | 7 | 7 | | 18 | 4 |
| ♦ Park County / Wayne A. Hertzler / Wayne A. Hertzler / 1977 | | | | | | | | | | | |
| 398 5/8 | 57 2/8 | 53 4/8 | 40 5/8 | 47 2/8 | 9 | 9 2/8 | 8 | 8 | | 27 | 5 |
| ♦ Lewis & Clark County / Richard Mosher / J.A. Iverson / 1953 | | | | | | | | | | | |
| 397 6/8 | 53 | 53 | 44 2/8 | 48 | 8 7/8 | 9 | 8 | 7 | | 31 | 6 |
| ♦ Cascade County / John W. Campbell / John W. Campbell / 1955 | | | | | | | | | | | |
| 395 4/8 | 56 2/8 | 51 2/8 | 43 6/8 | 46 1/8 | 10 2/8 | 9 5/8 | 6 | 6 | | 36 | 7 |
| ♦ Silver Bow County / Wayne Estep / Wayne Estep / 1966 | | | | | | | | | | | |
| 394 6/8 | 54 2/8 | 60 7/8 | 47 2/8 | 51 5/8 | 8 2/8 | 8 4/8 | 6 | 6 | | 40 | 8 |
| ♦ Jefferson County / John Willard / John Willard / 1953 | | | | | | | | | | | |
| 394 4/8 | 55 | 57 5/8 | 52 4/8 | 58 3/8 | 10 | 9 4/8 | 7 | 6 | 2 6/8 | 41 | 9 |
| ♦ Beaverhead County / Gwyn Brown / Gwyn Brown / 1944 | | | | | | | | | | | |
| 389 5/8 | 50 2/8 | 53 | 50 3/8 | 50 5/8 | 8 | 7 6/8 | 6 | 7 | | 66 | 10 |
| ♦ Park County / Thomas B. Adams / Jack Adams / 1932 | | | | | | | | | | | |
| 389 4/8 | 55 4/8 | 56 2/8 | 45 | 52 | 10 5/8 | 10 | 6 | 6 | | 68 | 11 |
| ♦ Helena / Picked Up / Robert L. Smith / 1964 | | | | | | | | | | | |
| 389 4/8 | 57 3/8 | 55 2/8 | 42 | 51 2/8 | 8 | 8 | 6 | 6 | | 68 | 11 |
| ♦ Bitterroot Area / Unknown / John Le Blanc / 1965 | | | | | | | | | | | |
| 388 | 53 2/8 | 53 6/8 | 48 2/8 | 52 1/8 | 9 | 9 3/8 | 6 | 6 | | 82 | 13 |
| ♦ Madison County / Terry Carlson / Christine Mullikin / 1961 | | | | | | | | | | | |

| Score | Length of Main Beam R | L | Inside Spread | Greatest Spread | Circumference at Smallest Place Between Burr and First Point R | L | Number of Points R | L | Total of Lengths Abnormal Points | All-Time Rank | State Rank |
|---|---|---|---|---|---|---|---|---|---|---|---|
| | ♦ *Locality Killed / By Whom Killed / Owner / Date Killed* | | | | | | | | | | |
| 387 4/8 | 56 5/8 | 58 2/8 | 44 2/8 | 52 6/8 | 9 | 9 | 6 | 6 | | 91 | 14 |
| | ♦ *Sage Creek / Joseph A. Vogel / Joseph A. Vogel / 1970* | | | | | | | | | | |
| 387 3/8 | 52 1/8 | 52 3/8 | 47 3/8 | 50 5/8 | 8 1/8 | 8 1/8 | 6 | 6 | | 93 | 15 |
| | ♦ *Park County / Lawrence P. Deering / Lawrence P. Deering / 1978* | | | | | | | | | | |
| 387 1/8 | 54 6/8 | 58 1/8 | 46 | 49 4/8 | 9 5/8 | 9 5/8 | 7 | 8 | 8 5/8 | 94 | 16 |
| | ♦ *Meagher County / B. McLees & H. Zehntner / Bud McLees / 1971* | | | | | | | | | | |
| 386 7/8 | 48 6/8 | 47 2/8 | 41 6/8 | 50 4/8 | 9 4/8 | 8 5/8 | 8 | 8 | 4 7/8 | 96 | 17 |
| | ♦ *Powell County / Mildred Eder / Mildred Eder / 1969* | | | | | | | | | | |
| 386 6/8 | 61 6/8 | 61 7/8 | 47 4/8 | 51 1/8 | 8 7/8 | 9 1/8 | 6 | 6 | | 98 | 18 |
| | ♦ *Flathead County / Floyd L. Jackson / Floyd L. Jackson / 1976* | | | | | | | | | | |
| 385 3/8 | 57 2/8 | 55 7/8 | 42 5/8 | 47 5/8 | 8 | 9 | 6 | 6 | | 114 | 19 |
| | ♦ *Sanders County / George R. Johnson / George R. Johnson / 1977* | | | | | | | | | | |
| 385 1/8 | 56 7/8 | 56 4/8 | 46 5/8 | 52 2/8 | 8 3/8 | 10 | 6 | 7 | 7 2/8 | 117 | 20 |
| | ♦ *Bozeman / Robert B. McKnight / Robert B. McKnight / 1966* | | | | | | | | | | |
| 384 3/8 | 59 | 58 4/8 | 46 3/8 | 50 2/8 | 10 5/8 | 9 3/8 | 6 | 6 | | 129 | 21 |
| | ♦ *Beaverhead County / Phil Matovich / Phil Matovich / 1960* | | | | | | | | | | |
| 384 | 58 7/8 | 56 4/8 | 44 | 50 4/8 | 9 6/8 | 9 1/8 | 6 | 7 | | 134 | 22 |
| | ♦ *Willow Creek / Mike Miles / Mike Miles / 1958* | | | | | | | | | | |
| 384 | 53 2/8 | 51 1/8 | 48 3/8 | 58 3/8 | 8 5/8 | 8 2/8 | 6 | 7 | 2 5/8 | 134 | 22 |
| | ♦ *Meagher County / Frank W. Fuller / Frank W. Fuller / 1963* | | | | | | | | | | |
| 382 7/8 | 53 4/8 | 51 4/8 | 47 4/8 | 54 3/8 | 9 7/8 | 10 2/8 | 7 | 8 | 2 7/8 | 146 | 24 |
| | ♦ *Blacktail Creek / Floyd E. Winn / Floyd E. Winn / 1959* | | | | | | | | | | |
| 382 4/8 | 54 | 55 1/8 | 40 6/8 | 47 3/8 | 8 4/8 | 9 1/8 | 7 | 7 | | 151 | 25 |
| | ♦ *Cascade County / Robert J. Gliko / Robert J. Gliko / 1983* | | | | | | | | | | |
| 382 2/8 | 55 4/8 | 55 | 47 4/8 | 51 7/8 | 7 4/8 | 7 2/8 | 6 | 6 | | 157 | 26 |
| | ♦ *Gallatin County / Henry Lambert / Charles F. Miller / 1923* | | | | | | | | | | |
| 382 1/8 | 57 3/8 | 55 7/8 | 44 3/8 | 47 4/8 | 8 1/8 | 8 2/8 | 7 | 7 | | 160 | 27 |
| | ♦ *Bob Marshall Wild. / Gene E. Trenary / Gene E. Trenary / 1958* | | | | | | | | | | |
| 382 1/8 | 54 3/8 | 54 6/8 | 45 7/8 | 50 1/8 | 8 | 8 2/8 | 6 | 6 | | 160 | 27 |
| | ♦ *Gallatin County / A. Francis Bailey / A. Francis Bailey / 1966* | | | | | | | | | | |
| 382 | 52 2/8 | 51 1/8 | 47 2/8 | 57 3/8 | 9 2/8 | 8 6/8 | 8 | 7 | | 162 | 29 |
| | ♦ *Missoula County / Fritz Frey / Clifford Frey / 1943* | | | | | | | | | | |
| 381 7/8 | 59 5/8 | 58 | 52 1/8 | 56 3/8 | 7 6/8 | 7 5/8 | 7 | 8 | | 164 | 30 |
| | ♦ *Gallatin County / H.K. Shields / H.K. Shields / 1958* | | | | | | | | | | |

| Score | Length of Main Beam R | Length of Main Beam L | Inside Spread | Greatest Spread | Circumference at Smallest Place Between Burr and First Point R | Circumference at Smallest Place Between Burr and First Point L | Number of Points R | Number of Points L | Total of Lengths Abnormal Points | All-Time Rank | State Rank |
|---|---|---|---|---|---|---|---|---|---|---|---|
| ♦ *Locality Killed / By Whom Killed / Owner / Date Killed* | | | | | | | | | | | |
| 381 6/8 | 52 2/8 | 52 | 49 7/8 | 55 1/8 | 10 2/8 | 9 3/8 | 6 | 7 | 3 1/8 | 165 | 31 |
| ♦ *Beaverhead County / C.L. Jensen / C.L. Jensen / 1960* | | | | | | | | | | | |
| 381 6/8 | 50 3/8 | 49 7/8 | 42 | 44 2/8 | 9 1/8 | 8 7/8 | 8 | 7 | 3 | 165 | 31 |
| ♦ *Madison County / Allan L. Mintken / Allan L. Mintken / 1986* | | | | | | | | | | | |
| 381 5/8 | 56 2/8 | 56 2/8 | 41 5/8 | 49 | 10 4/8 | 10 1/8 | 6 | 6 | | 168 | 33 |
| ♦ *Granite County / Jeff Conn / Jeff Conn / 1971* | | | | | | | | | | | |
| 381 3/8 | 57 2/8 | 57 7/8 | 41 1/8 | 54 2/8 | 9 6/8 | 9 4/8 | 7 | 6 | 2 | 171 | 34 |
| ♦ *Park County / Edward F. Skillman / Edward F. Skillman / 1968* | | | | | | | | | | | |
| 381 1/8 | 49 6/8 | 51 4/8 | 39 7/8 | 44 2/8 | 8 6/8 | 9 | 7 | 7 | | 175 | 35 |
| ♦ *Flathead County / Earl Weaver, Jr. / Earl Weaver, Jr. / 1962* | | | | | | | | | | | |
| 381 | 56 3/8 | 54 6/8 | 48 4/8 | 53 7/8 | 8 2/8 | 8 2/8 | 6 | 6 | 4 6/8 | 177 | 36 |
| ♦ *Gallatin County / Jack Bauer / Jack Bauer / 1961* | | | | | | | | | | | |
| 381 | 51 2/8 | 50 5/8 | 43 6/8 | 47 3/8 | 8 | 7 5/8 | 7 | 7 | | 177 | 36 |
| ♦ *Big Horn County / Jerry Barnes / Jerry Barnes / 1962* | | | | | | | | | | | |
| 381 | 54 | 53 4/8 | 48 6/8 | 52 4/8 | 8 | 7 6/8 | 6 | 7 | | 177 | 36 |
| ♦ *Gallatin County / Gerald Schroeder / Gerald Schroeder / 1977* | | | | | | | | | | | |
| 380 6/8 | 51 7/8 | 51 | 43 6/8 | 47 | 10 | 9 7/8 | 7 | 7 | | 181 | 39 |
| ♦ *Park County / John Caputo / John Caputo / 1968* | | | | | | | | | | | |
| 380 2/8 | 56 1/8 | 57 2/8 | 49 4/8 | 54 2/8 | 8 1/8 | 8 6/8 | 7 | 7 | | 188 | 40 |
| ♦ *Madison County / Phil Hensel / Phil Hensel / 1959* | | | | | | | | | | | |
| 380 2/8 | 58 7/8 | 58 3/8 | 42 2/8 | 46 2/8 | 9 4/8 | 8 6/8 | 7 | 6 | | 188 | 40 |
| ♦ *Granite County / Richard Shoner / Richard Shoner / 1977* | | | | | | | | | | | |
| 379 6/8 | 58 3/8 | 58 4/8 | 45 2/8 | 51 4/8 | 9 2/8 | 9 6/8 | 6 | 6 | | 197 | 42 |
| ♦ *Ruby Mts. / Jack Ballard / Jack Ballard / 1960* | | | | | | | | | | | |
| 379 6/8 | 57 2/8 | 57 2/8 | 40 4/8 | | 7 6/8 | 7 6/8 | 6 | 6 | | 197 | 42 |
| ♦ *Big Horn County / George F. Gamble / George F. Gamble / 1968* | | | | | | | | | | | |
| 379 6/8 | 54 | 54 6/8 | 45 6/8 | 49 5/8 | 7 7/8 | 8 1/8 | 6 | 6 | | 197 | 42 |
| ♦ *Daisy Pass / Larry R. Price / Larry R. Price / 1971* | | | | | | | | | | | |
| 379 4/8 | 51 7/8 | 52 3/8 | 39 | 45 2/8 | 9 7/8 | 9 7/8 | 6 | 6 | | 205 | 45 |
| ♦ *Madison County / LeRoy Schweitzer / LeRoy Schweitzer / 1964* | | | | | | | | | | | |
| 379 2/8 | 55 7/8 | 56 1/8 | 44 4/8 | 52 1/8 | 9 | 8 7/8 | 6 | 6 | | 210 | 46 |
| ♦ *Bozeman / K.L. Berry / K.L. Berry / 1959* | | | | | | | | | | | |
| 379 2/8 | 54 7/8 | 56 4/8 | 40 4/8 | 56 7/8 | 8 2/8 | 8 1/8 | 6 | 6 | | 210 | 46 |
| ♦ *Sanders County / Robert L. Coates / Robert L. Coates / 1974* | | | | | | | | | | | |

| Score | Length of Main Beam R | Length of Main Beam L | Inside Spread | Greatest Spread | Circumference at Smallest Place Between Burr and First Point R | Circumference at Smallest Place Between Burr and First Point L | Number of Points R | Number of Points L | Total of Lengths Abnormal Points | All-Time Rank | State Rank |
|---|---|---|---|---|---|---|---|---|---|---|---|
| ♦ *Locality Killed / By Whom Killed / Owner / Date Killed* | | | | | | | | | | | |
| 379 | 50 7/8 | 51 | 44 4/8 | 46 4/8 | 9 7/8 | 10 2/8 | 6 | 6 | | 215 | 48 |
| ♦ *Petroleum County / Lana J. Sluggett / Lana J. Sluggett / 1984* | | | | | | | | | | | |
| 378 6/8 | 55 | 54 4/8 | 45 | 48 3/8 | 8 | 7 4/8 | 6 | 6 | | 220 | 49 |
| ♦ *Gallatin County / Ted Shook / Ted Shook / 1966* | | | | | | | | | | | |
| 378 6/8 | 51 7/8 | 50 6/8 | 39 7/8 | 48 | 7 7/8 | 8 6/8 | 7 | 9 | 14 5/8 | 220 | 49 |
| ♦ *Sanders County / John Fitchett / John Fitchett / 1980* | | | | | | | | | | | |
| 378 4/8 | 58 3/8 | 56 3/8 | 43 6/8 | 48 1/8 | 8 4/8 | 8 3/8 | 6 | 6 | | 223 | 51 |
| ♦ *Beaverhead County / Milton F. Steele / Milton F. Steele / 1963* | | | | | | | | | | | |
| 378 | 49 3/8 | 50 2/8 | 39 5/8 | 46 3/8 | 8 1/8 | 8 6/8 | 7 | 7 | 2 3/8 | 229 | 52 |
| ♦ *Richard's Peak / Albert Sales / Richard Eastman / 1931* | | | | | | | | | | | |
| 377 6/8 | 56 6/8 | 55 6/8 | 41 6/8 | 53 | 8 2/8 | 8 2/8 | 7 | 10 | 14 2/8 | 231 | 53 |
| ♦ *Sanders County / Steve Barnes / Steve Barnes / 1973* | | | | | | | | | | | |
| 377 5/8 | 53 7/8 | 53 3/8 | 51 7/8 | 55 4/8 | 9 | 8 1/8 | 7 | 6 | 2 | 234 | 54 |
| ♦ *Beaverhead County / Edmund J. Giebel / Edmund J. Giebel / 1981* | | | | | | | | | | | |
| 377 4/8 | 54 3/8 | 51 5/8 | 45 5/8 | 52 6/8 | 8 6/8 | 8 6/8 | 7 | 7 | 1 1/8 | 236 | 55 |
| ♦ *Granite County / Tom Villeneue / Tom Villeneue / 1966* | | | | | | | | | | | |
| 377 3/8 | 60 | 58 | 41 7/8 | 46 | 8 5/8 | 8 4/8 | 6 | 6 | | 240 | 56 |
| ♦ *Sanders County / Allen White / Allen White / 1968* | | | | | | | | | | | |
| 377 3/8 | 53 1/8 | 52 | 46 1/8 | 47 6/8 | 8 4/8 | 9 1/8 | 6 | 6 | | 240 | 56 |
| ♦ *Missoula County / Tom Schenarts / Tom Schenarts / 1970* | | | | | | | | | | | |
| 377 2/8 | 53 5/8 | 53 6/8 | 49 2/8 | 53 4/8 | 8 2/8 | 8 2/8 | 6 | 7 | | 243 | 58 |
| ♦ *Gallatin Range / E. Dehart, Sr., P. Van Beek, & H. Prestine / Earl Dehart, Sr. / 1960* | | | | | | | | | | | |
| 376 6/8 | 51 2/8 | 52 4/8 | 48 2/8 | 51 7/8 | 8 4/8 | 8 3/8 | 8 | 7 | 1 6/8 | 254 | 59 |
| ♦ *Lewis & Clark County / Cameron G. Mielke / Cameron G. Mielke / 1964* | | | | | | | | | | | |
| 375 7/8 | 54 6/8 | 54 4/8 | 43 5/8 | 52 6/8 | 8 4/8 | 8 5/8 | 8 | 8 | | 269 | 60 |
| ♦ *Flathead County / Pat Roth / Pat Roth / 1966* | | | | | | | | | | | |
| 375 5/8 | 53 | 51 3/8 | 40 3/8 | 46 | 9 | 9 1/8 | 6 | 7 | | 275 | 61 |
| ♦ *Madison River / Dale A. Hancock / Dale A. Hancock / 1967* | | | | | | | | | | | |
| 375 5/8 | 54 3/8 | 54 1/8 | 43 7/8 | 52 1/8 | 8 2/8 | 8 3/8 | 7 | 6 | 9 | 275 | 61 |
| ♦ *Sanders County / Tony B. Cox / Tony B. Cox / 1980* | | | | | | | | | | | |
| 375 4/8 | 57 6/8 | 55 2/8 | 48 4/8 | 54 2/8 | 8 7/8 | 8 1/8 | 6 | 6 | | 278 | 63 |
| ♦ *Jefferson County / Ralph J. Huckaba / Ralph J. Huckaba / 1949* | | | | | | | | | | | |

| Score | Length of Main Beam | | Inside Spread | Great-est Spread | Circumference at Smallest Place Between Burr and First Point | | Number of Points | | Total of Lengths Abnor-mal Points | All-Time Rank | State Rank |
|---|---|---|---|---|---|---|---|---|---|---|---|
| | R | L | | | R | L | R | L | | | |
| ◆ *Locality Killed / By Whom Killed / Owner / Date Killed* | | | | | | | | | | | |
| 375 4/8 | 47 6/8 | 52 6/8 | 34 1/8 | 53 5/8 | 7 6/8 | 8 1/8 | 8 | 6 | 7 5/8 | 278 | 63 |
| ◆ *Powell County / Allan F. Kruse / Allan F. Kruse / 1977* | | | | | | | | | | | |
| 375 3/8 | 52 | 52 | 43 6/8 | 48 2/8 | 9 2/8 | 10 1/8 | 7 | 6 | 2 3/8 | 281 | 65 |
| ◆ *Jefferson County / Mrs. Lou Sweet / Mrs. Lou Sweet / 1924* | | | | | | | | | | | |
| 375 3/8 | 52 6/8 | 54 6/8 | 44 5/8 | 47 6/8 | 9 | 8 3/8 | 7 | 7 | | 281 | 65 |
| ◆ *Park County / Bruce Brown / Bruce Brown / 1967* | | | | | | | | | | | |
| 375 3/8 | 49 | 50 6/8 | 39 7/8 | 42 2/8 | 7 5/8 | 7 5/8 | 6 | 6 | | 281 | 65 |
| ◆ *Beaverhead County / Harold F. Krieger, Jr. / Harold F. Krieger, Jr. / 1970* | | | | | | | | | | | |
| 375 | 57 3/8 | 54 4/8 | 41 2/8 | 45 2/8 | 9 3/8 | 9 5/8 | 7 | 7 | | 294 | 68 |
| ◆ *Park County / Robert M. Brogan / Robert M. Brogan / 1972* | | | | | | | | | | | |
| 375 | 59 | 58 6/8 | 42 2/8 | 46 7/8 | 9 1/8 | 9 2/8 | 6 | 6 | | 294 | 68 |
| ◆ *Lewis & Clark County / James Bollinger / James Bollinger / 1982* | | | | | | | | | | | |

**MONTANA STATE RECORD**
**NON-TYPICAL AMERICAN ELK**
**SCORE: 402-7/8**
Locality: Powell Co.    Date: October 1987
Hunter: Donald A. Roberson

# MONTANA

## NON-TYPICAL AMERICAN ELK

| Score | Length of Main Beam R | Length of Main Beam L | Inside Spread | Greatest Spread | Circumference at Smallest Place Between Burr and First Point R | Circumference at Smallest Place Between Burr and First Point L | Number of Points R | Number of Points L | Total of Lengths Abnormal Points | All-Time Rank | State Rank |
|---|---|---|---|---|---|---|---|---|---|---|---|
| ♦ *Locality Killed / By Whom Killed / Owner / Date Killed* | | | | | | | | | | | |
| 402 7/8 | 48 6/8 | 50 | 39 | 47 5/8 | 8 2/8 | 8 3/8 | 8 | 9 | 19 7/8 | 7 | 1 |
| ♦ *Powell County / Donald A. Roberson / Donald A. Roberson / 1987* | | | | | | | | | | | |
| 401 7/8 | 51 6/8 | 50 | 49 2/8 | 63 4/8 | 9 4/8 | 9 4/8 | 9 | 7 | 29 5/8 | 9 | 2 |
| ♦ *Beaverhead County / Ben C. Holland / Ben C. Holland / 1953* | | | | | | | | | | | |
| 398 1/8 | 52 2/8 | 55 | 44 2/8 | 54 2/8 | 8 5/8 | 8 3/8 | 8 | 7 | 25 5/8 | 11 | 3 |
| ♦ *Park County / Picked Up / O. Cline Stelzig / 1972* | | | | | | | | | | | |
| 397 2/8 | 53 2/8 | 51 6/8 | 45 4/8 | 52 2/8 | 9 2/8 | 8 6/8 | 8 | 8 | 11 | 12 | 4 |
| ♦ *Powell County / Rex Sorenson / Univ. of Mont. Zool. Mus. / 1952* | | | | | | | | | | | |
| 386 5/8 | 51 7/8 | 50 6/8 | 45 7/8 | 60 5/8 | 8 7/8 | 8 4/8 | 8 | 7 | 15 4/8 | 13 | 5 |
| ♦ *Beaverhead County / Unknown / William H. Flesch / PR 1962* | | | | | | | | | | | |
| 407 6/8 | 54 6/8 | 54 2/8 | 46 4/8 | 51 | 9 | 8 | 8 | 8 | 29 4/8 | * | * |
| ♦ *Granite County / Scott Hicks / Scott Hicks / 1971* | | | | | | | | | | | |

Photograph Courtesy of Michael N. Kalafatic

**NEVADA STATE RECORD**
**TYPICAL AMERICAN ELK**
**SCORE: 381-3/8**
Locality: White Pine Co.    Date: September 1985
Hunter: Michael N. Kalafatic

# NEVADA

## TYPICAL AMERICAN ELK

| Score | Length of Main Beam | | Inside Spread | Greatest Spread | Circumference at Smallest Place Between Burr and First Point | | Number of Points | | Total of Lengths Abnormal Points | All-Time Rank | State Rank |
|---|---|---|---|---|---|---|---|---|---|---|---|
| | R | L | | | R | L | R | L | | | |
| | *Locality Killed* / *By Whom Killed* / *Owner* / *Date Killed* | | | | | | | | | | |
| 381 ⅜ | 53 ⅘ | 53 ⅞ | 43 ⅛ | 48 ⅜ | 9 ⅝ | 8 ⅝ | 6 | 6 | | 171 | 1 |
| ♦ *White Pine County* / *Michael N. Kalafatic* / *Michael N. Kalafatic* / *1985* | | | | | | | | | | | |

**NEW MEXICO STATE RECORD**
**TYPICAL AMERICAN ELK**
**SCORE: 398**
Locality: Mora Co.    Date: 1963
Hunter: Bernabe Alcon
Owner: Don Schaufler

# NEW MEXICO

## TYPICAL AMERICAN ELK

| Score | Length of Main Beam R | Length of Main Beam L | Inside Spread | Greatest Spread | Circumference at Smallest Place Between Burr and First Point R | Circumference at Smallest Place Between Burr and First Point L | Number of Points R | Number of Points L | Total of Lengths Abnormal Points | All-Time Rank | State Rank |
|---|---|---|---|---|---|---|---|---|---|---|---|
| ♦ *Locality Killed / By Whom Killed / Owner / Date Killed* | | | | | | | | | | | |
| 398 | 50 5/8 | 50 7/8 | 39 4/8 | 42 7/8 | 10 5/8 | 11 | 7 | 7 | | 28 | 1 |
| ♦ *Mora County / Bernabe Alcon / Don Schaufler / 1963* | | | | | | | | | | | |
| 393 2/8 | 63 1/8 | 64 4/8 | 44 2/8 | 49 1/8 | 9 5/8 | 9 6/8 | 6 | 7 | | 48 | 2 |
| ♦ *Socorro County / Floyd R. Owens / Floyd R. Owens / 1977* | | | | | | | | | | | |
| 387 | 55 | 55 4/8 | 54 4/8 | 56 6/8 | 8 7/8 | 8 2/8 | 8 | 7 | 4 4/8 | 95 | 3 |
| ♦ *Chama / Herb Klein / Herb Klein / 1952* | | | | | | | | | | | |
| 386 7/8 | 58 4/8 | 61 6/8 | 41 7/8 | 47 4/8 | 8 7/8 | 8 7/8 | 6 | 6 | | 96 | 4 |
| ♦ *Otero County / Picked Up / William M. Wheless III / 1981* | | | | | | | | | | | |
| 386 1/8 | 59 1/8 | 58 | 36 5/8 | 50 6/8 | 10 3/8 | 9 4/8 | 6 | 6 | | 104 | 5 |
| ♦ *Mescalero Apache Res. / Larry W. Bailey, Sr. / Larry W. Bailey, Sr. / 1974* | | | | | | | | | | | |
| 385 3/8 | 51 1/8 | 54 2/8 | 41 5/8 | 46 6/8 | 10 7/8 | 10 5/8 | 6 | 6 | | 114 | 6 |
| ♦ *Otero County / Gregory C. Saunders / Gregory C. Saunders / 1985* | | | | | | | | | | | |
| 380 3/8 | 56 3/8 | 58 | 44 1/8 | 47 5/8 | 7 5/8 | 7 5/8 | 7 | 6 | | 186 | 7 |
| ♦ *Catron County / Donald Parks, Jr. / Donald Parks, Jr. / 1988* | | | | | | | | | | | |
| 379 6/8 | 58 2/8 | 58 4/8 | 46 6/8 | 51 | 8 6/8 | 8 6/8 | 7 | 7 | | 197 | 8 |
| ♦ *Grant County / Tony R. Grijalva / Tony R. Grijalva / 1983* | | | | | | | | | | | |
| 379 3/8 | 51 2/8 | 47 | 42 3/8 | 51 7/8 | 9 4/8 | 9 7/8 | 6 | 6 | | 206 | 9 |
| ♦ *Otero County / Hubert R. Kennedy / Hubert R. Kennedy / 1985* | | | | | | | | | | | |
| 379 3/8 | 52 4/8 | 53 6/8 | 40 1/8 | 43 2/8 | 11 1/8 | 12 | 6 | 6 | | 206 | 9 |
| ♦ *Sierra County / James D. Wagner / James D. Wagner / 1986* | | | | | | | | | | | |
| 376 1/8 | 58 3/8 | 56 4/8 | 42 1/8 | 48 3/8 | 8 4/8 | 8 2/8 | 6 | 6 | | 266 | 11 |
| ♦ *Lincoln County / Jim Carter / Jim Carter / 1981* | | | | | | | | | | | |
| 375 2/8 | 55 3/8 | 55 3/8 | 41 2/8 | 46 | 8 3/8 | 8 3/8 | 6 | 6 | | 286 | 12 |
| ♦ *Colfax County / Slim Pickens / Margaret M. Lindley / 1981* | | | | | | | | | | | |
| 365 1/8 | 51 4/8 | 51 2/8 | 38 5/8 | 41 7/8 | 10 | 10 5/8 | 7 | 7 | | 304 | 13 |
| ♦ *Sandoval County / John C. McClendon / John C. McClendon / 1985* | | | | | | | | | | | |
| 360 2/8 | 53 6/8 | 52 4/8 | 41 6/8 | 48 | 9 6/8 | 9 | 6 | 7 | 4 4/8 | 306 | 14 |
| ♦ *Catron County / Robert H. Pickett, Jr. / Robert H. Pickett, Jr. / 1987* | | | | | | | | | | | |

**NEW MEXICO STATE RECORD**
**NON-TYPICAL AMERICAN ELK**
**SCORE: 414**
Locality: Taos Co.    Date: October 1974
Hunter: Lou A. DePaolis

# NEW MEXICO

## NON-TYPICAL AMERICAN ELK

| Score | Length of Main Beam R | Length of Main Beam L | Inside Spread | Great-est Spread | Circumference at Smallest Place Between Burr and First Point R | Circumference at Smallest Place Between Burr and First Point L | Number of Points R | Number of Points L | Total of Lengths Abnor-mal Points | All-Time Rank | State Rank |
|---|---|---|---|---|---|---|---|---|---|---|---|
| ◆ Locality Killed / By Whom Killed / Owner / Date Killed ||||||||||||
| 414 | 48 ⅞ | 48 ⅛ | 46 ⅞ | 55 ⅜ | 7 ⅜ | 6 ⅝ | 9 | 10 | 37 ⅜ | 3 | 1 |
| ◆ Taos County / Lou A. DePaolis / Lou A. DePaolis / 1974 ||||||||||||

Photograph Courtesy of James T. Sproul

**OREGON STATE RECORD**
**TYPICAL AMERICAN ELK**
**SCORE: 401-3/8**
Locality: Grant Co.    Date: October 1972
Hunter: James T. Sproul

# OREGON

## TYPICAL AMERICAN ELK

| Score | Length of Main Beam R | Length of Main Beam L | Inside Spread | Greatest Spread | Circumference at Smallest Place Between Burr and First Point R | Circumference at Smallest Place Between Burr and First Point L | Number of Points R | Number of Points L | Total of Lengths Abnormal Points | All-Time Rank | State Rank |
|---|---|---|---|---|---|---|---|---|---|---|---|
| ♦ *Locality Killed / By Whom Killed / Owner / Date Killed* | | | | | | | | | | | |
| 401 3/8 | 60 4/8 | 64 5/8 | 43 7/8 | 49 2/8 | 9 3/8 | 9 | 7 | 6 | | 19 | 1 |
| ♦ *Grant County / James T. Sproul / James T. Sproul / 1972* | | | | | | | | | | | |
| 400 | 56 2/8 | 57 | 49 | 52 2/8 | 9 1/8 | 9 1/8 | 7 | 7 | | 24 | 2 |
| ♦ *Crook County / Picked Up / Randall L. Ryerse / 1984* | | | | | | | | | | | |
| 395 1/8 | 56 4/8 | 57 2/8 | 46 5/8 | 59 1/8 | 10 2/8 | 9 3/8 | 7 | 8 | 3 | 38 | 3 |
| ♦ *Wallowa County / Lawton McDaniel / Lawton McDaniel / 1935* | | | | | | | | | | | |
| 392 3/8 | 53 4/8 | 54 4/8 | 46 3/8 | 51 2/8 | 8 3/8 | 8 6/8 | 6 | 6 | | 55 | 4 |
| ♦ *Umatilla County / Picked Up / Robert L. Brown / 1982* | | | | | | | | | | | |
| 390 2/8 | 55 | 55 4/8 | 49 2/8 | 55 4/8 | 8 6/8 | 8 6/8 | 7 | 7 | | 65 | 5 |
| ♦ *Hood River County / Bill Tensen / Bill Tensen / 1980* | | | | | | | | | | | |
| 389 | 51 | 48 3/8 | 41 6/8 | 47 | 8 2/8 | 8 2/8 | 6 | 6 | | 74 | 6 |
| ♦ *Meacham / H.M. Bailey / H.M. Bailey / 1963* | | | | | | | | | | | |
| 387 7/8 | 55 3/8 | 57 | 37 2/8 | 50 3/8 | 10 | 9 5/8 | 7 | 6 | 1 5/8 | 85 | 7 |
| ♦ *Grant County / Arnold Troph / Arnold Troph / 1966* | | | | | | | | | | | |
| 387 4/8 | 49 1/8 | 49 1/8 | 41 7/8 | 47 3/8 | 8 7/8 | 8 7/8 | 7 | 7 | 4 3/8 | 91 | 8 |
| ♦ *Grant County / Andy Chambers / Andy Chambers / 1959* | | | | | | | | | | | |
| 385 5/8 | 52 7/8 | 54 7/8 | 46 7/8 | 49 4/8 | 9 3/8 | 9 1/8 | 6 | 6 | | 110 | 9 |
| ♦ *Wheeler County / Ronny E. Rhoden / Ronny E. Rhoden / 1986* | | | | | | | | | | | |
| 382 2/8 | 55 7/8 | 53 3/8 | 39 2/8 | 50 2/8 | 9 2/8 | 9 1/8 | 7 | 7 | | 157 | 10 |
| ♦ *Grant County / Drake J. Davis / Drake J. Davis / 1981* | | | | | | | | | | | |
| 380 3/8 | 62 7/8 | 63 2/8 | 47 1/8 | 57 5/8 | 8 6/8 | 8 6/8 | 7 | 8 | 3 6/8 | 186 | 11 |
| ♦ *Harney County / Pat L. Wheeler / Pat L. Wheeler / 1967* | | | | | | | | | | | |
| 376 6/8 | 59 3/8 | 59 7/8 | 45 4/8 | 48 5/8 | 10 | 9 2/8 | 8 | 7 | 2 2/8 | 254 | 12 |
| ♦ *Crook County / Picked Up / Larry E. Miller / 1983* | | | | | | | | | | | |
| 375 | 57 1/8 | 58 1/8 | 42 6/8 | 48 | 9 1/8 | 8 6/8 | 6 | 6 | | 294 | 13 |
| ♦ *Wheeler County / William K. Bartlett / William K. Bartlett / 1986* | | | | | | | | | | | |
| 370 6/8 | 56 | 55 6/8 | 47 6/8 | 51 7/8 | 8 2/8 | 8 3/8 | 7 | 6 | 3 6/8 | 300 | 14 |
| ♦ *Grant County / Lawrence E. Mayfield / Lawrence E. Mayfield / 1984* | | | | | | | | | | | |

Photograph Courtesy of Todd Craig

**SOUTH DAKOTA STATE RECORD**
**TYPICAL AMERICAN ELK**
**SCORE: 363-6/8**
Locality: Custer Co.    Date: September 1986
Hunter: Todd Craig

# SOUTH DAKOTA
## TYPICAL AMERICAN ELK

| Score | Length of Main Beam R | L | Inside Spread | Great-est Spread | Circumference at Smallest Place Between Burr and First Point R | L | Number of Points R | L | Total of Lengths Abnor-mal Points | All-Time Rank | State Rank |
|---|---|---|---|---|---|---|---|---|---|---|---|
| | ♦ Locality Killed / By Whom Killed / Owner / Date Killed | | | | | | | | | | |
| 363 ⁵⁄₈ | 47 ⁴⁄₈ | 49 ⅛ | 40 ⅛ | 41 ⁵⁄₈ | 8 ⅜ | 8 ⅜ | 7 | 6 | 4 ⅞ | 305 | 1 |
| | ♦ Custer County / Todd Craig / Todd Craig / 1986 | | | | | | | | | | |

**TEXAS STATE RECORD**
**TYPICAL AMERICAN ELK**
**SCORE: 375**
Locality: Denton Co.    Date: 1934
Hunter: O.Z. Finley
Owner: Joe B. Finley, Jr.

# TEXAS

## TYPICAL AMERICAN ELK

| Score | Length of Main Beam R | Length of Main Beam L | Inside Spread | Greatest Spread | Circumference at Smallest Place Between Burr and First Point R | Circumference at Smallest Place Between Burr and First Point L | Number of Points R | Number of Points L | Total of Lengths Abnormal Points | All-Time Rank | State Rank |
|---|---|---|---|---|---|---|---|---|---|---|---|
| | ♦ Locality Killed / By Whom Killed / Owner / Date Killed | | | | | | | | | | |
| 375 | 57⅛ | 54 | 38 | 43 | 8 | 8 | 7 | 7 | | 294 | 1 |
| | ♦ Denton County / O.Z. Finley / Joe B. Finley, Jr. / 1934 | | | | | | | | | | |

**UTAH STATE RECORD**
**TYPICAL AMERICAN ELK**
**SCORE: 385-4/8**
Locality: Emery Co.     Date: November 1939
Hunter: Neville L. Wimmer
Owner: Russell N. Wimmer

# UTAH

## TYPICAL AMERICAN ELK

| Score | Length of Main Beam R | L | Inside Spread | Great- est Spread | Circumference at Smallest Place Between Burr and First Point R | L | Number of Points R | L | Total of Lengths Abnor- mal Points | All- Time Rank | State Rank |
|---|---|---|---|---|---|---|---|---|---|---|---|
| | ♦ Locality Killed / By Whom Killed / Owner / Date Killed | | | | | | | | | | |
| 385 4/8 | 56 2/8 | 57 3/8 | 37 4/8 | 46 5/8 | 8 2/8 | 8 2/8 | 6 | 6 | | 113 | 1 |
| | ♦ Emery County / Neville L. Wimmer / Russell N. Wimmer / 1939 | | | | | | | | | | |
| 374 4/8 | 53 2/8 | 54 2/8 | 40 2/8 | 46 3/8 | 7 7/8 | 8 2/8 | 6 | 6 | | 299 | 2 |
| | ♦ Garfield County / Brett R. Nybo / Brett R. Nybo / 1984 | | | | | | | | | | |

Photograph Courtesy of Clinton W. Morrow

**WASHINGTON SECOND PLACE**
**TYPICAL AMERICAN ELK**
**SCORE: 381-2/8**
Locality: Kittitas Co.    Date: 1957
Hunter: Clinton W. Morrow

# WASHINGTON

## TYPICAL AMERICAN ELK

| Score | Length of Main Beam R | Length of Main Beam L | Inside Spread | Greatest Spread | Circumference at Smallest Place Between Burr and First Point R | Circumference at Smallest Place Between Burr and First Point L | Number of Points R | Number of Points L | Total of Lengths Abnormal Points | All-Time Rank | State Rank |
|---|---|---|---|---|---|---|---|---|---|---|---|
| ♦ *Locality Killed / By Whom Killed / Owner / Date Killed* | | | | | | | | | | | |
| 393 1/8 | 56 3/8 | 59 2/8 | 47 1/8 | 52 1/8 | 8 6/8 | 8 6/8 | 6 | 6 | | 52 | 1 |
| ♦ *Kittitas County / Paul Anderson / Paul Anderson / 1927* | | | | | | | | | | | |
| 381 2/8 | 57 | 55 4/8 | 44 2/8 | 53 4/8 | 9 | 8 6/8 | 6 | 6 | | 174 | 2 |
| ♦ *Kittitas County / Clinton W. Morrow / Clinton W. Morrow / 1957* | | | | | | | | | | | |
| 380 2/8 | 57 4/8 | 57 3/8 | 46 4/8 | 48 6/8 | 8 4/8 | 8 3/8 | 7 | 7 | | 188 | 3 |
| ♦ *Lewis County / Charles Rudolph / Charles Rudolph / 1973* | | | | | | | | | | | |
| 379 2/8 | 53 4/8 | 52 2/8 | 44 | 50 6/8 | 8 | 8 4/8 | 6 | 6 | | 210 | 4 |
| ♦ *Yakima County / Donald G. Stein / Donald G. Stein / 1985* | | | | | | | | | | | |

**WYOMING STATE RECORD**
**TYPICAL AMERICAN ELK**
**SCORE: 441-6/8**
Locality: Big Horn Mts.    Date: 1890
Hunter: Unknown
Owner: Jackson Hole Museum

# WYOMING

## TYPICAL AMERICAN ELK

| Score | Length of Main Beam R | Length of Main Beam L | Inside Spread | Greatest Spread | Circumference at Smallest Place Between Burr and First Point R | Circumference at Smallest Place Between Burr and First Point L | Number of Points R | Number of Points L | Total of Lengths Abnormal Points | All-Time Rank | State Rank |
|---|---|---|---|---|---|---|---|---|---|---|---|
| ♦ *Locality Killed / By Whom Killed / Owner / Date Killed* | | | | | | | | | | | |
| 441 6/8 | 61 6/8 | 61 2/8 | 47 | 50 2/8 | 10 2/8 | 9 7/8 | 8 | 7 | | 2 | 1 |
| ♦ *Big Horn Mts. / Unknown / Jackson Hole Museum / 1890* | | | | | | | | | | | |
| 418 7/8 | 58 | 55 | 43 1/8 | 54 3/8 | 10 5/8 | 11 3/8 | 6 | 7 | 3 6/8 | 5 | 2 |
| ♦ *Wyoming / J.G. Millais / G. Kenneth Whitehead / 1886* | | | | | | | | | | | |
| 401 6/8 | 58 3/8 | 57 5/8 | 47 2/8 | 50 4/8 | 7 7/8 | 8 | 6 | 6 | | 17 | 3 |
| ♦ *Teton County / Douglas Spicer / Douglas Spicer / 1972* | | | | | | | | | | | |
| 400 2/8 | 56 | 55 2/8 | 46 | 53 7/8 | 8 2/8 | 8 4/8 | 7 | 7 | | 23 | 4 |
| ♦ *Jackson Hole / C. Atkins & O. Maynard / Thomas Myers / 1947* | | | | | | | | | | | |
| 397 7/8 | 52 | 55 1/8 | 52 1/8 | 62 4/8 | 8 1/8 | 7 6/8 | 7 | 7 | | 30 | 5 |
| ♦ *Sublette County / Ray Daugherty / Aldon L. Hale / 1950* | | | | | | | | | | | |
| 395 4/8 | 57 5/8 | 60 1/8 | 47 | 51 6/8 | 8 1/8 | 8 6/8 | 6 | 6 | | 36 | 6 |
| ♦ *Fremont County / Roger Linnell / Roger Linnell / 1955* | | | | | | | | | | | |
| 394 2/8 | 53 2/8 | 56 2/8 | 41 2/8 | 46 | 9 2/8 | 9 2/8 | 6 | 6 | | 43 | 7 |
| ♦ *Hoback Rim / Clyde Robbins / George Franz / 1940* | | | | | | | | | | | |
| 394 1/8 | 58 | 58 4/8 | 46 7/8 | 49 6/8 | 9 6/8 | 10 2/8 | 6 | 6 | | 46 | 8 |
| ♦ *Lincoln County / Roland Smith / Leon C. Smith / 1930* | | | | | | | | | | | |
| 393 2/8 | 53 5/8 | 51 6/8 | 46 2/8 | 49 | 10 2/8 | 10 | 6 | 6 | | 48 | 9 |
| ♦ *Big Horn County / Edwin Shaffer / Edwin Shaffer / 1946* | | | | | | | | | | | |
| 391 6/8 | 54 4/8 | 53 | 46 | 48 4/8 | 7 7/8 | 8 7/8 | 6 | 6 | | 57 | 10 |
| ♦ *Thoroughfare Creek / Thomas A. Yawkey / Thomas A. Yawkey / 1936* | | | | | | | | | | | |
| 391 4/8 | 52 2/8 | 52 7/8 | 51 2/8 | 53 2/8 | 8 5/8 | 9 | 7 | 6 | | 59 | 11 |
| ♦ *Big Horn Mts. / Robert K. Hamilton / Robert K. Hamilton / 1954* | | | | | | | | | | | |
| 390 3/8 | 57 1/8 | 54 1/8 | 40 1/8 | 48 6/8 | 9 2/8 | 9 1/8 | 7 | 7 | | 64 | 12 |
| ♦ *Hoback Canyon / Picked Up / Spanky Greenville / 1977* | | | | | | | | | | | |
| 389 4/8 | 53 7/8 | 54 7/8 | 46 | 52 6/8 | 8 7/8 | 8 7/8 | 6 | 6 | | 68 | 13 |
| ♦ *Big Horn County / Floyd A. Clark / Floyd A. Clark / 1976* | | | | | | | | | | | |

| Score | Length of Main Beam R | Length of Main Beam L | Inside Spread | Greatest Spread | Circumference at Smallest Place Between Burr and First Point R | Circumference at Smallest Place Between Burr and First Point L | Number of Points R | Number of Points L | Total of Lengths Abnormal Points | All-Time Rank | State Rank |
|---|---|---|---|---|---|---|---|---|---|---|---|
| ♦ *Locality Killed / By Whom Killed / Owner / Date Killed* | | | | | | | | | | | |
| 388 7/8 | 56 | 55 4/8 | 46 3/8 | 50 3/8 | 9 6/8 | 8 6/8 | 6 | 6 | | 75 | 14 |
| ♦ *Jackson Hole / Unknown / William Sonnenburg / PR 1912* | | | | | | | | | | | |
| 388 | 55 4/8 | 54 4/8 | 50 2/8 | 53 1/8 | 8 4/8 | 9 | 8 | 9 | 2 4/8 | 82 | 15 |
| ♦ *Converse / Jerry F. Cook / J.F. Cook & Mrs. P. Muchmore / 1965* | | | | | | | | | | | |
| 387 7/8 | 54 4/8 | 55 5/8 | 44 5/8 | 50 7/8 | 9 6/8 | 9 5/8 | 7 | 6 | 1 2/8 | 85 | 16 |
| ♦ *Kelly / Roger Penney / Bernard Bronk / 1963* | | | | | | | | | | | |
| 387 7/8 | 52 1/8 | 53 | 44 5/8 | 50 2/8 | 7 7/8 | 8 | 6 | 6 | | 85 | 16 |
| ♦ *Lincoln / Dexter R. Gardner / Dexter R. Gardner / 1967* | | | | | | | | | | | |
| 387 6/8 | 57 6/8 | 56 4/8 | 51 | 54 6/8 | 8 | 7 7/8 | 7 | 6 | | 88 | 18 |
| ♦ *Big Horn Mts. / Elgin T. Gates / Elgin T. Gates / 1954* | | | | | | | | | | | |
| 386 | 52 4/8 | 53 | 48 2/8 | 51 4/8 | 8 4/8 | 8 4/8 | 6 | 7 | | 106 | 19 |
| ♦ *Big Horn Mts. / Unknown / Fred Gray / 1966* | | | | | | | | | | | |
| 385 3/8 | 55 4/8 | 55 2/8 | 47 3/8 | 54 3/8 | 10 1/8 | 10 5/8 | 6 | 6 | | 114 | 20 |
| ♦ *Teton County / Gene J. Riordan / Timothy D. Riordan / 1960* | | | | | | | | | | | |
| 385 1/8 | 46 | 48 2/8 | 44 3/8 | 54 1/8 | 7 6/8 | 8 2/8 | 6 | 6 | | 117 | 21 |
| ♦ *Lincoln County / Ken Clark / Ken Clark / 1979* | | | | | | | | | | | |
| 384 3/8 | 59 3/8 | 59 2/8 | 49 1/8 | 49 1/8 | 7 6/8 | 7 5/8 | 7 | 6 | | 129 | 22 |
| ♦ *Jackson Hole / Francis X. Bouchard / Francis X. Bouchard / 1956* | | | | | | | | | | | |
| 383 1/8 | 58 1/8 | 54 4/8 | 53 1/8 | 54 | 9 | 9 6/8 | 6 | 6 | | 143 | 23 |
| ♦ *Snowy Range / Kermit Platt / Kermit Platt / 1961* | | | | | | | | | | | |
| 382 6/8 | 56 1/8 | 54 5/8 | 41 5/8 | 47 5/8 | 9 7/8 | 10 2/8 | 7 | 6 | 8 3/8 | 148 | 24 |
| ♦ *Rattlesnake Mt. / Bob Edgar / Bob Edgar / 1966* | | | | | | | | | | | |
| 382 4/8 | 49 | 48 5/8 | 36 6/8 | 46 3/8 | 8 5/8 | 8 6/8 | 6 | 6 | | 151 | 25 |
| ♦ *Teton County / Randy Johnston / Randy Johnston / 1970* | | | | | | | | | | | |
| 382 3/8 | 53 3/8 | 54 | 50 5/8 | 52 7/8 | 8 4/8 | 8 4/8 | 7 | 7 | | 155 | 26 |
| ♦ *Sublette County / Frank Dew / Frank Dew / 1931* | | | | | | | | | | | |
| 381 4/8 | 56 4/8 | 57 2/8 | 42 4/8 | 48 2/8 | 8 7/8 | 9 2/8 | 6 | 6 | | 170 | 27 |
| ♦ *Fremont County / John S. Maxson / John S. Maxson / 1954* | | | | | | | | | | | |
| 381 1/8 | 57 5/8 | 56 1/8 | 45 1/8 | 53 | 8 | 7 3/8 | 6 | 6 | | 175 | 28 |
| ♦ *Laramie Peak / Lawrence Prager / Lawrence Prager / 1958* | | | | | | | | | | | |
| 379 5/8 | 57 | 53 1/8 | 48 1/8 | 52 2/8 | 9 2/8 | 9 2/8 | 6 | 6 | | 203 | 29 |
| ♦ *Big Horn Mts. / Unknown / L.M. Brownell / 1956* | | | | | | | | | | | |
| 379 | 49 | 50 4/8 | 39 | 43 4/8 | 10 1/8 | 10 1/8 | 8 | 6 | | 215 | 30 |
| ♦ *Teton Park / S.M. Vilven / S.M. Vilven / 1964* | | | | | | | | | | | |

| Score | Length of Main Beam R | Length of Main Beam L | Inside Spread | Greatest Spread | Circumference at Smallest Place Between Burr and First Point R | Circumference at Smallest Place Between Burr and First Point L | Number of Points R | Number of Points L | Total of Lengths Abnormal Points | All-Time Rank | State Rank |
|---|---|---|---|---|---|---|---|---|---|---|---|
| ♦ *Locality Killed / By Whom Killed / Owner / Date Killed* | | | | | | | | | | | |
| 378 7/8 | 57 5/8 | 58 6/8 | 47 1/8 | 51 3/8 | 8 2/8 | 8 2/8 | 6 | 6 | | 218 | 31 |
| ♦ *Carbon County / Donal F. Mueller / Donal F. Mueller / 1964* | | | | | | | | | | | |
| 378 4/8 | 52 7/8 | 54 5/8 | 42 4/8 | 47 4/8 | 9 3/8 | 10 | 7 | 7 | | 223 | 32 |
| ♦ *Park County / Kenneth Smith / Kenneth Smith / 1954* | | | | | | | | | | | |
| 377 4/8 | 52 2/8 | 54 | 41 4/8 | 47 2/8 | 8 6/8 | 8 3/8 | 6 | 7 | | 236 | 33 |
| ♦ *Park County / Jon M. Mekeal / Jon M. Mekeal / 1984* | | | | | | | | | | | |
| 377 3/8 | 59 | 55 | 39 3/8 | 47 4/8 | 9 7/8 | 9 7/8 | 6 | 6 | | 240 | 34 |
| ♦ *Teton County / Walter V. Solinski / Walter V. Solinski / 1962* | | | | | | | | | | | |
| 377 2/8 | 56 | 55 2/8 | 40 2/8 | 48 2/8 | 11 1/8 | 11 | 6 | 6 | | 243 | 35 |
| ♦ *Park County / Mary J. Rickman / M.J. Rickman & E.R. Rickman, Jr. / 1965* | | | | | | | | | | | |
| 377 1/8 | 53 | 51 6/8 | 45 4/8 | 52 2/8 | 9 | 8 5/8 | 6 | 8 | 4 7/8 | 247 | 36 |
| ♦ *Sublette County / Ted Dew / Ted Dew / 1928* | | | | | | | | | | | |
| 376 7/8 | 55 | 55 6/8 | 38 2/8 | 43 6/8 | 9 5/8 | 10 2/8 | 7 | 6 | 1 7/8 | 251 | 37 |
| ♦ *Jackson Hole / H.M. Hanna / M.H. Haskell / PR 1890* | | | | | | | | | | | |
| 376 7/8 | 56 4/8 | 57 2/8 | 52 7/8 | 58 6/8 | 7 3/8 | 7 7/8 | 6 | 6 | | 251 | 37 |
| ♦ *Park County / Warren C. Cubbage / Warren C. Cubbage / 1957* | | | | | | | | | | | |
| 376 6/8 | 56 2/8 | 54 4/8 | 44 6/8 | 52 5/8 | 9 4/8 | 9 3/8 | 7 | 7 | 9 | 254 | 39 |
| ♦ *Big Horn Mts. / Unknown / A.W. Hendershot / 1912* | | | | | | | | | | | |
| 376 6/8 | 61 | 58 7/8 | 51 | 55 4/8 | 8 3/8 | 7 3/8 | 8 | 7 | | 254 | 39 |
| ♦ *Teton County / Ward Keevert / Ward Keevert / 1968* | | | | | | | | | | | |
| 376 4/8 | 55 1/8 | 53 4/8 | 49 6/8 | 53 | 8 2/8 | 8 5/8 | 8 | 7 | | 260 | 41 |
| ♦ *Albany County / Jerry F. Cook / Jerry F. Cook / 1965* | | | | | | | | | | | |
| 375 6/8 | 54 6/8 | 50 4/8 | 43 | 47 6/8 | 8 4/8 | 8 2/8 | 6 | 6 | | 270 | 42 |
| ♦ *Big Horn Mts. / Robert F. Retzlaff / Robert F. Retzlaff / 1957* | | | | | | | | | | | |
| 375 6/8 | 57 2/8 | 57 7/8 | 43 | 50 2/8 | 7 2/8 | 7 3/8 | 6 | 6 | | 270 | 42 |
| ♦ *Buck Creek / Andrew W. Heard, Jr. / Andrew W. Heard, Jr. / 1958* | | | | | | | | | | | |
| 375 6/8 | 55 1/8 | 54 4/8 | 39 4/8 | 46 6/8 | 8 7/8 | 8 2/8 | 6 | 6 | | 270 | 42 |
| ♦ *North Fall Creek / Picked Up / Bob F. Penny / 1981* | | | | | | | | | | | |
| 375 4/8 | 50 | 53 2/8 | 48 4/8 | 54 1/8 | 8 4/8 | 9 1/8 | 6 | 6 | | 278 | 45 |
| ♦ *Fremont County / Edward J. Patik / Edward J. Patik / 1962* | | | | | | | | | | | |
| 375 3/8 | 51 1/8 | 52 | 44 7/8 | 47 4/8 | 7 6/8 | 8 2/8 | 6 | 7 | | 281 | 46 |
| ♦ *Teton County / Unknown / Nathan E. Hindman / PR 1950* | | | | | | | | | | | |
| 375 3/8 | 58 7/8 | 56 6/8 | 43 1/8 | 48 4/8 | 8 3/8 | 9 1/8 | 6 | 7 | | 281 | 46 |
| ♦ *Snake River / W.H. Robinson / W.H. Robinson / 1957* | | | | | | | | | | | |

| Score | Length of Main Beam R | L | Inside Spread | Greatest Spread | Circumference at Smallest Place Between Burr and First Point R | L | Number of Points R | L | Total of Lengths Abnormal Points | All-Time Rank | State Rank |
|---|---|---|---|---|---|---|---|---|---|---|---|
| | | | | | *Locality Killed / By Whom Killed / Owner / Date Killed* | | | | | | |
| 375 2/8 | 54 4/8 | 55 3/8 | 49 | 54 4/8 | 9 3/8 | 9 6/8 | 6 | 7 | | 286 | 48 |
| | | | | ♦ *Jackson / Bill Blanchard / Bill Blanchard / 1954* | | | | | | | |
| 375 2/8 | 51 4/8 | 53 1/8 | 36 2/8 | 45 1/8 | 7 7/8 | 7 4/8 | 7 | 7 | | 286 | 48 |
| | | | | ♦ *Ten Sleep / Kenneth Hadland / Kenneth Hadland / 1959* | | | | | | | |
| 375 2/8 | 53 | 52 | 41 | 49 6/8 | 10 | 10 4/8 | 7 | 8 | | 286 | 48 |
| | | | | ♦ *Natrona County / Victor R. Jackson / Victor R. Jackson / 1976* | | | | | | | |
| 375 2/8 | 56 | 55 | 38 | 48 4/8 | 8 4/8 | 8 4/8 | 6 | 6 | | 286 | 48 |
| | | | | ♦ *Albany County / Don Stewart / Don Stewart / 1981* | | | | | | | |
| 368 2/8 | 50 5/8 | 50 4/8 | 42 4/8 | 48 6/8 | 8 | 9 1/8 | 6 | 6 | | 301 | 52 |
| | | | | ♦ *Carbon County / Larry J. Thoney / Larry J. Thoney / 1978* | | | | | | | |

A fall hunt in Petroleum County, Montana, in 1984 paid off handsomely by producing this massive typical American elk, with a score of 379 points, for Lana J. Sluggett.

**ALBERTA PROVINCE RECORD**
**TYPICAL AMERICAN ELK**
**SCORE: 419-5/8**
Locality: Panther River    Date: November 1977
Hunter: Clarence Brown

# ALBERTA

## TYPICAL AMERICAN ELK

| Score | Length of Main Beam R | Length of Main Beam L | Inside Spread | Greatest Spread | Circumference at Smallest Place Between Burr and First Point R | Circumference at Smallest Place Between Burr and First Point L | Number of Points R | Number of Points L | Total of Lengths Abnormal Points | All-Time Rank | Prov. Rank |
|---|---|---|---|---|---|---|---|---|---|---|---|
| ♦ *Locality Killed / By Whom Killed / Owner / Date Killed* | | | | | | | | | | | |
| 419 5/8 | 62 3/8 | 62 2/8 | 49 2/8 | 53 2/8 | 10 3/8 | 10 3/8 | 6 | 8 | 1 5/8 | 3 | 1 |
| ♦ *Panther River / Clarence Brown / Clarence Brown / 1977* | | | | | | | | | | | |
| 418 | 54 1/8 | 50 4/8 | 44 2/8 | 52 6/8 | 8 4/8 | 8 4/8 | 6 | 6 | | 6 | 2 |
| ♦ *Muddywater River / Bruce W. Hale / Bruce W. Hale / 1971* | | | | | | | | | | | |
| 402 5/8 | 59 1/8 | 59 6/8 | 44 1/8 | | 9 1/8 | 8 5/8 | 7 | 7 | | 13 | 3 |
| ♦ *Red Deer River / Henry Folkman / Henry Folkman / 1946* | | | | | | | | | | | |
| 400 7/8 | 59 3/8 | 59 3/8 | 47 5/8 | | 8 4/8 | 8 2/8 | 7 | 7 | | 20 | 4 |
| ♦ *Rock Lake / Ray Hindmarsh / Ray Hindmarsh / 1963* | | | | | | | | | | | |
| 399 2/8 | 59 5/8 | 57 4/8 | 47 3/8 | 53 2/8 | 7 7/8 | 7 5/8 | 8 | 7 | 3 7/8 | 26 | 5 |
| ♦ *Ram River / Ralph A. Fry / Ralph A. Fry / 1952* | | | | | | | | | | | |
| 398 | 50 3/8 | 53 5/8 | 46 6/8 | 49 4/8 | 8 4/8 | 8 4/8 | 6 | 6 | | 28 | 6 |
| ♦ *Pincher Creek / Monty F. Adams / Pat Adams / 1977* | | | | | | | | | | | |
| 396 1/8 | 51 5/8 | 50 2/8 | 49 7/8 | | 7 4/8 | 7 4/8 | 7 | 8 | | 35 | 7 |
| ♦ *Rock Lake / Harold R. Vaughn / Harold R. Vaughn / 1968* | | | | | | | | | | | |
| 394 2/8 | 56 7/8 | 57 2/8 | 42 6/8 | 49 1/8 | 9 2/8 | 7 6/8 | 7 | 6 | 1 4/8 | 43 | 8 |
| ♦ *Panther River / Picked Up / George Browne / 1938* | | | | | | | | | | | |
| 394 2/8 | 53 1/8 | 55 3/8 | 45 2/8 | 53 | 8 1/8 | 8 3/8 | 6 | 6 | | 43 | 8 |
| ♦ *Elkwater / Roy Crawford / Roy Crawford / 1976* | | | | | | | | | | | |
| 393 2/8 | 55 2/8 | 54 4/8 | 51 4/8 | 55 2/8 | 8 3/8 | 8 2/8 | 6 | 6 | | 48 | 10 |
| ♦ *Watertown Natl. Park / Alan Foster / Alan Foster / 1952* | | | | | | | | | | | |
| 392 5/8 | 58 7/8 | 58 4/8 | 48 5/8 | 52 5/8 | 8 7/8 | 9 | 7 | 7 | | 53 | 11 |
| ♦ *Panther River / Bill Brooks / Bill Brooks / 1955* | | | | | | | | | | | |
| 390 6/8 | 53 5/8 | 54 3/8 | 49 6/8 | 53 | 9 3/8 | 9 5/8 | 7 | 6 | | 62 | 12 |
| ♦ *Clearwater River / Bob Dial / Bob Dial / 1955* | | | | | | | | | | | |
| 388 2/8 | 59 1/8 | 59 | 54 | 57 | 7 5/8 | 7 6/8 | 6 | 6 | | 78 | 13 |
| ♦ *Cutoff Creek / Joe A. Riveira / Joe A. Riveira / 1986* | | | | | | | | | | | |

| Score | Length of Main Beam | | Inside Spread | Greatest Spread | Circumference at Smallest Place Between Burr and First Point | | Number of Points | | Total of Lengths Abnormal Points | All-Time Rank | Prov. Rank |
|---|---|---|---|---|---|---|---|---|---|---|---|
| | R | L | | | R | L | R | L | | | |
| *Locality Killed / By Whom Killed / Owner / Date Killed* | | | | | | | | | | | |
| 387 5/8 | 58 1/8 | 56 | 39 1/8 | 45 3/8 | 8 7/8 | 9 1/8 | 7 | 7 | | 90 | 14 |
| ◆ *Yarrow Creek / D. Belyea / D. Belyea / 1970* | | | | | | | | | | | |
| 386 5/8 | 59 3/8 | 60 | 52 1/8 | 55 | 9 6/8 | 9 1/8 | 7 | 7 | | 99 | 15 |
| ◆ *Panther River / Leonard L. Hengen / Leonard L. Hengen / 1977* | | | | | | | | | | | |
| 386 4/8 | 55 6/8 | 55 5/8 | 42 | 53 1/8 | 10 | 9 2/8 | 7 | 7 | | 100 | 16 |
| ◆ *Smoky River / Stephen Trulik / Stephen Trulik / 1963* | | | | | | | | | | | |
| 385 6/8 | 56 7/8 | 56 1/8 | 40 4/8 | 44 3/8 | 7 7/8 | 8 | 6 | 6 | | 109 | 17 |
| ◆ *Big Smoky River / Fred T. Huntington, Jr. / Fred T. Huntington, Jr. / 1961* | | | | | | | | | | | |
| 385 1/8 | 51 | 52 4/8 | 48 4/8 | 54 3/8 | 11 | 11 4/8 | 8 | 6 | 8 7/8 | 117 | 18 |
| ◆ *Grande Cache Lake / Kenneth A. Evans / Kenneth A. Evans / 1966* | | | | | | | | | | | |
| 384 6/8 | 55 3/8 | 54 3/8 | 36 4/8 | 39 7/8 | 9 2/8 | 9 | 6 | 6 | | 121 | 19 |
| ◆ *Clearwater River / William Lenz / William Lenz / 1966* | | | | | | | | | | | |
| 384 5/8 | 55 3/8 | 54 6/8 | 47 1/8 | 54 | 8 4/8 | 8 7/8 | 6 | 6 | | 125 | 20 |
| ◆ *Ram River / Joe Kramer / Joe Kramer / 1966* | | | | | | | | | | | |
| 383 3/8 | 53 5/8 | 55 | 50 1/8 | 51 2/8 | 8 2/8 | 8 | 6 | 6 | | 140 | 21 |
| ◆ *Maycroft / Steve Kubasek / Steve Kubasek / 1957* | | | | | | | | | | | |
| 383 | 52 1/8 | 52 3/8 | 51 4/8 | 53 1/8 | 9 5/8 | 9 | 6 | 6 | | 144 | 22 |
| ◆ *Panther River / Thomas Coupland / Echoglen Taxidermy / 1984* | | | | | | | | | | | |
| 382 7/8 | 54 3/8 | 52 7/8 | 43 5/8 | 47 3/8 | 8 6/8 | 8 5/8 | 6 | 6 | | 146 | 23 |
| ◆ *Castle River / Albert Truant / Albert Truant / 1970* | | | | | | | | | | | |
| 382 4/8 | 49 6/8 | 48 | 32 7/8 | 40 6/8 | 14 4/8 | 13 | 9 | 7 | 16 1/8 | 151 | 24 |
| ◆ *Elbow River / Harold F. Mailman / Harold F. Mailman / 1964* | | | | | | | | | | | |
| 381 6/8 | 55 2/8 | 57 1/8 | 41 | 47 | 9 6/8 | 9 6/8 | 7 | 7 | | 165 | 25 |
| ◆ *Red Deer River / Allan E. Brown / Allan E. Brown / 1980* | | | | | | | | | | | |
| 380 | 54 | 53 5/8 | 48 2/8 | 52 3/8 | 8 7/8 | 8 4/8 | 7 | 7 | | 193 | 26 |
| ◆ *Spring Creek / A.C. Bair / A.C. Bair / 1948* | | | | | | | | | | | |
| 379 6/8 | 50 1/8 | 51 4/8 | 45 4/8 | 52 1/8 | 9 4/8 | 9 4/8 | 6 | 6 | | 197 | 27 |
| ◆ *Rock Lake / Jim Soneff / Jim Soneff / 1961* | | | | | | | | | | | |
| 379 1/8 | 56 | 57 4/8 | 33 7/8 | 47 | 8 6/8 | 9 1/8 | 6 | 6 | | 214 | 28 |
| ◆ *Duvernay Bridge / Alec Mitchell / Alec Mitchell / 1917* | | | | | | | | | | | |
| 378 7/8 | 56 6/8 | 56 1/8 | 46 5/8 | 52 2/8 | 8 4/8 | 8 | 6 | 6 | | 218 | 29 |
| ◆ *Wildhay River / Richard Clouthier / Richard Clouthier / 1973* | | | | | | | | | | | |
| 378 5/8 | 52 | 55 1/8 | 47 1/8 | 51 4/8 | 8 7/8 | 8 6/8 | 7 | 6 | | 222 | 30 |
| ◆ *Dutch Creek / Harold King / Harold King / 1951* | | | | | | | | | | | |

| Score | Length of Main Beam R | Length of Main Beam L | Inside Spread | Greatest Spread | Circumference at Smallest Place Between Burr and First Point R | Circumference at Smallest Place Between Burr and First Point L | Number of Points R | Number of Points L | Total of Lengths Abnormal Points | All-Time Rank | Prov. Rank |
|---|---|---|---|---|---|---|---|---|---|---|---|
| ♦ *Locality Killed / By Whom Killed / Owner / Date Killed* | | | | | | | | | | | |
| 377 | 54 6/8 | 54 1/8 | 47 2/8 | 51 | 9 2/8 | 8 5/8 | 7 | 6 | | 248 | 31 |
| ♦ *Brazeau River / Ted Loblaw / Ted Loblaw / 1960* | | | | | | | | | | | |
| 377 | 49 4/8 | 48 1/8 | 39 | 48 3/8 | 7 1/8 | 7 4/8 | 7 | 7 | | 248 | 31 |
| ♦ *Clearwater River / Don H. Grimes / Don H. Grimes / 1985* | | | | | | | | | | | |
| 376 4/8 | 56 5/8 | 57 | 39 4/8 | 48 | 9 3/8 | 9 5/8 | 7 | 7 | | 260 | 33 |
| ♦ *Highwood River / L. Edwards / L. Edwards / 1956* | | | | | | | | | | | |
| 376 3/8 | 54 2/8 | 55 5/8 | 43 3/8 | 50 | 9 | 9 1/8 | 6 | 6 | | 262 | 34 |
| ♦ *Rocky Mt. House / George P. Ebl / George P. Ebl / 1966* | | | | | | | | | | | |
| 376 | 55 | 54 1/8 | 42 | 50 2/8 | 9 3/8 | 9 1/8 | 6 | 6 | | 267 | 35 |
| ♦ *Dormer River / D.C. Thomas / D.C. Thomas / 1978* | | | | | | | | | | | |
| 365 3/8 | 56 7/8 | 55 5/8 | 43 6/8 | 49 4/8 | 8 6/8 | 7 4/8 | 7 | 8 | 6 3/8 | 302 | 36 |
| ♦ *Barrier Mt. / James A. Bauer / James A. Bauer / 1985* | | | | | | | | | | | |

**ALBERTA PROVINCE RECORD**
**NON-TYPICAL AMERICAN ELK**
**SCORE: 402-2/8\***
Locality: Dogrib Creek    Date: November 1984
Hunter: Robert H. Jochim

# ALBERTA

## NON-TYPICAL AMERICAN ELK

| Score | Length of Main Beam R | Length of Main Beam L | Inside Spread | Greatest Spread | Circumference at Smallest Place Between Burr and First Point R | Circumference at Smallest Place Between Burr and First Point L | Number of Points R | Number of Points L | Total of Lengths Abnormal Points | All-Time Rank | Prov. Rank |
|---|---|---|---|---|---|---|---|---|---|---|---|
| ♦ *Locality Killed / By Whom Killed / Owner / Date Killed* | | | | | | | | | | | |
| 402 2/8 | 55 6/8 | 55 7/8 | 50 1/8 | 53 2/8 | 9 7/8 | 10 1/8 | 7 | 7 | 24 3/8 | * | * |
| ♦ *Dogrib Creek / Robert H. Jochim / Robert H. Jochim / 1984* | | | | | | | | | | | |

**BRITISH COLUMBIA PROVINCE RECORD**
**TYPICAL AMERICAN ELK**
**SCORE: 401-7/8**
Locality: Kootenay Lake    Date: Picked Up 1986
Owner: Rick D. Armstrong

# BRITISH COLUMBIA

## TYPICAL AMERICAN ELK

| Score | Length of Main Beam R | Length of Main Beam L | Inside Spread | Greatest Spread | Circumference at Smallest Place Between Burr and First Point R | Circumference at Smallest Place Between Burr and First Point L | Number of Points R | Number of Points L | Total of Lengths Abnormal Points | All-Time Rank | Prov. Rank |
|---|---|---|---|---|---|---|---|---|---|---|---|
| ♦ *Locality Killed / By Whom Killed / Owner / Date Killed* | | | | | | | | | | | |
| 401 7/8 | 55 3/8 | 54 4/8 | 45 3/8 | 50 6/8 | 9 6/8 | 9 4/8 | 6 | 6 | | 15 | 1 |
| ♦ *Kootenay Lake / Picked Up / Rick D. Armstrong / 1986* | | | | | | | | | | | |
| 388 2/8 | 56 1/8 | 54 7/8 | 40 | 50 7/8 | 9 2/8 | 9 7/8 | 7 | 6 | 4 6/8 | 78 | 2 |
| ♦ *Sentinel Mt. / Martin Braun / Martin Braun / 1986* | | | | | | | | | | | |

**MANITOBA PROVINCE RECORD
TYPICAL AMERICAN ELK
SCORE: 396-2/8**
Locality: Duck Mts.    Date: 1960
Hunter: Paul Kirkowich

# MANITOBA

## TYPICAL AMERICAN ELK

| Score | Length of Main Beam R | Length of Main Beam L | Inside Spread | Greatest Spread | Circumference at Smallest Place Between Burr and First Point R | Circumference at Smallest Place Between Burr and First Point L | Number of Points R | Number of Points L | Total of Lengths Abnormal Points | All-Time Rank | Prov. Rank |
|---|---|---|---|---|---|---|---|---|---|---|---|
| ♦ *Locality Killed / By Whom Killed / Owner / Date Killed* | | | | | | | | | | | |
| 396 2/8 | 48 | 50 4/8 | 32 4/8 | 44 4/8 | 10 | 9 4/8 | 7 | 7 | | 34 | 1 |
| ♦ *Duck Mt. / Paul Kirkowich / Paul Kirkowich / 1960* | | | | | | | | | | | |
| 380 | 51 5/8 | 51 6/8 | 41 6/8 | 45 3/8 | 7 6/8 | 8 3/8 | 6 | 6 | | 193 | 2 |
| ♦ *Duck Mt. / G.N. Burton / G.N. Burton / 1965* | | | | | | | | | | | |
| 378 2/8 | 43 4/8 | 47 3/8 | 40 | 47 6/8 | 9 6/8 | 9 6/8 | 9 | 8 | 14 2/8 | 226 | 3 |
| ♦ *Duck Mt. / John D. Harbarenko / John D. Harbarenko / 1973* | | | | | | | | | | | |

**MANITOBA PROVINCE RECORD
NON-TYPICAL AMERICAN ELK
SCORE: 405-3/8**
Locality: Vermillion River    Date: December 1986
Hunter: Ernie M. Bernat

# MANITOBA

## NON-TYPICAL AMERICAN ELK

| | Length of Main Beam | | Inside | Great-est | Circumference at Smallest Place Between Burr and First Point | | Number of Points | | Total of Lengths Abnor- | All- | Prov. |
|---|---|---|---|---|---|---|---|---|---|---|---|
| Score | R | L | Spread | Spread | R | L | R | L | mal Points | Time Rank | Rank |
| ♦ Locality Killed / By Whom Killed / Owner / Date Killed | | | | | | | | | | | |

| | | | | | | | | | | | |
|---|---|---|---|---|---|---|---|---|---|---|---|
| 405 ³⁄₈ | 59 ⁴⁄₈ | 58 ¹⁄₈ | 40 ²⁄₈ | 43 ⁶⁄₈ | 8 ⁴⁄₈ | 8 ²⁄₈ | 7 | 8 | 10 ³⁄₈ | 5 | 1 |
| ♦ Vermilion River / Ernie M. Bernat / Ernie M. Bernat / 1986 | | | | | | | | | | | |
| 402 | 51 ⁷⁄₈ | 46 ³⁄₈ | 38 ³⁄₈ | 48 ⁵⁄₈ | 8 ⁶⁄₈ | 8 ²⁄₈ | 8 | 9 | 29 ¹⁄₈ | 8 | 2 |
| ♦ Lundar / Picked Up / Fred Thorkelson / 1980 | | | | | | | | | | | |

Photograph Courtesy of Peter Hrbachek

**SASKATCHEWAN FOURTH PLACE**
**TYPICAL AMERICAN ELK**
**SCORE: 377-6/8**
Locality: Mistatim    Date: 1984
Hunter: Peter Hrbachek

78

# SASKATCHEWAN

## TYPICAL AMERICAN ELK

| Score | Length of Main Beam R | L | Inside Spread | Greatest Spread | Circumference at Smallest Place Between Burr and First Point R | L | Number of Points R | L | Total of Lengths Abnormal Points | All-Time Rank | Prov. Rank |
|---|---|---|---|---|---|---|---|---|---|---|---|
| 389 5/8 | 56 5/8 | 52 5/8 | 52 5/8 | | 9 2/8 | 9 2/8 | 7 | 7 | | 66 | 1 |
| ◆ Ft. A La Corne  /  Jim Crozier  /  Jim Crozier  /  1955 | | | | | | | | | | | |
| 389 2/8 | 49 7/8 | 48 1/8 | 40 | | 10 7/8 | 10 3/8 | 6 | 6 | | 72 | 2 |
| ◆ Saskatchewan  /  Unknown  /  B.P.O. Elks Lodge  /  PR 1956 | | | | | | | | | | | |
| 386 1/8 | 57 6/8 | 57 1/8 | 48 5/8 | 57 1/8 | 7 1/8 | 8 5/8 | 6 | 6 | | 104 | 3 |
| ◆ Forest Gate Store  /  Edwin L. Roberts  /  Edwin L. Roberts  /  1962 | | | | | | | | | | | |
| 377 6/8 | 53 3/8 | 53 4/8 | 41 6/8 | 53 3/8 | 9 | 9 5/8 | 9 | 9 | 8 6/8 | 231 | 4 |
| ◆ Mistatim  /  Peter Hrbachek  /  Peter Hrbachek  /  1984 | | | | | | | | | | | |
| 376 7/8 | 46 6/8 | 45 6/8 | 42 6/8 | 46 4/8 | 10 | 9 6/8 | 7 | 6 | 5 3/8 | 251 | 5 |
| ◆ Flotten Lake  /  Garry G. Ronald  /  Garry G. Ronald  /  1987 | | | | | | | | | | | |
| 375 1/8 | 52 | 53 4/8 | 39 3/8 | 46 5/8 | 9 | 10 | 6 | 6 | | 292 | 6 |
| ◆ Prince Albert  /  Unknown  /  Lucky Lake Sask. Elks  /  1926 | | | | | | | | | | | |

TOP 10 ROOSEVELT'S ELK LISTINGS INDEX

# Tabulations of Recorded Roosevelt's Elk

The trophy data shown on the following pages is taken from score charts in the Records Archives of the Boone and Crockett Club. A comparison of all-time rankings of this book with those of the last all-time records book (*Records of North American Big Game*, 9th Ed., 1988) will show some significant differences. This is generally caused by two factors: the addition of trophies accepted during the 20th Awards entry period (1986-1988) and elimination of the "double penalty" for excessive inside spread. The rankings shown in this book are official and supercede those of the all-time records and other publications.

Roosevelt's elk, named after the great conservationist who founded the Boone and Crockett Club, are larger bodied than American elk but have smaller racks. They occur in the coastal Pacific states, with geographic boundaries described for entry (see the all-time records book, 9th Ed. for a boundary description).

The scores and rank shown are final, except for trophies shown with an asterisk. The asterisk identifies entry scores subject to final certification by an Awards Panel of Judges. The asterisk can be removed (except in the case of a potential World's Record) by the submission of two additional, independent scorings by Official Measurers of the Boone and Crockett Club. The Records Committee of the Club will review the three scorings available (original plus two additional) and determine which, if any, will be accepted in lieu of the Judges Panel measurement. When the score has been accepted as final by the Records Committee, the asterisk will be removed in future editions of the all-time records book and other publications. In the case of a potential World's Record, the trophy *must* come before a Judges Panel at the end of an entry period. Only a Judges Panel can certify a World's Record and finalize its score. Asterisked trophies are shown at the end of their category, without rank.

**CALIFORNIA STATE RECORD**
**ROOSEVELT'S ELK**
**SCORE: 332-2/8**
Locality: Humboldt Co.    Date: Picked Up 1955
Owner: Leo Prshora

# CALIFORNIA

## ROOSEVELT'S ELK

| Score | Length of Main Beam R | Length of Main Beam L | Inside Spread | Greatest Spread | Circumference at Smallest Place Between Burr and First Point R | Circumference at Smallest Place Between Burr and First Point L | Number of Points R | Number of Points L | Total of Lengths Abnormal Points | All-Time Rank | State Rank |
|---|---|---|---|---|---|---|---|---|---|---|---|
| ♦ *Locality Killed / By Whom Killed / Owner / Date Killed* | | | | | | | | | | | |
| 332 2/8 | 51 6/8 | 51 4/8 | 41 2/8 | 46 2/8 | 8 6/8 | 9 1/8 | 8 | 6 | | 24 | 1 |
| ♦ *Humboldt County / Picked Up / Leo Prshora / 1955* | | | | | | | | | | | |
| 318 5/8 | 48 | 49 2/8 | 40 | 43 1/8 | 8 2/8 | 8 | 7 | 6 | | 44 | 2 |
| ♦ *Del Norte County / Richard K. Armas / Richard K. Armas / 1988* | | | | | | | | | | | |
| 306 4/8 | 47 | 47 5/8 | 43 5/8 | 45 5/8 | 7 5/8 | 7 6/8 | 6 | 6 | | 62 | 3 |
| ♦ *Humboldt County / Michael L. Johnson / Michael L. Johnson / 1976* | | | | | | | | | | | |

**OREGON STATE RECORD**
**WORLD'S RECORD**
**ROOSEVELT'S ELK**
**SCORE: 384-3/8**
Locality: Clatsop Co.    Date: 1949
Hunter: Robert Sharp

# OREGON

## ROOSEVELT'S ELK

| Score | Length of Main Beam R | Length of Main Beam L | Inside Spread | Greatest Spread | Circumference at Smallest Place Between Burr and First Point R | Circumference at Smallest Place Between Burr and First Point L | Number of Points R | Number of Points L | Total of Lengths Abnormal Points | All-Time Rank | State Rank |
|---|---|---|---|---|---|---|---|---|---|---|---|
| ♦ *Locality Killed / By Whom Killed / Owner / Date Killed* | | | | | | | | | | | |
| 384 3/8 | 48 4/8 | 49 | 41 1/8 | 49 1/8 | 8 7/8 | 9 4/8 | 9 | 8 | | 1 | 1 |
| ♦ *Clatsop County / Robert Sharp / Robert Sharp / 1949* | | | | | | | | | | | |
| 367 5/8 | 50 3/8 | 53 | 37 4/8 | 42 | 9 | 8 5/8 | 7 | 7 | | 4 | 2 |
| ♦ *Clatsop County / Pravomil Raichl / Pravomil Raichl / 1959* | | | | | | | | | | | |
| 366 5/8 | 43 | 45 5/8 | 35 4/8 | 48 3/8 | 9 6/8 | 9 5/8 | 7 | 8 | | 5 | 3 |
| ♦ *Columbia County / Floyd M. Lindberg / Floyd M. Lindberg / 1962* | | | | | | | | | | | |
| 362 6/8 | 45 7/8 | 45 5/8 | 37 4/8 | 43 4/8 | 9 4/8 | 9 1/8 | 7 | 7 | | 6 | 4 |
| ♦ *Lincoln County / James H. Flescher / James H. Flescher / 1955* | | | | | | | | | | | |
| 358 5/8 | 55 4/8 | 53 4/8 | 42 | 45 1/8 | 9 5/8 | 8 7/8 | 8 | 8 | 3 6/8 | 7 | 5 |
| ♦ *Tillamook County / Albert Hoffarber / Ray Hoffarber / 1940* | | | | | | | | | | | |
| 353 4/8 | 52 | 53 3/8 | 38 4/8 | 44 | 8 5/8 | 9 1/8 | 6 | 7 | | 8 | 6 |
| ♦ *Washington County / Kenneth R. Adamson / Kenneth R. Adamson / 1985* | | | | | | | | | | | |
| 347 6/8 | 41 3/8 | 42 3/8 | 46 2/8 | 48 4/8 | 8 2/8 | 8 | 7 | 7 | | 9 | 7 |
| ♦ *Tillamook County / Bud Davis / Herb W. Davis / 1957* | | | | | | | | | | | |
| 347 | 47 2/8 | 46 4/8 | 44 2/8 | 50 2/8 | 9 1/8 | 9 1/8 | 8 | 7 | | 10 | 8 |
| ♦ *Columbia County / Al Glenn / Al Glenn / 1955* | | | | | | | | | | | |
| 345 6/8 | 51 5/8 | 51 3/8 | 40 5/8 | 44 | 11 1/8 | 11 1/8 | 6 | 7 | 14 3/8 | 11 | 9 |
| ♦ *Columbia County / Unknown / Harold E. Stepp / 1962* | | | | | | | | | | | |
| 341 2/8 | 45 1/8 | 42 4/8 | 44 6/8 | 57 2/8 | 9 6/8 | 9 3/8 | 7 | 8 | | 13 | 10 |
| ♦ *Josephine County / Robert Veatch / Cass E. Raymond / PR 1890* | | | | | | | | | | | |
| 341 | 45 1/8 | 45 2/8 | 33 5/8 | 39 1/8 | 10 3/8 | 10 | 8 | 8 | | 14 | 11 |
| ♦ *Columbia County / Derl Roberts / Derl Roberts / 1965* | | | | | | | | | | | |
| 340 4/8 | 46 1/8 | 45 | 36 | 43 | 9 3/8 | 9 | 6 | 8 | 1 2/8 | 15 | 12 |
| ♦ *Columbia County / Bud Holmes / James C. Oroth / 1962* | | | | | | | | | | | |
| 338 | 43 4/8 | 44 1/8 | 41 1/8 | 47 3/8 | 9 7/8 | 9 1/8 | 7 | 7 | | 17 | 13 |
| ♦ *Tillamook County / Tony W. Hancock / Tony W. Hancock / 1985* | | | | | | | | | | | |

| Score | Length of Main Beam | | Inside Spread | Greatest Spread | Circumference at Smallest Place Between Burr and First Point | | Number of Points | | Total of Lengths Abnormal Points | All-Time Rank | State Rank |
|---|---|---|---|---|---|---|---|---|---|---|---|
| | R | L | | | R | L | R | L | | | |
| ♦ *Locality Killed / By Whom Killed / Owner / Date Killed* | | | | | | | | | | | |
| 336 ⁵⁄₈ | 50 ⁴⁄₈ | 47 ⁶⁄₈ | 39 | 43 | 8 | 8 ⁶⁄₈ | 6 | 7 | | 20 | 14 |
| ♦ *Tillamook County / Gary L. Cox / Gary L. Cox / 1965* | | | | | | | | | | | |
| 336 ⁴⁄₈ | 46 ⁶⁄₈ | 46 ⁶⁄₈ | 40 ³⁄₈ | 43 ²⁄₈ | 8 ⁷⁄₈ | 9 ¹⁄₈ | 7 | 6 | | 21 | 15 |
| ♦ *Oregon Coast Range / Unknown / Richard Leach / PR 1981* | | | | | | | | | | | |
| 335 ¹⁄₈ | 51 ²⁄₈ | 51 ⁷⁄₈ | 42 ¹⁄₈ | 46 ⁵⁄₈ | 10 ¹⁄₈ | 10 ³⁄₈ | 7 | 7 | | 23 | 16 |
| ♦ *Clatsop County / Picked Up / Andy Mendenhall, Jr. / 1978* | | | | | | | | | | | |
| 332 | 49 | 48 ⁴⁄₈ | 45 | 47 ²⁄₈ | 8 ¹⁄₈ | 8 ⁵⁄₈ | 7 | 6 | | 25 | 17 |
| ♦ *Tillamook County / Robert B. Thornton / Robert B. Thornton / 1964* | | | | | | | | | | | |
| 329 ⁵⁄₈ | 48 ⁷⁄₈ | 50 ¹⁄₈ | 39 ³⁄₈ | 45 ¹⁄₈ | 8 ⁵⁄₈ | 8 ²⁄₈ | 6 | 6 | | 26 | 18 |
| ♦ *Tillamook County / Gary H. Purdy / Gary H. Purdy / 1969* | | | | | | | | | | | |
| 327 ³⁄₈ | 48 ⁵⁄₈ | 50 ⁵⁄₈ | 42 ³⁄₈ | 50 ¹⁄₈ | 8 ³⁄₈ | 8 ¹⁄₈ | 8 | 7 | 9 ⁴⁄₈ | 29 | 19 |
| ♦ *Tillamook County / Picked Up / Dave Griffith / 1958* | | | | | | | | | | | |
| 327 ²⁄₈ | 50 ⁵⁄₈ | 50 | 40 ⁵⁄₈ | 44 | 8 ⁷⁄₈ | 9 ¹⁄₈ | 7 | 6 | 1 ⁵⁄₈ | 30 | 20 |
| ♦ *Clatsop County / Billy L. Jasper / Billy L. Jasper / 1946* | | | | | | | | | | | |
| 325 ³⁄₈ | 50 | 49 | 43 ⁶⁄₈ | 47 ⁶⁄₈ | 9 | 9 ⁶⁄₈ | 8 | 7 | 2 | 33 | 21 |
| ♦ *Columbia County / Edgar J. Rea / Edgar J. Rea / 1973* | | | | | | | | | | | |
| 323 | 45 ⁵⁄₈ | 47 | 37 ⁷⁄₈ | 40 ⁶⁄₈ | 7 ²⁄₈ | 7 ¹⁄₈ | 7 | 7 | | 36 | 22 |
| ♦ *Clatsop County / Clarence V. Jurhs / Clarence V. Jurhs / 1958* | | | | | | | | | | | |
| 322 ³⁄₈ | 47 ⁶⁄₈ | 44 ⁵⁄₈ | 38 ¹⁄₈ | 47 ¹⁄₈ | 8 ⁷⁄₈ | 9 ²⁄₈ | 8 | 7 | 16 ²⁄₈ | 37 | 23 |
| ♦ *Columbia County / William E. Curtis / Duane M. Bernard / 1952* | | | | | | | | | | | |
| 322 ²⁄₈ | 44 ⁶⁄₈ | 45 ²⁄₈ | 41 ³⁄₈ | 42 ¹⁄₈ | 8 ⁵⁄₈ | 9 ¹⁄₈ | 7 | 7 | | 38 | 24 |
| ♦ *Lincoln County / James R. Goodwin / James R. Goodwin / 1960* | | | | | | | | | | | |
| 322 ¹⁄₈ | 43 ²⁄₈ | 41 | 41 ²⁄₈ | 42 ⁷⁄₈ | 10 ³⁄₈ | 10 ³⁄₈ | 7 | 7 | 2 | 39 | 25 |
| ♦ *Clatsop County / Reed Holding / Reed Holding / 1939* | | | | | | | | | | | |
| 322 ¹⁄₈ | 45 ⁵⁄₈ | 45 ³⁄₈ | 42 ²⁄₈ | 45 | 11 ⁴⁄₈ | 11 | 6 | 6 | | 39 | 25 |
| ♦ *Polk County / R.L. Stamps / R.L. Stamps / 1985* | | | | | | | | | | | |
| 320 ⁴⁄₈ | 47 ¹⁄₈ | 51 ¹⁄₈ | 32 ⁵⁄₈ | 43 ⁶⁄₈ | 8 ⁶⁄₈ | 8 ⁶⁄₈ | 7 | 6 | | 41 | 27 |
| ♦ *Tillamook County / Stanley E. Kephart / Stanley E. Kephart / 1964* | | | | | | | | | | | |
| 320 ²⁄₈ | 43 ¹⁄₈ | 43 ⁵⁄₈ | 47 ¹⁄₈ | 50 | 8 ⁵⁄₈ | 8 ⁴⁄₈ | 7 | 7 | | 42 | 28 |
| ♦ *Columbia County / Harry R. Olsen / Harry R. Olsen / 1961* | | | | | | | | | | | |
| 317 ²⁄₈ | 41 ³⁄₈ | 41 ⁵⁄₈ | 37 ⁶⁄₈ | 45 | 9 | 8 ⁷⁄₈ | 6 | 7 | | 45 | 29 |
| ♦ *Columbia County / Max Oblack / Max Oblack / 1967* | | | | | | | | | | | |
| 316 ⁶⁄₈ | 51 ³⁄₈ | 49 | 39 | 42 ⁷⁄₈ | 8 ⁶⁄₈ | 9 ⁷⁄₈ | 6 | 7 | | 46 | 30 |
| ♦ *Columbia County / Harry R. Olsen / Harry R. Olsen / 1969* | | | | | | | | | | | |

| Score | Length of Main Beam R | L | Inside Spread | Greatest Spread | Circumference at Smallest Place Between Burr and First Point R | L | Number of Points R | L | Total of Lengths Abnormal Points | All-Time Rank | State Rank |
|---|---|---|---|---|---|---|---|---|---|---|---|
| 315 4/8 | 48 2/8 | 47 7/8 | 42 | 46 | 9 4/8 | 9 | 6 | 6 | | 49 | 31 |
| ♦ Columbia County / William E. Curtis / Duane M. Bernard / 1965 | | | | | | | | | | | |
| 314 6/8 | 46 6/8 | 46 6/8 | 42 2/8 | 43 | 8 | 8 5/8 | 7 | 8 | | 50 | 32 |
| ♦ Columbia County / Picked Up / Harold E. Stepp / 1962 | | | | | | | | | | | |
| 314 4/8 | 52 1/8 | 49 2/8 | 36 3/8 | 40 6/8 | 9 5/8 | 9 3/8 | 6 | 6 | | 51 | 33 |
| ♦ Coos County / Robert D. Dunson / Robert D. Dunson / 1982 | | | | | | | | | | | |
| 314 3/8 | 45 7/8 | 46 1/8 | 42 3/8 | 45 | 8 4/8 | 8 | 7 | 7 | | 52 | 34 |
| ♦ Clatsop County / Robert L. Brown / Robert L. Brown / 1966 | | | | | | | | | | | |
| 310 4/8 | 44 3/8 | 44 | 33 6/8 | 42 6/8 | 9 5/8 | 9 6/8 | 7 | 7 | | 55 | 35 |
| ♦ Clatsop County / Elman Peterson, Jr. / Elman Peterson, Jr. / 1968 | | | | | | | | | | | |
| 309 6/8 | 43 1/8 | 48 1/8 | 31 6/8 | 37 1/8 | 9 2/8 | 9 4/8 | 7 | 7 | | 57 | 36 |
| ♦ Clatsop County / Terry E. Andrews / Terry E. Andrews / 1984 | | | | | | | | | | | |
| 309 1/8 | 47 3/8 | 43 7/8 | 37 1/8 | 40 | 9 2/8 | 8 1/8 | 6 | 6 | | 58 | 37 |
| ♦ Clatsop County / Valentine T. Mueller / John A. Mueller / 1938 | | | | | | | | | | | |
| 308 3/8 | 48 | 48 | 41 5/8 | 45 2/8 | 9 7/8 | 9 2/8 | 6 | 7 | | 59 | 38 |
| ♦ Coos County / Dean Dunson / Dean Dunson / 1986 | | | | | | | | | | | |
| 307 4/8 | 46 1/8 | 45 6/8 | 40 6/8 | 43 1/8 | 7 1/8 | 7 7/8 | 7 | 7 | | 60 | 39 |
| ♦ Tillamook County / John A. Wehinger / John A. Wehinger / 1964 | | | | | | | | | | | |
| 306 6/8 | 50 2/8 | 50 4/8 | 38 6/8 | 43 1/8 | 7 6/8 | 8 | 6 | 6 | | 61 | 40 |
| ♦ Polk County / James E. Wallen / James E. Wallen / 1980 | | | | | | | | | | | |
| 306 | 40 4/8 | 39 3/8 | 40 4/8 | 43 1/8 | 9 1/8 | 9 4/8 | 7 | 7 | | 63 | 41 |
| ♦ Washington County / Michael R. Jamieson / Michael R. Jamieson / 1982 | | | | | | | | | | | |
| 304 6/8 | 49 | 41 1/8 | 39 1/8 | 44 | 9 7/8 | 9 3/8 | 6 | 7 | 3 5/8 | 64 | 42 |
| ♦ Clatsop County / William D. Mellinger / William D. Mellinger / 1958 | | | | | | | | | | | |
| 302 5/8 | 41 | 39 6/8 | 44 | 44 1/8 | 9 7/8 | 9 5/8 | 9 | 6 | 2 4/8 | 68 | 43 |
| ♦ Lincoln County / Michael Kosydar / Michael Kosydar / 1985 | | | | | | | | | | | |
| 301 6/8 | 43 | 43 7/8 | 36 2/8 | 41 5/8 | 8 6/8 | 9 4/8 | 8 | 8 | | 69 | 44 |
| ♦ Clatsop County / Pravomil Raichl / Pravomil Raichl / 1963 | | | | | | | | | | | |
| 300 2/8 | 43 | 40 6/8 | 37 1/8 | 41 2/8 | 9 | 8 4/8 | 6 | 6 | | 71 | 45 |
| ♦ Columbia County / Harry R. Olsen / Harry R. Olsen / 1963 | | | | | | | | | | | |
| 299 6/8 | 48 1/8 | 49 1/8 | 37 1/8 | 41 | 8 2/8 | 7 1/8 | 6 | 6 | | 72 | 46 |
| ♦ Lincoln County / Jullian Smallwood / Gerald Smallwood / 1945 | | | | | | | | | | | |
| 299 4/8 | 42 2/8 | 40 7/8 | 39 | 43 2/8 | 8 2/8 | 7 1/8 | 7 | 7 | | 74 | 47 |
| ♦ Lincoln County / Gene Nyhus / Gene Nyhus / 1950 | | | | | | | | | | | |

| Score | Length of Main Beam R | Length of Main Beam L | Inside Spread | Greatest Spread | Circumference at Smallest Place Between Burr and First Point R | Circumference at Smallest Place Between Burr and First Point L | Number of Points R | Number of Points L | Total of Lengths Abnormal Points | All-Time Rank | State Rank |
|---|---|---|---|---|---|---|---|---|---|---|---|
| ♦ *Locality Killed / By Whom Killed / Owner / Date Killed* | | | | | | | | | | | |
| 298 2/8 | 47 | 44 3/8 | 37 4/8 | 40 | 7 6/8 | 7 4/8 | 8 | 6 | | 76 | 48 |
| ♦ *Columbia County / Nicholas A. Berg / Nicholas A. Berg / 1963* | | | | | | | | | | | |
| 298 2/8 | 42 5/8 | 43 1/8 | 40 6/8 | 43 | 8 4/8 | 8 7/8 | 7 | 6 | | 76 | 48 |
| ♦ *Polk County / R.L. Stamps / R.L. Stamps / 1981* | | | | | | | | | | | |
| 296 | 46 | 46 6/8 | 36 6/8 | 42 3/8 | 7 7/8 | 7 7/8 | 7 | 7 | | 83 | 50 |
| ♦ *Yamhill County / Steven E. Anderson / Steven E. Anderson / 1983* | | | | | | | | | | | |
| 295 4/8 | 39 7/8 | 41 6/8 | 41 | 49 6/8 | 8 2/8 | 8 | 6 | 6 | | 85 | 51 |
| ♦ *Columbia County / Reed Holding / Reed Holding / 1950* | | | | | | | | | | | |
| 294 7/8 | 45 4/8 | 45 4/8 | 34 6/8 | 39 3/8 | 7 7/8 | 8 1/8 | 6 | 6 | | 86 | 52 |
| ♦ *Clatsop County / Picked Up / Robert L. Brown / 1965* | | | | | | | | | | | |
| 293 7/8 | 43 5/8 | 43 6/8 | 36 7/8 | 42 2/8 | 7 6/8 | 7 5/8 | 6 | 6 | | 87 | 53 |
| ♦ *Tillamook County / Steven F. Kellow / Steven F. Kellow / 1979* | | | | | | | | | | | |
| 291 4/8 | 38 2/8 | 38 7/8 | 33 7/8 | 36 2/8 | 8 2/8 | 8 1/8 | 8 | 7 | | 89 | 54 |
| ♦ *Tillamook County / Picked Up / Tim J. Christensen / 1975* | | | | | | | | | | | |
| 291 3/8 | 43 5/8 | 43 5/8 | 35 1/8 | 38 5/8 | 6 6/8 | 7 | 6 | 6 | | 90 | 55 |
| ♦ *Clatsop County / Picked Up / Robert L. Brown / 1979* | | | | | | | | | | | |
| 290 7/8 | 45 6/8 | 44 1/8 | 37 4/8 | 40 1/8 | 9 | 9 3/8 | 6 | 6 | | 91 | 56 |
| ♦ *Coos County / Gerald W. Hurst / Gerald W. Hurst / 1979* | | | | | | | | | | | |
| 283 4/8 | 42 7/8 | 44 1/8 | 35 2/8 | 42 5/8 | 6 7/8 | 6 7/8 | 7 | 6 | | 93 | 57 |
| ♦ *Columbia County / Thomas E. Eilertsen / Thomas E. Eilertsen / 1968* | | | | | | | | | | | |
| 279 7/8 | 47 7/8 | 45 | 39 3/8 | 40 | 8 3/8 | 8 2/8 | 6 | 5 | | 94 | 58 |
| ♦ *Tillamook County / Denis Schmitz / Denis Schmitz / 1987* | | | | | | | | | | | |
| 378 5/8 | 53 2/8 | 51 3/8 | 37 | 41 3/8 | 8 7/8 | 8 5/8 | 7 | 9 | | * | * |
| ♦ *Clatsop County / Fred M. Williamson / Charles R. Lindburg / 1947* | | | | | | | | | | | |
| 358 6/8 | 51 4/8 | 51 4/8 | 42 2/8 | 51 4/8 | 9 6/8 | 10 2/8 | 7 | 7 | | * | * |
| ♦ *Clatsop County / Donald A. Schoenborn / Larrys Sports Center / 1939* | | | | | | | | | | | |
| 340 2/8 | 46 5/8 | 46 | 38 4/8 | 45 2/8 | 7 2/8 | 7 7/8 | 8 | 7 | | * | * |
| ♦ *Columbia County / Harry R. Olsen / Harry R. Olsen / 1970* | | | | | | | | | | | |

Lou A. DePaolis took this fine, non-typical American elk in Taos County, New Mexico, in 1974. It scores 414 points, and it received the Third Place Award at the 20th Awards held in Albuquerque, New Mexico, 1989.

**WASHINGTON STATE RECORD
ROOSEVELT'S ELK
SCORE: 380-6/8**
Locality: Jefferson Co.    Date: November 1983
Hunter: Sam Argo

# WASHINGTON

## ROOSEVELT'S ELK

| Score | Length of Main Beam R | Length of Main Beam L | Inside Spread | Greatest Spread | Circumference at Smallest Place Between Burr and First Point R | Circumference at Smallest Place Between Burr and First Point L | Number of Points R | Number of Points L | Total of Lengths Abnormal Points | All-Time Rank | State Rank |
|---|---|---|---|---|---|---|---|---|---|---|---|
| ♦ *Locality Killed / By Whom Killed / Owner / Date Killed* | | | | | | | | | | | |
| 380 6/8 | 52 3/8 | 52 6/8 | 45 1/8 | 55 3/8 | 8 3/8 | 8 1/8 | 8 | 8 | | 2 | 1 |
| ♦ *Jefferson County / Sam Argo / Sam Argo / 1983* | | | | | | | | | | | |
| 376 3/8 | 53 2/8 | 52 3/8 | 41 5/8 | 48 5/8 | 10 1/8 | 10 3/8 | 8 | 7 | | 3 | 2 |
| ♦ *Clallam County / Picked Up / Roy C. Ewen / 1912* | | | | | | | | | | | |
| 344 2/8 | 49 2/8 | 47 5/8 | 40 | 45 4/8 | 8 4/8 | 8 5/8 | 7 | 7 | | 12 | 3 |
| ♦ *Jefferson County / Carroll E. Koenke / Carroll E. Koenke / 1966* | | | | | | | | | | | |
| 337 1/8 | 49 5/8 | 52 | 30 2/8 | 41 5/8 | 9 1/8 | 8 4/8 | 7 | 6 | | 18 | 4 |
| ♦ *Wahkiakum County / E.L. McKie & T. Faubian / E.L. McKie / 1962* | | | | | | | | | | | |
| 337 1/8 | 46 | 44 4/8 | 37 6/8 | 47 | 8 7/8 | 8 7/8 | 7 | 7 | | 18 | 4 |
| ♦ *Jefferson County / Dave D. Godfrey / Dave D. Godfrey / 1966* | | | | | | | | | | | |
| 336 2/8 | 46 | 48 3/8 | 40 | 46 6/8 | 8 3/8 | 9 1/8 | 7 | 7 | | 22 | 6 |
| ♦ *Clallam County / Howard M. Cameron / Lawrence C. Cameron / 1936* | | | | | | | | | | | |
| 327 4/8 | 47 4/8 | 46 | 44 4/8 | 44 4/8 | 10 3/8 | 11 | 6 | 6 | | 28 | 7 |
| ♦ *Clallam County / Daniel D. Hinchen / Daniel D. Hinchen / 1976* | | | | | | | | | | | |
| 326 4/8 | 54 1/8 | 54 2/8 | 40 | 51 2/8 | 7 5/8 | 7 7/8 | 7 | 7 | | 31 | 8 |
| ♦ *Pacific County / Donald Beasley / Donald Beasley / 1963* | | | | | | | | | | | |
| 326 1/8 | 49 6/8 | 49 2/8 | 33 6/8 | 38 5/8 | 8 1/8 | 8 1/8 | 7 | 7 | | 32 | 9 |
| ♦ *Wahkiakum County / Otis E. Wright / Otis E. Wright / 1966* | | | | | | | | | | | |
| 324 2/8 | 40 6/8 | 44 2/8 | 43 6/8 | 45 5/8 | 7 7/8 | 7 6/8 | 7 | 7 | | 35 | 10 |
| ♦ *Jefferson County / Newton P. Morris / Newton P. Morris / 1975* | | | | | | | | | | | |
| 320 2/8 | 49 6/8 | 48 2/8 | 42 4/8 | 44 4/8 | 8 4/8 | 8 1/8 | 6 | 6 | | 42 | 11 |
| ♦ *Mason County / Tony J. Bogachus / Tony J. Bogachus / 1955* | | | | | | | | | | | |
| 316 5/8 | 41 6/8 | 41 5/8 | 38 3/8 | 42 7/8 | 9 1/8 | 8 6/8 | 6 | 6 | | 47 | 12 |
| ♦ *Clallam County / Daniel M. Hilt / Daniel M. Hilt / 1982* | | | | | | | | | | | |
| 316 | 47 3/8 | 46 5/8 | 43 1/8 | 50 | 10 3/8 | 10 1/8 | 6 | 6 | | 48 | 13 |
| ♦ *Jefferson County / Hans Norbisrath / Hans Norbisrath / 1966* | | | | | | | | | | | |
| 311 2/8 | 47 6/8 | 40 3/8 | 41 2/8 | 43 4/8 | 8 6/8 | 8 6/8 | 7 | 7 | | 53 | 14 |
| ♦ *Jefferson County / Walter L. Campbell / Walter L. Campbell / 1987* | | | | | | | | | | | |

| Score | Length of Main Beam R | Length of Main Beam L | Inside Spread | Greatest Spread | Circumference at Smallest Place Between Burr and First Point R | Circumference at Smallest Place Between Burr and First Point L | Number of Points R | Number of Points L | Total of Lengths Abnormal Points | All-Time Rank | State Rank |
|---|---|---|---|---|---|---|---|---|---|---|---|
| ♦ *Locality Killed / By Whom Killed / Owner / Date Killed* | | | | | | | | | | | |
| 310 5/8 | 43 4/8 | 44 6/8 | 38 2/8 | 45 6/8 | 7 7/8 | 7 3/8 | 7 | 7 | | 54 | 15 |
| ♦ *Clallam County / Daniel M. Hilt / Daniel M. Hilt / 1958* | | | | | | | | | | | |
| 310 1/8 | 44 5/8 | 44 4/8 | 34 | 39 | 10 2/8 | 9 3/8 | 7 | 7 | 4 | 56 | 16 |
| ♦ *Jefferson County / Howard L. Hill / Michael R. Raffaell / 1969* | | | | | | | | | | | |
| 303 | 47 4/8 | 47 6/8 | 42 2/8 | 44 4/8 | 9 | 8 6/8 | 7 | 5 | | 65 | 17 |
| ♦ *Jefferson County / C.F. & C.H. Bernhardt / C.F. & C.H. Bernhardt / 1972* | | | | | | | | | | | |
| 302 6/8 | 50 | 50 | 36 7/8 | 40 7/8 | 7 3/8 | 7 7/8 | 6 | 6 | | 66 | 18 |
| ♦ *Jefferson County / Gary Talley / Gary Talley / 1981* | | | | | | | | | | | |
| 302 6/8 | 45 6/8 | 44 3/8 | 37 2/8 | 41 1/8 | 8 6/8 | 9 | 6 | 6 | | 66 | 18 |
| ♦ *Grays Harbor County / Donald M. Vestal / Dean Vestal / 1981* | | | | | | | | | | | |
| 301 1/8 | 46 5/8 | 44 | 34 2/8 | 40 1/8 | 8 5/8 | 8 2/8 | 7 | 7 | | 70 | 20 |
| ♦ *Jefferson County / C.F. & C.H. Bernhardt / C.F. & C.H. Bernhardt / 1973* | | | | | | | | | | | |
| 299 5/8 | 41 1/8 | 42 1/8 | 33 6/8 | 42 | 9 1/8 | 9 5/8 | 7 | 6 | | 73 | 21 |
| ♦ *Grays Harbor County / Robert Lentz / Robert Lentz / 1948* | | | | | | | | | | | |
| 297 6/8 | 46 | 45 7/8 | 42 7/8 | 43 7/8 | 7 3/8 | 7 3/8 | 6 | 6 | | 78 | 22 |
| ♦ *Clallam County / Arnold J. LaGambina / Arnold J. LaGambina / 1988* | | | | | | | | | | | |
| 297 1/8 | 47 2/8 | 45 6/8 | 36 7/8 | 42 1/8 | 9 | 9 | 7 | 7 | 4 2/8 | 79 | 23 |
| ♦ *Clallam County / Ronald W. Sanchez / Ronald W. Sanchez / 1988* | | | | | | | | | | | |
| 296 6/8 | 43 1/8 | 42 4/8 | 34 7/8 | 38 | 9 3/8 | 9 2/8 | 6 | 6 | | 80 | 24 |
| ♦ *Clallam County / Randy F. Mesenbrink / Randy F. Mesenbrink / 1977* | | | | | | | | | | | |
| 296 6/8 | 46 6/8 | 48 6/8 | 47 6/8 | 48 7/8 | 8 4/8 | 8 5/8 | 5 | 7 | 1 4/8 | 80 | 24 |
| ♦ *Clallam County / Aubrey F. Taylor / Aubrey F. Taylor / 1984* | | | | | | | | | | | |
| 296 1/8 | 39 | 39 3/8 | 35 2/8 | 43 3/8 | 8 2/8 | 7 7/8 | 7 | 7 | | 82 | 26 |
| ♦ *Jefferson County / Max E. Graves / Max E. Graves / 1970* | | | | | | | | | | | |
| 295 7/8 | 44 3/8 | 44 1/8 | 41 5/8 | 42 7/8 | 8 3/8 | 7 5/8 | 7 | 7 | | 84 | 27 |
| ♦ *Jefferson County / Newton P. Morris / Newton P. Morris / 1970* | | | | | | | | | | | |
| 293 1/8 | 42 | 42 1/8 | 41 3/8 | 41 6/8 | 8 2/8 | 8 7/8 | 6 | 6 | | 88 | 28 |
| ♦ *Jefferson County / William H. Boatman / William H. Boatman / 1951* | | | | | | | | | | | |
| 290 7/8 | 44 1/8 | 44 3/8 | 42 5/8 | 44 5/8 | 7 7/8 | 8 6/8 | 6 | 6 | 1 5/8 | 91 | 29 |
| ♦ *Jefferson County / William A. Harrison / William A. Harrison / 1984* | | | | | | | | | | | |
| 373 3/8 | 57 4/8 | 55 7/8 | 44 1/8 | 53 2/8 | 7 2/8 | 7 7/8 | 7 | 7 | | * | * |
| ♦ *Wahkiakum County / William Williams / William Williams / 1968* | | | | | | | | | | | |
| 342 7/8 | 47 2/8 | 49 6/8 | 43 1/8 | 50 | 8 2/8 | 7 5/8 | 8 | 7 | | * | * |
| ♦ *Clallam County / C.F. & C.H. Bernhardt / C.F. & C.H. Bernhardt / 1979* | | | | | | | | | | | |

Aubrey F. Taylor packing out the head and cape of the Roosevelt's elk he took in Clallam County, Washington, during the 1984 elk season. Taylor's bull scores 296-6/8 points.

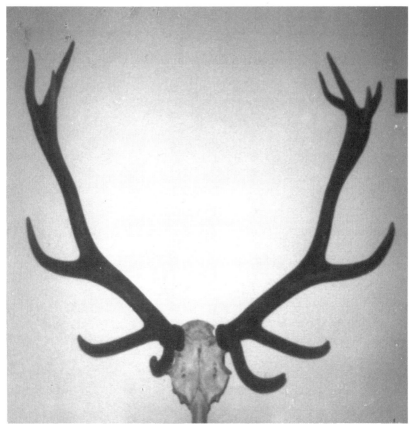

Photograph Courtesy of Wayne H. Zaccarelli

**BRITISH COLUMBIA SECOND PLACE**
**ROOSEVELT'S ELK**
**SCORE: 328-7/8**
Locality: Vancouver Island    Date: October 1981
Hunter: Wayne H. Zaccarelli

# BRITISH COLUMBIA

## ROOSEVELT'S ELK

| | Length of Main Beam | | Inside | Great-est | Circumference at Smallest Place Between Burr and First Point | | Number of Points | | Total of Lengths Abnor-mal | All-Time | Prov. |
|---|---|---|---|---|---|---|---|---|---|---|---|
| Score | R | L | Spread | Spread | R | L | R | L | Points | Rank | Rank |
| ♦ Locality Killed / By Whom Killed / Owner / Date Killed | | | | | | | | | | | |

| | | | | | | | | | | | |
|---|---|---|---|---|---|---|---|---|---|---|---|
| 339 6/8 | 45 5/8 | 45 4/8 | 42 6/8 | 46 6/8 | 8 3/8 | 8 | 8 | 7 | | 16 | 1 |
| ♦ Gold River / William H. Taylor / William H. Taylor / 1987 | | | | | | | | | | | |
| 328 7/8 | 46 4/8 | 46 4/8 | 38 4/8 | 44 | 8 7/8 | 8 5/8 | 7 | 7 | | 27 | 2 |
| ♦ Vancouver Island / Wayne H. Zaccarelli / Wayne H. Zaccarelli / 1981 | | | | | | | | | | | |
| 324 7/8 | 50 1/8 | 47 1/8 | 36 5/8 | 41 1/8 | 8 7/8 | 8 6/8 | 7 | 7 | | 34 | 3 |
| ♦ Ucona River / Norman W. Dougan / Norman W. Dougan / 1986 | | | | | | | | | | | |
| 298 3/8 | 43 5/8 | 44 1/8 | 38 3/8 | 41 | 8 | 8 1/8 | 6 | 6 | | 75 | 4 |
| ♦ White River / Harvey J. King / Harvey J. King / 1987 | | | | | | | | | | | |
| 373 3/8 | 50 4/8 | 50 | 34 3/8 | 44 1/8 | 8 7/8 | 9 2/8 | 6 | 8 | | * | * |
| ♦ Memekay River / Shane Jamieson / Shane Jamieson / 1987 | | | | | | | | | | | |
| 370 7/8 | 50 6/8 | 49 | 35 1/8 | 48 1/8 | 8 4/8 | 8 3/8 | 9 | 9 | | * | * |
| ♦ Ucona River / David R. Summers / David R. Summers / 1978 | | | | | | | | | | | |
| 364 6/8 | 54 | 54 3/8 | 40 1/8 | | 9 2/8 | 8 5/8 | 7 | 9 | 1 2/8 | * | * |
| ♦ Vancouver Island / Lawrence A. Ondzik / Alf Spineto / 1981 | | | | | | | | | | | |
| 356 2/8 | 46 | 46 4/8 | 39 7/8 | 49 2/8 | 11 2/8 | 9 5/8 | 8 | 7 | | * | * |
| ♦ White River / George Korhonen / George Korhonen / 1982 | | | | | | | | | | | |
| 344 4/8 | 52 | 50 2/8 | 41 2/8 | 48 | 10 | 10 | 6 | 6 | | * | * |
| ♦ Kelsey Bay / David Webber / David Webber / 1981 | | | | | | | | | | | |
| 341 2/8 | 46 1/8 | 47 7/8 | 40 7/8 | 49 | 9 | 9 2/8 | 7 | 7 | | * | * |
| ♦ Moakwa Creek / Harry Whitehead / Harry Whitehead / 1982 | | | | | | | | | | | |

TOP 10 MULE DEER LISTINGS INDEX

# Tabulations of Recorded Mule Deer

The trophy data shown on the following pages is taken from score charts in the Records Archives of the Boone and Crockett Club. A comparison of all-time rankings of this book with those of the last all-time records book (*Records of North American Big Game*, 9th Ed., 1988) will show some significant differences. This is generally caused by two factors: the addition of trophies accepted during the 20th Awards entry period (1986-1988) and elimination of the "double penalty" for excessive inside spread. The rankings shown in this book are official and supercede those of the all-time records and other publications.

Mule deer are the western counterpart of the common whitetail. They are easily identified by their large ears (like a mule's) and Y-fork antlers from other deer, making a geographic boundary for records keeping unnecessary. Geographic boundaries are described for the smaller antlered Columbia and Sitka blacktail deer, to prevent entry of common mule deer.

The scores and rank shown are final, except for trophies shown with an asterisk. The asterisk identifies entry scores subject to final certification by an Awards Panel of Judges. The asterisk can be removed (except in the case of a potential World's Record) by the submission of two additional, independent scorings by Official Measurers of the Boone and Crockett Club. The Records Committee of the Club will review the three scorings available (original plus two additional) and determine which, if any, will be accepted in lieu of the Judges Panel measurement. When the score has been accepted as final by the Records Committee, the asterisk will be removed in future editions of the all-time records book and other publications. In the case of a potential World's Record, the trophy *must* come before a Judges Panel at the end of an entry period. Only a Judges Panel can certify a World's Record and finalize its score. Asterisked trophies are shown at the end of their category, without rank.

**ARIZONA STATE RECORD**
**TYPICAL MULE DEER**
**SCORE: 209-5/8**
Locality: Coconino Co.    Date: Prior to 1985
Hunter: Unknown
Owner: John C. McClendon

# ARIZONA

## TYPICAL MULE DEER

| Score | Length of Main Beam R | Length of Main Beam L | Inside Spread | Greatest Spread | Circumference at Smallest Place Between Burr and First Point R | Circumference at Smallest Place Between Burr and First Point L | Number of Points R | Number of Points L | Total of Lengths Abnormal Points | All-Time Rank | State Rank |
|---|---|---|---|---|---|---|---|---|---|---|---|
| ♦ *Locality Killed / By Whom Killed / Owner / Date Killed* | | | | | | | | | | | |
| 209 5/8 | 27 5/8 | 26 5/8 | 30 6/8 | 35 3/8 | 4 7/8 | 5 2/8 | 6 | 8 | 10 | 15 | 1 |
| ♦ *Coconino County / Unknown / John C. McClendon / PR 1985* | | | | | | | | | | | |
| 208 6/8 | 27 6/8 | 26 7/8 | 26 2/8 | 30 | 5 1/8 | 5 | 6 | 5 | 3 4/8 | 23 | 2 |
| ♦ *North Kaibab / Horace T. Fowler / Horace T. Fowler / 1938* | | | | | | | | | | | |
| 206 3/8 | 27 1/8 | 26 5/8 | 24 3/8 | 35 6/8 | 5 1/8 | 5 1/8 | 6 | 7 | 6 4/8 | 41 | 3 |
| ♦ *Coconino County / Robert C. Kaufman / Robert C. Kaufman / 1978* | | | | | | | | | | | |
| 203 4/8 | 25 7/8 | 29 5/8 | 27 6/8 | 36 | 5 4/8 | 5 2/8 | 5 | 5 | | 72 | 4 |
| ♦ *Kaibab Forest / Herb Graham / Herb Graham / 1939* | | | | | | | | | | | |
| 203 1/8 | 26 2/8 | 26 6/8 | 27 1/8 | 31 | 5 6/8 | 5 6/8 | 5 | 5 | 7 5/8 | 82 | 5 |
| ♦ *North Kaibab / Monico Marquez / Monico Marquez / 1957* | | | | | | | | | | | |
| 200 5/8 | 25 7/8 | 25 | 27 5/8 | 32 | 5 3/8 | 5 | 5 | 5 | | 149 | 6 |
| ♦ *Yavapai County / Joseph C. Pecha / Joseph C. Pecha / 1983* | | | | | | | | | | | |
| 200 | 29 6/8 | 29 7/8 | 24 4/8 | 29 5/8 | 5 3/8 | 5 2/8 | 6 | 6 | 7 | 171 | 7 |
| ♦ *Mouqi / Tom Corey / Tom Corey / 1964* | | | | | | | | | | | |
| 199 7/8 | 25 7/8 | 27 2/8 | 25 7/8 | 29 7/8 | 4 7/8 | 5 | 7 | 6 | 5 4/8 | 178 | 8 |
| ♦ *Coconino County / John L. Johnson / John L. Johnson / 1972* | | | | | | | | | | | |
| 199 2/8 | 26 1/8 | 25 1/8 | 24 1/8 | 28 7/8 | 5 6/8 | 5 5/8 | 6 | 6 | 4 5/8 | 196 | 9 |
| ♦ *Hidden Canyon / Milton Wyman / Milton Wyman / 1972* | | | | | | | | | | | |
| 199 | 24 2/8 | 24 2/8 | 21 | 29 2/8 | 5 | 5 2/8 | 5 | 6 | 1 4/8 | 206 | 10 |
| ♦ *Mohave County / William M. Berger, Jr. / William M. Berger, Jr. / 1973* | | | | | | | | | | | |
| 198 4/8 | 28 | 26 1/8 | 28 2/8 | 31 3/8 | 5 | 5 | 5 | 6 | 1 | 218 | 11 |
| ♦ *Kaibab Forest / W.O. Hart / W.O. Hart / 1946* | | | | | | | | | | | |
| 198 4/8 | 27 | 26 2/8 | 28 6/8 | 34 | 5 | 5 | 5 | 5 | | 218 | 11 |
| ♦ *North Kaibab / Simon C. Krevitsky / Simon C. Krevitsky / 1963* | | | | | | | | | | | |
| 198 3/8 | 25 | 25 5/8 | 26 | 28 6/8 | 6 | 5 7/8 | 6 | 6 | 5 4/8 | 226 | 13 |
| ♦ *Mt. Trumbull / E.O. Brown / E.O. Brown / 1960* | | | | | | | | | | | |

| Score | Length of Main Beam R | L | Inside Spread | Greatest Spread | Circumference at Smallest Place Between Burr and First Point R | L | Number of Points R | L | Total of Lengths Abnormal Points | All-Time Rank | State Rank |
|---|---|---|---|---|---|---|---|---|---|---|---|
| | \u2666 *Locality Killed / By Whom Killed / Owner / Date Killed* | | | | | | | | | | |
| 198 2/8 | 24 4/8 | 25 | 25 3/8 | 30 1/8 | 5 1/8 | 4 7/8 | 5 | 5 | | 229 | 14 |
| | \u2666 *Coconino County / Dale C. Morse / Dale C. Morse / 1977* | | | | | | | | | | |
| 197 7/8 | 25 2/8 | 25 1/8 | 24 5/8 | 30 | 4 6/8 | 4 7/8 | 5 | 6 | 1 4/8 | 247 | 15 |
| | \u2666 *Kaibab Forest / Eoans Pababla / Eoans Pababla / 1957* | | | | | | | | | | |
| 196 7/8 | 24 | 24 5/8 | 26 4/8 | 34 1/8 | 5 1/8 | 5 2/8 | 5 | 6 | 1 2/8 | 296 | 16 |
| | \u2666 *North Kaibab / Alex J. Haas / Alex J. Haas / 1961* | | | | | | | | | | |
| 196 6/8 | 24 | 24 1/8 | 23 6/8 | 32 2/8 | 5 7/8 | 6 1/8 | 5 | 6 | 1 4/8 | 300 | 17 |
| | \u2666 *Coconino County / James D. Wagner / James D. Wagner / 1986* | | | | | | | | | | |
| 196 | 27 5/8 | 26 6/8 | 23 3/8 | 32 7/8 | 5 3/8 | 5 2/8 | 7 | 6 | 7 3/8 | 346 | 18 |
| | \u2666 *Kaibab Forest / Graves Peeler / John E. Conner Museum / PR 1930* | | | | | | | | | | |
| 196 | 27 1/8 | 26 | 21 6/8 | | 5 3/8 | 5 3/8 | 5 | 7 | | 346 | 18 |
| | \u2666 *North Kaibab / John D. McNeley / John D. McNeley / 1948* | | | | | | | | | | |
| 196 | 23 6/8 | 24 1/8 | 22 4/8 | 26 1/8 | 5 | 5 1/8 | 5 | 5 | | 346 | 18 |
| | \u2666 *Kaibab Forest / Elgin T. Gates / Elgin T. Gates / 1958* | | | | | | | | | | |
| 195 3/8 | 28 7/8 | 28 4/8 | 25 5/8 | 28 3/8 | 5 2/8 | 5 2/8 | 5 | 7 | 2 6/8 | 383 | 21 |
| | \u2666 *Mohave County / Bob B. Coker / Bob B. Coker / 1972* | | | | | | | | | | |
| 195 1/8 | 26 5/8 | 26 1/8 | 24 7/8 | 31 7/8 | 4 7/8 | 5 1/8 | 6 | 7 | 5 6/8 | 397 | 22 |
| | \u2666 *Coconino County / Gary R. Clark / Gary R. Clark / 1972* | | | | | | | | | | |

Photograph courtesy of Artie McGram

Artie McGram with California's second largest non-typical mule deer. McGram took this 34-point monster in 1987 in Shasta County, California. It scores 305-6/8 points and received the First Place Award at the 20th Awards held in Albuquerque, New Mexico, in 1989.

**ARIZONA STATE RECORD**
**NON-TYPICAL MULE DEER**
**SCORE: 324-1/8**
Locality: North Kaibab    Date: November 1943
Hunter: William L. Murphy
Owner: Michael R. Karam

# ARIZONA
## NON-TYPICAL MULE DEER

| Score | Length of Main Beam R | L | Inside Spread | Greatest Spread | Circumference at Smallest Place Between Burr and First Point R | L | Number of Points R | L | Total of Lengths Abnormal Points | All-Time Rank | State Rank |
|---|---|---|---|---|---|---|---|---|---|---|---|
| | | ◆ *Locality Killed / By Whom Killed / Owner / Date Killed* | | | | | | | | | |
| 324 1/8 | 25 5/8 | 25 1/8 | 32 7/8 | 43 4/8 | 6 5/8 | 6 5/8 | 16 | 17 | 115 2/8 | 3 | 1 |
| | ◆ *North Kaibab / William L. Murphy / Michael R. Karam / 1943* | | | | | | | | | | |
| 311 6/8 | 26 7/8 | 24 7/8 | 24 1/8 | 32 5/8 | 6 1/8 | 6 5/8 | 22 | 21 | 105 1/8 | 5 | 2 |
| | ◆ *Kaibab / Vernor Wilson / Don Schaufler / 1941* | | | | | | | | | | |
| 282 3/8 | 22 5/8 | 21 3/8 | 22 1/8 | 40 2/8 | 4 5/8 | 5 1/8 | 18 | 15 | 103 6/8 | 29 | 3 |
| | ◆ *North Kaibab / Robert C. Rantz / Robert C. Rantz / 1969* | | | | | | | | | | |
| 279 6/8 | 26 6/8 | 24 2/8 | 17 3/8 | 37 6/8 | 6 4/8 | 5 4/8 | 18 | 10 | 89 5/8 | 33 | 4 |
| | ◆ *Kaibab Forest / M. Powell & D. Auld, Jr. / Milroy Powell / 1950* | | | | | | | | | | |
| 274 1/8 | 27 1/8 | 26 6/8 | 25 6/8 | 35 7/8 | 5 6/8 | 5 3/8 | 11 | 10 | 55 5/8 | 45 | 5 |
| | ◆ *Kaibab Forest / Unknown / Don Schaufler / PR 1950* | | | | | | | | | | |
| 270 3/8 | 24 | 25 | 27 4/8 | 39 3/8 | 5 6/8 | 6 | 10 | 10 | 69 3/8 | 61 | 6 |
| | ◆ *Kaibab Forest / Dean Naylor / D.B. Sanford / 1948* | | | | | | | | | | |
| 270 2/8 | 29 2/8 | 32 1/8 | 28 | 42 3/8 | 4 6/8 | 4 6/8 | 12 | 13 | 60 | 62 | 7 |
| | ◆ *North Kaibab / Thomas M. Knoles, Jr. / Thomas M. Knoles, Jr. / 1944* | | | | | | | | | | |
| 268 6/8 | 28 3/8 | 28 4/8 | 24 6/8 | 37 | 5 5/8 | 5 5/8 | 12 | 13 | 58 2/8 | 63 | 8 |
| | ◆ *Kaibab Forest / Milroy Powell / Milroy Powell / 1952* | | | | | | | | | | |
| 263 | 26 3/8 | 27 5/8 | 25 4/8 | 33 4/8 | 5 | 5 | 12 | 12 | 79 | 90 | 9 |
| | ◆ *Kaibab Forest / Unknown / Bob Housholder / 1940* | | | | | | | | | | |
| 262 4/8 | 28 2/8 | 29 | 28 | 41 2/8 | 5 4/8 | 5 4/8 | 14 | 12 | 71 6/8 | 92 | 10 |
| | ◆ *Kaibab Forest / Jack Verner / Jack Verner / 1947* | | | | | | | | | | |
| 261 | 25 2/8 | 26 2/8 | 25 6/8 | | 5 | 5 1/8 | 12 | 12 | | 102 | 11 |
| | ◆ *Kaibab Forest / Unknown / Larry Arndt / 1930* | | | | | | | | | | |
| 260 4/8 | 25 5/8 | 27 | 26 6/8 | 41 5/8 | 5 7/8 | 5 7/8 | 13 | 14 | 81 6/8 | 105 | 12 |
| | ◆ *Kaibab Forest / David Bevly / David Bevly / 1949* | | | | | | | | | | |
| 260 | 27 2/8 | 25 6/8 | 32 6/8 | 34 6/8 | 5 6/8 | 6 2/8 | 13 | 11 | 64 2/8 | 109 | 13 |
| | ◆ *Mohave County / John W. Sokatch / John W. Sokatch / 1978* | | | | | | | | | | |

| Score | Length of Main Beam R | L | Inside Spread | Greatest Spread | Circumference at Smallest Place Between Burr and First Point R | L | Number of Points R | L | Total of Lengths Abnormal Points | All-Time Rank | State Rank |
|---|---|---|---|---|---|---|---|---|---|---|---|
| | | | | | ◆ Locality Killed / By Whom Killed / Owner / Date Killed | | | | | | |
| 258 7/8 | 28 5/8 | 27 7/8 | 28 1/8 | 35 4/8 | 4 6/8 | 4 7/8 | 13 | 13 | 49 7/8 | 119 | 14 |
| | ◆ North Kaibab / Marvin Fridenmaker / Marvin Fridenmaker / 1968 | | | | | | | | | | |
| 257 5/8 | 27 2/8 | 29 | 28 7/8 | 39 | 5 5/8 | 5 5/8 | 15 | 14 | 60 | 131 | 15 |
| | ◆ Kaibab Forest / Graves Peeler / John E. Connor Museum / 1946 | | | | | | | | | | |
| 257 5/8 | 25 7/8 | 26 5/8 | 25 1/8 | 39 5/8 | 5 6/8 | 5 5/8 | 12 | 11 | 54 2/8 | 131 | 15 |
| | ◆ Kaibab Forest / Graves Peeler / John E. Connor Museum / 1947 | | | | | | | | | | |
| 257 5/8 | 24 2/8 | 26 7/8 | 20 6/8 | 34 | 5 3/8 | 5 4/8 | 11 | 13 | 59 7/8 | 131 | 15 |
| | ◆ Hell's Hole / D.L. DeMente / D.L. DeMente / 1965 | | | | | | | | | | |
| 256 2/8 | 27 4/8 | 28 2/8 | 26 6/8 | 32 4/8 | 4 7/8 | 5 1/8 | 10 | 8 | 55 4/8 | 146 | 18 |
| | ◆ Mt. Trumbull / Ervin M. Schmutz / Ervin M. Schmutz / 1965 | | | | | | | | | | |
| 255 4/8 | 23 3/8 | 23 5/8 | 25 5/8 | 37 | 5 6/8 | 5 7/8 | 12 | 12 | 56 5/8 | 153 | 19 |
| | ◆ Coconino County / Glenn A. Hunt / Glenn A. Hunt / 1985 | | | | | | | | | | |
| 253 6/8 | 25 | 26 1/8 | 25 6/8 | 39 5/8 | 6 1/8 | 6 1/8 | 9 | 12 | 54 2/8 | 161 | 20 |
| | ◆ Mohave County / Manuel Machado / Manuel Machado / 1973 | | | | | | | | | | |
| 252 5/8 | 26 7/8 | 28 7/8 | 29 1/8 | 36 | 5 3/8 | 5 5/8 | 15 | 13 | 60 6/8 | 171 | 21 |
| | ◆ Kaibab Forest / Graves Peeler / Graves Peeler / PR 1951 | | | | | | | | | | |
| 250 | 25 | 27 1/8 | 21 4/8 | 32 5/8 | 6 5/8 | 6 4/8 | 14 | 14 | 61 | 192 | 22 |
| | ◆ Mohave County / Douglas C. Mallory / Douglas C. Mallory / 1980 | | | | | | | | | | |
| 249 6/8 | 23 3/8 | 21 6/8 | 23 3/8 | 42 | 6 2/8 | 5 7/8 | 12 | 12 | 77 5/8 | 193 | 23 |
| | ◆ Mt. Dellenbaugh / Ted Riggs / Don Schaufler / 1965 | | | | | | | | | | |
| 249 1/8 | 25 4/8 | 26 | 25 1/8 | 32 4/8 | 5 1/8 | 5 1/8 | 8 | 11 | 36 2/8 | 199 | 24 |
| | ◆ Kaibab / Robert G. McDonald / Robert G. McDonald / 1969 | | | | | | | | | | |
| 248 4/8 | 25 4/8 | 25 1/8 | 26 | 31 6/8 | 5 6/8 | 5 5/8 | 13 | 11 | 45 | 205 | 25 |
| | ◆ Kaibab Forest / H.W. Meisch / H.W. Meisch / 1942 | | | | | | | | | | |
| 248 3/8 | 26 3/8 | 26 6/8 | 23 4/8 | 41 2/8 | 5 4/8 | 5 3/8 | 10 | 16 | 62 3/8 | 206 | 26 |
| | ◆ Kaibab Forest / O.M. Corbett / O.M. Corbett / 1953 | | | | | | | | | | |
| 248 2/8 | 25 | 25 3/8 | 26 7/8 | 38 6/8 | 6 6/8 | 7 | 12 | 12 | 57 3/8 | 207 | 27 |
| | ◆ Kaibab Forest / Graves Peeler / Graves Peeler / PR 1951 | | | | | | | | | | |
| 247 5/8 | 25 2/8 | 25 4/8 | 22 2/8 | 28 4/8 | 6 1/8 | 6 | 12 | 16 | 63 1/8 | 217 | 28 |
| | ◆ Mohave County / Brad L. Johnson / Brad L. Johnson / 1986 | | | | | | | | | | |
| 246 3/8 | 24 7/8 | 24 6/8 | 25 1/8 | 30 1/8 | 5 2/8 | 5 2/8 | 11 | 14 | 49 6/8 | 236 | 29 |
| | ◆ Kaibab Forest / Elgin T. Gates / Elgin T. Gates / 1960 | | | | | | | | | | |
| 246 | 27 1/8 | 26 5/8 | 31 6/8 | 37 3/8 | 5 5/8 | 5 5/8 | 8 | 8 | 36 7/8 | 241 | 30 |
| | ◆ Mohave County / Bernard E. Anderson / Bernard E. Anderson / 1969 | | | | | | | | | | |

| Score | Length of Main Beam R | L | Inside Spread | Greatest Spread | Circumference at Smallest Place Between Burr and First Point R | L | Number of Points R | L | Total of Lengths Abnormal Points | All-Time Rank | State Rank |
|---|---|---|---|---|---|---|---|---|---|---|---|
| | *Locality Killed / By Whom Killed / Owner / Date Killed* | | | | | | | | | | |
| 245 | 24 6/8 | 22 5/8 | 18 5/8 | 33 3/8 | 6 5/8 | 7 | 12 | 14 | 55 1/8 | 250 | 31 |
| | ♦ *Mt. Trumbull / Tony Stromei / Tony Stromei / 1960* | | | | | | | | | | |
| 244 4/8 | 24 6/8 | 26 6/8 | 26 | 32 2/8 | 5 | 4 6/8 | 11 | 11 | 56 | 258 | 32 |
| | ♦ *Kaibab Forest / C.M. Randal, Jr. / C.M. Randal, Jr. / 1953* | | | | | | | | | | |
| 244 2/8 | 24 4/8 | 26 2/8 | 28 4/8 | 38 1/8 | 5 6/8 | 5 5/8 | 9 | 8 | 38 4/8 | 259 | 33 |
| | ♦ *Kaibab Forest / Ray Ramsey / Ray Ramsey / 1952* | | | | | | | | | | |
| 240 5/8 | 26 4/8 | 27 6/8 | 23 2/8 | 32 7/8 | 6 | 5 7/8 | 10 | 13 | 43 7/8 | 308 | 34 |
| | ♦ *Kaibab Forest / Bert E. George / Bert E. George / 1949* | | | | | | | | | | |
| 240 2/8 | 27 3/8 | 27 1/8 | 21 7/8 | 35 3/8 | 5 2/8 | 5 2/8 | 9 | 11 | 43 1/8 | 315 | 35 |
| | ♦ *Mt. Dellenbaugh / Edwin R. Riggs / Edwin R. Riggs / 1964* | | | | | | | | | | |

**CALIFORNIA STATE RECORD**
**TYPICAL MULE DEER**
**SCORE: 195-7/8**
Locality: Lassen Co.    Date: September 1943
Hunter: Sulo E. Lakso
Owner: Tracy A. Jenkins

# CALIFORNIA

## TYPICAL MULE DEER

| Score | Length of Main Beam R | Length of Main Beam L | Inside Spread | Greatest Spread | Circumference at Smallest Place Between Burr and First Point R | Circumference at Smallest Place Between Burr and First Point L | Number of Points R | Number of Points L | Total of Lengths Abnormal Points | All-Time Rank | State Rank |
|---|---|---|---|---|---|---|---|---|---|---|---|
| ♦ *Locality Killed / By Whom Killed / Owner / Date Killed* | | | | | | | | | | | |
| 195 7/8 | 27 6/8 | 25 7/8 | 26 4/8 | 31 1/8 | 4 6/8 | 4 6/8 | 5 | 7 | 4 7/8 | 354 | 1 |
| ♦ *Lassen County / Sulo E. Lakso / Tracy A. Jenkins / 1943* | | | | | | | | | | | |

Photograph by Wm. H. Nesbitt

**CALIFORNIA STATE RECORD**
**NON-TYPICAL MULE DEER**
**SCORE: 319-4/8**
Locality: Mariposa Co.    Date: November 1972
Hunter: Harold R. Laird
Owner: Don Schaufler

# CALIFORNIA

## NON-TYPICAL MULE DEER

| Score | Length of Main Beam R | L | Inside Spread | Greatest Spread | Circumference at Smallest Place Between Burr and First Point R | L | Number of Points R | L | Total of Lengths Abnormal Points | All-Time Rank | State Rank |
|---|---|---|---|---|---|---|---|---|---|---|---|
| 319 4/8 | 24 2/8 | 24 | 23 5/8 | 35 6/8 | 7 1/8 | 7 1/8 | 27 | 23 | 132 3/8 | 4 | 1 |

♦ *Mariposa County / Harold R. Laird / Don Schaufler / 1972*

| 305 6/8 | 23 7/8 | 24 1/8 | 21 3/8 | 35 2/8 | 6 1/8 | 6 4/8 | 17 | 17 | 102 5/8 | 8 | 2 |

♦ *Shasta County / Artie McGram / Artie McGram / 1987*

| 246 6/8 | 23 4/8 | 21 | 26 3/8 | 36 3/8 | 6 2/8 | 6 4/8 | 13 | 14 | 67 4/8 | 233 | 3 |

♦ *Modoc County / Bill Foster / Foster's Bighorn Rest. / 1930*

| 240 4/8 | 26 4/8 | 27 | 21 4/8 | 33 | 6 2/8 | 5 6/8 | 10 | 9 | 51 | 310 | 4 |

♦ *Modoc County / Niilo Niemi / Niilo Niemi / 1968*

**COLORADO STATE RECORD**
**WORLD'S RECORD**
**TYPICAL MULE DEER**
**SCORE: 226-4/8**
Locality: Dolores Co.      Date: October 1972
Hunter: Doug Burris, Jr.
Owner: Loaned to B&C National Collection

# COLORADO

## TYPICAL MULE DEER

| Score | Length of Main Beam R | L | Inside Spread | Greatest Spread | Circumference at Smallest Place Between Burr and First Point R | L | Number of Points R | L | Total of Lengths Abnormal Points | All-Time Rank | State Rank |
|---|---|---|---|---|---|---|---|---|---|---|---|
| 226 4/8 | 30 1/8 | 28 6/8 | 30 7/8 | 33 2/8 | 5 2/8 | 5 3/8 | 6 | 5 | 2 5/8 | 1 | 1 |
| ◆ Dolores County / Doug Burris, Jr. / Loaned to B&C Natl. Collection / 1972 | | | | | | | | | | | |
| 214 3/8 | 27 5/8 | 27 1/8 | 31 3/8 | 35 | 4 7/8 | 4 7/8 | 5 | 5 | | 5 | 2 |
| ◆ Gypsum Creek / Paul A. Muehlbauer / Paul A. Muehlbauer / 1967 | | | | | | | | | | | |
| 212 | 29 | 27 | 21 4/8 | 25 6/8 | 5 4/8 | 5 4/8 | 5 | 5 | | 8 | 3 |
| ◆ Grand County / Wesley B. Brock / Wesley B. Brock / 1963 | | | | | | | | | | | |
| 210 2/8 | 29 1/8 | 29 2/8 | 27 | 31 4/8 | 5 2/8 | 5 2/8 | 6 | 5 | 3 | 12 | 4 |
| ◆ Southern Ute Res. / Jack D. Johnston / Jack D. Johnston / 1963 | | | | | | | | | | | |
| 210 2/8 | 27 7/8 | 27 7/8 | 31 4/8 | 34 | 5 1/8 | 5 | 5 | 6 | 3 7/8 | 12 | 4 |
| ◆ Delta County / Tom Donaldson / Tom Donaldson / 1972 | | | | | | | | | | | |
| 209 5/8 | 29 7/8 | 29 2/8 | 29 2/8 | 35 6/8 | 5 | 5 3/8 | 5 | 7 | 8 1/8 | 15 | 6 |
| ◆ Montrose County / Mike Thomas / Mike Thomas / 1974 | | | | | | | | | | | |
| 209 2/8 | 27 6/8 | 27 1/8 | 27 4/8 | 32 4/8 | 5 6/8 | 5 6/8 | 5 | 5 | | 19 | 7 |
| ◆ Amherst Mt. / Herbert Graham / Mrs. W.J. Graham / 1963 | | | | | | | | | | | |
| 209 | 24 4/8 | 25 4/8 | 24 1/8 | 27 7/8 | 6 1/8 | 6 2/8 | 5 | 7 | 2 5/8 | 21 | 8 |
| ◆ Saguache County / William B. Pennington / William B. Pennington / 1967 | | | | | | | | | | | |
| 208 6/8 | 24 4/8 | 24 6/8 | 17 4/8 | 25 6/8 | 5 3/8 | 5 3/8 | 6 | 6 | 3 3/8 | 23 | 9 |
| ◆ Garfield County / George Shearer / Richard L. Baker / 1952 | | | | | | | | | | | |
| 208 5/8 | 26 7/8 | 27 1/8 | 27 2/8 | 32 7/8 | 5 | 5 | 5 | 5 | | 26 | 10 |
| ◆ Mesa County / Robert L. Zaina / Robert L. Zaina / 1960 | | | | | | | | | | | |
| 207 3/8 | 28 1/8 | 29 4/8 | 28 7/8 | 34 | 5 6/8 | 5 5/8 | 9 | 7 | 18 2/8 | 30 | 11 |
| ◆ Mesa County / Wally Bruegman / Wally Bruegman / 1972 | | | | | | | | | | | |
| 207 2/8 | 28 5/8 | 27 1/8 | 28 1/8 | 36 6/8 | 6 5/8 | 6 4/8 | 6 | 6 | 2 5/8 | 32 | 12 |
| ◆ Montrose County / Bill Crouch / Don Schaufler / 1974 | | | | | | | | | | | |
| 207 1/8 | 26 6/8 | 26 2/8 | 24 1/8 | 28 7/8 | 5 6/8 | 5 4/8 | 6 | 5 | 2 4/8 | 33 | 13 |
| ◆ Golden / Harold B. Moser / Harold B. Moser / 1967 | | | | | | | | | | | |
| 207 | 28 | 28 2/8 | 29 | 32 | 6 | 6 | 6 | 5 | 3 | 34 | 14 |
| ◆ Montrose / Warren S. Bachhofer / Warren S. Bachhofer / 1966 | | | | | | | | | | | |

111

| Score | Length of Main Beam R | L | Inside Spread | Greatest Spread | Circumference at Smallest Place Between Burr and First Point R | L | Number of Points R | L | Total of Lengths Abnormal Points | All-Time Rank | State Rank |
|---|---|---|---|---|---|---|---|---|---|---|---|
| | *Locality Killed / By Whom Killed / Owner / Date Killed* | | | | | | | | | | |
| 206 7/8 | 26 1/8 | 25 7/8 | 21 3/8 | 24 6/8 | 4 6/8 | 4 7/8 | 5 | 5 | | 37 | 15 |
| ♦ *Montrose County / W.L. Boynton / W.L. Boynton / 1973* | | | | | | | | | | | |
| 206 6/8 | 27 | 27 4/8 | 29 4/8 | 36 7/8 | 6 2/8 | 6 1/8 | 5 | 8 | 9 4/8 | 39 | 16 |
| ♦ *Pagosa Springs / Richard V. Price / Richard V. Price / 1962* | | | | | | | | | | | |
| 206 6/8 | 26 3/8 | 25 6/8 | 28 2/8 | 31 4/8 | 5 1/8 | 4 7/8 | 6 | 5 | 1 5/8 | 39 | 16 |
| ♦ *Pagosa Springs / Henry Trujillo, Jr. / Henry Trujillo, Jr. / 1963* | | | | | | | | | | | |
| 206 3/8 | 27 2/8 | 27 7/8 | 28 1/8 | 32 4/8 | 5 1/8 | 5 | 5 | 4 | | 41 | 18 |
| ♦ *Eagle County / Harold Taylor / Fred Palmer / 1960* | | | | | | | | | | | |
| 206 2/8 | 26 5/8 | 27 5/8 | 23 4/8 | 25 7/8 | 5 5/8 | 5 7/8 | 5 | 5 | | 44 | 19 |
| ♦ *Mesa County / Picked Up / James S. Bennett / 1974* | | | | | | | | | | | |
| 206 | 24 | 22 1/8 | 25 | 34 1/8 | 6 | 6 1/8 | 5 | 5 | | 48 | 20 |
| ♦ *Eagle / Harold L. Loesch / Harold L. Loesch / 1967* | | | | | | | | | | | |
| 205 6/8 | 24 3/8 | 24 3/8 | 23 4/8 | 26 3/8 | 5 4/8 | 5 4/8 | 5 | 5 | | 49 | 21 |
| ♦ *Eagle County / Mark A. McCormick / Mark A. McCormick / 1981* | | | | | | | | | | | |
| 205 4/8 | 29 1/8 | 28 4/8 | 27 5/8 | 31 6/8 | 5 1/8 | 5 2/8 | 6 | 6 | 3 5/8 | 51 | 22 |
| ♦ *Carbondale / Richard Cobb / Richard Cobb / 1962* | | | | | | | | | | | |
| 205 4/8 | 25 3/8 | 27 3/8 | 22 7/8 | 26 | 5 4/8 | 5 4/8 | 6 | 5 | 1 1/8 | 51 | 22 |
| ♦ *Kremmling / Larry Bell / Larry Bell / 1962* | | | | | | | | | | | |
| 204 7/8 | 27 2/8 | 27 | 23 5/8 | 30 4/8 | 5 5/8 | 5 4/8 | 6 | 5 | 1 | 57 | 24 |
| ♦ *Delta County / Frank Peterson / Frank Peterson / 1956* | | | | | | | | | | | |
| 204 7/8 | 26 4/8 | 26 1/8 | 26 3/8 | 29 6/8 | 5 2/8 | 5 2/8 | 5 | 5 | | 57 | 24 |
| ♦ *Southern Ute Res. / Nolan Martins / Nolan Martins / 1967* | | | | | | | | | | | |
| 204 5/8 | 25 5/8 | 24 3/8 | 19 4/8 | 29 | 5 5/8 | 5 4/8 | 7 | 5 | 3 5/8 | 59 | 26 |
| ♦ *Eagle County / Robert V. Doerr / Robert V. Doerr / 1982* | | | | | | | | | | | |
| 204 3/8 | 26 1/8 | 26 4/8 | 20 5/8 | 26 5/8 | 5 6/8 | 5 5/8 | 5 | 5 | | 60 | 27 |
| ♦ *Grand Junction / Charles M. Bentley / Charles M. Bentley / 1962* | | | | | | | | | | | |
| 204 | 27 | 27 3/8 | 24 | 33 2/8 | 5 4/8 | 5 3/8 | 5 | 5 | | 65 | 28 |
| ♦ *Pitkin County / Jens O. Solberg / Jens O. Solberg / 1950* | | | | | | | | | | | |
| 203 7/8 | 24 5/8 | 26 | 24 4/8 | 28 4/8 | 5 7/8 | 5 6/8 | 6 | 6 | 3 3/8 | 66 | 29 |
| ♦ *North Park / Edison A. Pillmore / Mrs. E.A. Pillmore / 1949* | | | | | | | | | | | |
| 203 7/8 | 26 3/8 | 27 5/8 | 26 3/8 | 38 6/8 | 5 2/8 | 5 3/8 | 6 | 6 | 4 6/8 | 66 | 29 |
| ♦ *Mesa Creek / Ed Craig / Jerome Craig / 1951* | | | | | | | | | | | |
| 203 5/8 | 28 3/8 | 27 3/8 | 24 4/8 | 30 4/8 | 5 7/8 | 5 6/8 | 6 | 5 | 1 5/8 | 69 | 31 |
| ♦ *La Plata County / B.E. Gressett / B.E. Gressett / 1950* | | | | | | | | | | | |

| Score | Length of Main Beam R | L | Inside Spread | Greatest Spread | Circumference at Smallest Place Between Burr and First Point R | L | Number of Points R | L | Total of Lengths Abnormal Points | All-Time Rank | State Rank |
|---|---|---|---|---|---|---|---|---|---|---|---|
| ♦ *Locality Killed  /  By Whom Killed  /  Owner  /  Date Killed* | | | | | | | | | | | |
| 203 5/8 | 24 5/8 | 25 5/8 | 25 6/8 | 32 3/8 | 4 5/8 | 4 6/8 | 5 | 5 | | 69 | 31 |
| ♦ *Mesa County  /  William P. Burger  /  William P. Burger  /  1957* | | | | | | | | | | | |
| 203 4/8 | 27 5/8 | 28 3/8 | 25 | 28 2/8 | 4 5/8 | 4 6/8 | 5 | 7 | 3 | 72 | 33 |
| ♦ *Garfield County  /  John T. Sewell  /  John T. Sewell  /  1985* | | | | | | | | | | | |
| 203 2/8 | 25 7/8 | 28 | 22 4/8 | 25 | 4 4/8 | 4 4/8 | 6 | 5 | 2 2/8 | 77 | 34 |
| ♦ *White River  /  Ron Vance  /  Ronald Crawford  /  1943* | | | | | | | | | | | |
| 203 2/8 | 28 | 28 4/8 | 29 6/8 | 34 | 5 2/8 | 5 2/8 | 5 | 5 | | 77 | 34 |
| ♦ *De Beque  /  Francis A. Moore  /  Francis A. Moore  /  1962* | | | | | | | | | | | |
| 203 2/8 | 27 1/8 | 26 6/8 | 22 2/8 | 30 3/8 | 4 7/8 | 4 6/8 | 5 | 5 | 2 4/8 | 77 | 34 |
| ♦ *Collbran  /  Joe R. Colingo  /  Joe R. Colingo  /  1973* | | | | | | | | | | | |
| 203 1/8 | 22 5/8 | 22 7/8 | 27 6/8 | 34 2/8 | 5 3/8 | 6 3/8 | 6 | 6 | 6 6/8 | 82 | 37 |
| ♦ *Hayden  /  M.W. Giboney  /  M.W. Giboney  /  1959* | | | | | | | | | | | |
| 203 | 25 | 23 5/8 | 24 | 31 3/8 | 5 2/8 | 5 2/8 | 5 | 5 | | 84 | 38 |
| ♦ *Mesa County  /  James K. Scott  /  James K. Scott  /  1966* | | | | | | | | | | | |
| 203 | 26 3/8 | 25 5/8 | 27 1/8 | 31 | 5 4/8 | 5 6/8 | 9 | 8 | 15 7/8 | 84 | 38 |
| ♦ *Montrose County  /  Earl L. Markley  /  Earl L. Markley  /  1968* | | | | | | | | | | | |
| 202 6/8 | 25 3/8 | 24 7/8 | 19 2/8 | 23 2/8 | 6 6/8 | 6 7/8 | 5 | 5 | | 90 | 40 |
| ♦ *Ouray County  /  Jewel E. Schottel  /  Jewel E. Schottel  /  1966* | | | | | | | | | | | |
| 202 5/8 | 26 3/8 | 25 5/8 | 21 5/8 | 26 | 5 1/8 | 5 | 5 | 5 | | 92 | 41 |
| ♦ *Ouray County  /  Louis V. Schlosser  /  Louis V. Schlosser  /  1965* | | | | | | | | | | | |
| 202 4/8 | 30 4/8 | 30 | 21 2/8 | 28 4/8 | 6 | 5 7/8 | 6 | 4 | 5 6/8 | 94 | 42 |
| ♦ *Collbran  /  Jack Thompson  /  Jack Thompson  /  1968* | | | | | | | | | | | |
| 202 4/8 | 26 7/8 | 24 7/8 | 21 6/8 | 28 1/8 | 5 1/8 | 5 | 4 | 6 | 2 2/8 | 94 | 42 |
| ♦ *Garfield County  /  James S. Harden  /  James S. Harden  /  1982* | | | | | | | | | | | |
| 202 3/8 | 25 6/8 | 26 1/8 | 23 5/8 | 30 1/8 | 5 3/8 | 5 3/8 | 7 | 6 | 3 6/8 | 98 | 44 |
| ♦ *Boulder County  /  Bob Wallace  /  Bob Wallace  /  1963* | | | | | | | | | | | |
| 202 2/8 | 25 6/8 | 26 | 26 5/8 | 33 4/8 | 5 1/8 | 5 | 5 | 7 | 3 2/8 | 101 | 45 |
| ♦ *Pagosa Springs  /  Allen R. Arnwine  /  Allen R. Arnwine  /  1960* | | | | | | | | | | | |
| 202 2/8 | 30 2/8 | 29 6/8 | 20 6/8 | 30 4/8 | 4 7/8 | 4 7/8 | 4 | 5 | 2 6/8 | 101 | 45 |
| ♦ *Archuleta County  /  Duane Yearwood  /  Duane Yearwood  /  1973* | | | | | | | | | | | |
| 202 | 26 4/8 | 25 4/8 | 29 4/8 | 36 | 5 1/8 | 5 3/8 | 5 | 6 | 3 2/8 | 104 | 47 |
| ♦ *Gunnison Natl. For.  /  James M. Newsom  /  James M. Newsom  /  1963* | | | | | | | | | | | |
| 202 | 27 4/8 | 27 1/8 | 24 2/8 | 29 2/8 | 5 2/8 | 5 1/8 | 5 | 6 | 4 4/8 | 104 | 47 |
| ♦ *Montrose County  /  Kenneth Klees  /  Kenneth Klees  /  1966* | | | | | | | | | | | |

| Score | Length of Main Beam R | L | Inside Spread | Greatest Spread | Circumference at Smallest Place Between Burr and First Point R | L | Number of Points R | L | Total of Lengths Abnormal Points | All-Time Rank | State Rank |
|---|---|---|---|---|---|---|---|---|---|---|---|
| | ♦ *Locality Killed / By Whom Killed / Owner / Date Killed* | | | | | | | | | | |
| 201 7/8 | 26 5/8 | 27 2/8 | 26 3/8 | 28 6/8 | 4 6/8 | 4 5/8 | 6 | 5 | 1 4/8 | 111 | 49 |
| | ♦ *Dolores County / Leonard J. Ashcraft / Leonard J. Ashcraft / 1958* | | | | | | | | | | |
| 201 5/8 | 26 2/8 | 26 4/8 | 23 3/8 | 31 5/8 | 5 1/8 | 5 | 5 | 5 | | 114 | 50 |
| | ♦ *Gunnison County / Robert D. Rader / Robert D. Rader / 1966* | | | | | | | | | | |
| 201 5/8 | 26 6/8 | 25 5/8 | 28 4/8 | 35 4/8 | 5 2/8 | 5 | 6 | 6 | 5 7/8 | 114 | 50 |
| | ♦ *Eagle County / Richard C. Bergquist / Richard C. Bergquist / 1981* | | | | | | | | | | |
| 201 4/8 | 27 | 26 | 26 | 33 2/8 | 5 | 5 | 5 | 5 | | 117 | 52 |
| | ♦ *Garfield County / Unknown / Ronald E. McKinney / 1954* | | | | | | | | | | |
| 201 4/8 | 23 | 24 | 20 | 26 2/8 | 5 4/8 | 5 2/8 | 6 | 6 | 2 | 117 | 52 |
| | ♦ *Moffat County / Carl E. Jacobson / Carl E. Jacobson / 1967* | | | | | | | | | | |
| 201 3/8 | 25 4/8 | 26 1/8 | 30 1/8 | 37 6/8 | 6 1/8 | 6 | 5 | 5 | | 122 | 54 |
| | ♦ *Archuleta County / Joe Moore / Joe Moore / 1962* | | | | | | | | | | |
| 201 3/8 | 25 5/8 | 26 4/8 | 25 3/8 | 30 6/8 | 5 4/8 | 5 4/8 | 5 | 5 | | 122 | 54 |
| | ♦ *Grand Junction / William C. Byrd / William C. Byrd / 1967* | | | | | | | | | | |
| 201 3/8 | 25 6/8 | 24 6/8 | 23 1/8 | 28 | 5 4/8 | 5 4/8 | 5 | 5 | | 122 | 54 |
| | ♦ *Montrose County / Grant Morlang / Grant Morlang / 1972* | | | | | | | | | | |
| 201 2/8 | 28 | 29 | 28 | 38 | 5 | 4 6/8 | 6 | 6 | 6 2/8 | 130 | 57 |
| | ♦ *Bayfield / D. Rockwell / D. Rockwell / 1956* | | | | | | | | | | |
| 201 1/8 | 26 2/8 | 26 2/8 | 25 3/8 | 32 3/8 | 5 | 4 7/8 | 5 | 5 | 4/8 | 133 | 58 |
| | ♦ *Cameo / Thomas C. Krauss / Thomas C. Krauss / 1962* | | | | | | | | | | |
| 201 1/8 | 26 4/8 | 27 2/8 | 26 6/8 | 34 | 6 3/8 | 6 5/8 | 5 | 7 | 2 5/8 | 133 | 58 |
| | ♦ *Bayfield / Les Patrick / Les Patrick / 1966* | | | | | | | | | | |
| 201 | 29 | 26 2/8 | 22 6/8 | 31 5/8 | 6 1/8 | 6 1/8 | 6 | 8 | 14 6/8 | 137 | 60 |
| | ♦ *Grand Junction / Ernest Mancuso / Ernest Mancuso / 1954* | | | | | | | | | | |
| 201 | 25 | 25 1/8 | 24 4/8 | 32 2/8 | 4 7/8 | 5 | 5 | 5 | | 137 | 60 |
| | ♦ *Dolores County / Mark Loverin / Mark Loverin / 1978* | | | | | | | | | | |
| 201 | 26 2/8 | 26 2/8 | 23 6/8 | 26 6/8 | 5 1/8 | 5 1/8 | 5 | 5 | | 137 | 60 |
| | ♦ *La Plata County / Larry Pennington / Larry Pennington / 1978* | | | | | | | | | | |
| 200 7/8 | 28 | 28 4/8 | 25 4/8 | 33 | 5 2/8 | 5 2/8 | 6 | 6 | 10 5/8 | 140 | 63 |
| | ♦ *Collbran / Homer O. Hartley / Homer O. Hartley / 1962* | | | | | | | | | | |
| 200 6/8 | 27 1/8 | 25 2/8 | 22 4/8 | 25 4/8 | 5 7/8 | 5 6/8 | 5 | 5 | | 143 | 64 |
| | ♦ *Eagle County / John Robertson / John Robertson / 1958* | | | | | | | | | | |
| 200 6/8 | 27 | 27 3/8 | 26 | 31 1/8 | 5 | 5 1/8 | 5 | 5 | | 143 | 64 |
| | ♦ *Southern Ute Res. / Jerry E. Morgan / Jerry E. Morgan / 1965* | | | | | | | | | | |

| Score | Length of Main Beam | | Inside Spread | Greatest Spread | Circumference at Smallest Place Between Burr and First Point | | Number of Points | | Total of Lengths Abnormal Points | All-Time Rank | State Rank |
|---|---|---|---|---|---|---|---|---|---|---|---|
| | R | L | | | R | L | R | L | | | |
| ♦ *Locality Killed / By Whom Killed / Owner / Date Killed* | | | | | | | | | | | |
| 200 6/8 | 26 | 26 6/8 | 23 4/8 | 30 2/8 | 5 6/8 | 5 4/8 | 6 | 7 | 7 6/8 | 143 | 64 |
| ♦ *Delta / Emil Warber, Jr. / Emil Warber, Jr. / 1966* | | | | | | | | | | | |
| 200 5/8 | 27 | 25 2/8 | 26 5/8 | 31 2/8 | 5 | 5 1/8 | 5 | 5 | | 149 | 67 |
| ♦ *La Plata County / Unknown / Ronald F. Lax / 1979* | | | | | | | | | | | |
| 200 4/8 | 25 | 25 4/8 | 25 | 31 1/8 | 4 6/8 | 5 | 5 | 5 | | 153 | 68 |
| ♦ *Eagle County / Jack Stevens / Jack Stevens / 1975* | | | | | | | | | | | |
| 200 3/8 | 27 4/8 | 27 4/8 | 26 1/8 | 31 4/8 | 5 4/8 | 5 3/8 | 7 | 7 | 7 | 158 | 69 |
| ♦ *Uncompahgre Natl. For. / R.M. Holbrook / R.M. Holbrook / 1972* | | | | | | | | | | | |
| 200 3/8 | 26 7/8 | 29 1/8 | 24 4/8 | 30 1/8 | 5 1/8 | 5 1/8 | 5 | 7 | 3 3/8 | 158 | 69 |
| ♦ *Gypsum / Gene D. Lintz / Gene D. Lintz / 1974* | | | | | | | | | | | |
| 200 2/8 | 26 4/8 | 26 | 27 | 34 | 5 6/8 | 5 6/8 | 5 | 6 | 1 6/8 | 161 | 71 |
| ♦ *Mesa County / Mitchell J. Sacco / Mitchell J. Sacco / 1966* | | | | | | | | | | | |
| 200 2/8 | 29 7/8 | 28 3/8 | 23 6/8 | 29 | 4 7/8 | 4 6/8 | 5 | 5 | | 161 | 71 |
| ♦ *Southern Ute Res. / Arthur Burch / Steven Burch / 1966* | | | | | | | | | | | |
| 200 2/8 | 27 4/8 | 27 | 26 7/8 | 34 1/8 | 5 | 4 7/8 | 6 | 5 | 2 5/8 | 161 | 71 |
| ♦ *Ouray County / Joseph T. Hollingshead / Joseph T. Hollingshead / 1967* | | | | | | | | | | | |
| 200 2/8 | 25 7/8 | 24 1/8 | 19 6/8 | 25 5/8 | 4 6/8 | 4 5/8 | 5 | 5 | | 161 | 71 |
| ♦ *Montrose County / Nelson Harding / Nelson Harding / 1985* | | | | | | | | | | | |
| 200 1/8 | 27 2/8 | 28 6/8 | 25 7/8 | 31 3/8 | 4 6/8 | 4 6/8 | 5 | 5 | | 168 | 75 |
| ♦ *Mesa County / John M. Domingos / John M. Domingos / 1965* | | | | | | | | | | | |
| 200 | 26 2/8 | 27 | 27 | 30 5/8 | 5 5/8 | 5 5/8 | 5 | 6 | 1 4/8 | 171 | 76 |
| ♦ *Summit County / Picked Up / Bill Knorr / 1959* | | | | | | | | | | | |
| 200 | 24 2/8 | 25 4/8 | 25 2/8 | 30 | 4 7/8 | 4 6/8 | 5 | 5 | | 171 | 76 |
| ♦ *Piedra River / Glenn A. Smith / Glenn A. Smith / 1960* | | | | | | | | | | | |
| 200 | 27 | 27 4/8 | 28 5/8 | 33 1/8 | 6 1/8 | 6 1/8 | 5 | 5 | | 171 | 76 |
| ♦ *Silt / George McCoy / George McCoy / 1961* | | | | | | | | | | | |
| 200 | 27 4/8 | 28 7/8 | 29 3/8 | 32 5/8 | 6 3/8 | 6 3/8 | 6 | 5 | 1 1/8 | 171 | 76 |
| ♦ *Garfield County / Picked Up / John F. Frost / 1963* | | | | | | | | | | | |
| 200 | 27 1/8 | 26 | 24 4/8 | 30 | 4 7/8 | 4 7/8 | 5 | 5 | | 171 | 76 |
| ♦ *Eagle County / Dale R. Leonard / David P. Moore / 1976* | | | | | | | | | | | |
| 199 7/8 | 22 6/8 | 23 2/8 | 22 6/8 | 30 2/8 | 5 1/8 | 5 1/8 | 7 | 6 | 4 7/8 | 178 | 81 |
| ♦ *Jackson County / G.B. Berger, Jr. / Denver Mus. Nat. Hist. / 1934* | | | | | | | | | | | |
| 199 7/8 | 24 4/8 | 25 3/8 | 26 1/8 | 28 7/8 | 5 6/8 | 5 6/8 | 5 | 5 | | 178 | 81 |
| ♦ *Disappointment Creek / Clifford Le Neve / Clifford Le Neve / 1954* | | | | | | | | | | | |

| Score | Length of Main Beam | | Inside Spread | Greatest Spread | Circumference at Smallest Place Between Burr and First Point | | Number of Points | | Total of Lengths Abnormal Points | All-Time Rank | State Rank |
|---|---|---|---|---|---|---|---|---|---|---|---|
| | R | L | | | R | L | R | L | | | |
| 199 7/8 | 24 1/8 | 24 7/8 | 23 1/8 | 28 5/8 | 5 | 5 1/8 | 5 | 5 | | 178 | 81 |
| ♦ Uncompahgre Natl. For. / H.E. Gerhart / H.E. Gerhart / 1963 | | | | | | | | | | | |
| 199 6/8 | 29 7/8 | 29 | 21 5/8 | 32 6/8 | 5 2/8 | 5 2/8 | 6 | 8 | 14 3/8 | 183 | 84 |
| ♦ Montrose County / James O. McCleary / John E. McCleary / 1951 | | | | | | | | | | | |
| 199 4/8 | 28 2/8 | 27 3/8 | 28 | 37 1/8 | 6 1/8 | 6 2/8 | 7 | 8 | 20 4/8 | 187 | 85 |
| ♦ Pagosa Springs / Perry Dixon / Perry Dixon / 1957 | | | | | | | | | | | |
| 199 4/8 | 25 | 25 4/8 | 26 | 31 2/8 | 4 6/8 | 5 | 5 | 5 | | 187 | 85 |
| ♦ Dolores County / Kenneth L. Peters / Kenneth L. Peters / 1976 | | | | | | | | | | | |
| 199 3/8 | 27 3/8 | 26 | 25 1/8 | 27 7/8 | 5 4/8 | 6 | 4 | 4 | | 193 | 87 |
| ♦ Silt / V.M. Spiller / V.M. Spiller / 1961 | | | | | | | | | | | |
| 199 2/8 | 27 4/8 | 26 1/8 | 26 4/8 | 28 4/8 | 5 1/8 | 5 1/8 | 5 | 5 | | 196 | 88 |
| ♦ Eagle County / Howard Stoker / Howard Stoker / 1965 | | | | | | | | | | | |
| 199 2/8 | 25 2/8 | 25 1/8 | 25 1/8 | 30 1/8 | 5 2/8 | 5 2/8 | 7 | 6 | 7 5/8 | 196 | 88 |
| ♦ Garfield County / Gary W. Hartley / Gary W. Hartley / 1978 | | | | | | | | | | | |
| 198 7/8 | 26 4/8 | 24 2/8 | 19 3/8 | 24 7/8 | 5 7/8 | 5 7/8 | 7 | 5 | 2 4/8 | 209 | 90 |
| ♦ Burns / Charles D. Rush / Charles D. Rush / 1967 | | | | | | | | | | | |
| 198 5/8 | 26 2/8 | 27 2/8 | 24 5/8 | 32 4/8 | 5 | 5 | 6 | 7 | 5 4/8 | 213 | 91 |
| ♦ Carbondale / Ralph Clock / Ralph Clock / 1961 | | | | | | | | | | | |
| 198 4/8 | 29 | 27 2/8 | 32 7/8 | 37 6/8 | 5 5/8 | 5 4/8 | 6 | 9 | 18 6/8 | 218 | 92 |
| ♦ Del Norte / Esequiel Trujillo / Esequiel Trujillo / 1947 | | | | | | | | | | | |
| 198 4/8 | 26 | 25 4/8 | 21 4/8 | 26 4/8 | 5 3/8 | 5 2/8 | 5 | 4 | 2 2/8 | 218 | 92 |
| ♦ Routt County / Lloyd D. Kindsfater / Lloyd D. Kindsfater / 1966 | | | | | | | | | | | |
| 198 4/8 | 29 | 28 7/8 | 22 4/8 | 26 1/8 | 5 1/8 | 5 1/8 | 4 | 5 | | 218 | 92 |
| ♦ Dark Canyon / O.P. McGuire / O.P. McGuire / 1966 | | | | | | | | | | | |
| 198 4/8 | 29 5/8 | 30 | 28 4/8 | 32 3/8 | 4 6/8 | 4 5/8 | 6 | 7 | 11 2/8 | 218 | 92 |
| ♦ La Plata County / Pauline J. Bostic / Pauline J. Bostic / 1971 | | | | | | | | | | | |
| 198 3/8 | 26 6/8 | 26 5/8 | 28 | 35 2/8 | 5 2/8 | 5 2/8 | 6 | 6 | 2 5/8 | 226 | 96 |
| ♦ Moffat County / Lucille Gooch / George Gooch / 1951 | | | | | | | | | | | |
| 198 2/8 | 26 4/8 | 27 4/8 | 26 4/8 | 32 4/8 | 4 7/8 | 4 7/8 | 6 | 8 | 6 | 229 | 97 |
| ♦ Summit County / Picked Up / Louis Ceriani / PR 1965 | | | | | | | | | | | |
| 198 2/8 | 26 2/8 | 26 | 26 6/8 | 31 | 5 2/8 | 5 4/8 | 5 | 5 | | 229 | 97 |
| ♦ Gunnison County / Bobby J. Watson / Bobby J. Watson / 1975 | | | | | | | | | | | |
| 198 1/8 | 25 3/8 | 26 1/8 | 23 7/8 | 34 | 5 6/8 | 5 7/8 | 5 | 6 | 3 6/8 | 234 | 99 |
| ♦ Bayfield / C. Ben Boyd / C. Ben Boyd / 1967 | | | | | | | | | | | |

*♦ Locality Killed / By Whom Killed / Owner / Date Killed*

| Score | Length of Main Beam | | Inside Spread | Greatest Spread | Circumference at Smallest Place Between Burr and First Point | | Number of Points | | Total of Lengths Abnormal Points | All-Time Rank | State Rank |
|---|---|---|---|---|---|---|---|---|---|---|---|
| | R | L | | | R | L | R | L | | | |
| | ♦ *Locality Killed / By Whom Killed / Owner / Date Killed* | | | | | | | | | | |
| 198 1/8 | 27 4/8 | 27 2/8 | 23 2/8 | 27 4/8 | 5 | 5 | 7 | 6 | 10 3/8 | 234 | 99 |
| | ♦ *Montrose County / Robert A. Klatt / Robert A. Klatt / 1975* | | | | | | | | | | |
| 198 | 25 2/8 | 25 5/8 | 22 4/8 | 30 | 6 1/8 | 6 | 8 | 5 | 11 | 239 | 101 |
| | ♦ *Garfield County / Leroy Failor / Leroy Failor / 1944* | | | | | | | | | | |
| 198 | 23 7/8 | 25 4/8 | 27 1/8 | 29 1/8 | 4 7/8 | 4 7/8 | 7 | 7 | | 239 | 101 |
| | ♦ *Gunnison County / E.D. Palmer / E.D. Palmer / 1962* | | | | | | | | | | |
| 198 | 24 | 24 7/8 | 22 4/8 | 29 2/8 | 6 1/8 | 5 6/8 | 7 | 6 | 7 4/8 | 239 | 101 |
| | ♦ *Eagle County / Larry Schlasinger / Larry Schlasinger / 1978* | | | | | | | | | | |
| 198 | 27 | 26 1/8 | 28 6/8 | 37 4/8 | 4 6/8 | 5 3/8 | 4 | 5 | | 239 | 101 |
| | ♦ *Hinsdale County / Alan L. VanDenBerg / Alan L. VanDenBerg / 1978* | | | | | | | | | | |
| 197 7/8 | 27 6/8 | 27 7/8 | 28 5/8 | 32 2/8 | 5 1/8 | 5 3/8 | 5 | 5 | | 247 | 105 |
| | ♦ *San Miguel County / Everett Stutler / Everett Stutler / 1965* | | | | | | | | | | |
| 197 7/8 | 26 1/8 | 27 4/8 | 24 1/8 | 29 6/8 | 4 7/8 | 5 | 5 | 5 | | 247 | 105 |
| | ♦ *Rio Blanco County / Gary L. Bicknell / Gary L. Bicknell / 1967* | | | | | | | | | | |
| 197 7/8 | 28 6/8 | 28 6/8 | 25 6/8 | 30 4/8 | 5 | 5 | 6 | 5 | 3 5/8 | 247 | 105 |
| | ♦ *Eagle County / Lee Frudden / Lee Frudden / 1978* | | | | | | | | | | |
| 197 4/8 | 24 | 26 | 21 2/8 | 27 5/8 | 5 4/8 | 5 6/8 | 5 | 5 | | 264 | 108 |
| | ♦ *Moffat County / Russ H. Winslow / Russ H. Winslow / 1967* | | | | | | | | | | |
| 197 4/8 | 22 1/8 | 24 | 24 | 28 4/8 | 5 6/8 | 5 5/8 | 6 | 5 | 4 2/8 | 264 | 108 |
| | ♦ *Gunnison County / Thomas Gray, Jr. / Thomas Gray, Jr. / 1980* | | | | | | | | | | |
| 197 3/8 | 26 7/8 | 26 5/8 | 24 5/8 | 26 7/8 | 5 | 5 | 5 | 6 | 1 | 269 | 110 |
| | ♦ *White River Natl. For. / Picked Up / Jack Thompson / PR 1957* | | | | | | | | | | |
| 197 3/8 | 27 1/8 | 27 4/8 | 24 2/8 | 34 4/8 | 5 | 5 | 5 | 7 | 9 3/8 | 269 | 110 |
| | ♦ *Montrose / H.R. Clark / H.R. Clark / 1961* | | | | | | | | | | |
| 197 3/8 | 26 6/8 | 26 | 25 4/8 | 31 2/8 | 5 2/8 | 5 2/8 | 5 | 6 | 1 1/8 | 269 | 110 |
| | ♦ *Pagosa Springs / John D. Guess / John D. Guess / 1966* | | | | | | | | | | |
| 197 3/8 | 26 | 26 2/8 | 23 2/8 | 28 | 5 6/8 | 5 5/8 | 6 | 6 | 6 5/8 | 269 | 110 |
| | ♦ *Gunnison County / Mark L. Hanna / Mark L. Hanna / 1980* | | | | | | | | | | |
| 197 2/8 | 27 7/8 | 27 | 26 2/8 | | 5 2/8 | 5 | 5 | 8 | | 277 | 114 |
| | ♦ *Chaffee County / Marguerite Hill / Marguerite Hill / 1956* | | | | | | | | | | |
| 197 1/8 | 28 1/8 | 27 3/8 | 22 7/8 | 29 1/8 | 5 | 5 | 5 | 6 | 2 | 285 | 115 |
| | ♦ *Mesa County / Willis A. Kinsey / Willis A. Kinsey / 1978* | | | | | | | | | | |
| 197 | 27 4/8 | 26 3/8 | 29 3/8 | 34 | 5 4/8 | 5 6/8 | 5 | 5 | | 288 | 116 |
| | ♦ *Jackson County / Alvin Bush / Jerry Haldeman / 1961* | | | | | | | | | | |

| Score | Length of Main Beam R | L | Inside Spread | Greatest Spread | Circumference at Smallest Place Between Burr and First Point R | L | Number of Points R | L | Total of Lengths Abnormal Points | All-Time Rank | State Rank |
|---|---|---|---|---|---|---|---|---|---|---|---|
| | | | | | *Locality Killed / By Whom Killed / Owner / Date Killed* | | | | | | |
| 197 | 24 2/8 | 25 4/8 | 25 2/8 | 30 6/8 | 5 3/8 | 5 6/8 | 5 | 5 | | 288 | 116 |
| ♦ Grand County / Woodrow W. Dixon / Woodrow W. Dixon / 1962 | | | | | | | | | | | |
| 197 | 26 6/8 | 26 | 28 4/8 | 35 | 5 3/8 | 5 3/8 | 6 | 5 | 5 2/8 | 288 | 116 |
| ♦ Archuleta County / Hugh W. Gardner / Hugh W. Gardner / 1971 | | | | | | | | | | | |
| 196 6/8 | 25 1/8 | 25 4/8 | 24 4/8 | 28 5/8 | 5 2/8 | 5 5/8 | 5 | 5 | | 300 | 119 |
| ♦ Delta / Howard G. Reed / Howard G. Reed / 1968 | | | | | | | | | | | |
| 196 6/8 | 24 2/8 | 23 4/8 | 23 1/8 | 31 2/8 | 6 3/8 | 6 2/8 | 5 | 6 | 2 1/8 | 300 | 119 |
| ♦ De Beque / Walter C. Friauf / Walter C. Friauf / 1970 | | | | | | | | | | | |
| 196 6/8 | 26 1/8 | 26 | 22 2/8 | 28 3/8 | 5 | 5 | 5 | 5 | | 300 | 119 |
| ♦ San Juan Natl. For. / W.E. Seymour, Jr. / W.E. Seymour, Jr. / 1974 | | | | | | | | | | | |
| 196 5/8 | 26 | 26 6/8 | 24 1/8 | 32 1/8 | 4 4/8 | 4 6/8 | 5 | 5 | | 307 | 122 |
| ♦ Slater / W.J. Bracken / W.J. Bracken / 1959 | | | | | | | | | | | |
| 196 5/8 | 26 2/8 | 26 7/8 | 23 3/8 | 31 | 6 5/8 | 5 3/8 | 8 | 8 | 18 2/8 | 307 | 122 |
| ♦ Moffat County / Tran Canton / Tran Canton / 1960 | | | | | | | | | | | |
| 196 5/8 | 27 6/8 | 24 2/8 | 22 5/8 | 25 2/8 | 5 4/8 | 5 4/8 | 5 | 5 | | 307 | 122 |
| ♦ Grand Mesa / Marvin L. Shepard / Marvin L. Shepard / 1960 | | | | | | | | | | | |
| 196 5/8 | 26 5/8 | 26 4/8 | 27 2/8 | 33 5/8 | 4 7/8 | 4 7/8 | 6 | 6 | 3 | 307 | 122 |
| ♦ Mesa County / Bill Styers / Bill Styers / 1964 | | | | | | | | | | | |
| 196 5/8 | 24 7/8 | 25 | 23 5/8 | 26 3/8 | 4 4/8 | 4 5/8 | 5 | 5 | | 307 | 122 |
| ♦ Maybell / James W. Johnson / James W. Johnson / 1968 | | | | | | | | | | | |
| 196 4/8 | 23 2/8 | 22 6/8 | 19 6/8 | 26 | 5 1/8 | 5 | 5 | 5 | | 318 | 127 |
| ♦ Garfield County / Elmer Nelson / Elmer Nelson / 1962 | | | | | | | | | | | |
| 196 4/8 | 22 1/8 | 22 1/8 | 23 5/8 | 32 | 5 3/8 | 5 4/8 | 5 | 6 | 3 2/8 | 318 | 127 |
| ♦ Summit County / Steve Orecchio / Steve Orecchio / 1967 | | | | | | | | | | | |
| 196 4/8 | 25 3/8 | 24 5/8 | 23 | 29 7/8 | 5 5/8 | 5 7/8 | 5 | 5 | | 318 | 127 |
| ♦ Southern Ute Res. / William C. Forsyth / William C. Forsyth / 1974 | | | | | | | | | | | |
| 196 3/8 | 26 4/8 | 26 | 24 4/8 | 29 3/8 | 5 2/8 | 5 3/8 | 6 | 5 | 1 3/8 | 326 | 130 |
| ♦ Durango / Ronald Chitwood / Ronald Chitwood / 1964 | | | | | | | | | | | |
| 196 3/8 | 28 1/8 | 28 1/8 | 26 1/8 | 29 5/8 | 4 7/8 | 5 | 5 | 4 | | 326 | 130 |
| ♦ Uncompahgre Plateau / Earl L. Markley / Earl L. Markley / 1969 | | | | | | | | | | | |
| 196 2/8 | 27 2/8 | 27 3/8 | 20 6/8 | 31 4/8 | 5 6/8 | 5 2/8 | 5 | 8 | 8 | 330 | 132 |
| ♦ Meeker / Mike Murphy / Mike Murphy / 1971 | | | | | | | | | | | |
| 196 2/8 | 25 4/8 | 25 4/8 | 25 5/8 | 31 4/8 | 5 | 5 1/8 | 5 | 5 | | 330 | 132 |
| ♦ Meeker / Max R. Zoeller / Max R. Zoeller / 1972 | | | | | | | | | | | |

| Score | Length of Main Beam | | Inside Spread | Greatest Spread | Circumference at Smallest Place Between Burr and First Point | | Number of Points | | Total of Lengths Abnormal Points | All-Time Rank | State Rank |
|---|---|---|---|---|---|---|---|---|---|---|---|
| | R | L | | | R | L | R | L | | | |
| *Locality Killed  /  By Whom Killed  /  Owner  /  Date Killed* | | | | | | | | | | | |
| 196 1/8 | 25 2/8 | 25 | 23 5/8 | 29 2/8 | 5 4/8 | 5 3/8 | 4 | 4 | | 341 | 134 |
| ♦ *Uncompahgre Natl. For.  /  Harry L. Whitlock  /  Harry L. Whitlock  /  1968* | | | | | | | | | | | |
| 196 1/8 | 25 5/8 | 25 3/8 | 25 5/8 | 28 4/8 | 4 6/8 | 4 7/8 | 5 | 5 | | 341 | 134 |
| ♦ *Eagle County  /  Jeffery D. Harrison  /  Jeffery D. Harrison  /  1981* | | | | | | | | | | | |
| 196 | 27 6/8 | 27 4/8 | 27 2/8 | 33 4/8 | 5 6/8 | 5 6/8 | 5 | 5 | | 346 | 136 |
| ♦ *Huerfano County  /  F.C. Hibben  /  F.C. Hibben  /  1963* | | | | | | | | | | | |
| 195 7/8 | 26 6/8 | 26 7/8 | 26 5/8 | 26 7/8 | 5 4/8 | 5 4/8 | 6 | 6 | 11 4/8 | 354 | 137 |
| ♦ *Southern Ute Res.  /  Richard Schmidt  /  Southern Ute Tribe  /  1960* | | | | | | | | | | | |
| 195 7/8 | 27 4/8 | 26 5/8 | 24 7/8 | 27 2/8 | 5 5/8 | 5 5/8 | 5 | 5 | | 354 | 137 |
| ♦ *San Miguel County  /  Jerry E. Albin  /  Jerry E. Albin  /  1972* | | | | | | | | | | | |
| 195 6/8 | 25 2/8 | 26 4/8 | 24 6/8 | 30 7/8 | 4 6/8 | 4 6/8 | 5 | 5 | | 360 | 139 |
| ♦ *Gunnison  /  Randall R. Kieft  /  Randall R. Kieft  /  1967* | | | | | | | | | | | |
| 195 6/8 | 24 6/8 | 25 2/8 | 22 6/8 | 29 6/8 | 5 | 5 | 5 | 7 | 3 2/8 | 360 | 139 |
| ♦ *Montrose County  /  Larry D. Bitta  /  Larry D. Bitta  /  1969* | | | | | | | | | | | |
| 195 6/8 | 22 7/8 | 24 6/8 | 23 5/8 | 29 6/8 | 5 3/8 | 5 2/8 | 5 | 6 | 1 5/8 | 360 | 139 |
| ♦ *Gunnison County  /  George L. Hoffman, Jr.  /  George L. Hoffman, Jr.  /  1972* | | | | | | | | | | | |
| 195 6/8 | 25 6/8 | 25 3/8 | 24 1/8 | 28 4/8 | 6 1/8 | 6 2/8 | 6 | 6 | 2 3/8 | 360 | 139 |
| ♦ *Eagle County  /  James B. Mesecke  /  James B. Mesecke  /  1985* | | | | | | | | | | | |
| 195 5/8 | 25 1/8 | 25 4/8 | 21 3/8 | 27 2/8 | 4 6/8 | 4 4/8 | 5 | 4 | | 367 | 143 |
| ♦ *Pitkin County  /  William F. Kirby  /  William F. Kirby  /  1966* | | | | | | | | | | | |
| 195 5/8 | 27 5/8 | 25 3/8 | 20 5/8 | 24 6/8 | 4 7/8 | 4 6/8 | 5 | 5 | | 367 | 143 |
| ♦ *Delta County  /  Royce J. Carville  /  Royce J. Carville  /  1974* | | | | | | | | | | | |
| 195 5/8 | 25 3/8 | 25 4/8 | 21 3/8 | 28 | 5 2/8 | 5 | 5 | 6 | 1 4/8 | 367 | 143 |
| ♦ *Grand County  /  C. Jay Stout  /  C. Jay Stout  /  1981* | | | | | | | | | | | |
| 195 5/8 | 26 5/8 | 27 | 24 3/8 | 32 2/8 | 5 2/8 | 5 2/8 | 9 | 5 | 19 | 367 | 143 |
| ♦ *Archuleta County  /  Matthew J. Arkins  /  Matthew J. Arkins  /  1986* | | | | | | | | | | | |
| 195 4/8 | 24 2/8 | 24 7/8 | 24 2/8 | 33 4/8 | 5 2/8 | 5 2/8 | 7 | 6 | 9 4/8 | 375 | 147 |
| ♦ *Garfield County  /  Billy R. Babb  /  Billy R. Babb  /  1969* | | | | | | | | | | | |
| 195 4/8 | 24 2/8 | 25 | 20 4/8 | 24 1/8 | 5 6/8 | 5 7/8 | 5 | 5 | | 375 | 147 |
| ♦ *Montrose  /  Tony L. Hill  /  Tony L. Hill  /  1969* | | | | | | | | | | | |
| 195 3/8 | 26 4/8 | 25 7/8 | 26 3/8 | 29 6/8 | 5 2/8 | 5 1/8 | 6 | 5 | 9 6/8 | 383 | 149 |
| ♦ *Moffat County  /  Frank J. Kubin  /  Frank J. Kubin  /  1978* | | | | | | | | | | | |
| 195 2/8 | 29 1/8 | 27 7/8 | 25 7/8 | 31 7/8 | 5 3/8 | 5 4/8 | 7 | 6 | 4 7/8 | 389 | 150 |
| ♦ *Gunnison County  /  Herman F. Tomky  /  Russell J. Tomky  /  1937* | | | | | | | | | | | |

| Score | Length of Main Beam R | Length of Main Beam L | Inside Spread | Greatest Spread | Circumference at Smallest Place Between Burr and First Point R | Circumference at Smallest Place Between Burr and First Point L | Number of Points R | Number of Points L | Total of Lengths Abnormal Points | All-Time Rank | State Rank |
|---|---|---|---|---|---|---|---|---|---|---|---|
| ♦ *Locality Killed / By Whom Killed / Owner / Date Killed* | | | | | | | | | | | |
| 195 2/8 | 24 4/8 | 24 3/8 | 24 6/8 | 32 | 4 5/8 | 4 6/8 | 5 | 6 | 5 2/8 | 389 | 150 |
| ♦ *Moffat County / Orville R. Meineke / Craig Sports / 1964* | | | | | | | | | | | |
| 195 2/8 | 26 4/8 | 27 1/8 | 27 | 35 | 5 5/8 | 5 7/8 | 7 | 7 | 6 2/8 | 389 | 150 |
| ♦ *Montrose County / Edward A. Ipser / Edward A. Ipser / 1965* | | | | | | | | | | | |
| 195 2/8 | 26 4/8 | 27 | 25 7/8 | 32 3/8 | 5 1/8 | 5 1/8 | 7 | 6 | 10 5/8 | 389 | 150 |
| ♦ *Marble / David R. Allen / David R. Allen / 1968* | | | | | | | | | | | |
| 195 1/8 | 26 3/8 | 26 1/8 | 24 1/8 | 27 2/8 | 6 | 5 7/8 | 6 | 5 | 3 2/8 | 397 | 154 |
| ♦ *Montrose County / Eldon L. Webb / Eldon L. Webb / 1965* | | | | | | | | | | | |
| 195 | 26 | 25 5/8 | 23 4/8 | 26 1/8 | 4 5/8 | 5 | 5 | 5 | | 405 | 155 |
| ♦ *Larimer County / Michael D. Blehm / Michael D. Blehm / 1972* | | | | | | | | | | | |
| 195 | 24 6/8 | 24 7/8 | 22 4/8 | 26 2/8 | 5 | 5 1/8 | 5 | 5 | | 405 | 155 |
| ♦ *Rio Blanco County / Gene Lawrence / Gene Lawrence / 1977* | | | | | | | | | | | |
| 193 6/8 | 27 6/8 | 27 2/8 | 29 4/8 | 37 | 5 5/8 | 5 3/8 | 4 | 6 | 3 2/8 | 415 | 157 |
| ♦ *Cimmaron / Reynolds L. Vanstrom / Reynolds L. Vanstrom / 1960* | | | | | | | | | | | |
| 192 5/8 | 27 1/8 | 25 1/8 | 30 4/8 | 35 4/8 | 5 3/8 | 5 4/8 | 6 | 8 | 9 5/8 | 417 | 158 |
| ♦ *Delta / Alvin T. Stivers / Alvin T. Stivers / 1965* | | | | | | | | | | | |
| 192 | 26 4/8 | 25 7/8 | 27 7/8 | 33 | 5 3/8 | 5 3/8 | 5 | 5 | | 418 | 159 |
| ♦ *Delta County / James W. Arellano / James W. Arellano / 1977* | | | | | | | | | | | |
| 190 3/8 | 24 7/8 | 25 3/8 | 26 | 28 6/8 | 4 4/8 | 4 4/8 | 5 | 5 | | 421 | 160 |
| ♦ *Mesa / Robert W. Hill / Robert W. Hill / 1963* | | | | | | | | | | | |
| 189 1/8 | 25 | 28 4/8 | 21 | 31 2/8 | 5 | 5 2/8 | 7 | 7 | 6 7/8 | 425 | 161 |
| ♦ *La Plata County / James L. Leyshon / James L. Leyshon / 1986* | | | | | | | | | | | |
| 188 3/8 | 21 1/8 | 21 6/8 | 18 6/8 | 27 6/8 | 4 3/8 | 4 3/8 | 5 | 6 | 1 3/8 | 429 | 162 |
| ♦ *Larimer County / Fred W. Loy / Fred W. Loy / 1965* | | | | | | | | | | | |
| 187 | 24 4/8 | 25 | 28 1/8 | 30 2/8 | 5 | 5 1/8 | 5 | 5 | | 433 | 163 |
| ♦ *Moffat County / Warren C. Nuzum / Warren C. Nuzum / 1987* | | | | | | | | | | | |
| 186 7/8 | 24 | 24 6/8 | 23 | 28 4/8 | 4 5/8 | 4 6/8 | 6 | 5 | 1 3/8 | 435 | 164 |
| ♦ *Garfield County / Gary L. Hecht / Gary L. Hecht / 1986* | | | | | | | | | | | |
| 186 6/8 | 23 6/8 | 23 6/8 | 24 | 30 5/8 | 5 4/8 | 5 3/8 | 5 | 5 | | 437 | 165 |
| ♦ *Routt County / Willie Jones / Willie Jones / 1976* | | | | | | | | | | | |
| 186 5/8 | 25 | 23 2/8 | 26 | 32 1/8 | 4 6/8 | 4 7/8 | 5 | 6 | 1 5/8 | 439 | 166 |
| ♦ *Fremont County / Donald B. Anderson, Jr. / Donald B. Anderson, Jr. / 1986* | | | | | | | | | | | |
| 186 2/8 | 24 5/8 | 25 5/8 | 25 | 29 5/8 | 5 2/8 | 5 2/8 | 4 | 5 | | 440 | 167 |
| ♦ *Routt County / William A.S. Heuer / William A.S. Heuer / 1981* | | | | | | | | | | | |

Photograph courtesy of Doug Burris, Jr.

Doug Burris, Jr., relaxing in front of his fireplace with three of his finest hunting trophies. At center is the World's Record typical mule deer Burris took in Dolores County, Colorado, in 1972. It scores 226-4/8 points and received the First Place Award and the coveted Sagamore Hill Medal at the 15th Awards held in Atlanta, Georgia, in 1974.

**COLORADO STATE RECORD
NON-TYPICAL MULE DEER
SCORE: 306-2/8**
Locality: Norwood    Date: 1954
Hunter: Steve H. Herndon
Owners: Vernon D. & Dan F. Holleman

# COLORADO
## NON-TYPICAL MULE DEER

| Score | Length of Main Beam R | L | Inside Spread | Greatest Spread | Circumference at Smallest Place Between Burr and First Point R | L | Number of Points R | L | Total of Lengths Abnormal Points | All-Time Rank | State Rank |
|---|---|---|---|---|---|---|---|---|---|---|---|
| 306 2/8 | 28 6/8 | 27 4/8 | 22 6/8 | 38 5/8 | 5 6/8 | 5 4/8 | 14 | 23 | 86 4/8 | 6 | 1 |
| ◆ Norwood / Steve H. Herndon / V.D. & D.F. Holleman / 1954 | | | | | | | | | | | |
| 303 6/8 | 26 4/8 | 26 7/8 | 24 3/8 | 32 3/8 | 5 2/8 | 5 | 13 | 11 | 85 7/8 | 9 | 2 |
| ◆ Eagle County / James Austill / Don Schaufler / 1962 | | | | | | | | | | | |
| 302 4/8 | 25 1/8 | 26 2/8 | 25 2/8 | 41 | 5 7/8 | 6 3/8 | 18 | 14 | 84 4/8 | 10 | 3 |
| ◆ Paonia / Louis H. Huntington, Jr. / Louis H. Huntington, Jr. / 1965 | | | | | | | | | | | |
| 300 | 27 | 25 6/8 | 23 1/8 | 41 | 5 3/8 | 5 3/8 | 14 | 12 | 80 5/8 | 13 | 4 |
| ◆ Mesa County / George Blackmon, Jr. / Don Schaufler / 1961 | | | | | | | | | | | |
| 299 5/8 | 26 6/8 | 28 1/8 | 29 1/8 | 41 1/8 | 6 2/8 | 5 2/8 | 19 | 17 | 113 4/8 | 14 | 5 |
| ◆ Elk Creek / Andrew Daum / National Collection / 1886 | | | | | | | | | | | |
| 296 2/8 | 30 1/8 | 30 2/8 | 26 5/8 | 37 | 5 7/8 | 5 7/8 | 12 | 14 | 83 1/8 | 17 | 6 |
| ◆ Mesa County / Unknown / Don Schaufler / PR 1981 | | | | | | | | | | | |
| 286 3/8 | 29 4/8 | 29 6/8 | 35 4/8 | 37 3/8 | 5 1/8 | 5 1/8 | 13 | 13 | 61 1/8 | 21 | 7 |
| ◆ Eagle County / Albert L. Mulnix / Don Schaufler / 1928 | | | | | | | | | | | |
| 278 7/8 | 24 4/8 | 26 | 18 | 29 1/8 | 4 7/8 | 5 1/8 | 8 | 11 | 75 1/8 | 35 | 8 |
| ◆ Montrose County / Keith Thaute / Keith Thaute / 1961 | | | | | | | | | | | |
| 278 7/8 | 26 7/8 | 30 | 24 6/8 | 42 1/8 | 6 2/8 | 6 3/8 | 12 | 12 | 78 5/8 | 35 | 8 |
| ◆ Eagle County / Dale L. Becker / Dale L. Becker / 1978 | | | | | | | | | | | |
| 277 1/8 | 25 1/8 | 24 7/8 | 25 3/8 | 41 1/8 | 5 2/8 | 5 5/8 | 12 | 10 | 63 5/8 | 39 | 10 |
| ◆ Colorado / Indian / Charles McAden / 1930 | | | | | | | | | | | |
| 276 4/8 | 26 5/8 | 25 | 23 | 44 1/8 | 4 7/8 | 5 | 11 | 12 | 78 | 41 | 11 |
| ◆ Glenwood Springs / Larry Prehm / Spanky Greenville / 1967 | | | | | | | | | | | |
| 273 6/8 | 23 2/8 | 24 2/8 | 23 3/8 | 40 1/8 | 5 4/8 | 5 6/8 | 15 | 15 | 73 3/8 | 51 | 12 |
| ◆ Hayden / Roy I. Roney / Colo. Div. of Wildl. / 1930 | | | | | | | | | | | |
| 272 5/8 | 29 | 28 | 21 5/8 | 27 6/8 | 5 3/8 | 5 2/8 | 16 | 14 | 62 | 55 | 13 |
| ◆ Glenwood Springs / William L. Kurtz / William L. Kurtz / 1967 | | | | | | | | | | | |

| Score | Length of Main Beam R | L | Inside Spread | Greatest Spread | Circumference at Smallest Place Between Burr and First Point R | L | Number of Points R | L | Total of Lengths Abnormal Points | All-Time Rank | State Rank |
|---|---|---|---|---|---|---|---|---|---|---|---|
| | ♦ Locality Killed / By Whom Killed / Owner / Date Killed | | | | | | | | | | |
| 272 4/8 | 28 3/8 | 27 1/8 | 21 2/8 | 31 6/8 | 6 3/8 | 6 2/8 | 19 | 17 | 59 2/8 | 56 | 14 |
| | ♦ Eagle County / Eddie Stephenson, Jr. / Eddie Stephenson, Jr. / 1978 | | | | | | | | | | |
| 268 3/8 | 25 4/8 | 27 5/8 | 23 | 34 4/8 | 6 1/8 | 6 | 17 | 11 | 64 7/8 | 66 | 15 |
| | ♦ Delta County / Shirley Smith / Shirley Smith / 1962 | | | | | | | | | | |
| 267 1/8 | 23 7/8 | 25 3/8 | 24 2/8 | 32 | 5 2/8 | 5 4/8 | 15 | 11 | 67 3/8 | 68 | 16 |
| | ♦ Eagle County / Josef Langegger / Josef Langegger / 1969 | | | | | | | | | | |
| 264 3/8 | 26 | 27 5/8 | 21 4/8 | 32 5/8 | 5 4/8 | 5 3/8 | 13 | 10 | 57 3/8 | 83 | 17 |
| | ♦ Gunnison County / Gordon E. Blay / Gorden E. Blay / 1975 | | | | | | | | | | |
| 263 4/8 | 26 5/8 | 26 4/8 | 23 6/8 | 39 2/8 | 5 | 5 | 12 | 12 | 58 4/8 | 87 | 18 |
| | ♦ Montrose / Robert L. Price / Robert L. Price / 1963 | | | | | | | | | | |
| 262 3/8 | 30 7/8 | 29 3/8 | 29 4/8 | | 5 3/8 | 5 6/8 | 10 | 11 | 51 5/8 | 93 | 19 |
| | ♦ Brush Creek / Pete Taullie / Pete Taullie / 1967 | | | | | | | | | | |
| 261 1/8 | 23 | 23 1/8 | 21 3/8 | 37 4/8 | 5 4/8 | 5 2/8 | 12 | 13 | 62 4/8 | 101 | 20 |
| | ♦ Rio Blanco County / L.C. Denny, Jr. / L.C. Denny, Jr.. / 1961 | | | | | | | | | | |
| 259 6/8 | 24 2/8 | 25 4/8 | 21 3/8 | 36 7/8 | 5 3/8 | 5 3/8 | 13 | 13 | 78 5/8 | 114 | 21 |
| | ♦ Routt County / R.V. Rhoads / Cecil R. Weston / 1949 | | | | | | | | | | |
| 258 3/8 | 27 | 28 4/8 | 25 1/8 | 38 6/8 | 5 1/8 | 5 1/8 | 11 | 10 | 54 | 124 | 22 |
| | ♦ Monte Vista / Geis Nettlebeck / Phil Skinner / 1956 | | | | | | | | | | |
| 257 3/8 | 24 6/8 | 26 3/8 | 23 1/8 | 38 4/8 | 4 6/8 | 4 7/8 | 12 | 8 | 60 4/8 | 138 | 23 |
| | ♦ New Castle / Unknown / A.E. Hudson / 1952 | | | | | | | | | | |
| 255 2/8 | 28 | 27 3/8 | 28 2/8 | 39 6/8 | 5 7/8 | 5 5/8 | 14 | 12 | 41 4/8 | 154 | 24 |
| | ♦ Garfield County / Louis Lindauer / Louis Lindauer / 1932 | | | | | | | | | | |
| 255 1/8 | 25 | 25 7/8 | 26 5/8 | 46 3/8 | 4 7/8 | 5 | 7 | 9 | 47 4/8 | 156 | 25 |
| | ♦ Eagle County / Dennis Martinson / Dennis Martinson / 1980 | | | | | | | | | | |
| 255 | 21 5/8 | 22 4/8 | 19 7/8 | 29 3/8 | 5 5/8 | 5 4/8 | 9 | 9 | 56 7/8 | 158 | 26 |
| | ♦ Dunkley Flat / Richard A. Gorden / Richard A. Gorden / 1966 | | | | | | | | | | |
| 254 2/8 | 30 | 28 6/8 | 23 4/8 | | 6 2/8 | 6 4/8 | 7 | 8 | | 160 | 27 |
| | ♦ Columbine / M.A. Story / M.A. Story / 1955 | | | | | | | | | | |
| 253 4/8 | 24 6/8 | 25 1/8 | 25 6/8 | 39 6/8 | 5 2/8 | 5 1/8 | 11 | 10 | 47 5/8 | 162 | 28 |
| | ♦ Silt / George McCoy / George McCoy / 1961 | | | | | | | | | | |
| 253 3/8 | 25 3/8 | 23 4/8 | 26 1/8 | 43 4/8 | 5 4/8 | 5 4/8 | 13 | 17 | 61 2/8 | 164 | 29 |
| | ♦ Meeker / George R. Howey / Robert L. Howey / 1917 | | | | | | | | | | |
| 253 3/8 | 27 6/8 | 26 6/8 | 21 | | 5 2/8 | 5 3/8 | 11 | 13 | | 164 | 29 |
| | ♦ Georgetown / George Lappin / Doug Grubbe / 1947 | | | | | | | | | | |

| Score | Length of Main Beam R | L | Inside Spread | Greatest Spread | Circumference at Smallest Place Between Burr and First Point R | L | Number of Points R | L | Total of Lengths Abnormal Points | All-Time Rank | State Rank |
|---|---|---|---|---|---|---|---|---|---|---|---|
| | ◆ *Locality Killed / By Whom Killed / Owner / Date Killed* | | | | | | | | | | |
| 253 | 25 5/8 | 25 4/8 | 25 2/8 | 41 3/8 | 5 6/8 | 6 | 11 | 11 | 52 2/8 | 170 | 31 |
| | ◆ *Paonia / F.F. Parham / F.F. Parham / 1961* | | | | | | | | | | |
| 252 2/8 | 30 | 30 | 26 6/8 | 39 | 6 | 5 4/8 | 15 | 14 | 47 | 172 | 32 |
| | ◆ *Garfield County / B.J. Slack / B.J. Slack / 1973* | | | | | | | | | | |
| 252 | 24 7/8 | 23 | 24 5/8 | 31 | 5 | 5 | 9 | 13 | 69 7/8 | 175 | 33 |
| | ◆ *Eagle County / Richard G. Lundock / Richard G. Lundock / 1945* | | | | | | | | | | |
| 251 5/8 | 27 4/8 | 25 2/8 | 23 6/8 | 29 5/8 | 5 2/8 | 5 2/8 | 9 | 14 | 46 3/8 | 179 | 34 |
| | ◆ *Gunnison County / John M. Ringler / John M. Ringler / 1956* | | | | | | | | | | |
| 251 5/8 | 24 1/8 | 26 1/8 | 21 | 38 4/8 | 5 1/8 | 5 4/8 | 10 | 14 | 52 7/8 | 179 | 34 |
| | ◆ *Roan Creek / Anthony Morabito / Anthony Morabito / 1965* | | | | | | | | | | |
| 251 1/8 | 27 5/8 | 25 6/8 | 25 7/8 | 40 7/8 | 5 3/8 | 5 2/8 | 10 | 9 | 46 | 181 | 36 |
| | ◆ *Meeker / Henry Zietz, Jr. / Henry Zietz, Jr. / 1955* | | | | | | | | | | |
| 250 6/8 | 29 | 29 1/8 | 35 1/8 | 43 5/8 | 5 4/8 | 5 3/8 | 11 | 13 | 52 3/8 | 185 | 37 |
| | ◆ *Pagosa Springs / Thomas Jarrett / Thomas Jarrett / 1962* | | | | | | | | | | |
| 250 3/8 | 29 | 28 4/8 | 27 4/8 | 41 4/8 | 5 1/8 | 4 6/8 | 10 | 12 | 39 5/8 | 188 | 38 |
| | ◆ *Moffat County / Unknown / Carrol Grounds / 1960* | | | | | | | | | | |
| 250 3/8 | 26 2/8 | 24 7/8 | 25 4/8 | 36 6/8 | 5 | 5 | 10 | 10 | 50 5/8 | 188 | 38 |
| | ◆ *Cedaredge / E.K. Plante / E.K. Plante / 1963* | | | | | | | | | | |
| 250 1/8 | 26 | 26 | 24 | 34 4/8 | 5 4/8 | 5 6/8 | 15 | 11 | 56 1/8 | 191 | 40 |
| | ◆ *Montezuma County / Jack E. Reed / Jack E. Reed / 1981* | | | | | | | | | | |
| 249 3/8 | 25 | 24 2/8 | 19 6/8 | 35 2/8 | 5 4/8 | 5 3/8 | 12 | 9 | 47 7/8 | 195 | 41 |
| | ◆ *Routt County / Howard Stoker / Howard Stoker / 1958* | | | | | | | | | | |
| 249 2/8 | 23 5/8 | 23 4/8 | 20 7/8 | 35 1/8 | 5 | 4 5/8 | 12 | 10 | 55 3/8 | 197 | 42 |
| | ◆ *Mesa County / Gene Cavanagh / Gene Cavanagh / 1967* | | | | | | | | | | |
| 249 | 25 1/8 | 23 4/8 | 23 1/8 | 43 4/8 | 5 1/8 | 5 | 14 | 10 | 69 1/8 | 200 | 43 |
| | ◆ *Minturn / John F. Baldauf / L.F. Nowotny / 1941* | | | | | | | | | | |
| 249 | 26 7/8 | 26 7/8 | 26 7/8 | 35 4/8 | 5 1/8 | 5 1/8 | 8 | 10 | 39 5/8 | 200 | 43 |
| | ◆ *New Castle / William Wiedenfeld / William Wiedenfeld / 1969* | | | | | | | | | | |
| 248 1/8 | 25 7/8 | 24 7/8 | 22 6/8 | 31 5/8 | 5 | 5 1/8 | 11 | 10 | 36 3/8 | 208 | 45 |
| | ◆ *Rio Blanco County / Claude E. Shults / Claude E. Shults / 1956* | | | | | | | | | | |
| 248 1/8 | 25 4/8 | 25 | 23 | 34 6/8 | 5 2/8 | 5 | 15 | 18 | 66 5/8 | 208 | 45 |
| | ◆ *San Juan Natl. For. / Leland R. Tate / Leland R. Tate / 1973* | | | | | | | | | | |
| 248 | 25 5/8 | 26 4/8 | 24 7/8 | 29 6/8 | 5 2/8 | 5 | 11 | 10 | 50 1/8 | 210 | 47 |
| | ◆ *Columbine / Bobby McLaughlin / Bobby McLaughlin / 1962* | | | | | | | | | | |

| Score | Length of Main Beam R | Length of Main Beam L | Inside Spread | Greatest Spread | Circumference at Smallest Place Between Burr and First Point R | Circumference at Smallest Place Between Burr and First Point L | Number of Points R | Number of Points L | Total of Lengths Abnormal Points | All-Time Rank | State Rank |
|---|---|---|---|---|---|---|---|---|---|---|---|
| ♦ *Locality Killed / By Whom Killed / Owner / Date Killed* | | | | | | | | | | | |
| 247 7/8 | 26 | 25 3/8 | 25 | 38 | 5 6/8 | 6 | 16 | 11 | 66 5/8 | 213 | 48 |
| ♦ *Norwood / Walter L. Reisbeck / Walter L. Reisbeck / 1951* | | | | | | | | | | | |
| 247 5/8 | 26 | 24 1/8 | 26 5/8 | 36 2/8 | 7 3/8 | 7 5/8 | 16 | 20 | 69 3/8 | 217 | 49 |
| ♦ *Hinsdale County / Fred Jardine / Fred Jardine / 1966* | | | | | | | | | | | |
| 247 4/8 | 28 3/8 | 28 5/8 | 28 3/8 | 35 5/8 | 5 1/8 | 5 | 9 | 10 | 40 7/8 | 220 | 50 |
| ♦ *Archuleta County / Vince Plaskett / Vince Plaskett / 1970* | | | | | | | | | | | |
| 247 3/8 | 28 6/8 | 28 1/8 | 25 2/8 | 33 4/8 | 5 | 5 | 10 | 9 | 38 7/8 | 222 | 51 |
| ♦ *Eagle County / Earl M. Johnson / Earl M. Johnson / 1966* | | | | | | | | | | | |
| 247 1/8 | 28 3/8 | 27 7/8 | 25 | 32 7/8 | 6 1/8 | 6 | 10 | 15 | 41 5/8 | 225 | 52 |
| ♦ *San Miguel County / W.F. Grice / W.F. Grice / 1978* | | | | | | | | | | | |
| 247 | 23 4/8 | 24 2/8 | 21 1/8 | 30 4/8 | 4 7/8 | 4 7/8 | 11 | 8 | 50 3/8 | 229 | 53 |
| ♦ *Montrose County / Thomas M. Bost / Thomas M. Bost / 1967* | | | | | | | | | | | |
| 246 7/8 | 23 5/8 | 23 | 26 4/8 | 38 | 5 1/8 | 5 1/8 | 11 | 10 | 56 | 231 | 54 |
| ♦ *Craig / Fred E. Trouth / Fred E. Trouth / 1960* | | | | | | | | | | | |
| 246 6/8 | 24 2/8 | 23 3/8 | 25 1/8 | 43 | 5 2/8 | 5 2/8 | 13 | 11 | 57 | 233 | 55 |
| ♦ *Eagle County / William M. Nickels / William M. Nickels / 1963* | | | | | | | | | | | |
| 246 3/8 | 25 2/8 | 25 | 26 | 33 | 5 4/8 | 5 2/8 | 9 | 11 | 56 1/8 | 236 | 56 |
| ♦ *Glenwood Springs / Grady P. Lester / Grady P. Lester / 1959* | | | | | | | | | | | |
| 246 2/8 | 28 1/8 | 26 6/8 | 28 2/8 | 35 4/8 | 5 1/8 | 4 6/8 | 8 | 9 | 41 1/8 | 238 | 57 |
| ♦ *Eagle County / Charles H. Thornberg / Charles H. Thornberg / 1949* | | | | | | | | | | | |
| 246 1/8 | 26 6/8 | 25 4/8 | 25 4/8 | 37 1/8 | 5 3/8 | 5 4/8 | 12 | 10 | 32 3/8 | 240 | 58 |
| ♦ *Mesa County / Joseph J. Pitcherella / Joseph J. Pitcherella / 1972* | | | | | | | | | | | |
| 246 | 23 5/8 | 26 1/8 | 24 1/8 | 32 4/8 | 6 3/8 | 5 6/8 | 14 | 13 | 57 3/8 | 241 | 59 |
| ♦ *Mesa County / Harry A. Gay / Harry A. Gay / 1962* | | | | | | | | | | | |
| 245 5/8 | 27 5/8 | 28 | 23 3/8 | 35 2/8 | 5 1/8 | 5 2/8 | 13 | 11 | 65 | 244 | 60 |
| ♦ *Rio Blanco County / Charlie Grove / Dorothy Shults / 1934* | | | | | | | | | | | |
| 245 5/8 | 27 2/8 | 28 2/8 | 23 2/8 | 30 2/8 | 5 3/8 | 5 4/8 | 9 | 8 | 41 5/8 | 244 | 60 |
| ♦ *Eagle County / James Caraccioli / James Caraccioli / 1978* | | | | | | | | | | | |
| 245 3/8 | 28 2/8 | 24 | 31 6/8 | 40 | 5 1/8 | 5 1/8 | 10 | 7 | 52 5/8 | 246 | 62 |
| ♦ *Saquache County / Walter A. Larsen / Walter A. Larsen / 1962* | | | | | | | | | | | |
| 244 7/8 | 28 3/8 | 28 5/8 | 25 | 31 4/8 | 5 5/8 | 6 4/8 | 9 | 11 | 29 5/8 | 252 | 63 |
| ♦ *Eagle / Robert Rambo / Robert Rambo / 1963* | | | | | | | | | | | |
| 244 5/8 | 25 5/8 | 25 4/8 | 20 3/8 | 32 2/8 | 5 1/8 | 5 1/8 | 13 | 10 | 54 | 254 | 64 |
| ♦ *Delta County / Neil A. Briscoe, Jr. / Neil A. Briscoe, Jr. / 1969* | | | | | | | | | | | |

| Score | Length of Main Beam R | L | Inside Spread | Greatest Spread | Circumference at Smallest Place Between Burr and First Point R | L | Number of Points R | L | Total of Lengths Abnormal Points | All-Time Rank | State Rank |
|---|---|---|---|---|---|---|---|---|---|---|---|
| | | | | | | | | | | | |
| 244 2/8 | 28 4/8 | 28 7/8 | 30 1/8 | 41 | 5 2/8 | 5 4/8 | 9 | 8 | 36 3/8 | 259 | 65 |

♦ *Oak Creek / Scott C. Hinkle / Scott C. Hinkle / 1961*

| | | | | | | | | | | | |
|---|---|---|---|---|---|---|---|---|---|---|---|
| 244 2/8 | 27 3/8 | 29 2/8 | 29 6/8 | 35 4/8 | 5 2/8 | 5 5/8 | 9 | 9 | 38 4/8 | 259 | 65 |

♦ *Montrose County / Jim Herndon / Mrs. Jim Herndon / 1974*

| | | | | | | | | | | | |
|---|---|---|---|---|---|---|---|---|---|---|---|
| 244 2/8 | 23 1/8 | 25 | 23 6/8 | 34 1/8 | 5 2/8 | 5 3/8 | 12 | 11 | 49 6/8 | 259 | 65 |

♦ *Mesa County / Thomas S. Hundley / Thomas S. Hundley / 1986*

| | | | | | | | | | | | |
|---|---|---|---|---|---|---|---|---|---|---|---|
| 244 1/8 | 24 2/8 | 25 1/8 | 27 | 37 4/8 | 5 1/8 | 5 1/8 | 14 | 9 | 49 2/8 | 266 | 68 |

♦ *Mesa County / Edward B. Walsh / Mrs. Edward B. Walsh / 1960*

| | | | | | | | | | | | |
|---|---|---|---|---|---|---|---|---|---|---|---|
| 243 6/8 | 26 | 24 5/8 | 22 4/8 | 39 4/8 | 6 2/8 | 6 4/8 | 10 | 12 | 62 | 271 | 69 |

♦ *San Miguel County / Ben Crandell / Ben Crandell / 1939*

| | | | | | | | | | | | |
|---|---|---|---|---|---|---|---|---|---|---|---|
| 243 4/8 | 23 6/8 | 22 7/8 | 21 | 40 5/8 | 5 4/8 | 5 5/8 | 10 | 13 | 56 | 274 | 70 |

♦ *Clear Creek County / Louis I. Kingsley / Louis I. Kingsley / 1981*

| | | | | | | | | | | | |
|---|---|---|---|---|---|---|---|---|---|---|---|
| 243 2/8 | 28 4/8 | 28 1/8 | 25 5/8 | 37 3/8 | 4 6/8 | 4 7/8 | 10 | 10 | 44 1/8 | 276 | 71 |

♦ *Colorado / Unknown / Brad A. Bauer / 1954*

| | | | | | | | | | | | |
|---|---|---|---|---|---|---|---|---|---|---|---|
| 243 1/8 | 29 2/8 | 28 2/8 | 28 6/8 | 43 6/8 | 4 6/8 | 5 2/8 | 8 | 9 | 30 3/8 | 277 | 72 |

♦ *Harrison Gulch / George R. Mattern / George R. Mattern / 1958*

| | | | | | | | | | | | |
|---|---|---|---|---|---|---|---|---|---|---|---|
| 242 2/8 | 23 2/8 | 23 | 20 2/8 | 36 2/8 | 5 3/8 | 5 6/8 | 12 | 17 | 71 2/8 | 288 | 73 |

♦ *Middle Park / Picked Up / Karl H. Knorr / PR 1961*

| | | | | | | | | | | | |
|---|---|---|---|---|---|---|---|---|---|---|---|
| 242 2/8 | 25 4/8 | 25 3/8 | 23 2/8 | 32 3/8 | 5 | 4 7/8 | 9 | 12 | 46 | 288 | 73 |

♦ *Rabbit Ears Pass / Douglas Valentine / Douglas Valentine / 1964*

| | | | | | | | | | | | |
|---|---|---|---|---|---|---|---|---|---|---|---|
| 242 1/8 | 26 | 25 4/8 | 28 | 32 4/8 | 5 2/8 | 5 2/8 | 12 | 10 | 50 1/8 | 290 | 75 |

♦ *Hinsdale County / Bill Crose / Bill Crose / 1973*

| | | | | | | | | | | | |
|---|---|---|---|---|---|---|---|---|---|---|---|
| 242 | 22 6/8 | 23 5/8 | 18 6/8 | 32 4/8 | 5 4/8 | 5 7/8 | 12 | 14 | 49 4/8 | 293 | 76 |

♦ *Garfield County / Daniel J. Stanek / Daniel J. Stanek / 1981*

| | | | | | | | | | | | |
|---|---|---|---|---|---|---|---|---|---|---|---|
| 241 7/8 | 26 4/8 | 26 2/8 | 30 6/8 | 36 4/8 | 4 5/8 | 4 6/8 | 10 | 9 | 48 5/8 | 295 | 77 |

♦ *La Plata County / Randall N. Bostick / Randall N. Bostick / 1984*

| | | | | | | | | | | | |
|---|---|---|---|---|---|---|---|---|---|---|---|
| 241 4/8 | 25 1/8 | 25 7/8 | 23 3/8 | 32 3/8 | 4 4/8 | 4 4/8 | 10 | 9 | 40 5/8 | 298 | 78 |

♦ *Summit County / Robert R. Ross / Robert R. Ross / 1974*

| | | | | | | | | | | | |
|---|---|---|---|---|---|---|---|---|---|---|---|
| 241 2/8 | 26 6/8 | 25 1/8 | 18 6/8 | 27 4/8 | 5 | 5 | 10 | 11 | 51 4/8 | 304 | 79 |

♦ *Oak Creek / Richard J. Peltier / Richard J. Peltier / 1967*

| | | | | | | | | | | | |
|---|---|---|---|---|---|---|---|---|---|---|---|
| 240 7/8 | 27 | 27 2/8 | 25 2/8 | 30 3/8 | 5 2/8 | 5 1/8 | 6 | 6 | 39 1/8 | 306 | 80 |

♦ *New Castle / Harold F. Auld / Harold F. Auld / 1960*

| | | | | | | | | | | | |
|---|---|---|---|---|---|---|---|---|---|---|---|
| 240 6/8 | 27 | 25 6/8 | 27 1/8 | 39 | 5 7/8 | 5 1/8 | 10 | 8 | 33 | 307 | 81 |

♦ *Eagle County / Steve B. Humann / Steve B. Humann / 1982*

127

| Score | Length of Main Beam R | Length of Main Beam L | Inside Spread | Greatest Spread | Circumference at Smallest Place Between Burr and First Point R | Circumference at Smallest Place Between Burr and First Point L | Number of Points R | Number of Points L | Total of Lengths Abnormal Points | All-Time Rank | State Rank |
|---|---|---|---|---|---|---|---|---|---|---|---|
| ♦ *Locality Killed / By Whom Killed / Owner / Date Killed* | | | | | | | | | | | |
| 240 4/8 | 23 6/8 | 22 | 22 6/8 | 34 1/8 | 5 1/8 | 5 4/8 | 10 | 11 | 48 6/8 | 310 | 82 |
| ♦ *Eagle County / James P. Hale / James P. Hale / 1979* | | | | | | | | | | | |
| 240 4/8 | 23 | 24 4/8 | 21 5/8 | 37 1/8 | 5 2/8 | 5 2/8 | 15 | 14 | 53 1/8 | 310 | 82 |
| ♦ *Garfield County / James E. Powell, Jr. / James E. Powell, Jr. / 1983* | | | | | | | | | | | |
| 240 | 25 7/8 | 24 4/8 | 23 2/8 | 34 2/8 | 5 4/8 | 5 6/8 | 12 | 10 | 51 2/8 | 318 | 84 |
| ♦ *Grand Valley / Ed Peters, Jr. / Ed Peters, Jr. / 1962* | | | | | | | | | | | |
| 240 | 26 1/8 | 28 5/8 | 27 1/8 | 40 3/8 | 4 6/8 | 4 7/8 | 9 | 8 | 38 7/8 | 318 | 84 |
| ♦ *San Juan Wild. / Tommie Cornelius / Tommie Cornelius / 1967* | | | | | | | | | | | |
| 232 | 23 1/8 | 24 | 18 3/8 | 34 3/8 | 5 3/8 | 5 3/8 | 10 | 17 | 36 7/8 | 326 | 86 |
| ♦ *Grand County / William L. Henry / William L. Henry / 1986* | | | | | | | | | | | |
| 297 5/8 | 26 1/8 | 26 3/8 | 26 5/8 | 34 7/8 | 6 4/8 | 6 6/8 | 17 | 15 | 90 4/8 | * | * |
| ♦ *Larimer County / Jack Autrey / Warren C. Autrey / 1941* | | | | | | | | | | | |
| 266 4/8 | 26 4/8 | 25 4/8 | 22 7/8 | 41 7/8 | 5 5/8 | 5 6/8 | 15 | 13 | 62 7/8 | * | * |
| ♦ *Ouray County / Eugene D. Guilaroff / Eugene D. Guilaroff / 1971* | | | | | | | | | | | |

Photograph courtesy of H. Ritman Jons

A very happy H. Ritman Jons with a fine Utah typical mule deer. With a score of 199-1/8 points, you know why Jons is smiling. He hunted Morgan County in 1987 to find this prize.

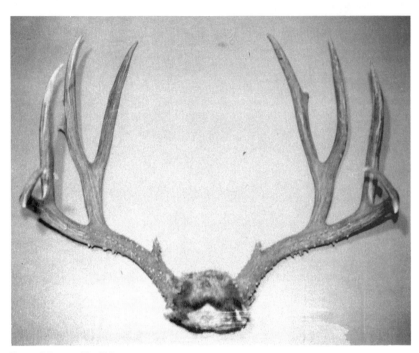

**IDAHO STATE RECORD**
**TYPICAL MULE DEER**
**SCORE: 215-5/8**
Locality: Franklin Co.    Date: October 1961
Hunter: Ray Talbot
Owner: Don Schaufler

# IDAHO

## TYPICAL MULE DEER

| Score | Length of Main Beam R | L | Inside Spread | Greatest Spread | Circumference at Smallest Place Between Burr and First Point R | L | Number of Points R | L | Total of Lengths Abnormal Points | All-Time Rank | State Rank |
|---|---|---|---|---|---|---|---|---|---|---|---|
| | ♦ Locality Killed / By Whom Killed / Owner / Date Killed | | | | | | | | | | |
| 215 5/8 | 27 3/8 | 27 1/8 | 28 6/8 | 30 4/8 | 5 4/8 | 5 4/8 | 5 | 6 | 1 6/8 | 3 | 1 |
| | ♦ Franklin County / Ray Talbot / Don Schaufler / 1961 | | | | | | | | | | |
| 212 6/8 | 26 6/8 | 26 7/8 | 25 4/8 | 32 2/8 | 5 2/8 | 5 2/8 | 5 | 5 | | 6 | 2 |
| | ♦ Gem County / Kirk Payne / Kirk Payne / 1967 | | | | | | | | | | |
| 211 7/8 | 30 3/8 | 30 1/8 | 25 3/8 | 27 4/8 | 5 | 5 | 5 | 6 | 2 6/8 | 9 | 3 |
| | ♦ Adams County / Boyd W. Dennis / Boyd W. Dennis / 1970 | | | | | | | | | | |
| 209 | 26 7/8 | 27 | 24 2/8 | 28 6/8 | 5 6/8 | 5 6/8 | 5 | 5 | | 21 | 4 |
| | ♦ Boise County / Charles Root / Soron Root / 1970 | | | | | | | | | | |
| 208 | 26 6/8 | 26 6/8 | 31 6/8 | 34 | 5 3/8 | 5 1/8 | 6 | 5 | 2 6/8 | 27 | 5 |
| | ♦ Franklin County / Herb Voyler, Jr. / Herb Voyler, Jr. / 1972 | | | | | | | | | | |
| 206 7/8 | 29 | 29 2/8 | 29 7/8 | 34 7/8 | 5 3/8 | 5 3/8 | 6 | 5 | 2 3/8 | 37 | 6 |
| | ♦ Washington County / E. Jack Raby / E. Jack Raby / 1968 | | | | | | | | | | |
| 206 1/8 | 24 7/8 | 25 1/8 | 25 2/8 | 29 6/8 | 5 1/8 | 5 1/8 | 5 | 5 | | 46 | 7 |
| | ♦ Idaho County / William B. Joyner / William B. Joyner / 1965 | | | | | | | | | | |
| 203 4/8 | 28 | 26 5/8 | 30 5/8 | | 5 4/8 | 5 2/8 | 6 | 5 | 1 6/8 | 72 | 8 |
| | ♦ Adams County / Roy Eastlick / Roy Eastlick / 1975 | | | | | | | | | | |
| 202 7/8 | 24 2/8 | 26 3/8 | 26 3/8 | 29 1/8 | 6 | 5 7/8 | 5 | 5 | | 86 | 9 |
| | ♦ Adams County / James S. Denney / James S. Denney / 1939 | | | | | | | | | | |
| 202 7/8 | 26 5/8 | 26 | 23 7/8 | 30 7/8 | 4 7/8 | 4 7/8 | 6 | 7 | 5 6/8 | 86 | 9 |
| | ♦ Idaho County / Myron L. Gilbert / Myron L. Gilbert / 1975 | | | | | | | | | | |
| 202 5/8 | 27 1/8 | 26 1/8 | 25 1/8 | 30 1/8 | 5 | 5 1/8 | 5 | 5 | | 92 | 11 |
| | ♦ Adams County / David J. Couch / David J. Couch / 1970 | | | | | | | | | | |
| 202 4/8 | 26 1/8 | 26 2/8 | 28 2/8 | 35 | 4 7/8 | 4 7/8 | 5 | 6 | 1 1/8 | 94 | 12 |
| | ♦ Bear Lake County / Alan R. Crane / Alan R. Crane / 1962 | | | | | | | | | | |
| 202 | 26 1/8 | 26 4/8 | 21 1/8 | 24 5/8 | 5 | 4 7/8 | 5 | 5 | | 104 | 13 |
| | ♦ Idaho County / John H. Davis / John H. Davis / 1981 | | | | | | | | | | |

131

# IDAHO TYPICAL MULE DEER *(continued)*

| Score | Length of Main Beam R | L | Inside Spread | Greatest Spread | Circumference at Smallest Place Between Burr and First Point R | L | Number of Points R | L | Total of Lengths Abnormal Points | All-Time Rank | State Rank |
|---|---|---|---|---|---|---|---|---|---|---|---|
| | ♦ Locality Killed / By Whom Killed / Owner / Date Killed | | | | | | | | | | |
| 201 3/8 | 27 6/8 | 27 6/8 | 26 4/8 | 36 5/8 | 5 4/8 | 5 4/8 | 7 | 7 | 12 5/8 | 122 | 14 |
| | ♦ Blaine County / Brent Jones / Brent Jones / 1965 | | | | | | | | | | |
| 201 3/8 | 28 3/8 | 29 7/8 | 34 2/8 | 37 4/8 | 5 3/8 | 5 6/8 | 4 | 5 | | 122 | 14 |
| | ♦ Butte County / John A. Little / John A. Little / 1981 | | | | | | | | | | |
| 200 6/8 | 25 1/8 | 25 1/8 | 26 7/8 | 30 5/8 | 5 3/8 | 5 2/8 | 5 | 7 | 3 2/8 | 143 | 16 |
| | ♦ Boise County / Delbert W. Crawford / Delbert W. Crawford / 1969 | | | | | | | | | | |
| 200 4/8 | 26 7/8 | 28 6/8 | 27 6/8 | 34 6/8 | 5 1/8 | 5 1/8 | 5 | 6 | | 153 | 17 |
| | ♦ Bear Lake County / Frank Bidart / Frank Bidart / 1965 | | | | | | | | | | |
| 200 4/8 | 27 | 25 6/8 | 23 6/8 | 30 4/8 | 5 1/8 | 5 | 7 | 6 | 8 6/8 | 153 | 17 |
| | ♦ Bear Lake County / Lee Bridges / Lee Bridges / 1966 | | | | | | | | | | |
| 200 4/8 | 26 4/8 | 26 6/8 | 23 | 25 6/8 | 5 3/8 | 5 3/8 | 5 | 5 | | 153 | 17 |
| | ♦ Caribou County / Herb Voyler, Jr. / Herb Voyler, Jr. / 1972 | | | | | | | | | | |
| 200 4/8 | 27 1/8 | 26 | 30 5/8 | 39 | 5 4/8 | 5 3/8 | 6 | 5 | 1 6/8 | 153 | 17 |
| | ♦ Adams County / Roy Eastlick / Roy Eastlick / 1974 | | | | | | | | | | |
| 199 4/8 | 26 1/8 | 28 4/8 | 28 7/8 | 30 | 4 6/8 | 4 7/8 | 7 | 7 | 6 6/8 | 187 | 21 |
| | ♦ Salmon River / C.A. Schwope / C.A. Schwope / 1959 | | | | | | | | | | |
| 199 4/8 | 24 1/8 | 24 1/8 | 21 2/8 | 27 | 5 5/8 | 5 5/8 | 5 | 5 | | 187 | 21 |
| | ♦ Bonneville County / Leonard J. Vella / Leonard J. Vella / 1972 | | | | | | | | | | |
| 198 5/8 | 24 4/8 | 24 7/8 | 24 1/8 | 30 4/8 | 5 3/8 | 5 5/8 | 6 | 6 | | 213 | 23 |
| | ♦ Swan Valley / Harry G. Brinkley, Jr. / Harry G. Brinkley, Jr. / 1966 | | | | | | | | | | |
| 198 5/8 | 25 | 24 7/8 | 23 5/8 | 27 5/8 | 4 7/8 | 4 7/8 | 5 | 5 | | 213 | 23 |
| | ♦ Elmore County / William Hartwig / William Hartwig / 1984 | | | | | | | | | | |
| 198 3/8 | 25 | 25 4/8 | 19 5/8 | 25 5/8 | 4 5/8 | 4 5/8 | 5 | 5 | | 226 | 25 |
| | ♦ Bonneville County / Tony Dawson / Tony Dawson / 1973 | | | | | | | | | | |
| 198 2/8 | 28 2/8 | 28 3/8 | 27 | 32 3/8 | 5 4/8 | 5 3/8 | 5 | 7 | 5 4/8 | 229 | 26 |
| | ♦ Bonneville County / Thomas N. Thiel / Thomas N. Thiel / 1987 | | | | | | | | | | |
| 198 1/8 | 25 3/8 | 26 | 25 2/8 | 32 6/8 | 5 4/8 | 5 4/8 | 5 | 4 | 4 7/8 | 234 | 27 |
| | ♦ Irwin / Chet Warwick / Chet Warwick / 1959 | | | | | | | | | | |
| 198 | 25 | 25 | 22 4/8 | 30 2/8 | 5 6/8 | 5 6/8 | 5 | 5 | | 239 | 28 |
| | ♦ Montpelier / Charles R. Mann / Charles R. Mann / 1973 | | | | | | | | | | |
| 197 7/8 | 28 3/8 | 28 2/8 | 25 7/8 | 30 4/8 | 5 6/8 | 5 5/8 | 7 | 6 | 11 6/8 | 247 | 29 |
| | ♦ Blaine County / James D. Scarrow / James D. Scarrow / 1983 | | | | | | | | | | |
| 197 6/8 | 24 3/8 | 26 4/8 | 27 3/8 | 29 1/8 | 5 | 5 1/8 | 5 | 5 | | 253 | 30 |
| | ♦ Bonneville County / Preston L. Winchell / Preston L. Winchell / 1974 | | | | | | | | | | |

| Score | Length of Main Beam R | Length of Main Beam L | Inside Spread | Greatest Spread | Circumference at Smallest Place Between Burr and First Point R | Circumference at Smallest Place Between Burr and First Point L | Number of Points R | Number of Points L | Total of Lengths Abnormal Points | All-Time Rank | State Rank |
|---|---|---|---|---|---|---|---|---|---|---|---|
| | *Locality Killed* | | *By Whom Killed* | | *Owner* | | *Date Killed* | | | | |
| 197 5/8 | 24 3/8 | 24 1/8 | 24 7/8 | 29 3/8 | 4 7/8 | 5 | 5 | 5 | | 258 | 31 |
| | ◆ *Ashton / Earl Johnson / O.M. Corbett / 1959* | | | | | | | | | | |
| 197 4/8 | 27 2/8 | 27 1/8 | 23 6/8 | 30 2/8 | 4 3/8 | 4 3/8 | 4 | 5 | | 264 | 32 |
| | ◆ *Bonneville County / LaDon Harriell / LaDon Harriell / 1982* | | | | | | | | | | |
| 197 3/8 | 26 5/8 | 27 5/8 | 26 3/8 | 31 1/8 | 4 6/8 | 4 7/8 | 6 | 6 | 4 4/8 | 269 | 33 |
| | ◆ *Fremont County / Stanley A. Gilgen / Stanley A. Gilgen / 1964* | | | | | | | | | | |
| 197 2/8 | 26 5/8 | 25 7/8 | 26 4/8 | 30 5/8 | 5 2/8 | 5 3/8 | 5 | 6 | 4 2/8 | 277 | 34 |
| | ◆ *Blaine County / Bart Hofmann / Bart Hofmann / 1980* | | | | | | | | | | |
| 197 | 24 7/8 | 25 7/8 | 22 | 29 | 5 3/8 | 5 3/8 | 5 | 5 | | 288 | 35 |
| | ◆ *Franklin County / Robert C. Porter / Robert C. Porter / 1972* | | | | | | | | | | |
| 197 | 25 2/8 | 24 1/8 | 25 | 27 5/8 | 4 7/8 | 4 6/8 | 5 | 5 | | 288 | 35 |
| | ◆ *Camas County / Bret C. Silver / Bret C. Silver / 1980* | | | | | | | | | | |
| 196 7/8 | 24 5/8 | 24 4/8 | 22 5/8 | 27 2/8 | 5 6/8 | 5 5/8 | 5 | 5 | | 296 | 37 |
| | ◆ *Boise County / Andrew T. Rogers / Andrew T. Rogers / 1967* | | | | | | | | | | |
| 196 6/8 | 24 4/8 | 23 6/8 | 24 4/8 | 30 7/8 | 5 3/8 | 5 2/8 | 7 | 5 | 6 2/8 | 300 | 38 |
| | ◆ *Bear Lake County / Nels H. Pehrson / Ralph V. Pehrson / 1936* | | | | | | | | | | |
| 196 6/8 | 23 3/8 | 24 1/8 | 22 4/8 | 30 5/8 | 5 1/8 | 5 2/8 | 5 | 5 | | 300 | 38 |
| | ◆ *Bonneville County / William G. Pine / William G. Pine / 1969* | | | | | | | | | | |
| 196 5/8 | 22 | 22 6/8 | 21 5/8 | 29 6/8 | 5 | 5 1/8 | 7 | 6 | 3 2/8 | 307 | 40 |
| | ◆ *Lemhi County / Hubert M. Livingston / Hubert M. Livingston / 1967* | | | | | | | | | | |
| 196 2/8 | 25 4/8 | 25 6/8 | 22 4/8 | 31 2/8 | 5 2/8 | 5 3/8 | 6 | 6 | 5 | 330 | 41 |
| | ◆ *Bingham County / Thomas D. Robison / Thomas D. Robison / 1972* | | | | | | | | | | |
| 196 1/8 | 26 | 27 7/8 | 24 4/8 | 29 5/8 | 5 7/8 | 5 6/8 | 5 | 7 | 4 5/8 | 341 | 42 |
| | ◆ *Boise County / H.L. Rice / H.L. Rice / 1966* | | | | | | | | | | |
| 196 | 25 4/8 | 28 | 23 | 26 | 5 5/8 | 5 6/8 | 5 | 6 | 2 | 346 | 43 |
| | ◆ *Franklin County / Larry W. Cross / Larry W. Cross / 1974* | | | | | | | | | | |
| 195 7/8 | 26 2/8 | 25 7/8 | 26 2/8 | 31 4/8 | 5 6/8 | 5 5/8 | 7 | 7 | 8 1/8 | 354 | 44 |
| | ◆ *Bannock County / William J. Barry / William J. Barry / 1956* | | | | | | | | | | |
| 195 7/8 | 27 | 28 4/8 | 28 4/8 | 33 | 5 3/8 | 5 4/8 | 7 | 7 | 4 7/8 | 354 | 44 |
| | ◆ *Franklin County / Melvin S. Thomson / Melvin S. Thomson / 1987* | | | | | | | | | | |
| 195 4/8 | 26 | 26 1/8 | 25 4/8 | 27 6/8 | 5 | 5 | 5 | 6 | 1 4/8 | 375 | 46 |
| | ◆ *Bear Lake County / Joseph R. Given / Joseph R. Given / 1985* | | | | | | | | | | |
| 195 1/8 | 25 | 25 6/8 | 22 4/8 | 28 4/8 | 5 | 4 7/8 | 5 | 8 | 5 1/8 | 397 | 47 |
| | ◆ *Salmon River / Gary Bevan / Gary Bevan / 1970* | | | | | | | | | | |

| Score | Length of Main Beam R | Length of Main Beam L | Inside Spread | Greatest Spread | Circumference at Smallest Place Between Burr and First Point R | Circumference at Smallest Place Between Burr and First Point L | Number of Points R | Number of Points L | Total of Lengths Abnormal Points | All-Time Rank | State Rank |
|---|---|---|---|---|---|---|---|---|---|---|---|
| ♦ *Locality Killed / By Whom Killed / Owner / Date Killed* | | | | | | | | | | | |
| 190 7/8 | 27 4/8 | 27 7/8 | 27 | 32 1/8 | 4 5/8 | 5 | 6 | 6 | 3 5/8 | 420 | 48 |
| ♦ *Elmore County / Michael H. Felton / Michael H. Felton / 1980* | | | | | | | | | | | |
| 187 | 25 2/8 | 24 6/8 | 26 3/8 | 32 | 4 6/8 | 4 7/8 | 5 | 5 | | 433 | 49 |
| ♦ *Bonneville County / Rockie L. Walker / Rockie L. Walker / 1986* | | | | | | | | | | | |
| 186 7/8 | 24 6/8 | 22 3/8 | 19 7/8 | 28 6/8 | 4 5/8 | 4 5/8 | 5 | 5 | | 435 | 50 |
| ♦ *Idaho County / Tom M. Schachten / Tom M. Schachten / 1987* | | | | | | | | | | | |
| 185 5/8 | 26 2/8 | 26 2/8 | 20 7/8 | 27 7/8 | 5 5/8 | 5 5/8 | 5 | 8 | 4 | 444 | 51 |
| ♦ *Franklin County / R. Ashley Lyman III / R. Ashley Lyman III / 1964* | | | | | | | | | | | |
| 210 6/8 | 28 2/8 | 29 1/8 | 24 4/8 | 28 2/8 | 5 | 5 | 5 | 5 | | * | * |
| ♦ *Idaho County / Urban H. Riener / John D. Morgan / 1979* | | | | | | | | | | | |

Photograph courtesy of Pauline J. Bostic

Pauline J. Bostic with the typical mule deer she took in La Plata County, Colorado, in 1971. Bostic's trophy still scores 198-4/8 points after the deduction of 11-2/8 inches for the total of lengths of three abnormal points.

**IDAHO STATE RECORD**
**NON-TYPICAL MULE DEER**
**SCORE: 300-7/8**
Locality: Bonneville Co.    Date: November 1985
Hunter: Brett J. Sauer
Owner: Don Schaufler

# IDAHO

## NON-TYPICAL MULE DEER

| Score | Length of Main Beam R | Length of Main Beam L | Inside Spread | Greatest Spread | Circumference at Smallest Place Between Burr and First Point R | Circumference at Smallest Place Between Burr and First Point L | Number of Points R | Number of Points L | Total of Lengths Abnormal Points | All-Time Rank | State Rank |
|---|---|---|---|---|---|---|---|---|---|---|---|
| ♦ *Locality Killed / By Whom Killed / Owner / Date Killed* | | | | | | | | | | | |
| 300 7/8 | 24 | 22 6/8 | 29 4/8 | 33 7/8 | 5 5/8 | 5 3/8 | 17 | 16 | 108 3/8 | 12 | 1 |
| ♦ *Bonneville County / Brett J. Sauer / Don Schaufler / 1985* | | | | | | | | | | | |
| 288 2/8 | 25 | 25 7/8 | 26 | 41 | 6 | 6 | 16 | 13 | 95 1/8 | 20 | 2 |
| ♦ *Hailey / Robby Miller / Don Schaufler / 1969* | | | | | | | | | | | |
| 280 4/8 | 27 | 26 6/8 | 23 4/8 | 34 6/8 | 6 | 6 | 15 | 14 | 65 2/8 | 31 | 3 |
| ♦ *Gem County / Ronald S. Holbrook / Ronald S. Holbrook / 1982* | | | | | | | | | | | |
| 279 5/8 | 21 7/8 | 22 5/8 | 30 4/8 | 39 | 6 3/8 | 6 2/8 | 18 | 17 | 104 4/8 | 34 | 4 |
| ♦ *Cuprum / Ed Martin / Ed Martin / 1966* | | | | | | | | | | | |
| 278 3/8 | 27 2/8 | 28 | 26 | 34 7/8 | 5 2/8 | 5 3/8 | 11 | 13 | 63 5/8 | 37 | 5 |
| ♦ *Soda Springs / Jack White / Don Schaufler / 1957* | | | | | | | | | | | |
| 274 2/8 | 22 3/8 | 25 | 23 2/8 | 26 1/8 | 6 6/8 | 6 1/8 | 13 | 13 | 89 4/8 | 46 | 6 |
| ♦ *Sublett / Mrs. Jack Keen / Mr. & Mrs. Jack Keen / 1957* | | | | | | | | | | | |
| 274 2/8 | 24 4/8 | 25 7/8 | 24 5/8 | 34 6/8 | 5 6/8 | 5 3/8 | 14 | 13 | 68 3/8 | 46 | 6 |
| ♦ *Fremont County / David L. Maurer / David L. Maurer / 1979* | | | | | | | | | | | |
| 274 1/8 | 21 7/8 | 23 6/8 | 22 2/8 | 32 4/8 | 4 7/8 | 5 | 11 | 11 | 70 7/8 | 48 | 8 |
| ♦ *North Fork / James D. Edwards / Idaho Fish & Game Dept. / 1967* | | | | | | | | | | | |
| 272 7/8 | 24 1/8 | 26 2/8 | 27 1/8 | 31 6/8 | 5 4/8 | 5 5/8 | 15 | 16 | 66 1/8 | 54 | 9 |
| ♦ *Caribou County / Picked Up / Don Schaufler / 1948* | | | | | | | | | | | |
| 265 | 24 | 24 2/8 | 19 4/8 | 35 1/8 | 4 7/8 | 5 | 13 | 15 | 67 6/8 | 81 | 10 |
| ♦ *Custer County / John L. Simmons / John L. Simmons / 1986* | | | | | | | | | | | |
| 264 5/8 | 26 | 26 5/8 | 22 4/8 | 35 4/8 | 5 4/8 | 5 6/8 | 18 | 13 | 65 7/8 | 82 | 11 |
| ♦ *Bannock County / Jarel Neeser / Jarel Neeser / 1974* | | | | | | | | | | | |
| 263 1/8 | 27 4/8 | 26 1/8 | 26 4/8 | 42 | 6 2/8 | 6 1/8 | 20 | 13 | 73 1/8 | 89 | 12 |
| ♦ *Bigwood River / Robert C. Young / Robert C. Young / 1956* | | | | | | | | | | | |
| 261 3/8 | 25 4/8 | 24 | 27 2/8 | | 5 2/8 | 5 | 10 | 10 | | 99 | 13 |
| ♦ *Blaine County / Roger A. Crowder / Roger A. Crowder / 1957* | | | | | | | | | | | |

| Score | Length of Main Beam R | L | Inside Spread | Greatest Spread | Circumference at Smallest Place Between Burr and First Point R | L | Number of Points R | L | Total of Lengths Abnormal Points | All-Time Rank | State Rank |
|---|---|---|---|---|---|---|---|---|---|---|---|
| | ♦ *Locality Killed / By Whom Killed / Owner / Date Killed* | | | | | | | | | | |
| 260 6/8 | 26 5/8 | 26 3/8 | 22 3/8 | 36 4/8 | 4 7/8 | 4 7/8 | 10 | 13 | 63 1/8 | 103 | 14 |
| | ♦ *Ada County / Howard R. Cromwell / Raymond R. Cross / 1975* | | | | | | | | | | |
| 260 2/8 | 23 1/8 | 24 3/8 | 25 4/8 | 36 1/8 | 5 7/8 | 6 | 15 | 17 | 68 7/8 | 106 | 15 |
| | ♦ *Boise / George M. Tweedy / George M. Tweedy / 1946* | | | | | | | | | | |
| 260 | 22 7/8 | 25 | 20 | 35 5/8 | 5 | 5 | 12 | 12 | 61 6/8 | 109 | 16 |
| | ♦ *Caribou County / Arthur H. Summers / Arthur H. Summers / 1966* | | | | | | | | | | |
| 259 7/8 | 25 1/8 | 25 2/8 | 22 2/8 | 39 2/8 | 5 | 5 | 8 | 10 | 50 1/8 | 111 | 17 |
| | ♦ *Caribou County / Jerry Hunt / Jerry Hunt / 1966* | | | | | | | | | | |
| 259 6/8 | 25 7/8 | 24 7/8 | 29 | 37 4/8 | 6 3/8 | 5 7/8 | 15 | 14 | 66 3/8 | 114 | 18 |
| | ♦ *Gooding County / Charles Hollingsworth / Charles Hollingsworth / 1970* | | | | | | | | | | |
| 259 4/8 | 24 3/8 | 24 | 25 3/8 | 41 6/8 | 5 | 5 2/8 | 13 | 15 | 66 7/8 | 117 | 19 |
| | ♦ *Boise County / LeRoy Massey / LeRoy Massey / 1959* | | | | | | | | | | |
| 258 6/8 | 27 5/8 | 27 6/8 | 24 5/8 | 31 4/8 | 5 | 5 | 15 | 10 | 49 7/8 | 120 | 20 |
| | ♦ *Valley County / Larry Dwonch / Larry Dwonch / 1972* | | | | | | | | | | |
| 258 1/8 | 27 3/8 | 26 4/8 | 23 6/8 | 40 3/8 | 5 1/8 | 5 1/8 | 13 | 14 | 70 1/8 | 126 | 21 |
| | ♦ *Atlanta / Kenneth E. Potts / Kenneth E. Potts / 1968* | | | | | | | | | | |
| 257 4/8 | 25 3/8 | 26 | 27 2/8 | 35 | 5 4/8 | 5 4/8 | 9 | 14 | 69 | 134 | 22 |
| | ♦ *Blaine County / Philip T. Homer / Philip T. Homer / 1983* | | | | | | | | | | |
| 256 7/8 | 23 7/8 | 22 4/8 | 21 4/8 | 34 1/8 | 4 1/8 | 4 6/8 | 12 | 13 | 71 5/8 | 141 | 23 |
| | ♦ *Elmore County / Paul Vetter / Paul Vetter / 1972* | | | | | | | | | | |
| 256 1/8 | 22 7/8 | 22 4/8 | 20 1/8 | 30 5/8 | 4 5/8 | 5 | 14 | 12 | 70 2/8 | 147 | 24 |
| | ♦ *Irwin / Hale K. Charlton / Hale K. Charlton / 1966* | | | | | | | | | | |
| 256 | 26 7/8 | 26 5/8 | 22 6/8 | 35 2/8 | 9 4/8 | 6 5/8 | 16 | 9 | 62 6/8 | 149 | 25 |
| | ♦ *Gem County / Jay P. Baker / Jay P. Baker / 1981* | | | | | | | | | | |
| 255 1/8 | 25 6/8 | 26 6/8 | 29 4/8 | 37 | 5 6/8 | 5 4/8 | 10 | 11 | 48 5/8 | 156 | 26 |
| | ♦ *Hells Canyon / Basil C. Bradbury / Basil C. Bradbury / 1955* | | | | | | | | | | |
| 253 2/8 | 24 3/8 | 25 2/8 | 20 5/8 | 35 6/8 | 5 2/8 | 5 5/8 | 15 | 17 | 72 1/8 | 168 | 27 |
| | ♦ *Salmon / Ben H. Quick / Ben H. Quick / 1960* | | | | | | | | | | |
| 251 6/8 | 24 | 25 4/8 | 20 | 38 1/8 | 5 1/8 | 5 | 13 | 14 | 57 | 178 | 28 |
| | ♦ *Gem County / A.K. England / Roscoe E. Ferris / 1969* | | | | | | | | | | |
| 251 | 25 1/8 | 26 1/8 | 26 1/8 | 40 | 5 1/8 | 5 1/8 | 13 | 14 | 54 3/8 | 183 | 29 |
| | ♦ *Adams County / Clark Childers / Clark Childers / 1955* | | | | | | | | | | |

| Score | Length of Main Beam R | Length of Main Beam L | Inside Spread | Greatest Spread | Circumference at Smallest Place Between Burr and First Point R | Circumference at Smallest Place Between Burr and First Point L | Number of Points R | Number of Points L | Total of Lengths Abnormal Points | All-Time Rank | State Rank |
|---|---|---|---|---|---|---|---|---|---|---|---|
| 250 4/8 | 29 1/8 | 26 7/8 | 22 4/8 | 31 5/8 | 6 2/8 | 8 | 7 | 13 | 42 2/8 | 186 | 30 |
| ♦ *Kunard Valley / Ralph D. Hogan / Ralph D. Hogan / 1966* | | | | | | | | | | | |
| 249 3/8 | 27 | 27 4/8 | 27 5/8 | 35 5/8 | 6 1/8 | 6 2/8 | 7 | 11 | 48 1/8 | 195 | 31 |
| ♦ *Adams County / Howard E. Paradis / Howard E. Paradis / 1966* | | | | | | | | | | | |
| 248 5/8 | 26 6/8 | 25 6/8 | 33 6/8 | 45 4/8 | 6 2/8 | 5 2/8 | 14 | 10 | 51 1/8 | 204 | 32 |
| ♦ *Franklin County / Joan Butterworth / Quinten Butterworth / 1961* | | | | | | | | | | | |
| 247 6/8 | 24 7/8 | 23 5/8 | 22 2/8 | 34 4/8 | 5 | 5 1/8 | 11 | 16 | 69 6/8 | 216 | 33 |
| ♦ *Shoshone County / Gary J. Finney / Gary J. Finney / 1983* | | | | | | | | | | | |
| 247 3/8 | 22 5/8 | 22 6/8 | 22 5/8 | 33 1/8 | 4 4/8 | 4 4/8 | 11 | 9 | 52 6/8 | 222 | 34 |
| ♦ *Fremont County / Donald R. Craig / Donald R. Craig / 1982* | | | | | | | | | | | |
| 247 1/8 | 26 2/8 | 25 | 27 2/8 | 37 | 4 6/8 | 4 5/8 | 12 | 9 | 35 7/8 | 225 | 35 |
| ♦ *Whitebird / Harold Gustin / Wayne Demaray / 1965* | | | | | | | | | | | |
| 246 7/8 | 27 2/8 | 21 3/8 | 29 2/8 | 40 4/8 | 5 2/8 | 5 4/8 | 14 | 14 | 65 1/8 | 231 | 36 |
| ♦ *Needle Peak / Michael G. Cameron / Michael G. Cameron / 1966* | | | | | | | | | | | |
| 245 1/8 | 24 | 23 2/8 | 20 2/8 | 37 5/8 | 5 3/8 | 5 4/8 | 12 | 9 | 47 5/8 | 249 | 37 |
| ♦ *Power County / Mark B. Cooper / Mark B. Cooper / 1984* | | | | | | | | | | | |
| 245 | 25 6/8 | 25 5/8 | 29 6/8 | 31 6/8 | 5 5/8 | 5 4/8 | 17 | 15 | 45 4/8 | 250 | 38 |
| ♦ *Bonner County / Dick Sherwood / Dick Sherwood / 1963* | | | | | | | | | | | |
| 243 1/8 | 25 4/8 | 23 4/8 | 25 1/8 | 37 3/8 | 5 4/8 | 5 7/8 | 8 | 11 | 38 6/8 | 277 | 39 |
| ♦ *Fremont County / Larry D. Hawker / Larry D. Hawker / 1970* | | | | | | | | | | | |
| 242 7/8 | 22 4/8 | 23 7/8 | 26 4/8 | 39 6/8 | 5 4/8 | 5 3/8 | 10 | 12 | 49 6/8 | 282 | 40 |
| ♦ *Gem County / Roland Bright / Roland Bright / 1965* | | | | | | | | | | | |
| 242 5/8 | 25 | 26 3/8 | 18 3/8 | 25 4/8 | 6 | 5 6/8 | 11 | 10 | 44 | 284 | 41 |
| ♦ *Baison / Daniel E. Osborne / Daniel E. Osborne / 1959* | | | | | | | | | | | |
| 242 4/8 | 27 2/8 | 25 3/8 | 29 4/8 | 37 | 5 | 5 | 10 | 11 | 62 | 286 | 42 |
| ♦ *Blaine County / Roger A. Crowder / Roger A. Crowder / 1957* | | | | | | | | | | | |
| 242 1/8 | 28 | 27 6/8 | 22 1/8 | 32 4/8 | 6 1/8 | 6 1/8 | 9 | 11 | 36 6/8 | 290 | 43 |
| ♦ *Bear Lake County / Robert N. Gale / Robert N. Gale / 1970* | | | | | | | | | | | |
| 241 3/8 | 22 3/8 | 23 7/8 | 20 4/8 | 36 | 5 1/8 | 5 2/8 | 10 | 12 | 51 7/8 | 300 | 44 |
| ♦ *Adams County / Peter Renberg / Peter Renberg / 1963* | | | | | | | | | | | |
| 241 3/8 | 26 6/8 | 24 7/8 | 24 3/8 | 35 4/8 | 5 | 5 1/8 | 12 | 13 | 43 4/8 | 300 | 44 |
| ♦ *Salmon River / Richard Shilling / Richard Shilling / 1965* | | | | | | | | | | | |

| Score | Length of Main Beam R | L | Inside Spread | Greatest Spread | Circumference at Smallest Place Between Burr and First Point R | L | Number of Points R | L | Total of Lengths Abnormal Points | All-Time Rank | State Rank |
|---|---|---|---|---|---|---|---|---|---|---|---|
| ◆ *Locality Killed / By Whom Killed / Owner / Date Killed* | | | | | | | | | | | |
| 240 1/8 | 23 4/8 | 23 1/8 | 23 2/8 | 36 7/8 | 5 6/8 | 5 5/8 | 12 | 12 | 43 1/8 | 316 | 46 |
| ◆ *Elmore County / Phillip K. Messer / Phillip K. Messer / 1971* | | | | | | | | | | | |
| 237 3/8 | 27 2/8 | 23 7/8 | 20 2/8 | 35 5/8 | 4 6/8 | 5 4/8 | 8 | 13 | 59 1/8 | 323 | 47 |
| ◆ *Hawley Creek / Clifford Nealis / Clifford Nealis / 1960* | | | | | | | | | | | |
| 237 3/8 | 23 6/8 | 23 2/8 | 23 3/8 | 37 | 5 5/8 | 5 7/8 | 11 | 12 | 52 4/8 | 323 | 47 |
| ◆ *Bonneville County / Bert L. Freed / Bert L. Freed / 1987* | | | | | | | | | | | |
| 227 1/8 | 27 5/8 | 26 | 22 4/8 | 33 | 4 7/8 | 4 6/8 | 8 | 7 | 44 5/8 | 329 | 49 |
| ◆ *Nez Perce County / Richard S. Lowe / Richard S. Lowe / 1986* | | | | | | | | | | | |
| 252 7/8 | 22 4/8 | 18 6/8 | 19 1/8 | 36 1/8 | 5 4/8 | 5 4/8 | 11 | 22 | 82 6/8 | * | * |
| ◆ *Boise County / Dennis D. Snider / Dennis D. Snider / 1983* | | | | | | | | | | | |

A lot of folks think a week of hunting is a long time. Bruce K. McRae took this non-typical mule deer on the 13th day of his 1986 hunt in Teton County, Wyoming. It has 23 total antler points and a final score of 232-5/8.

Photograph by Corey Johnston

**KANSAS STATE RECORD**
**NON-TYPICAL MULE DEER**
**SCORE: 260-6/8**
Locality: Rooks Co.    Date: December 1965
Hunter: Lee Odle

# KANSAS

## NON-TYPICAL MULE DEER

| Score | Length of Main Beam | | Inside Spread | Great-est Spread | Circumference at Smallest Place Between Burr and First Point | | Number of Points | | Total of Lengths Abnor-mal Points | All-Time Rank | State Rank |
|---|---|---|---|---|---|---|---|---|---|---|---|
| | R | L | | | R | L | R | L | | | |

♦ *Locality Killed / By Whom Killed / Owner / Date Killed*

| 260 ⁶/₈ | 29 ⁴/₈ | 27 ⁷/₈ | 28 ⁶/₈ | 36 ⁷/₈ | 5 ⁴/₈ | 5 ⁷/₈ | 10 | 14 | 58 ⁴/₈ | 103 | 1 |

♦ *Rooks County / Lee Odle / Lee Odle / 1965*

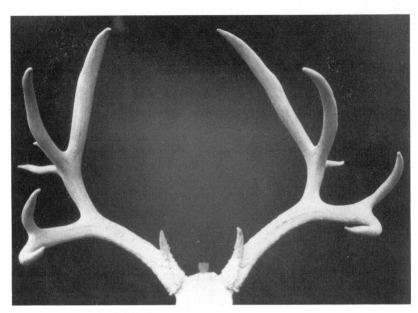

## MONTANA STATE RECORD
## TYPICAL MULE DEER
## SCORE: 202
Locality: Lincoln Co.    Date: November 1963
Hunter: William E. Hubbard

# MONTANA

## TYPICAL MULE DEER

| Score | Length of Main Beam | | Inside Spread | Greatest Spread | Circumference at Smallest Place Between Burr and First Point | | Number of Points | | Total of Lengths Abnormal Points | All-Time Rank | State Rank |
|---|---|---|---|---|---|---|---|---|---|---|---|
| | R | L | | | R | L | R | L | | | |
| | *Locality Killed / By Whom Killed / Owner / Date Killed* | | | | | | | | | | |
| 202 | 26 7/8 | 27 2/8 | 27 6/8 | 33 2/8 | 6 3/8 | 6 3/8 | 6 | 6 | 7 | 104 | 1 |
| | *Lincoln County / William E. Hubbard / William E. Hubbard / 1963* | | | | | | | | | | |
| 201 4/8 | 28 1/8 | 28 3/8 | 22 7/8 | 27 1/8 | 5 6/8 | 5 4/8 | 5 | 7 | 2 3/8 | 117 | 2 |
| | *Ravalli County / Sherman L. Williams / Sherman L. Williams / 1973* | | | | | | | | | | |
| 199 7/8 | 25 3/8 | 24 5/8 | 25 1/8 | 29 1/8 | 5 4/8 | 5 4/8 | 5 | 5 | | 178 | 3 |
| | *Stillwater County / Basil C. Bradbury / Basil C. Bradbury / 1965* | | | | | | | | | | |
| 197 6/8 | 27 4/8 | 26 2/8 | 24 4/8 | 28 6/8 | 4 6/8 | 4 6/8 | 5 | 5 | | 253 | 4 |
| | *Jefferson County / James W. Rowe / James W. Rowe / 1964* | | | | | | | | | | |
| 197 2/8 | 24 4/8 | 24 4/8 | 23 2/8 | 27 2/8 | 4 6/8 | 4 6/8 | 5 | 6 | 1 2/8 | 277 | 5 |
| | *Flathead County / James E. Betters / James E. Betters / 1986* | | | | | | | | | | |
| 196 7/8 | 25 5/8 | 24 | 21 5/8 | 29 4/8 | 5 2/8 | 5 4/8 | 5 | 5 | | 296 | 6 |
| | *Lincoln County / Dennis J. Hauke / Dennis J. Hauke / 1973* | | | | | | | | | | |
| 196 4/8 | 24 5/8 | 25 5/8 | 25 1/8 | 33 2/8 | 5 2/8 | 5 1/8 | 7 | 5 | 2 1/8 | 318 | 7 |
| | *Flathead River / Stanley Rauscher / Stanley Rauscher / 1959* | | | | | | | | | | |
| 196 4/8 | 23 5/8 | 23 5/8 | 23 | 27 | 5 2/8 | 5 2/8 | 5 | 5 | | 318 | 7 |
| | *Powell County / Raymond A. Fitzgerald / Raymond A. Fitzgerald / 1983* | | | | | | | | | | |
| 196 3/8 | 24 6/8 | 25 1/8 | 24 4/8 | 26 4/8 | 5 3/8 | 5 3/8 | 6 | 5 | 1 1/8 | 326 | 9 |
| | *Powell County / Stanley F. Malcolm / Stanley F. Malcolm / 1958* | | | | | | | | | | |
| 196 2/8 | 27 4/8 | 27 1/8 | 25 1/8 | 29 7/8 | 4 5/8 | 5 1/8 | 7 | 5 | 3 3/8 | 330 | 10 |
| | *Lincoln County / Tommy Boothman / Tommy Boothman / 1960* | | | | | | | | | | |
| 196 | 25 | 24 4/8 | 24 | 28 3/8 | 5 3/8 | 5 | 5 | 5 | | 346 | 11 |
| | *Corwin Springs / Donald Strazzabosco / Donald Strazzabosco / 1966* | | | | | | | | | | |
| 195 5/8 | 26 5/8 | 27 1/8 | 26 1/8 | 29 5/8 | 4 7/8 | 4 6/8 | 5 | 5 | | 367 | 12 |
| | *Ravalli County / William H. Cowan / William H. Cowan / 1959* | | | | | | | | | | |

| Score | Length of Main Beam R | L | Inside Spread | Greatest Spread | Circumference at Smallest Place Between Burr and First Point R | L | Number of Points R | L | Total of Lengths Abnormal Points | All-Time Rank | State Rank |
|---|---|---|---|---|---|---|---|---|---|---|---|
| | | | | | ◆ *Locality Killed / By Whom Killed / Owner / Date Killed* | | | | | | |
| 195 4/8 | 25 2/8 | 27 1/8 | 22 7/8 | 29 6/8 | 5 6/8 | 5 4/8 | 6 | 6 | 6 7/8 | 375 | 13 |
| | ◆ *Flathead County / Sharon M. Gaughan / Sharon M. Gaughan / 1980* | | | | | | | | | | |
| 195 4/8 | 26 3/8 | 26 5/8 | 25 2/8 | 28 | 5 6/8 | 5 5/8 | 5 | 5 | | 375 | 13 |
| | ◆ *Sanders County / William B. Hart / William B. Hart / 1984* | | | | | | | | | | |
| 195 | 27 1/8 | 26 1/8 | 22 4/8 | 27 4/8 | 5 6/8 | 5 6/8 | 5 | 5 | | 405 | 15 |
| | ◆ *Sun River / Dick Lyman / Dick Lyman / 1966* | | | | | | | | | | |
| 187 5/8 | 25 6/8 | 26 1/8 | 24 1/8 | 26 3/8 | 5 4/8 | 5 | 5 | 5 | | 432 | 16 |
| | ◆ *Flathead County / Jeffrey A. Bechtel / Jeffrey A. Bechtel / 1983* | | | | | | | | | | |

Photograph courtesy of Barbara M. Conley

Barbara M. Conley with her typical mule deer buck that scores 193-3/8 points. Conley hunted on Lost Creek in Washoe County, Nevada, in 1987 to find this trophy.

Photograph Courtesy of Peter Zemljak

**MONTANA STATE RECORD**
**NON-TYPICAL MULE DEER**
**SCORE: 275-7/8**
Locality: Highland Mts.    Date: 1962
Hunter: Peter Zemljak, Sr.
Owner: Peter Zemljak

# MONTANA

## NON-TYPICAL MULE DEER

| Score | Length of Main Beam R | Length of Main Beam L | Inside Spread | Greatest Spread | Circumference at Smallest Place Between Burr and First Point R | Circumference at Smallest Place Between Burr and First Point L | Number of Points R | Number of Points L | Total of Lengths Abnormal Points | All-Time Rank | State Rank |
|---|---|---|---|---|---|---|---|---|---|---|---|
| ♦ *Locality Killed / By Whom Killed / Owner / Date Killed* | | | | | | | | | | | |
| 275 7/8 | 29 2/8 | 25 4/8 | 34 3/8 | 41 5/8 | 5 5/8 | 5 6/8 | 16 | 13 | 92 3/8 | 42 | 1 |
| ♦ *Highland Mts. / Peter Zemljak, Sr. / Peter Zemljak / 1962* | | | | | | | | | | | |
| 275 1/8 | 23 6/8 | 22 4/8 | 20 5/8 | 43 4/8 | 5 7/8 | 6 | 14 | 15 | 82 2/8 | 44 | 2 |
| ♦ *Ruby Mts. / Peter Zemljak / Peter Zemljak / 1960* | | | | | | | | | | | |
| 270 5/8 | 23 6/8 | 24 2/8 | 21 1/8 | 38 3/8 | 4 3/8 | 4 3/8 | 10 | 12 | 73 4/8 | 60 | 3 |
| ♦ *Big Horn County / R. Turnsback & J. Van Elsen / William Erdmann / 1961* | | | | | | | | | | | |
| 268 4/8 | 21 3/8 | 23 6/8 | 17 4/8 | 32 2/8 | 6 5/8 | 6 5/8 | 17 | 16 | 86 | 65 | 4 |
| ♦ *Cascade County / Unknown / Kent Austin / PR 1980* | | | | | | | | | | | |
| 266 2/8 | 24 4/8 | 24 7/8 | 21 | 37 6/8 | 5 3/8 | 5 4/8 | 12 | 18 | 83 4/8 | 72 | 5 |
| ♦ *Park County / Benton R. Venable / Benton R. Venable / 1945* | | | | | | | | | | | |
| 265 7/8 | 25 5/8 | 26 4/8 | 27 6/8 | 39 1/8 | 5 4/8 | 5 6/8 | 8 | 12 | 54 5/8 | 75 | 6 |
| ♦ *Sidney / Buster Dodson / F.P. Murray / 1954* | | | | | | | | | | | |
| 265 7/8 | 23 5/8 | 24 1/8 | 22 7/8 | 31 7/8 | 5 5/8 | 5 6/8 | 20 | 15 | 80 6/8 | 75 | 6 |
| ♦ *Powder River County / Michael A. Siewert / Michael A. Siewert / 1987* | | | | | | | | | | | |
| 262 5/8 | 26 2/8 | 24 | 23 7/8 | 31 7/8 | 4 6/8 | 4 6/8 | 14 | 13 | 83 2/8 | 91 | 8 |
| ♦ *Dawson County / Johnny Scheitlin / Bob Scheitlin / 1949* | | | | | | | | | | | |
| 262 1/8 | 26 5/8 | 26 2/8 | 29 3/8 | 36 7/8 | 5 2/8 | 4 7/8 | 17 | 12 | 64 4/8 | 95 | 9 |
| ♦ *Montana / Unknown / Nick M. Messmer / PR 1943* | | | | | | | | | | | |
| 252 2/8 | 23 4/8 | 22 | 14 5/8 | 33 3/8 | 5 6/8 | 5 6/8 | 16 | 15 | 80 1/8 | 172 | 10 |
| ♦ *Glacier County / Bob Scriver / Philip Schlegel / 1934* | | | | | | | | | | | |
| 250 3/8 | 26 5/8 | 26 2/8 | 28 1/8 | 33 3/8 | 4 6/8 | 5 | 10 | 12 | 62 4/8 | 188 | 11 |
| ♦ *Petroleum County / Lawrence T. Keenan / Lawrence T. Keenan / 1979* | | | | | | | | | | | |
| 247 3/8 | 27 5/8 | 28 4/8 | 33 6/8 | 41 | 6 1/8 | 6 4/8 | 11 | 12 | 47 7/8 | 222 | 12 |
| ♦ *Missoula County / Harold Wample / Ralph Raymond / 1949* | | | | | | | | | | | |
| 247 1/8 | 30 4/8 | 30 3/8 | 28 3/8 | 36 5/8 | 6 1/8 | 6 2/8 | 11 | 11 | 38 2/8 | 225 | 13 |
| ♦ *Drummond / Tom Brosovich / Tom Brosovich / 1957* | | | | | | | | | | | |

| Score | Length of Main Beam R | Length of Main Beam L | Inside Spread | Greatest Spread | Circumference at Smallest Place Between Burr and First Point R | Circumference at Smallest Place Between Burr and First Point L | Number of Points R | Number of Points L | Total of Lengths Abnormal Points | All-Time Rank | State Rank |
|---|---|---|---|---|---|---|---|---|---|---|---|
| ♦ *Locality Killed / By Whom Killed / Owner / Date Killed* | | | | | | | | | | | |
| 246 2/8 | 23 4/8 | 24 1/8 | 26 4/8 | 35 1/8 | 5 1/8 | 5 1/8 | 12 | 11 | 57 5/8 | 238 | 14 |
| ♦ *Ravalli County / Lloyd G. Hunter / Lloyd G. Hunter / 1963* | | | | | | | | | | | |
| 244 5/8 | 25 1/8 | 25 3/8 | 22 1/8 | 29 5/8 | 5 1/8 | 5 2/8 | 9 | 10 | 42 4/8 | 254 | 15 |
| ♦ *Park County / Unknown / Don Schaufler / PR 1968* | | | | | | | | | | | |
| 242 5/8 | 27 3/8 | 26 7/8 | 25 5/8 | 43 2/8 | 5 7/8 | 5 6/8 | 12 | 9 | 47 2/8 | 284 | 16 |
| ♦ *Sanders County / Robert D. Frisk / Robert D. Frisk / 1974* | | | | | | | | | | | |
| 241 7/8 | 21 | 18 | 14 7/8 | 29 2/8 | 4 3/8 | 5 3/8 | 12 | 15 | 75 6/8 | 295 | 17 |
| ♦ *Sanders County / Buzz Faro / Buzz Faro / 1963* | | | | | | | | | | | |
| 241 | 26 2/8 | 27 3/8 | 26 3/8 | | 4 6/8 | 4 6/8 | 11 | 11 | 53 1/8 | 305 | 18 |
| ♦ *Lewis & Clark County / Mike Filcher / Mike Filcher / 1972* | | | | | | | | | | | |
| 240 3/8 | 22 3/8 | 24 5/8 | 21 2/8 | 25 6/8 | 5 5/8 | 5 7/8 | 13 | 12 | 56 5/8 | 314 | 19 |
| ♦ *Missoula County / Richard A. Gendrow / Richard A. Gendrow / 1973* | | | | | | | | | | | |
| 239 4/8 | 25 1/8 | 25 5/8 | 19 2/8 | 30 1/8 | 5 3/8 | 5 2/8 | 14 | 13 | 50 4/8 | 321 | 20 |
| ♦ *Pondera County / Dan Mougeot / Dan Mougeot / 1961* | | | | | | | | | | | |
| 229 | 23 2/8 | 21 7/8 | 19 2/8 | 30 4/8 | 4 7/8 | 5 | 9 | 11 | 46 6/8 | 328 | 21 |
| ♦ *Ravalli County / James Milleson / James Milleson / 1984* | | | | | | | | | | | |

Photograph courtesy of Michael D. Atwood

Michael D. Atwood and the non-typical mule deer he took in Utah County, Utah, during the 1967 hunting season. Atwood's buck has 29 antler points and scores 262 for its final score.

**NEBRASKA STATE RECORD**
**TYPICAL MULE DEER**
**SCORE: 196-2/8**
Locality: Dawes Co.    Date: November 1968
Hunter: Terry L. Sandstrom

# NEBRASKA

## TYPICAL MULE DEER

| Score | Length of Main Beam R | Length of Main Beam L | Inside Spread | Greatest Spread | Circumference at Smallest Place Between Burr and First Point R | Circumference at Smallest Place Between Burr and First Point L | Number of Points R | Number of Points L | Total of Lengths Abnormal Points | All-Time Rank | State Rank |
|---|---|---|---|---|---|---|---|---|---|---|---|
| 196 2/8 | 26 | 26 4/8 | 26 | 28 | 5 1/8 | 5 4/8 | 5 | 5 | | 330 | 1 |
| ◆ Dawes County / Terry L. Sandstrom / Terry L. Sandstrom / 1968 | | | | | | | | | | | |
| 195 3/8 | 26 3/8 | 26 | 26 1/8 | 28 7/8 | 4 6/8 | 4 6/8 | 5 | 5 | | 383 | 2 |
| ◆ Frontier County / Brent S. Klein / Brent S. Klein / 1984 | | | | | | | | | | | |

**NEBRASKA STATE RECORD**
**NON-TYPICAL MULE DEER**
**SCORE: 256-7/8**
Locality: Chadron   Date: November 1960
Hunter: Art Thomsen

# NEBRASKA

## NON-TYPICAL MULE DEER

| Score | Length of Main Beam R | Length of Main Beam L | Inside Spread | Greatest Spread | Circumference at Smallest Place Between Burr and First Point R | Circumference at Smallest Place Between Burr and First Point L | Number of Points R | Number of Points L | Total of Lengths Abnormal Points | All-Time Rank | State Rank |
|---|---|---|---|---|---|---|---|---|---|---|---|
| ♦ *Locality Killed / By Whom Killed / Owner / Date Killed* | | | | | | | | | | | |
| 256 7/8 | 26 5/8 | 27 2/8 | 22 6/8 | 28 1/8 | 5 3/8 | 5 6/8 | 20 | 14 | 60 7/8 | 141 | 1 |
| ♦ *Chadron / Art Thomsen / Art Thomsen / 1960* | | | | | | | | | | | |
| 249 6/8 | 24 7/8 | 25 2/8 | 22 | 35 | 5 | 4 7/8 | 10 | 14 | 57 | 193 | 2 |
| ♦ *Red Willow County / Delman H. Tuller / Delman H. Tuller / 1965* | | | | | | | | | | | |

Photograph by Wm. H. Nesbitt

**NEVADA STATE RECORD**
**TYPICAL MULE DEER**
**SCORE: 205-4/8**
Locality: Lincoln Co.    Date: October 1983
Hunter: Erich P. Burkhard

# NEVADA

## TYPICAL MULE DEER

| Score | Length of Main Beam R | Length of Main Beam L | Inside Spread | Greatest Spread | Circumference at Smallest Place Between Burr and First Point R | Circumference at Smallest Place Between Burr and First Point L | Number of Points R | Number of Points L | Total of Lengths Abnormal Points | All-Time Rank | State Rank |
|---|---|---|---|---|---|---|---|---|---|---|---|
| ♦ *Locality Killed / By Whom Killed / Owner / Date Killed* | | | | | | | | | | | |
| 205 4/8 | 26 4/8 | 26 4/8 | 25 2/8 | 35 4/8 | 5 1/8 | 4 6/8 | 6 | 5 | 1 4/8 | 51 | 1 |
| ♦ *Lincoln County / Erich P. Burkhard / Erich P. Burkhard / 1983* | | | | | | | | | | | |
| 203 4/8 | 27 2/8 | 24 | 24 2/8 | 27 4/8 | 5 4/8 | 5 3/8 | 5 | 5 | | 72 | 2 |
| ♦ *Elko County / C.H. Wahl / C.H. Wahl / 1953* | | | | | | | | | | | |
| 200 7/8 | 30 4/8 | 25 7/8 | 28 3/8 | 36 | 4 6/8 | 4 4/8 | 5 | 5 | | 140 | 3 |
| ♦ *Elko County / Harry Irland / Mrs. Harry Irland / 1919* | | | | | | | | | | | |
| 200 1/8 | 24 7/8 | 23 6/8 | 28 3/8 | 33 2/8 | 5 5/8 | 5 6/8 | 5 | 5 | | 168 | 4 |
| ♦ *Ruby Mt. / Earl Frantzen / Earl Frantzen / 1941* | | | | | | | | | | | |
| 199 5/8 | 25 4/8 | 24 2/8 | 21 7/8 | 27 4/8 | 6 1/8 | 6 | 5 | 5 | | 185 | 5 |
| ♦ *Humboldt County / Robert L. Swinney / Robert L. Swinney / 1982* | | | | | | | | | | | |
| 197 2/8 | 23 | 24 | 25 | 30 4/8 | 4 6/8 | 4 4/8 | 7 | 5 | 7 6/8 | 277 | 6 |
| ♦ *Elko County / John C. Burman / John C. Burman / 1980* | | | | | | | | | | | |
| 195 1/8 | 25 | 25 2/8 | 22 1/8 | 25 6/8 | 5 1/8 | 5 1/8 | 5 | 5 | | 397 | 7 |
| ♦ *Elko County / Donald G. Heidtman / Donald G. Heidtman / 1954* | | | | | | | | | | | |
| 193 3/8 | 26 7/8 | 27 2/8 | 23 3/8 | 33 1/8 | 4 7/8 | 4 7/8 | 5 | 5 | | 416 | 8 |
| ♦ *Washoe County / Barbara M. Conley / Barbara M. Conley / 1987* | | | | | | | | | | | |
| 188 5/8 | 26 4/8 | 26 2/8 | 23 5/8 | 29 4/8 | 5 | 5 2/8 | 8 | 5 | 8 | 427 | 9 |
| ♦ *Washoe County / Christine L. Matley / Christine L. Matley / 1986* | | | | | | | | | | | |
| 204 6/8 | 26 2/8 | 26 2/8 | 24 6/8 | 32 7/8 | 4 7/8 | 4 6/8 | 5 | 5 | | * | * |
| ♦ *Elko County / Donnie L. Thompson / Donnie L. Thompson / 1982* | | | | | | | | | | | |

**NEVADA STATE RECORD**
**NON-TYPICAL MULE DEER**
**SCORE: 299-1/8**
Locality: Eureka Co.    Date: October 1968
Hunter: Dan Avery, Jr.
Owner: Don Schaufler

# NEVADA

## NON-TYPICAL MULE DEER

| Score | Length of Main Beam | | Inside Spread | Greatest Spread | Circumference at Smallest Place Between Burr and First Point | | Number of Points | | Total of Lengths Abnormal Points | All-Time Rank | State Rank |
|---|---|---|---|---|---|---|---|---|---|---|---|
| | R | L | | | R | L | R | L | | | |
| *Locality Killed / By Whom Killed / Owner / Date Killed* | | | | | | | | | | | |
| 299 1/8 | 27 1/8 | 28 3/8 | 24 4/8 | 40 | 5 6/8 | 5 4/8 | 13 | 16 | 86 1/8 | 15 | 1 |
| ♦ *Eureka County / Dan Avery, Jr. / Don Schaufler / 1968* | | | | | | | | | | | |
| 286 1/8 | 24 4/8 | 25 | 26 4/8 | 38 2/8 | 5 | 5 | 12 | 13 | 85 3/8 | 22 | 2 |
| ♦ *Elko County / Joseph W. Dooley / Raymond R. Cross / 1954* | | | | | | | | | | | |
| 264 | 25 5/8 | 26 1/8 | 22 7/8 | 40 2/8 | 6 3/8 | 5 1/8 | 14 | 13 | 46 5/8 | 85 | 3 |
| ♦ *Elko County / Jim Stichter / Jim Stichter / 1965* | | | | | | | | | | | |
| 258 5/8 | 25 3/8 | 25 4/8 | 21 | 35 7/8 | 5 2/8 | 5 3/8 | 12 | 10 | 56 1/8 | 122 | 4 |
| ♦ *Elko County / Edward J. Giauque / Edward J. Giauque / 1960* | | | | | | | | | | | |
| 247 | 29 1/8 | 28 6/8 | 24 5/8 | 42 3/8 | 6 | 5 4/8 | 14 | 16 | 43 7/8 | 229 | 5 |
| ♦ *Elko County / Walter B. Hester / Walter B. Hester / 1957* | | | | | | | | | | | |
| 243 | 25 6/8 | 27 1/8 | 29 | 37 2/8 | 5 3/8 | 5 3/8 | 11 | 10 | 45 4/8 | 279 | 6 |
| ♦ *Elko County / Paul Giuliani / Paul Giuliani / 1971* | | | | | | | | | | | |
| 240 5/8 | 22 | 23 2/8 | 21 | 28 5/8 | 4 7/8 | 4 7/8 | 10 | 9 | 46 3/8 | 308 | 7 |
| ♦ *Elko County / George M. Boman / George M. Boman / 1956* | | | | | | | | | | | |

**NEW MEXICO STATE RECORD**
**TYPICAL MULE DEER**
**SCORE: 211-7/8**
Locality: Chama    Date: November 1965
Hunter: Joseph A. Garcia
Owner: John D. Morgan

# NEW MEXICO

## TYPICAL MULE DEER

| Score | Length of Main Beam R | L | Inside Spread | Greatest Spread | Circumference at Smallest Place Between Burr and First Point R | L | Number of Points R | L | Total of Lengths Abnormal Points | All-Time Rank | State Rank |
|---|---|---|---|---|---|---|---|---|---|---|---|
| 211 7/8 | 28 6/8 | 28 | 27 6/8 | 34 4/8 | 6 5/8 | 6 5/8 | 5 | 6 | 1 7/8 | 9 | 1 |
| ◆ Chama / Joseph A. Garcia / John D. Morgan / 1965 | | | | | | | | | | | |
| 209 5/8 | 27 4/8 | 27 1/8 | 28 1/8 | 32 1/8 | 5 5/8 | 5 5/8 | 5 | 7 | 2 2/8 | 15 | 2 |
| ◆ Rio Arriba County / Kelly Baird / Kelly Baird / 1984 | | | | | | | | | | | |
| 208 6/8 | 26 | 27 1/8 | 26 4/8 | 28 | 5 2/8 | 5 2/8 | 4 | 5 | | 23 | 3 |
| ◆ Rio Arriba County / James R. Odiorne, Jr. / James R. Odiorne, Jr. / 1978 | | | | | | | | | | | |
| 207 3/8 | 26 5/8 | 26 5/8 | 25 5/8 | 30 4/8 | 5 2/8 | 5 2/8 | 6 | 6 | 2 5/8 | 30 | 4 |
| ◆ Jicarilla Apache Res. / Kenneth Campbell / Kenneth Campbell / 1969 | | | | | | | | | | | |
| 206 3/8 | 27 4/8 | 26 3/8 | 26 7/8 | 30 6/8 | 5 2/8 | 5 3/8 | 5 | 5 | | 41 | 5 |
| ◆ Rio Arriba County / Jim Roddie / Jim Roddie / 1971 | | | | | | | | | | | |
| 206 2/8 | 26 | 27 4/8 | 26 4/8 | 29 4/8 | 5 5/8 | 5 5/8 | 6 | 5 | 1 6/8 | 44 | 6 |
| ◆ Rio Arriba County / Harley Hinds / Oran M. Roberts / 1963 | | | | | | | | | | | |
| 204 1/8 | 28 6/8 | 30 4/8 | 24 1/8 | 31 1/8 | 4 5/8 | 4 7/8 | 6 | 5 | 7 6/8 | 63 | 7 |
| ◆ Jicarilla Apache Res. / Juan Monarco / Juan Monarco / 1960 | | | | | | | | | | | |
| 203 7/8 | 29 3/8 | 29 4/8 | 25 5/8 | 28 5/8 | 5 6/8 | 5 5/8 | 5 | 5 | | 66 | 8 |
| ◆ Jicarilla Apache Res. / Dick Wright / Dick Wright / 1966 | | | | | | | | | | | |
| 203 4/8 | 27 | 28 1/8 | 24 4/8 | 26 7/8 | 5 4/8 | 5 4/8 | 5 | 6 | 1 | 72 | 9 |
| ◆ Rio Arriba County / Arnold Wendt / John W. Hughes / 1965 | | | | | | | | | | | |
| 202 7/8 | 27 5/8 | 27 4/8 | 26 6/8 | | 6 | 5 7/8 | 5 | 7 | | 86 | 10 |
| ◆ Jicarilla Apache Res. / Anthony Julian / Anthony Julian / 1961 | | | | | | | | | | | |
| 202 6/8 | 28 2/8 | 29 2/8 | 25 4/8 | 27 6/8 | 5 3/8 | 5 2/8 | 5 | 5 | | 90 | 11 |
| ◆ Rio Arriba County / James F. Leveritt, Jr. / James F. Leveritt, Jr. / 1980 | | | | | | | | | | | |
| 202 4/8 | 27 4/8 | 27 6/8 | 27 | 28 6/8 | 5 3/8 | 5 2/8 | 6 | 6 | 4 2/8 | 94 | 12 |
| ◆ Rio Arriba County / Gerald J. Weber / Gerald J. Weber / 1970 | | | | | | | | | | | |
| 202 3/8 | 29 5/8 | 28 4/8 | 30 1/8 | 30 3/8 | 5 1/8 | 5 1/8 | 5 | 6 | 2 6/8 | 98 | 13 |
| ◆ Jicarilla Apache Res. / Theodore Serafin / Theodore Serafin / 1959 | | | | | | | | | | | |

*Locality Killed / By Whom Killed / Owner / Date Killed*

| Score | Length of Main Beam R | Length of Main Beam L | Inside Spread | Greatest Spread | Circumference at Smallest Place Between Burr and First Point R | Circumference at Smallest Place Between Burr and First Point L | Number of Points R | Number of Points L | Total of Lengths Abnormal Points | All-Time Rank | State Rank |
|---|---|---|---|---|---|---|---|---|---|---|---|
| | ♦ *Locality Killed / By Whom Killed / Owner / Date Killed* | | | | | | | | | | |
| 201 4/8 | 26 6/8 | 24 7/8 | 28 4/8 | 30 4/8 | 6 3/8 | 6 | 5 | 5 | | 117 | 14 |
| | ♦ *Chama / James W. Smith II / James W. Smith II / 1969* | | | | | | | | | | |
| 201 3/8 | 26 3/8 | 26 3/8 | 25 4/8 | 27 4/8 | 5 5/8 | 5 5/8 | 6 | 5 | 2 3/8 | 122 | 15 |
| | ♦ *Rio Arriba County / Donald W. Johnson / Donald W. Johnson / 1970* | | | | | | | | | | |
| 201 2/8 | 26 6/8 | 27 6/8 | 26 6/8 | 31 | 6 | 6 | 5 | 6 | 2 2/8 | 130 | 16 |
| | ♦ *Jicarilla Apache Res. / Anthony Julian / Anthony Julian / 1961* | | | | | | | | | | |
| 201 2/8 | 28 4/8 | 28 3/8 | 24 | 29 6/8 | 5 1/8 | 5 3/8 | 5 | 5 | | 130 | 16 |
| | ♦ *Chama / Emitt W. Mundy / Emitt W. Mundy / 1961* | | | | | | | | | | |
| 201 1/8 | 25 6/8 | 26 1/8 | 26 4/8 | 31 1/8 | 5 | 5 4/8 | 5 | 6 | 1 6/8 | 133 | 18 |
| | ♦ *Jicarilla Apache Res. / Arnold Cassador / Arnold Cassador / 1967* | | | | | | | | | | |
| 199 3/8 | 27 | 27 6/8 | 23 7/8 | 27 6/8 | 5 4/8 | 5 4/8 | 4 | 4 | | 193 | 19 |
| | ♦ *Rio Arriba County / John A. Farrell / John A. Farrell / 1966* | | | | | | | | | | |
| 199 3/8 | 26 7/8 | 25 7/8 | 24 4/8 | 27 1/8 | 5 6/8 | 5 5/8 | 5 | 6 | 2 5/8 | 193 | 19 |
| | ♦ *Rio Arriba County / Johnny L. Montgomery / Johnny L. Montgomery / 1967* | | | | | | | | | | |
| 199 1/8 | 28 3/8 | 27 2/8 | 27 6/8 | 31 | 6 | 5 6/8 | 8 | 6 | 8 7/8 | 202 | 21 |
| | ♦ *Jicarilla Apache Res. / David L. Chandler / David L. Chandler / 1961* | | | | | | | | | | |
| 198 7/8 | 26 5/8 | 27 1/8 | 26 5/8 | 30 4/8 | 5 7/8 | 6 | 5 | 7 | 4 6/8 | 209 | 22 |
| | ♦ *Jicarilla Apache Res. / Anthony Julian / Jicarilla Apache Tribe / 1961* | | | | | | | | | | |
| 198 6/8 | 32 7/8 | 32 4/8 | 25 3/8 | 35 1/8 | 6 3/8 | 7 | 7 | 6 | 15 5/8 | 211 | 23 |
| | ♦ *Dulce / Picked Up / Everett M. Vigil / 1967* | | | | | | | | | | |
| 198 5/8 | 26 | 25 3/8 | 28 | 31 6/8 | 5 4/8 | 5 7/8 | 5 | 7 | 4 1/8 | 213 | 24 |
| | ♦ *Rio Arriba County / Stanley Davis / Stanley Davis / 1965* | | | | | | | | | | |
| 197 4/8 | 26 | 26 2/8 | 23 2/8 | 26 2/8 | 5 2/8 | 5 1/8 | 5 | 6 | 1 | 264 | 25 |
| | ♦ *Rio Arriba County / Jerry Longenbaugh / Jerry Longenbaugh / 1969* | | | | | | | | | | |
| 197 3/8 | 25 5/8 | 27 1/8 | 26 1/8 | 28 4/8 | 5 3/8 | 5 4/8 | 5 | 5 | | 269 | 26 |
| | ♦ *Apache Mesa / Tom Martine / Tom Martine / 1970* | | | | | | | | | | |
| 197 | 26 4/8 | 26 4/8 | 27 5/8 | 32 | 5 2/8 | 5 4/8 | 5 | 5 | | 288 | 27 |
| | ♦ *Rio Arriba County / Ross Lopez / Ross Lopez / 1964* | | | | | | | | | | |
| 196 2/8 | 26 1/8 | 23 7/8 | 23 4/8 | 28 2/8 | 6 | 5 7/8 | 5 | 6 | 2 6/8 | 330 | 28 |
| | ♦ *Chama / Laura Wilson / Laura Wilson / 1967* | | | | | | | | | | |
| 196 2/8 | 27 | 27 1/8 | 24 7/8 | 30 2/8 | 5 4/8 | 5 4/8 | 7 | 9 | 12 5/8 | 330 | 28 |
| | ♦ *Rio Arriba County / B.D. Shipwash / B.D. Shipwash / 1969* | | | | | | | | | | |
| 196 1/8 | 27 2/8 | 27 7/8 | 27 | 33 1/8 | 5 1/8 | 5 1/8 | 6 | 9 | 9 1/8 | 341 | 30 |
| | ♦ *Chama / Jerry Washburn / Jerry Washburn / 1960* | | | | | | | | | | |

| Score | Length of Main Beam R | L | Inside Spread | Greatest Spread | Circumference at Smallest Place Between Burr and First Point R | L | Number of Points R | L | Total of Lengths Abnormal Points | All-Time Rank | State Rank |
|---|---|---|---|---|---|---|---|---|---|---|---|
| | | | | | | *Locality Killed / By Whom Killed / Owner / Date Killed* | | | | | |
| 196 1/8 | 26 3/8 | 27 3/8 | 22 3/8 | 27 1/8 | 6 | 6 1/8 | 7 | 6 | 5 6/8 | 341 | 30 |
| ◆ *Jicarilla Apache Res. / Tim Vicenti / Tim Vicenti / 1960* | | | | | | | | | | | |
| 196 | 29 4/8 | 29 2/8 | 25 2/8 | 28 7/8 | 5 | 5 | 5 | 5 | | 346 | 32 |
| ◆ *Jicarilla Apache Res. / Collins F. Kellogg / Collins F. Kellogg / 1973* | | | | | | | | | | | |
| 195 5/8 | 30 5/8 | 29 | 26 4/8 | 31 2/8 | 6 2/8 | 6 2/8 | 6 | 8 | 7 3/8 | 367 | 33 |
| ◆ *Jicarilla Apache Res. / Eldrid Vigil / Eldrid Vigil / 1962* | | | | | | | | | | | |
| 195 4/8 | 26 3/8 | 25 1/8 | 26 2/8 | 31 1/8 | 5 3/8 | 5 2/8 | 5 | 5 | | 375 | 34 |
| ◆ *Raton / Unknown / John H. Steinle III / 1963* | | | | | | | | | | | |
| 195 3/8 | 25 4/8 | 24 2/8 | 24 5/8 | 30 5/8 | 5 | 5 | 5 | 4 | | 383 | 35 |
| ◆ *Rio Arriba County / Robert W. Highfill / Robert W. Highfill / 1964* | | | | | | | | | | | |
| 195 1/8 | 25 4/8 | 24 2/8 | 24 1/8 | 27 4/8 | 5 5/8 | 5 6/8 | 5 | 5 | | 397 | 36 |
| ◆ *Rio Arriba County / Eddie W. Brieno, Jr. / Eddie W. Brieno, Jr. / 1965* | | | | | | | | | | | |
| 195 | 25 1/8 | 25 1/8 | 25 | 28 3/8 | 4 4/8 | 4 7/8 | 5 | 5 | | 405 | 37 |
| ◆ *Rio Arriba County / Pat Wilson / John Lind, Jr. / 1967* | | | | | | | | | | | |
| 194 | 25 1/8 | 25 4/8 | 27 4/8 | 30 1/8 | 5 4/8 | 5 4/8 | 5 | 5 | | 413 | 38 |
| ◆ *Rio Arriba County / C.J. McElroy / C.J. McElroy / 1970* | | | | | | | | | | | |
| 188 5/8 | 24 4/8 | 23 7/8 | 24 4/8 | 30 2/8 | 5 2/8 | 5 2/8 | 5 | 6 | 1 7/8 | 427 | 39 |
| ◆ *Rio Arriba County / George R. Payne / George R. Payne / 1973* | | | | | | | | | | | |

**NEW MEXICO STATE RECORD**
**NON-TYPICAL MULE DEER**
**SCORE: 306-2/8**
Locality: Chama    Date: October 1963
Hunter: Joseph A. Garcia
Owner: Don Schaufler

# NEW MEXICO

## NON-TYPICAL MULE DEER

| Score | Length of Main Beam R | Length of Main Beam L | Inside Spread | Greatest Spread | Circumference at Smallest Place Between Burr and First Point R | Circumference at Smallest Place Between Burr and First Point L | Number of Points R | Number of Points L | Total of Lengths Abnormal Points | All-Time Rank | State Rank |
|---|---|---|---|---|---|---|---|---|---|---|---|
| ♦ *Locality Killed / By Whom Killed / Owner / Date Killed* | | | | | | | | | | | |
| 306 2/8 | 29 | 28 5/8 | 28 7/8 | 40 6/8 | 5 4/8 | 5 5/8 | 18 | 18 | 103 3/8 | 6 | 1 |
| ♦ *Chama / Joseph A. Garcia / Don Schaufler / 1963* | | | | | | | | | | | |
| 288 6/8 | 30 4/8 | 31 6/8 | 26 5/8 | 49 2/8 | 6 5/8 | 6 3/8 | 12 | 10 | 51 3/8 | 19 | 2 |
| ♦ *Chama / Frank B. Maestas / W.H. Mundy, Jr. / 1962* | | | | | | | | | | | |
| 267 5/8 | 26 4/8 | 25 7/8 | 26 3/8 | 29 6/8 | 4 7/8 | 4 6/8 | 13 | 18 | 58 2/8 | 67 | 3 |
| ♦ *Jicarilla Apache Res. / Byrd L. Minter, Jr. / Byrd L. Minter, Jr. / 1961* | | | | | | | | | | | |
| 265 5/8 | 24 7/8 | 26 7/8 | 27 2/8 | 36 1/8 | 6 7/8 | 6 5/8 | 16 | 14 | 67 | 78 | 4 |
| ♦ *Chama / Stephanie D. Tartaglia / Stephanie D. Tartaglia / 1966* | | | | | | | | | | | |
| 263 2/8 | 24 | 24 | 20 3/8 | 28 6/8 | 5 2/8 | 5 2/8 | 15 | 10 | 59 1/8 | 88 | 5 |
| ♦ *Rio Arriba County / Kenneth Campbell / Kenneth Campbell / 1970* | | | | | | | | | | | |
| 262 3/8 | 30 2/8 | 27 6/8 | 28 2/8 | 39 | 6 2/8 | 6 4/8 | 10 | 15 | 51 1/8 | 93 | 6 |
| ♦ *Tierra Amarilla / Pat Lovato, Jr. / Pat Lovato, Jr. / 1966* | | | | | | | | | | | |
| 259 7/8 | 28 4/8 | 27 4/8 | 29 4/8 | 38 1/8 | 5 7/8 | 5 5/8 | 12 | 15 | 53 3/8 | 111 | 7 |
| ♦ *Catron County / Jeff K. Gunnell / Jeff K. Gunnell / 1981* | | | | | | | | | | | |
| 258 | 20 4/8 | 22 1/8 | 19 3/8 | 32 3/8 | 4 2/8 | 4 5/8 | 13 | 13 | 89 1/8 | 128 | 8 |
| ♦ *Cimarron / Ralph L. Smith / Don Schaufler / 1957* | | | | | | | | | | | |
| 257 7/8 | 27 1/8 | 26 | 26 7/8 | 41 6/8 | 5 7/8 | 5 6/8 | 14 | 14 | 69 | 129 | 9 |
| ♦ *Jicarilla Apache Res. / Henry Callado / Henry Callado / 1961* | | | | | | | | | | | |
| 256 5/8 | 25 7/8 | 27 2/8 | 25 6/8 | 35 4/8 | 5 3/8 | 5 3/8 | 14 | 13 | 57 1/8 | 144 | 10 |
| ♦ *Jicarilla Apache Res. / Picked Up / S.L. Canterbury III / 1967* | | | | | | | | | | | |
| 255 2/8 | 26 | 26 5/8 | 25 1/8 | 33 | 4 7/8 | 4 5/8 | 9 | 9 | 42 1/8 | 154 | 11 |
| ♦ *Rio Arriba County / Gene Garcia / Gene Garcia / 1964* | | | | | | | | | | | |
| 249 | 27 7/8 | 29 7/8 | 25 6/8 | 36 | 5 3/8 | 5 1/8 | 11 | 8 | 47 | 200 | 12 |
| ♦ *Jemez Mts. / Max S. Jenson / Max S. Jenson / 1962* | | | | | | | | | | | |

| Score | Length of Main Beam R | L | Inside Spread | Greatest Spread | Circumference at Smallest Place Between Burr and First Point R | L | Number of Points R | L | Total of Lengths Abnormal Points | All-Time Rank | State Rank |
|---|---|---|---|---|---|---|---|---|---|---|---|
| | ♦ Locality Killed / By Whom Killed / Owner / Date Killed | | | | | | | | | | |
| 245 6/8 | 27 1/8 | 28 2/8 | 24 4/8 | 34 4/8 | 5 6/8 | 5 7/8 | 11 | 9 | 30 | 243 | 13 |
| | ♦ *Rio Arriba County / Kenneth W. Lee / Kenneth W. Lee / 1971* | | | | | | | | | | |
| 245 2/8 | 26 5/8 | 27 4/8 | 21 2/8 | 29 7/8 | 5 6/8 | 5 6/8 | 10 | 10 | 45 6/8 | 247 | 14 |
| | ♦ *Jicarilla Apache Res. / Arthur Wanoskea / Arthur Wanoskea / 1960* | | | | | | | | | | |
| 243 4/8 | 22 2/8 | 18 4/8 | 23 5/8 | 32 6/8 | 4 6/8 | 4 5/8 | 14 | 11 | 70 6/8 | 274 | 15 |
| | ♦ *Cibola County / Fred R. Valdez, Jr. / Don Schaufler / 1986* | | | | | | | | | | |
| 241 4/8 | 26 4/8 | 27 | 27 | 31 | 5 | 5 3/8 | 8 | 7 | 26 | 298 | 16 |
| | ♦ *Socorro County / James T. Everheart / James T. Everheart / 1973* | | | | | | | | | | |
| 231 7/8 | 25 5/8 | 30 2/8 | 25 2/8 | 37 1/8 | 5 | 4 7/8 | 11 | 9 | 36 1/8 | 327 | 17 |
| | ♦ *Rio Arriba County / Dan F. Holleman / Vernon D. Holleman / 1966* | | | | | | | | | | |

Shelly R. Risner with the typical mule deer scoring 205-2/8 points she shot in 1986 in Carbon County, Wyoming. Risner's buck took the Second Place Award at the 20th Awards that were held in Albuquerque, New Mexico, in 1989.

Photograph Courtesy of Robert L. Klisares

**NORTH DAKOTA STATE RECORD**
**TYPICAL MULE DEER**
**SCORE: 196-4/8**
Locality: Missouri River    Date: Prior to 1958
Hunter: Unknown
Owner: Robert L. Klisares

# NORTH DAKOTA

## TYPICAL MULE DEER

| Score | Length of Main Beam R | Length of Main Beam L | Inside Spread | Great- est Spread | Circumference at Smallest Place Between Burr and First Point R | Circumference at Smallest Place Between Burr and First Point L | Number of Points R | Number of Points L | Total of Lengths Abnor- mal Points | All- Time Rank | State Rank |
|---|---|---|---|---|---|---|---|---|---|---|---|
| ♦ Locality Killed / By Whom Killed / Owner / Date Killed | | | | | | | | | | | |
| 196 4/8 | 26 3/8 | 27 5/8 | 27 5/8 | 36 2/8 | 5 | 4 7/8 | 5 | 6 | 5 1/8 | 318 | 1 |
| ♦ Missouri River / Unknown / Robert L. Klisares / PR 1958 | | | | | | | | | | | |

## OREGON STATE RECORD
## TYPICAL MULE DEER
### SCORE: 209-4/8
Locality: Wallowa Co.    Date: September 1920
Hunter: John C. Evans
Owner: Stan J. Neitling, Jr.

# OREGON

## TYPICAL MULE DEER

| Score | Length of Main Beam R | L | Inside Spread | Greatest Spread | Circumference at Smallest Place Between Burr and First Point R | L | Number of Points R | L | Total of Lengths Abnormal Points | All-Time Rank | State Rank |
|---|---|---|---|---|---|---|---|---|---|---|---|
| | ♦ Locality Killed / By Whom Killed / Owner / Date Killed | | | | | | | | | | |
| 209 4/8 | 28 7/8 | 29 6/8 | 28 | 30 1/8 | 5 7/8 | 5 7/8 | 6 | 8 | 8 4/8 | 18 | 1 |
| | ♦ Wallowa County / John C. Evans / Stan J. Neitling, Jr. / 1920 | | | | | | | | | | |
| 205 3/8 | 26 6/8 | 27 | 26 7/8 | 29 1/8 | 5 3/8 | 5 3/8 | 5 | 5 | | 55 | 2 |
| | ♦ Starkey / H.M. Bailey / H.M. Bailey / 1963 | | | | | | | | | | |
| 202 3/8 | 26 3/8 | 25 5/8 | 24 5/8 | 30 7/8 | 5 6/8 | 5 6/8 | 8 | 7 | 11 4/8 | 98 | 3 |
| | ♦ Baker County / Brett N. Hayes / Brett N. Hayes / 1982 | | | | | | | | | | |
| 201 5/8 | 26 2/8 | 27 3/8 | 24 3/8 | 29 3/8 | 5 4/8 | 5 4/8 | 5 | 5 | | 114 | 4 |
| | ♦ Baker County / Terry Williams / Terry Williams / 1988 | | | | | | | | | | |
| 201 4/8 | 26 3/8 | 25 3/8 | 24 2/8 | 28 7/8 | 5 3/8 | 5 2/8 | 5 | 5 | | 117 | 5 |
| | ♦ Malheur County / David L. Bauer / David L. Bauer / 1971 | | | | | | | | | | |
| 200 6/8 | 26 2/8 | 28 | 25 6/8 | 29 7/8 | 5 4/8 | 5 4/8 | 5 | 5 | | 143 | 6 |
| | ♦ Malheur County / Raymond Duncan / Raymond Duncan / 1949 | | | | | | | | | | |
| 199 6/8 | 25 1/8 | 25 3/8 | 25 | 31 2/8 | 5 1/8 | 5 1/8 | 5 | 5 | | 183 | 7 |
| | ♦ Grant County / Steve M. Stevenson / Steve M. Stevenson / 1982 | | | | | | | | | | |
| 198 1/8 | 26 5/8 | 25 5/8 | 28 | 30 4/8 | 4 6/8 | 4 7/8 | 5 | 5 | | 234 | 8 |
| | ♦ Wallowa County / Dan L. Gober / Dan L. Gober / 1980 | | | | | | | | | | |
| 197 2/8 | 29 4/8 | 30 2/8 | 28 6/8 | 33 3/8 | 5 4/8 | 5 5/8 | 7 | 6 | 4 | 277 | 9 |
| | ♦ Harney County / Guy E. Osborne / Guy E. Osborne / 1963 | | | | | | | | | | |
| 197 1/8 | 26 5/8 | 27 6/8 | 26 3/8 | 35 3/8 | 5 2/8 | 5 1/8 | 5 | 5 | 10 | 285 | 10 |
| | ♦ Ashwood / Harvey Rhoads / Harvey Rhoads / 1962 | | | | | | | | | | |
| 196 6/8 | 25 4/8 | 24 4/8 | 26 1/8 | 27 1/8 | 5 1/8 | 4 6/8 | 5 | 5 | | 300 | 11 |
| | ♦ Clackamas County / Picked Up / Curt M. Funk / 1983 | | | | | | | | | | |
| 196 2/8 | 27 1/8 | 27 5/8 | 26 | 28 1/8 | 5 2/8 | 5 | 5 | 5 | | 330 | 12 |
| | ♦ Baker County / Vivian M. Zikmund / Vivian M. Zikmund / 1986 | | | | | | | | | | |

| Score | Length of Main Beam R | L | Inside Spread | Greatest Spread | Circumference at Smallest Place Between Burr and First Point R | L | Number of Points R | L | Total of Lengths Abnormal Points | All-Time Rank | State Rank |
|---|---|---|---|---|---|---|---|---|---|---|---|
| | ♦ *Locality Killed / By Whom Killed / Owner / Date Killed* | | | | | | | | | | |
| 195 6/8 | 27 4/8 | 29 | 26 2/8 | 28 5/8 | 5 5/8 | 5 4/8 | 7 | 9 | 9 | 360 | 13 |
| ♦ *Keating / Al Delepierre / Francis A. Delepierre / 1966* | | | | | | | | | | | |
| 195 6/8 | 28 1/8 | 28 4/8 | 28 4/8 | 31 1/8 | 5 1/8 | 5 3/8 | 5 | 5 | | 360 | 13 |
| ♦ *Grant County / Larry Parlette / Larry Parlette / 1967* | | | | | | | | | | | |
| 195 3/8 | 25 | 25 2/8 | 25 1/8 | 27 3/8 | 4 4/8 | 4 4/8 | 6 | 5 | 2 | 383 | 15 |
| ♦ *Wallowa County / Michael R. Shirley / Michael R. Shirley / 1986* | | | | | | | | | | | |
| 186 6/8 | 24 | 22 7/8 | 18 2/8 | 25 4/8 | 5 5/8 | 5 2/8 | 6 | 6 | 3 2/8 | 437 | 16 |
| ♦ *Grant County / Leslie M. Brady / Leslie M. Brady / 1986* | | | | | | | | | | | |

172

Matthew J. Arkins hunted on horseback in the San Juan National Forest, Colorado, in 1986. When he saw this typical mule deer, he knew it was the one he was seeking. Arkins' trophy scores 195-5/8 points.

**OREGON STATE RECORD**
**NON-TYPICAL MULE DEER**
**SCORE: 297-7/8**
Locality: Malheur Co.    Date: October 1971
Hunter: Bradley Barclay

# OREGON

## NON-TYPICAL MULE DEER

| Score | Length of Main Beam R | Length of Main Beam L | Inside Spread | Greatest Spread | Circumference at Smallest Place Between Burr and First Point R | Circumference at Smallest Place Between Burr and First Point L | Number of Points R | Number of Points L | Total of Lengths Abnormal Points | All-Time Rank | State Rank |
|---|---|---|---|---|---|---|---|---|---|---|---|
| ♦ *Locality Killed / By Whom Killed / Owner / Date Killed* | | | | | | | | | | | |
| 297 7/8 | 29 1/8 | 27 5/8 | 35 4/8 | 39 6/8 | 5 4/8 | 5 3/8 | 20 | 18 | 99 2/8 | 16 | 1 |
| ♦ *Malheur County / Bradley Barclay / Bradley Barclay / 1971* | | | | | | | | | | | |
| 277 1/8 | 26 1/8 | 24 6/8 | 24 3/8 | 38 7/8 | 5 6/8 | 5 5/8 | 13 | 13 | 74 2/8 | 39 | 2 |
| ♦ *Bly / Alice C. O'Brien / Don Schaufler / 1949* | | | | | | | | | | | |
| 273 6/8 | 26 | 26 4/8 | 26 1/8 | 41 7/8 | 5 | 5 | 15 | 18 | 91 1/8 | 51 | 3 |
| ♦ *Klamath County / J.J. McDaniels / J.J. McDaniels / 1952* | | | | | | | | | | | |
| 270 6/8 | 28 6/8 | 28 2/8 | 27 6/8 | 37 3/8 | 5 7/8 | 5 7/8 | 15 | 15 | 71 | 59 | 4 |
| ♦ *Crook County / C.F. Cheney / C.F. Cheney / 1962* | | | | | | | | | | | |
| 266 | 25 3/8 | 24 2/8 | 27 7/8 | 35 3/8 | 5 6/8 | 5 5/8 | 16 | 20 | 73 7/8 | 74 | 5 |
| ♦ *Grant County / Harold T. Oathes / Harold T. Oathes / 1965* | | | | | | | | | | | |
| 262 | 24 2/8 | 24 6/8 | 16 5/8 | 34 4/8 | 4 6/8 | 4 7/8 | 14 | 16 | 87 7/8 | 96 | 6 |
| ♦ *John Day River / Glen E. Park / Glen E. Park / 1962* | | | | | | | | | | | |
| 247 4/8 | 25 2/8 | 24 7/8 | 24 3/8 | 36 6/8 | 6 2/8 | 5 6/8 | 12 | 16 | 71 7/8 | 220 | 7 |
| ♦ *Bend / L.M. Martinson / L.M. Martinson / 1949* | | | | | | | | | | | |
| 243 | 25 7/8 | 25 6/8 | 20 | | 5 2/8 | 5 | 15 | 12 | | 279 | 8 |
| ♦ *Crook County / Wes Mitts / Wes Mitts / 1936* | | | | | | | | | | | |
| 242 | 26 2/8 | 26 6/8 | 28 1/8 | 35 | 5 4/8 | 5 4/8 | 10 | 8 | 31 2/8 | 293 | 9 |
| ♦ *Klamath County / Corinne Fields / Corinne Fields / 1946* | | | | | | | | | | | |
| 241 7/8 | 24 5/8 | 24 2/8 | 25 | | 5 2/8 | 5 2/8 | 11 | 19 | | 295 | 10 |
| ♦ *Jefferson County / Spencer L. Darrar / Spencer L. Darrar / 1953* | | | | | | | | | | | |
| 240 1/8 | 24 2/8 | 24 | 19 6/8 | 36 6/8 | 5 6/8 | 5 7/8 | 13 | 12 | 61 7/8 | 316 | 11 |
| ♦ *Harney County / R.G. Creager / R.G. Creager / 1957* | | | | | | | | | | | |
| 268 4/8 | 25 6/8 | 23 | 22 7/8 | 37 3/8 | 5 4/8 | 5 6/8 | 17 | 14 | 89 7/8 | * | * |
| ♦ *Deschutes County / Devon Talley / Devon Talley / 1983* | | | | | | | | | | | |

Photograph Courtesy of Kenny E. Yeaton

**SOUTH DAKOTA STATE RECORD**
**TYPICAL MULE DEER**
**SCORE: 185-4/8**
Locality: Brule Co.    Date: November 1985
Hunter: Kenny E. Yeaton

# SOUTH DAKOTA

## TYPICAL MULE DEER

| Score | Length of Main Beam R | L | Inside Spread | Greatest Spread | Circumference at Smallest Place Between Burr and First Point R | L | Number of Points R | L | Total of Lengths Abnormal Points | All-Time Rank | State Rank |
|---|---|---|---|---|---|---|---|---|---|---|---|
| | | | | | | | | | | | |

♦ *Locality Killed  /  By Whom Killed  /  Owner  /  Date Killed*

| | | | | | | | | | | | |
|---|---|---|---|---|---|---|---|---|---|---|---|
| 185 4/8 | 24 2/8 | 24 2/8 | 23 6/8 | 28 1/8 | 4 7/8 | 4 7/8 | 6 | 6 | 3 6/8 | 445 | 1 |

♦ *Brule County  /  Kenny E. Yeaton  /  Kenny E. Yeaton  /  1985*

**SOUTH DAKOTA STATE RECORD**
**NON-TYPICAL MULE DEER**
**SCORE: 266-5/8**
Locality: Philip    Date: November 1959
Hunter: Clifford Ramsey

# SOUTH DAKOTA

## NON-TYPICAL MULE DEER

| Score | Length of Main Beam R | L | Inside Spread | Greatest Spread | Circumference at Smallest Place Between Burr and First Point R | L | Number of Points R | L | Total of Lengths Abnormal Points | All-Time Rank | State Rank |
|---|---|---|---|---|---|---|---|---|---|---|---|
| \* Locality Killed / By Whom Killed / Owner / Date Killed ||||||||||||
| 266 5/8 | 25 5/8 | 25 2/8 | 20 6/8 | 28 5/8 | 5 | 5 | 13 | 11 | 85 7/8 | 71 | 1 |
| \* Philip / Clifford Ramsey / Clifford Ramsey / 1959 ||||||||||||
| 246 6/8 | 24 6/8 | 24 7/8 | 22 1/8 | 34 4/8 | 4 5/8 | 4 6/8 | 10 | 14 | 54 5/8 | 233 | 2 |
| \* Lawrence County / Unknown / Old Style Saloon / 1945 ||||||||||||

Photograph by Gary Hoffpauir

**UTAH STATE RECORD**
**TYPICAL MULE DEER**
**SCORE: 212-1/8**
Locality: San Juan Co.    Date: October 1973
Hunter: V.R. Rayburn

# UTAH

## TYPICAL MULE DEER

| Score | Length of Main Beam | | Inside Spread | Greatest Spread | Circumference at Smallest Place Between Burr and First Point | | Number of Points | | Total of Lengths Abnormal Points | All-Time Rank | State Rank |
|---|---|---|---|---|---|---|---|---|---|---|---|
| | R | L | | | R | L | R | L | | | |

♦ Locality Killed / By Whom Killed / Owner / Date Killed

| Score | R | L | Inside Spread | Greatest Spread | R | L | R | L | Abnormal | All-Time | State |
|---|---|---|---|---|---|---|---|---|---|---|---|
| 212 1/8 | 26 3/8 | 26 5/8 | 26 4/8 | 30 4/8 | 6 1/8 | 6 1/8 | 8 | 6 | 6 5/8 | 7 | 1 |
| 210 | 26 2/8 | 26 4/8 | 25 4/8 | 31 6/8 | 5 2/8 | 5 1/8 | 6 | 6 | 3 6/8 | 14 | 2 |
| 209 2/8 | 28 | 29 4/8 | 28 4/8 | 34 4/8 | 4 7/8 | 4 6/8 | 5 | 5 | | 19 | 3 |
| 208 | 29 | 26 4/8 | 34 3/8 | 35 1/8 | 5 | 5 1/8 | 5 | 5 | | 27 | 4 |
| 207 4/8 | 27 4/8 | 26 | 24 | 32 2/8 | 4 7/8 | 4 7/8 | 5 | 5 | | 29 | 5 |
| 206 1/8 | 26 3/8 | 26 3/8 | 26 7/8 | 34 2/8 | 6 | 6 | 5 | 8 | 8 6/8 | 46 | 6 |
| 205 6/8 | 26 6/8 | 27 6/8 | 25 1/8 | 37 2/8 | 5 4/8 | 5 2/8 | 5 | 7 | 8 2/8 | 49 | 7 |
| 204 2/8 | 26 | 26 2/8 | 22 2/8 | 30 2/8 | 5 4/8 | 5 4/8 | 5 | 5 | | 62 | 8 |
| 204 1/8 | 24 6/8 | 26 | 27 6/8 | 34 5/8 | 4 7/8 | 4 7/8 | 6 | 5 | 1 1/8 | 63 | 9 |
| 203 5/8 | 28 6/8 | 30 2/8 | 30 1/8 | 34 3/8 | 5 | 5 | 5 | 5 | 7 2/8 | 69 | 10 |
| 203 2/8 | 25 6/8 | 26 6/8 | 23 3/8 | 27 3/8 | 4 6/8 | 4 7/8 | 6 | 5 | 1 7/8 | 77 | 11 |
| 202 2/8 | 27 2/8 | 28 1/8 | 31 3/8 | 42 4/8 | 5 2/8 | 5 2/8 | 10 | 7 | 12 7/8 | 101 | 12 |
| 201 7/8 | 27 2/8 | 27 3/8 | 27 3/8 | 35 | 6 1/8 | 5 6/8 | 6 | 6 | 9 2/8 | 111 | 13 |

♦ San Juan County / V.R. Rayburn / V.R. Rayburn / 1973

♦ Manti-Lasal Mts. / William Norton / William Norton / 1970

♦ Rich County / Dee Hildt / Dee Hildt / 1968

♦ Utah County / Ned H. Losser / Ned H. Losser / 1972

♦ Washington County / John K. Frei / Don Schaufler / 1987

♦ Peterson / Picked Up / Paul Crittenden / PR 1965

♦ Kanab / Loyd A. Folkstad / Loyd A. Folkstad / 1968

♦ Garfield County / James D. Perkins / James D. Perkins / 1969

♦ Morgan County / Kenneth R. Dickamore / Kenneth R. Dickamore / 1967

♦ Grand County / Glen Dumas / S. Kim Bonnett / PR 1960

♦ Garfield County / James D. Perkins / Mrs. James D. Perkins / 1965

♦ Carbon County / Robert R. Henderson / Robert R. Henderson / 1965

♦ Daggett County / Earl Eldredge / Phil Brotherson / 1940

| Score | Length of Main Beam R | Length of Main Beam L | Inside Spread | Greatest Spread | Circumference at Smallest Place Between Burr and First Point R | Circumference at Smallest Place Between Burr and First Point L | Number of Points R | Number of Points L | Total of Lengths Abnormal Points | All-Time Rank | State Rank |
|---|---|---|---|---|---|---|---|---|---|---|---|
| ♦ *Locality Killed / By Whom Killed / Owner / Date Killed* | | | | | | | | | | | |
| 201 3/8 | 30 1/8 | 28 2/8 | 28 7/8 | 32 4/8 | 4 5/8 | 4 6/8 | 5 | 5 | | 122 | 14 |
| ♦ *Wasatch County / Paul Probst / Paul Probst / 1971* | | | | | | | | | | | |
| 201 1/8 | 29 1/8 | 29 2/8 | 31 | 43 4/8 | 5 2/8 | 5 3/8 | 7 | 8 | 11 3/8 | 133 | 15 |
| ♦ *Sanpete County / Roger M. Allred / Roger M. Allred / 1958* | | | | | | | | | | | |
| 200 6/8 | 26 7/8 | 26 3/8 | 23 | 28 | 4 6/8 | 4 7/8 | 5 | 5 | | 143 | 16 |
| ♦ *Provo Canyon / Karl D. Zaugg / Karl D. Zaugg / 1948* | | | | | | | | | | | |
| 200 5/8 | 27 | 26 4/8 | 26 4/8 | 35 2/8 | 4 6/8 | 5 | 7 | 9 | 12 7/8 | 149 | 17 |
| ♦ *Ogden / Carl F. Worden / Carl F. Worden / 1948* | | | | | | | | | | | |
| 200 2/8 | 25 2/8 | 27 2/8 | 25 2/8 | 35 3/8 | 4 7/8 | 5 | 6 | 5 | 3 2/8 | 161 | 18 |
| ♦ *Sevier County / Mayben J. Crane / Mayben J. Crane / 1987* | | | | | | | | | | | |
| 199 4/8 | 25 5/8 | 26 4/8 | 23 6/8 | 27 4/8 | 4 7/8 | 5 | 5 | 6 | 2 4/8 | 187 | 19 |
| ♦ *Sanpete County / Kevin P. Price / Kevin P. Price / 1973* | | | | | | | | | | | |
| 199 2/8 | 27 5/8 | 28 | 25 4/8 | 30 4/8 | 5 2/8 | 5 2/8 | 5 | 5 | | 196 | 20 |
| ♦ *Strawberry / Steve Payne / Steve Payne / 1962* | | | | | | | | | | | |
| 199 2/8 | 26 4/8 | 26 2/8 | 27 4/8 | 30 4/8 | 5 6/8 | 5 5/8 | 5 | 5 | | 196 | 20 |
| ♦ *Grand County / Picked Up / Jon P. Leatham / 1976* | | | | | | | | | | | |
| 199 1/8 | 25 | 24 3/8 | 24 3/8 | 30 2/8 | 5 6/8 | 5 5/8 | 6 | 5 | 4 2/8 | 202 | 22 |
| ♦ *San Juan County / Phyllis O. Crookston / Phyllis O. Crookston / 1971* | | | | | | | | | | | |
| 199 1/8 | 25 4/8 | 25 3/8 | 23 3/8 | 27 2/8 | 5 6/8 | 6 | 5 | 5 | | 202 | 22 |
| ♦ *Morgan County / H. Ritman Jons / H. Ritman Jons / 1987* | | | | | | | | | | | |
| 199 | 26 6/8 | 27 1/8 | 26 2/8 | 30 5/8 | 4 7/8 | 5 1/8 | 5 | 5 | | 206 | 24 |
| ♦ *Echo / Wilford Zaugg / Wilford Zaugg / 1958* | | | | | | | | | | | |
| 198 4/8 | 25 5/8 | 25 6/8 | 20 4/8 | 25 2/8 | 5 | 5 | 5 | 5 | | 218 | 25 |
| ♦ *Tabiona / Picked Up / H.A. Zumbrock / 1957* | | | | | | | | | | | |
| 198 | 25 1/8 | 25 2/8 | 22 4/8 | 25 3/8 | 5 1/8 | 5 | 4 | 4 | | 239 | 26 |
| ♦ *Davis County / Carl D. Craig / Jay D. Craig / 1939* | | | | | | | | | | | |
| 198 | 25 4/8 | 24 6/8 | 25 1/8 | 30 4/8 | 5 4/8 | 5 3/8 | 6 | 5 | 1 1/8 | 239 | 26 |
| ♦ *Smithfield Canyon / Stanley Richardson / Stanley Richardson / 1961* | | | | | | | | | | | |
| 197 6/8 | 25 4/8 | 25 7/8 | 23 6/8 | 33 | 5 2/8 | 5 2/8 | 6 | 5 | 2 2/8 | 253 | 28 |
| ♦ *Elk Ridge / Bill King / Joseph Fitting / 1956* | | | | | | | | | | | |
| 197 5/8 | 25 1/8 | 25 | 27 5/8 | 36 4/8 | 5 1/8 | 5 3/8 | 8 | 6 | 6 | 258 | 29 |
| ♦ *Summit County / Wendell M. Smith / Nathan H. Smith / 1954* | | | | | | | | | | | |
| 197 5/8 | 26 7/8 | 27 3/8 | 26 | 32 5/8 | 5 | 4 7/8 | 6 | 5 | 4 3/8 | 258 | 29 |
| ♦ *Uintah County / Robert C. Chapoose, Jr. / Robert C. Chapoose, Jr. / 1987* | | | | | | | | | | | |

| Score | Length of Main Beam R | L | Inside Spread | Greatest Spread | Circumference at Smallest Place Between Burr and First Point R | L | Number of Points R | L | Total of Lengths Abnormal Points | All-Time Rank | State Rank |
|---|---|---|---|---|---|---|---|---|---|---|---|
| 197 3/8 | 26 7/8 | 25 | 22 3/8 | 26 2/8 | 5 4/8 | 5 3/8 | 5 | 5 | | 269 | 31 |
| *Currant Creek / Morris Kidd / Morris Kidd / 1960* | | | | | | | | | | | |
| 197 3/8 | 28 1/8 | 28 6/8 | 23 4/8 | 27 5/8 | 5 3/8 | 5 4/8 | 7 | 6 | 7 5/8 | 269 | 31 |
| *Garfield County / James R. McCourt / James R. McCourt / 1985* | | | | | | | | | | | |
| 197 2/8 | 26 2/8 | 26 1/8 | 21 2/8 | 28 4/8 | 4 3/8 | 4 4/8 | 5 | 5 | | 277 | 33 |
| *Weber County / Abe B. Murdock / Abe B. Murdock / 1972* | | | | | | | | | | | |
| 197 1/8 | 25 1/8 | 24 3/8 | 25 5/8 | 30 2/8 | 4 2/8 | 4 3/8 | 5 | 5 | | 285 | 34 |
| *Morgan County / Gayle Allen / Gayle Allen / 1948* | | | | | | | | | | | |
| 197 | 25 3/8 | 27 | 22 3/8 | 25 6/8 | 5 | 4 7/8 | 5 | 6 | 1 1/8 | 288 | 35 |
| *Utah County / L. Doug Carlton / L. Doug Carlton / 1982* | | | | | | | | | | | |
| 196 5/8 | 25 6/8 | 25 5/8 | 24 2/8 | 30 4/8 | 5 | 4 7/8 | 7 | 6 | 4 3/8 | 307 | 36 |
| *Summit County / Jerry L. Henriod / Jerry L. Henriod / 1967* | | | | | | | | | | | |
| 196 4/8 | 24 2/8 | 25 1/8 | 21 | 26 7/8 | 6 1/8 | 6 1/8 | 5 | 5 | | 318 | 37 |
| *Vernal / Selby G. Tanner / Selby G. Tanner / 1966* | | | | | | | | | | | |
| 196 4/8 | 26 2/8 | 26 1/8 | 25 2/8 | 30 7/8 | 5 2/8 | 5 6/8 | 6 | 5 | 1 4/8 | 318 | 37 |
| *Morgan County / Elwood Williams / Elwood Williams / 1968* | | | | | | | | | | | |
| 196 2/8 | 22 5/8 | 22 5/8 | 21 6/8 | 35 | 5 3/8 | 5 3/8 | 6 | 7 | 5 | 330 | 39 |
| *Millard County / Burnell Washburn / Burnell Washburn / 1967* | | | | | | | | | | | |
| 195 7/8 | 28 5/8 | 28 | 26 5/8 | 32 6/8 | 5 5/8 | 5 5/8 | 7 | 8 | 22 6/8 | 354 | 40 |
| *Cache County / Richard E. Reeder / Richard E. Reeder / 1968* | | | | | | | | | | | |
| 195 5/8 | 26 1/8 | 26 1/8 | 24 | 30 5/8 | 5 | 5 | 6 | 5 | 1 1/8 | 367 | 41 |
| *Washington County / Scott M. Bulloch / Scott M. Bulloch / 1985* | | | | | | | | | | | |
| 195 4/8 | 25 1/8 | 25 4/8 | 22 6/8 | 30 | 5 2/8 | 5 2/8 | 5 | 5 | | 375 | 42 |
| *Grover / Vicki Davis / R.J. Davis / 1959* | | | | | | | | | | | |
| 195 2/8 | 25 | 26 4/8 | 24 4/8 | 31 | 5 7/8 | 5 5/8 | 5 | 5 | | 389 | 43 |
| *Davis County / Mitchell L. Cochran / Mitchell L. Cochran / 1972* | | | | | | | | | | | |
| 195 1/8 | 24 4/8 | 24 3/8 | 22 2/8 | 25 3/8 | 5 6/8 | 5 5/8 | 6 | 5 | 1 3/8 | 397 | 44 |
| *Utah / Unknown / Jarvie Taxidermy / 1959* | | | | | | | | | | | |
| 195 1/8 | 27 3/8 | 28 2/8 | 27 1/8 | 31 2/8 | 5 5/8 | 5 5/8 | 5 | 5 | | 397 | 44 |
| *Kane County / Cecil Hunt / Cecil Hunt / 1987* | | | | | | | | | | | |
| 194 6/8 | 25 4/8 | 24 6/8 | 23 1/8 | 31 3/8 | 4 3/8 | 4 3/8 | 6 | 5 | 1 5/8 | 410 | 46 |
| *Utah / Unknown / Jarvie Taxidermy / 1947* | | | | | | | | | | | |
| 194 6/8 | 28 | 27 5/8 | 26 7/8 | 30 4/8 | 4 5/8 | 4 7/8 | 6 | 8 | 15 7/8 | 410 | 46 |
| *Grand County / Richard V. Beesley / Richard V. Beesley / 1986* | | | | | | | | | | | |

| Score | Length of Main Beam R | L | Inside Spread | Greatest Spread | Circumference at Smallest Place Between Burr and First Point R | L | Number of Points R | L | Total of Lengths Abnormal Points | All-Time Rank | State Rank |
|---|---|---|---|---|---|---|---|---|---|---|---|
| 194 5/8 | 25 7/8 | 25 4/8 | 25 1/8 | 30 4/8 | 4 6/8 | 5 2/8 | 5 | 5 | | 412 | 48 |
| ◆ *Weber River / Desmond Shields / Desmond Shields / 1960* | | | | | | | | | | | |
| 191 1/8 | 26 5/8 | 24 6/8 | 24 3/8 | 28 5/8 | 4 7/8 | 4 7/8 | 5 | 5 | | 419 | 49 |
| ◆ *Uintah County / Robert B. Keel / Robert B. Keel / 1986* | | | | | | | | | | | |
| 189 4/8 | 25 2/8 | 25 1/8 | 27 1/8 | 29 4/8 | 4 4/8 | 4 5/8 | 5 | 5 | | 423 | 50 |
| ◆ *Emery County / Marvin H. Christensen / Marvin H. Christensen / 1974* | | | | | | | | | | | |
| 189 3/8 | 24 7/8 | 25 1/8 | 24 3/8 | 27 3/8 | 5 1/8 | 5 3/8 | 5 | 5 | | 424 | 51 |
| ◆ *San Juan County / Keele Johnson / Keele Johnson / 1986* | | | | | | | | | | | |
| 188 2/8 | 23 | 23 2/8 | 16 2/8 | 26 6/8 | 4 7/8 | 4 7/8 | 5 | 5 | | 430 | 52 |
| ◆ *Daggett County / Roy D. Sessions / Roy D. Sessions / 1979* | | | | | | | | | | | |
| 187 6/8 | 23 6/8 | 23 6/8 | 23 1/8 | 29 | 5 5/8 | 5 3/8 | 5 | 6 | 7 1/8 | 431 | 53 |
| ◆ *Kane County / Theo J. McAllister / Theo J. McAllister / 1985* | | | | | | | | | | | |
| 186 1/8 | 24 6/8 | 26 4/8 | 25 1/8 | 32 2/8 | 5 6/8 | 5 5/8 | 7 | 5 | 10 6/8 | 441 | 54 |
| ◆ *Sanpete County / Deland G. James / Emma James / 1935* | | | | | | | | | | | |
| 185 7/8 | 25 2/8 | 25 | 23 6/8 | 29 2/8 | 4 5/8 | 4 4/8 | 5 | 7 | 2 5/8 | 442 | 55 |
| ◆ *Juab County / Chris J. Carter / Chris J. Carter / 1987* | | | | | | | | | | | |

Photograph courtesy of Alton Hunsaker

Alton Hunsaker with the second largest non-typical mule deer ever taken. Hunsaker took this buck, which scores 330-1/8 points, in Box Elder County, Utah, in 1943. This buck was listed in early editions of the records book with the hunter unknown. Hunsaker established himself as the hunter for this trophy when he presented this photograph to the Club's records office.

**UTAH STATE RECORD**
**NON-TYPICAL MULE DEER**
**SCORE: 330-1/8**
Locality: Box Elder Co.     Date: 1943
Hunter: Alton Hunsaker
Owner: Julie Ahey

# UTAH

## NON-TYPICAL MULE DEER

| Score | Length of Main Beam R | L | Inside Spread | Greatest Spread | Circumference at Smallest Place Between Burr and First Point R | L | Number of Points R | L | Total of Lengths Abnormal Points | All-Time Rank | State Rank |
|---|---|---|---|---|---|---|---|---|---|---|---|
| | | | | | | | | | | | |

♦ Locality Killed / By Whom Killed / Owner / Date Killed

| Score | R | L | Inside Spread | Greatest Spread | R | L | R | L | Abnormal Points | All-Time Rank | State Rank |
|---|---|---|---|---|---|---|---|---|---|---|---|
| 330 1/8 | 23 1/8 | 22 | 9 4/8 | 31 | 8 2/8 | 8 3/8 | 21 | 28 | 142 7/8 | 2 | 1 |
| 302 | 26 7/8 | 26 2/8 | 21 5/8 | 40 7/8 | 6 3/8 | 6 5/8 | 21 | 15 | 108 3/8 | 11 | 2 |
| 286 1/8 | 27 | 26 6/8 | 26 1/8 | 34 4/8 | 5 2/8 | 5 3/8 | 12 | 20 | 86 | 22 | 3 |
| 284 3/8 | 27 4/8 | 24 3/8 | 26 | 38 2/8 | 5 1/8 | 5 2/8 | 15 | 15 | 84 7/8 | 25 | 4 |
| 284 | 25 7/8 | 26 3/8 | 24 1/8 | 43 6/8 | 5 2/8 | 5 4/8 | 15 | 15 | 82 1/8 | 26 | 5 |
| 283 | 28 | 29 2/8 | 24 3/8 | 37 1/8 | 8 | 7 1/8 | 14 | 13 | 69 5/8 | 27 | 6 |
| 277 2/8 | 23 6/8 | 25 1/8 | 25 6/8 | 47 4/8 | 5 2/8 | 5 5/8 | 11 | 10 | 55 3/8 | 38 | 7 |
| 274 1/8 | 28 3/8 | 28 | 23 | 36 6/8 | 5 4/8 | 5 7/8 | 10 | 4 | 53 5/8 | 48 | 8 |
| 273 1/8 | 27 7/8 | 29 2/8 | 26 6/8 | 40 6/8 | 6 1/8 | 6 | 8 | 12 | 52 3/8 | 50 | 9 |
| 273 5/8 | 28 3/8 | 28 2/8 | 23 7/8 | 42 4/8 | 6 | 6 1/8 | 15 | 16 | 54 6/8 | 53 | 10 |
| 271 2/8 | 24 3/8 | 24 4/8 | 20 | 38 3/8 | 4 6/8 | 5 1/8 | 13 | 14 | 92 6/8 | 58 | 11 |
| 266 7/8 | 22 5/8 | 22 7/8 | 18 6/8 | 37 5/8 | 5 1/8 | 5 1/8 | 8 | 8 | 67 3/8 | 69 | 12 |
| 265 6/8 | 25 6/8 | 25 6/8 | 24 1/8 | 41 | 5 1/8 | 5 4/8 | 11 | 13 | 79 5/8 | 77 | 13 |

♦ Box Elder County / Alton Hunsaker / Julie Ahey / 1943

♦ Iron County / Darwin Hulett / Don Schaufler / 1950

♦ Utah County / Joe Allen / Todd L. Johnson / PR 1950

♦ Duchesne County / Clyde Lambert / Lucy L. Back / 1935

♦ Provo River / Melvin T. Ashton / Don Schaufler / 1961

♦ Rose Creek / Verl N. Creager / Verl N. Creager / 1960

♦ Morgan County / Jim Kilfoil / Gilbert Francis / 1938

♦ Beaver / Murray Bohn / Parowan Rod & Gun Club / 1920

♦ Kane County / Waldon Ballard / Alice Ballard / 1950

♦ Morgan County / Harold B. Rollins / Harold B. Rollins / 1944

♦ East Canyon / Joseph H. Greenig / Mrs. J.H. Greenig / 1947

♦ Draper / Glenn W. Furrow / Glenn W. Furrow / 1962

♦ Cache County / Jerry S. Wuthrich / Jerry S. Wuthrich / 1966

| Score | Length of Main Beam R | L | Inside Spread | Great-est Spread | Circumference at Smallest Place Between Burr and First Point R | L | Number of Points R | L | Total of Lengths Abnor-mal Points | All-Time Rank | State Rank |
|---|---|---|---|---|---|---|---|---|---|---|---|
| | ♦ Locality Killed / By Whom Killed / Owner / Date Killed | | | | | | | | | | |
| 264 2/8 | 24 4/8 | 26 2/8 | 21 | 26 7/8 | 5 3/8 | 5 3/8 | 7 | 13 | 61 6/8 | 84 | 14 |
| | ♦ Southern Utah / Unknown / Earl Mecham / 1932 | | | | | | | | | | |
| 263 6/8 | 26 5/8 | 26 5/8 | 22 2/8 | 37 | 5 | 5 | 16 | 14 | 53 4/8 | 86 | 15 |
| | ♦ Sanpete County / Wayne Dwyer / Raymond R. Cross / 1974 | | | | | | | | | | |
| 262 | 25 7/8 | 23 7/8 | 21 | 37 7/8 | 4 7/8 | 5 | 14 | 15 | 71 2/8 | 96 | 16 |
| | ♦ Utah County / Michael D. Atwood / Michael D. Atwood / 1967 | | | | | | | | | | |
| 261 5/8 | 25 | 26 3/8 | 23 6/8 | 41 4/8 | 4 7/8 | 5 | 10 | 12 | 71 5/8 | 98 | 17 |
| | ♦ Heber Mountain / DuWayne C. Bailey / DuWayne C. Bailey / 1963 | | | | | | | | | | |
| 260 1/8 | 26 | 27 2/8 | 24 3/8 | 37 1/8 | 4 6/8 | 5 1/8 | 16 | 20 | 75 4/8 | 108 | 18 |
| | ♦ Newcastle / Unknown / Utah Div. of Wildl. Resc. / 1961 | | | | | | | | | | |
| 259 7/8 | 25 7/8 | 24 | 24 6/8 | 35 2/8 | 4 7/8 | 4 6/8 | 11 | 13 | 76 5/8 | 111 | 19 |
| | ♦ Kanab / Arthur Glover / Arthur Glover / 1947 | | | | | | | | | | |
| 259 3/8 | 27 3/8 | 29 2/8 | 24 6/8 | 42 | 5 6/8 | 5 4/8 | 13 | 13 | 52 5/8 | 118 | 20 |
| | ♦ Iron County / Mont Hunter / Mont Hunter / 1939 | | | | | | | | | | |
| 258 4/8 | 25 4/8 | 26 6/8 | 24 4/8 | 36 | 5 6/8 | 5 4/8 | 11 | 9 | 53 6/8 | 123 | 21 |
| | ♦ Grand County / Vernon K. Heller / Vernon K. Heller / 1971 | | | | | | | | | | |
| 258 1/8 | 27 1/8 | 25 6/8 | 23 2/8 | 29 7/8 | 5 7/8 | 5 7/8 | 11 | 13 | 89 7/8 | 126 | 22 |
| | ♦ Morgan County / Martin Harris / Rodney D. Layton / 1935 | | | | | | | | | | |
| 257 4/8 | 28 7/8 | 28 6/8 | 27 7/8 | 37 3/8 | 4 6/8 | 4 7/8 | 18 | 10 | 52 1/8 | 134 | 23 |
| | ♦ Utah County / J. Clyde Burgess / Dave Burgess / 1949 | | | | | | | | | | |
| 257 4/8 | 23 6/8 | 24 1/8 | 20 2/8 | 29 5/8 | 5 6/8 | 5 4/8 | 12 | 10 | 49 6/8 | 134 | 23 |
| | ♦ Sanpete County / Dan J. Keller / Dan J. Keller / 1986 | | | | | | | | | | |
| 257 1/8 | 25 2/8 | 24 7/8 | 19 | 31 6/8 | 5 6/8 | 5 3/8 | 10 | 8 | 49 7/8 | 139 | 25 |
| | ♦ Juab County / P.L. Jones / Nelson L. Jones / 1949 | | | | | | | | | | |
| 257 | 26 7/8 | 26 | 24 2/8 | 31 6/8 | 5 | 4 7/8 | 12 | 12 | 57 6/8 | 140 | 26 |
| | ♦ Cache County / Harold S. Shandrew / Harold S. Shandrew / 1958 | | | | | | | | | | |
| 256 1/8 | 23 7/8 | 24 7/8 | 25 | 33 5/8 | 4 7/8 | 5 1/8 | 12 | 13 | 54 2/8 | 147 | 27 |
| | ♦ East Zion / Raymond Pocta / Raymond Pocta / 1963 | | | | | | | | | | |
| 256 | 24 4/8 | 26 7/8 | 25 1/8 | 34 2/8 | 5 | 4 6/8 | 13 | 10 | 62 1/8 | 149 | 28 |
| | ♦ Garfield County / James D. Perkins / James D. Perkins / 1959 | | | | | | | | | | |
| 255 6/8 | 26 5/8 | 26 7/8 | 26 5/8 | 37 7/8 | 5 2/8 | 5 2/8 | 11 | 9 | 51 5/8 | 152 | 29 |
| | ♦ Cache County / Roland Leishman / Roland Leishman / 1980 | | | | | | | | | | |
| 253 3/8 | 20 1/8 | 22 1/8 | 22 6/8 | 28 5/8 | 5 2/8 | 5 3/8 | 15 | 22 | 90 | 164 | 30 |
| | ♦ Utah County / Paul H. Mitchell / Paul H. Mitchell / 1953 | | | | | | | | | | |

| Score | Length of Main Beam R | L | Inside Spread | Greatest Spread | Circumference at Smallest Place Between Burr and First Point R | L | Number of Points R | L | Total of Lengths Abnormal Points | All-Time Rank | State Rank |
|---|---|---|---|---|---|---|---|---|---|---|---|
| | ♦ *Locality Killed / By Whom Killed / Owner / Date Killed* | | | | | | | | | | |
| 252 1/8 | 25 1/8 | 24 1/8 | 21 5/8 | 31 5/8 | 4 6/8 | 4 7/8 | 11 | 10 | 54 | 174 | 31 |
| | ♦ *Salina Canyon / James C. Larsen / James C. Larsen / 1969* | | | | | | | | | | |
| 251 7/8 | 22 | 24 1/8 | 17 1/8 | 29 4/8 | 4 6/8 | 4 5/8 | 10 | 10 | 68 6/8 | 177 | 32 |
| | ♦ *Salem / John Vincent / John Vincent / 1956* | | | | | | | | | | |
| 251 1/8 | 28 1/8 | 27 7/8 | 26 3/8 | 31 5/8 | 6 | 6 1/8 | 10 | 9 | 42 6/8 | 181 | 33 |
| | ♦ *Iron County / James C. Howard / James C. Howard / 1987* | | | | | | | | | | |
| 247 1/8 | 25 7/8 | 25 | 23 7/8 | 38 5/8 | 5 6/8 | 5 4/8 | 7 | 10 | 38 | 225 | 34 |
| | ♦ *Carbon County / Ralph A. Sanich / Ralph A. Sanich / 1986* | | | | | | | | | | |
| 244 2/8 | 25 1/8 | 24 5/8 | 22 5/8 | 37 | 5 | 5 | 12 | 13 | 69 3/8 | 259 | 35 |
| | ♦ *Wasatch County / Unknown / Ted Clegg / 1938* | | | | | | | | | | |
| 244 2/8 | 25 6/8 | 26 3/8 | 22 7/8 | 29 6/8 | 5 2/8 | 5 4/8 | 12 | 13 | 53 1/8 | 259 | 35 |
| | ♦ *San Juan County / Phil Acton / Phil Acton / 1966* | | | | | | | | | | |
| 244 | 26 4/8 | 27 1/8 | 24 6/8 | 31 1/8 | 4 6/8 | 4 6/8 | 9 | 10 | 55 | 269 | 37 |
| | ♦ *East Canyon / Ronald E. Coburn / Ronald E. Coburn / 1961* | | | | | | | | | | |
| 243 7/8 | 23 6/8 | 23 7/8 | 26 | 36 3/8 | 4 6/8 | 4 6/8 | 10 | 11 | 66 | 270 | 38 |
| | ♦ *Utah County / Zenneth K. Chamberlain / Zenneth K. Chamberlain / 1956* | | | | | | | | | | |
| 243 5/8 | 23 6/8 | 23 2/8 | 26 6/8 | 37 6/8 | 4 4/8 | 4 6/8 | 7 | 9 | 42 7/8 | 273 | 39 |
| | ♦ *Cache County / Albert C. Steffenhagen / A. Ladell Atkinson / 1924* | | | | | | | | | | |
| 241 3/8 | 27 1/8 | 26 7/8 | 26 1/8 | 32 6/8 | 5 5/8 | 5 4/8 | 13 | 11 | 37 6/8 | 300 | 40 |
| | ♦ *Kane County / Aivars O. Berkis / Aivars O. Berkis / 1987* | | | | | | | | | | |
| 240 4/8 | 23 6/8 | 23 5/8 | 23 2/8 | 31 4/8 | 5 1/8 | 5 2/8 | 11 | 14 | 57 6/8 | 310 | 41 |
| | ♦ *Morgan County / Pietro De Santis / Pietro De Santis / 1982* | | | | | | | | | | |

Photograph Courtesy of Howard W. Hoskins

**WASHINGTON STATE RECORD**
**TYPICAL MULE DEER**
**SCORE: 202**
Locality: Chelan Co.    Date: Prior to 1970
Hunter: Unknown
Owner: Howard W. Hoskins

# WASHINGTON

## TYPICAL MULE DEER

| Score | Length of Main Beam R | L | Inside Spread | Greatest Spread | Circumference at Smallest Place Between Burr and First Point R | L | Number of Points R | L | Total of Lengths Abnormal Points | All-Time Rank | State Rank |
|---|---|---|---|---|---|---|---|---|---|---|---|
| | | | | | | | | | | | |
| 202 | 27 ²/₈ | 27 ¹/₈ | 27 ⁵/₈ | 32 ²/₈ | 5 ⁴/₈ | 5 ⁵/₈ | 5 | 5 | | 104 | 1 |
| ♦ Chelan County / Unknown / Howard W. Hoskins / PR 1970 | | | | | | | | | | | |
| 200 ³/₈ | 27 ⁵/₈ | 27 ⁴/₈ | 27 ¹/₈ | 29 ⁷/₈ | 5 ⁴/₈ | 5 ²/₈ | 4 | 4 | | 158 | 2 |
| ♦ Okanogan County / E.R. Crooks / E.R. Crooks / 1939 | | | | | | | | | | | |
| 200 ²/₈ | 27 ⁵/₈ | 28 ⁵/₈ | 26 | 30 ⁶/₈ | 4 ⁷/₈ | 5 | 4 | 4 | | 161 | 3 |
| ♦ Asotin County / Grant E. Holcomb / Grant E. Holcomb / 1975 | | | | | | | | | | | |
| 200 ¹/₈ | 27 ³/₈ | 27 ⁶/₈ | 27 ³/₈ | | 5 ³/₈ | 5 ⁴/₈ | 5 | 5 | | 168 | 4 |
| ♦ Cashmere / John F. Schurle / William H. Schott / 1913 | | | | | | | | | | | |
| 196 ⁵/₈ | 27 ¹/₈ | 26 ⁶/₈ | 25 ⁵/₈ | 31 ⁵/₈ | 6 | 6 | 6 | 6 | 3 ⁵/₈ | 307 | 5 |
| ♦ Chelan County / George Bolton / Welcome Sauer / 1930 | | | | | | | | | | | |
| 196 | 25 ¹/₈ | 25 ⁴/₈ | 25 ⁶/₈ | 34 ⁶/₈ | 5 ⁷/₈ | 6 | 5 | 5 | | 346 | 6 |
| ♦ Ferry County / Owen R. Burgess / Owen R. Burgess / 1982 | | | | | | | | | | | |

Photograph Courtesy of Ernest Fait

**WASHINGTON FOURTH PLACE**
**NON-TYPICAL MULE DEER**
**SCORE: 257-6/8**
Locality: Leclerc Creek    Date: November 1960
Hunter: Ernest Fait

# WASHINGTON

## NON-TYPICAL MULE DEER

| Score | Length of Main Beam R | Length of Main Beam L | Inside Spread | Greatest Spread | Circumference at Smallest Place Between Burr and First Point R | Circumference at Smallest Place Between Burr and First Point L | Number of Points R | Number of Points L | Total of Lengths Abnormal Points | All-Time Rank | State Rank |
|---|---|---|---|---|---|---|---|---|---|---|---|
| ♦ *Locality Killed / By Whom Killed / Owner / Date Killed* | | | | | | | | | | | |
| 266 1/8 | 22 4/8 | 22 7/8 | 16 4/8 | 32 6/8 | 5 4/8 | 5 1/8 | 16 | 13 | 94 5/8 | 73 | 1 |
| ♦ *Stevens County / Joe C. Mally / Steve Mally / 1933* | | | | | | | | | | | |
| 265 2/8 | 25 6/8 | 24 2/8 | 18 | 38 1/8 | 5 6/8 | 5 2/8 | 22 | 18 | 88 4/8 | 80 | 2 |
| ♦ *Blue Mts. / Frank Henriksen / Frank Henriksen / 1961* | | | | | | | | | | | |
| 261 2/8 | 25 2/8 | 26 2/8 | 24 3/8 | 35 | 4 6/8 | 5 1/8 | 13 | 19 | 90 3/8 | 100 | 3 |
| ♦ *Iron Creek / Win Coultas / Win Coultas / 1924* | | | | | | | | | | | |
| 257 6/8 | 28 3/8 | 27 1/8 | 24 2/8 | 34 2/8 | 5 4/8 | 5 4/8 | 9 | 13 | 69 4/8 | 130 | 4 |
| ♦ *Leclerc Creek / Ernest Fait / Ernest Fait / 1960* | | | | | | | | | | | |
| 250 7/8 | 26 4/8 | 27 2/8 | 24 | 29 1/8 | 5 4/8 | 6 | 19 | 13 | 54 1/8 | 184 | 5 |
| ♦ *Chelan County / Ben R. Williamson / Vera T. Williamson / 1951* | | | | | | | | | | | |
| 250 4/8 | 26 1/8 | 27 3/8 | 28 4/8 | 35 3/8 | 5 1/8 | 5 | 12 | 10 | 53 3/8 | 186 | 6 |
| ♦ *Washington / Unknown / Pat Redding / PR 1973* | | | | | | | | | | | |
| 248 6/8 | 27 | 25 4/8 | 28 | 39 3/8 | 5 5/8 | 5 6/8 | 9 | 14 | 62 | 203 | 7 |
| ♦ *Okanogan County / Fred C. Heuer / Raymond R. Cross / 1940* | | | | | | | | | | | |
| 247 7/8 | 23 6/8 | 24 | 20 7/8 | 34 5/8 | 5 | 5 | 14 | 13 | 60 2/8 | 213 | 8 |
| ♦ *Asotin County / David G. Bennett / David G. Bennett / 1971* | | | | | | | | | | | |
| 243 | 25 | 25 5/8 | 20 4/8 | 33 | 7 1/8 | 5 2/8 | 15 | 11 | 73 | 279 | 9 |
| ♦ *Winthrop / Bruce Miller / Bruce Miller / 1941* | | | | | | | | | | | |

Photograph by Alex Rota

**WYOMING STATE RECORD**
**TYPICAL MULE DEER**
**SCORE: 217**
Locality: Hoback Canyon    Date: 1925
Hunter: Unknown
Owner: Jackson Hole Museum

# WYOMING

## TYPICAL MULE DEER

| Score | Length of Main Beam R | L | Inside Spread | Greatest Spread | Circumference at Smallest Place Between Burr and First Point R | L | Number of Points R | L | Total of Lengths Abnormal Points | All-Time Rank | State Rank |
|---|---|---|---|---|---|---|---|---|---|---|---|
| | ♦ Locality Killed / By Whom Killed / Owner / Date Killed | | | | | | | | | | |
| 217 | 28 4/8 | 28 2/8 | 26 6/8 | 30 6/8 | 5 5/8 | 5 6/8 | 6 | 6 | 3 | 2 | 1 |
| | ♦ Hoback Canyon / Unknown / Jackson Hole Museum / 1925 | | | | | | | | | | |
| 215 5/8 | 26 7/8 | 28 1/8 | 29 4/8 | 36 3/8 | 5 3/8 | 5 3/8 | 5 | 7 | 5 2/8 | 3 | 2 |
| | ♦ Uinta County / Gary L. Albertson / Don Schaufler / 1960 | | | | | | | | | | |
| 211 6/8 | 29 7/8 | 29 6/8 | 30 3/8 | 38 4/8 | 4 5/8 | 4 5/8 | 7 | 8 | 7 3/8 | 11 | 3 |
| | ♦ Teton County / Robert V. Parke / Robert V. Parke / 1967 | | | | | | | | | | |
| 207 | 31 6/8 | 27 2/8 | 27 4/8 | 31 6/8 | 7 | 7 | 6 | 6 | 15 | 34 | 4 |
| | ♦ Split Rock / Herb Klein / Herb Klein / 1960 | | | | | | | | | | |
| 207 | 26 7/8 | 28 | 26 5/8 | 30 4/8 | 5 3/8 | 5 3/8 | 5 | 6 | 2 7/8 | 34 | 4 |
| | ♦ Lincoln County / Al Firenze, Sr. / Al Firenze, Jr. / 1969 | | | | | | | | | | |
| 205 4/8 | 26 6/8 | 25 7/8 | 24 6/8 | 30 1/8 | 5 | 5 | 5 | 5 | | 51 | 6 |
| | ♦ Lincoln County / John E. Myers / John E. Myers / 1968 | | | | | | | | | | |
| 205 2/8 | 27 1/8 | 27 6/8 | 28 1/8 | 32 2/8 | 4 5/8 | 5 | 5 | 5 | | 56 | 7 |
| | ♦ Carbon County / Shelly R. Risner / Shelly R. Risner / 1986 | | | | | | | | | | |
| 203 2/8 | 25 3/8 | 25 7/8 | 24 6/8 | 33 1/8 | 4 6/8 | 4 5/8 | 6 | 7 | 3 6/8 | 77 | 8 |
| | ♦ Crook County / Ora McGurn / George L. Cooper / 1957 | | | | | | | | | | |
| 202 7/8 | 24 5/8 | 23 | 22 1/8 | 27 5/8 | 5 3/8 | 5 2/8 | 5 | 5 | | 86 | 9 |
| | ♦ Lincoln County / Monte J. Brough / Monte J. Brough / 1968 | | | | | | | | | | |
| 202 | 26 | 24 6/8 | 27 4/8 | 32 1/8 | 5 | 4 7/8 | 5 | 5 | | 104 | 10 |
| | ♦ Sweetwater County / Arnold A. Bethke / Arnold A. Bethke / 1976 | | | | | | | | | | |
| 201 6/8 | 26 | 26 5/8 | 21 2/8 | 27 4/8 | 5 | 5 | 5 | 4 | | 113 | 11 |
| | ♦ Afton / Bernard Domries / Bernard Domries / 1967 | | | | | | | | | | |
| 201 3/8 | 26 5/8 | 25 7/8 | 23 3/8 | 26 | 5 2/8 | 5 2/8 | 6 | 7 | 4 2/8 | 122 | 12 |
| | ♦ Sublette County / Jerry C. Lopez / Jerry C. Lopez / 1985 | | | | | | | | | | |
| 200 5/8 | 25 2/8 | 25 2/8 | 25 2/8 | 30 3/8 | 5 | 5 2/8 | 6 | 5 | 2 1/8 | 149 | 13 |
| | ♦ Lincoln County / John Myers / John Myers / 1973 | | | | | | | | | | |

| Score | Length of Main Beam | | Inside Spread | Greatest Spread | Circumference at Smallest Place Between Burr and First Point | | Number of Points | | Total of Lengths Abnormal Points | All-Time Rank | State Rank |
|---|---|---|---|---|---|---|---|---|---|---|---|
| | R | L | | | R | L | R | L | | | |
| 200 2/8 | 25 | 25 1/8 | 22 4/8 | 37 4/8 | 5 6/8 | 5 6/8 | 6 | 6 | 2 6/8 | 161 | 14 |
| ◆ Battle Mt. / Ron Vance / Ronald Crawford / 1963 | | | | | | | | | | | |
| 200 | 25 7/8 | 25 4/8 | 21 7/8 | 29 4/8 | 5 5/8 | 5 5/8 | 5 | 7 | 3 7/8 | 171 | 15 |
| ◆ Hot Springs County / Basil C. Bradbury / Basil C. Bradbury / 1977 | | | | | | | | | | | |
| 199 1/8 | 27 | 26 2/8 | 27 2/8 | 29 5/8 | 5 5/8 | 5 4/8 | 5 | 6 | 1 1/8 | 202 | 16 |
| ◆ Laramie County / David L. Shannon / David L. Shannon / 1981 | | | | | | | | | | | |
| 199 | 25 1/8 | 26 3/8 | 23 4/8 | 27 2/8 | 5 4/8 | 5 1/8 | 5 | 5 | | 206 | 17 |
| ◆ Park County / Lois M. Pelzel / Lois M. Pelzel / 1965 | | | | | | | | | | | |
| 198 5/8 | 25 1/8 | 25 2/8 | 23 1/8 | 27 7/8 | 4 7/8 | 5 | 5 | 7 | 2 4/8 | 213 | 18 |
| ◆ Carbon County / M. Gary Muske / M. Gary Muske / 1968 | | | | | | | | | | | |
| 198 4/8 | 28 5/8 | 28 4/8 | 24 5/8 | 28 5/8 | 5 3/8 | 5 3/8 | 5 | 6 | 1 5/8 | 218 | 19 |
| ◆ Afton / Ray M. Vincent / Ray M. Vincent / 1967 | | | | | | | | | | | |
| 198 1/8 | 25 4/8 | 26 1/8 | 26 2/8 | 34 | 5 2/8 | 5 2/8 | 5 | 5 | | 234 | 20 |
| ◆ Natrona County / Kerry J. Clegg / Kerry J. Clegg / 1983 | | | | | | | | | | | |
| 197 6/8 | 27 2/8 | 28 | 25 2/8 | 29 6/8 | 4 6/8 | 4 6/8 | 5 | 5 | | 253 | 21 |
| ◆ Encampment / Ralph E. Platt, Jr. / Ralph E. Platt, Jr. / 1936 | | | | | | | | | | | |
| 197 6/8 | 26 5/8 | 27 5/8 | 23 7/8 | 33 4/8 | 4 6/8 | 5 | 8 | 8 | 12 3/8 | 253 | 21 |
| ◆ Teton County / John W. Farlow, Jr. / John W. Farlow, Jr. / 1971 | | | | | | | | | | | |
| 197 4/8 | 26 3/8 | 25 7/8 | 24 7/8 | 30 1/8 | 4 6/8 | 4 7/8 | 5 | 6 | 2 5/8 | 264 | 23 |
| ◆ Uinta County / Ken L. Vernon / Ken L. Vernon / 1968 | | | | | | | | | | | |
| 197 2/8 | 27 3/8 | 27 3/8 | 27 1/8 | 36 1/8 | 5 2/8 | 5 4/8 | 6 | 5 | 1 7/8 | 277 | 24 |
| ◆ Afton / Robert Williams / Robert Williams / 1960 | | | | | | | | | | | |
| 196 5/8 | 25 5/8 | 25 3/8 | 25 6/8 | 27 4/8 | 5 2/8 | 5 | 5 | 5 | | 307 | 25 |
| ◆ Johnson County / Unknown / Toby J. Johnson / 1940 | | | | | | | | | | | |
| 196 5/8 | 26 | 25 7/8 | 22 6/8 | 27 3/8 | 4 4/8 | 4 6/8 | 6 | 5 | 2 1/8 | 307 | 25 |
| ◆ Dubois / P.C. Alfred Dorow / P.C. Alfred Dorow / 1960 | | | | | | | | | | | |
| 196 5/8 | 23 7/8 | 24 | 22 5/8 | 31 4/8 | 4 6/8 | 4 7/8 | 5 | 5 | | 307 | 25 |
| ◆ Lincoln County / Chester P. Michalski / Chester P. Michalski / 1974 | | | | | | | | | | | |
| 196 3/8 | 26 3/8 | 27 1/8 | 25 1/8 | 31 4/8 | 5 6/8 | 5 4/8 | 6 | 6 | 7 | 326 | 28 |
| ◆ Sublette County / S. Kim Bonnett / S. Kim Bonnett / 1978 | | | | | | | | | | | |
| 196 2/8 | 27 1/8 | 27 3/8 | 25 1/8 | 31 | 5 3/8 | 5 2/8 | 5 | 6 | 2 3/8 | 330 | 29 |
| ◆ Sweetwater County / Donald H. Pabst / Donald H. Pabst / 1962 | | | | | | | | | | | |
| 196 2/8 | 24 | 25 | 20 6/8 | 27 6/8 | 4 2/8 | 4 5/8 | 5 | 5 | | 330 | 29 |
| ◆ Big Horn Mts. / Ruth Davis / Ruth Davis / 1968 | | | | | | | | | | | |

*Locality Killed / By Whom Killed / Owner / Date Killed*

| Score | Length of Main Beam R | L | Inside Spread | Greatest Spread | Circumference at Smallest Place Between Burr and First Point R | L | Number of Points R | L | Total of Lengths Abnormal Points | All-Time Rank | State Rank |
|---|---|---|---|---|---|---|---|---|---|---|---|
| | | | | | ♦ *Locality Killed  /  By Whom Killed  /  Owner  /  Date Killed* | | | | | | |
| 195 6/8 | 25 3/8 | 24 3/8 | 24 6/8 | 29 1/8 | 4 5/8 | 4 5/8 | 5 | 5 | | 360 | 31 |
| | | | | | ♦ *Teton County  /  Joel M. Leatham  /  Joel M. Leatham  /  1979* | | | | | | |
| 195 3/8 | 27 3/8 | 26 1/8 | 26 5/8 | 29 7/8 | 4 6/8 | 4 6/8 | 5 | 5 | | 383 | 32 |
| | | | | | ♦ *Natrona County  /  Richard Ullery  /  Richard Ullery  /  1977* | | | | | | |
| 195 2/8 | 28 5/8 | 29 7/8 | 29 | 31 5/8 | 5 5/8 | 5 7/8 | 5 | 5 | | 389 | 33 |
| | | | | | ♦ *Niobrara County  /  David E. Pauna  /  David E. Pauna  /  1976* | | | | | | |
| 195 2/8 | 23 3/8 | 24 6/8 | 21 4/8 | 27 3/8 | 5 1/8 | 5 2/8 | 5 | 5 | | 389 | 33 |
| | | | | | ♦ *Sublette County  /  John R. Birchett  /  John R. Birchett  /  1981* | | | | | | |
| 195 | 24 2/8 | 24 4/8 | 22 3/8 | 31 1/8 | 6 2/8 | 6 1/8 | 7 | 5 | 5 3/8 | 405 | 35 |
| | | | | | ♦ *Sublette County  /  Norm Busselle  /  Norm Busselle  /  1977* | | | | | | |
| 194 | 23 3/8 | 25 1/8 | 22 4/8 | 25 6/8 | 4 6/8 | 4 7/8 | 5 | 5 | | 413 | 36 |
| | | | | | ♦ *Sublette County  /  James J. McBride  /  James J. McBride  /  1979* | | | | | | |
| 188 7/8 | 26 4/8 | 27 | 23 6/8 | 32 5/8 | 4 6/8 | 4 6/8 | 8 | 7 | 10 5/8 | 426 | 37 |
| | | | | | ♦ *Sublette County  /  George Shuleshko  /  George Shuleshko  /  1986* | | | | | | |
| 185 7/8 | 24 3/8 | 24 3/8 | 22 1/8 | 29 | 4 5/8 | 4 7/8 | 6 | 5 | 1 4/8 | 442 | 38 |
| | | | | | ♦ *Lincoln County  /  James P. Speck  /  James P. Speck  /  1987* | | | | | | |

**WYOMING FOURTH PLACE**
**NON-TYPICAL MULE DEER**
**SCORE: 260-2/8**
Locality: Pinedale    Date: 1965
Hunter: James H. Straley
Owner: Monte W. Straley

# WYOMING

## NON-TYPICAL MULE DEER

| Score | Length of Main Beam R | Length of Main Beam L | Inside Spread | Greatest Spread | Circumference at Smallest Place Between Burr and First Point R | Circumference at Smallest Place Between Burr and First Point L | Number of Points R | Number of Points L | Total of Lengths Abnormal Points | All-Time Rank | State Rank |
|---|---|---|---|---|---|---|---|---|---|---|---|
| ♦ *Locality Killed / By Whom Killed / Owner / Date Killed* | | | | | | | | | | | |
| 293 7/8 | 26 4/8 | 24 6/8 | 27 6/8 | 39 1/8 | 5 6/8 | 5 4/8 | 18 | 16 | 99 1/8 | 18 | 1 |
| ♦ *Wyoming / J.B. Marvin, Jr. / National Collection / PR 1924* | | | | | | | | | | | |
| 272 3/8 | 28 4/8 | 28 2/8 | 28 4/8 | 42 3/8 | 5 1/8 | 5 5/8 | 11 | 12 | 81 3/8 | 57 | 2 |
| ♦ *Albany County / S.A. Lawson / Acad. Nat. Sci., Phil. / 1905* | | | | | | | | | | | |
| 266 7/8 | 26 | 25 1/8 | 22 4/8 | 33 | 6 4/8 | 6 1/8 | 13 | 15 | 73 3/8 | 69 | 3 |
| ♦ *Wyoming / J.L. Kemmerer / Am. Mus. Nat. History / 1905* | | | | | | | | | | | |
| 260 2/8 | 26 7/8 | 25 | 21 2/8 | 28 5/8 | 4 6/8 | 4 5/8 | 12 | 13 | 73 6/8 | 106 | 4 |
| ♦ *Pinedale / James H. Straley / Monte W. Straley / 1965* | | | | | | | | | | | |
| 259 5/8 | 27 2/8 | 26 6/8 | 24 1/8 | 33 4/8 | 5 2/8 | 5 2/8 | 12 | 13 | 59 6/8 | 116 | 5 |
| ♦ *Glendo / Rudolph B. Johnson / Rudolph B. Johnson / 1961* | | | | | | | | | | | |
| 258 6/8 | 21 | 22 | 16 2/8 | 30 4/8 | 10 | 5 | 18 | 18 | 86 2/8 | 120 | 6 |
| ♦ *Sweetwater County / John A. Fabian / John A. Fabian / 1974* | | | | | | | | | | | |
| 257 4/8 | 24 5/8 | 23 | 19 2/8 | 35 3/8 | 5 4/8 | 5 4/8 | 11 | 11 | 57 | 134 | 7 |
| ♦ *Encampment / Sam Whitney / Mrs. Sam Whitney / 1946* | | | | | | | | | | | |
| 256 6/8 | 24 6/8 | 26 4/8 | 20 4/8 | 33 1/8 | 5 | 5 1/8 | 12 | 15 | 60 2/8 | 143 | 8 |
| ♦ *Hoback Basin / Buck Heide / Buck Heide / 1968* | | | | | | | | | | | |
| 253 3/8 | 24 4/8 | 24 3/8 | 20 4/8 | 34 3/8 | 5 3/8 | 5 3/8 | 11 | 11 | 52 7/8 | 164 | 9 |
| ♦ *Rawlins / A.H. Henkel / A.H. Henkel / 1952* | | | | | | | | | | | |
| 253 1/8 | 24 2/8 | 23 2/8 | 24 6/8 | 37 2/8 | 5 4/8 | 5 1/8 | 16 | 12 | 67 7/8 | 169 | 10 |
| ♦ *Sweetwater County / John C. Erickson / M. Painovich & J. Etcheverry / 1932* | | | | | | | | | | | |
| 249 2/8 | 24 3/8 | 23 5/8 | 27 | 36 7/8 | 4 6/8 | 4 6/8 | 10 | 10 | 63 1/8 | 197 | 11 |
| ♦ *Lincoln County / Robert J. Stallone / Robert J. Stallone / 1986* | | | | | | | | | | | |
| 248 | 26 | 27 1/8 | 22 | 36 1/8 | 5 | 5 | 12 | 9 | 45 4/8 | 210 | 12 |
| ♦ *Pinedale / Lyle Rosendahl / Lyle Rosendahl / 1960* | | | | | | | | | | | |
| 244 7/8 | 25 6/8 | 26 4/8 | 22 1/8 | 39 7/8 | 4 7/8 | 4 7/8 | 11 | 9 | 42 2/8 | 252 | 13 |
| ♦ *Lincoln County / Brian H. Suter / Brian H. Suter / 1981* | | | | | | | | | | | |

| Score | Length of Main Beam | | Inside Spread | Greatest Spread | Circumference at Smallest Place Between Burr and First Point | | Number of Points | | Total of Lengths Abnormal Points | All-Time Rank | State Rank |
|---|---|---|---|---|---|---|---|---|---|---|---|
| | R | L | | | R | L | R | L | | | |
| ♦ *Locality Killed / By Whom Killed / Owner / Date Killed* | | | | | | | | | | | |
| 244 5/8 | 25 5/8 | 24 2/8 | 22 1/8 | 40 6/8 | 5 6/8 | 5 6/8 | 13 | 14 | 54 | 254 | 14 |
| ♦ *Teton County / Vern Shinkle / Vern Shinkle / 1968* | | | | | | | | | | | |
| 244 2/8 | 22 6/8 | 21 6/8 | 19 4/8 | 30 6/8 | 4 4/8 | 4 7/8 | 9 | 13 | 67 1/8 | 259 | 15 |
| ♦ *Fremont County / Warren V. Spriggs / Warren V. Spriggs / 1962* | | | | | | | | | | | |
| 244 1/8 | 25 | 26 2/8 | 29 2/8 | 34 | 5 5/8 | 5 6/8 | 11 | 12 | 45 3/8 | 266 | 16 |
| ♦ *Split Rock / Herb Klein / Herb Klein / 1957* | | | | | | | | | | | |
| 244 1/8 | 24 1/8 | 24 2/8 | 28 | 34 | 4 4/8 | 4 4/8 | 9 | 10 | 75 5/8 | 266 | 16 |
| ♦ *Big Horn County / Picked Up / Henry D. Frey / 1978* | | | | | | | | | | | |
| 242 7/8 | 24 4/8 | 24 1/8 | 22 6/8 | 28 4/8 | 4 7/8 | 5 | 10 | 11 | 72 7/8 | 282 | 18 |
| ♦ *Sheridan / J.M. Blakeman / J.M. Blakeman / 1952* | | | | | | | | | | | |
| 232 5/8 | 24 4/8 | 25 7/8 | 17 5/8 | 30 5/8 | 4 3/8 | 4 3/8 | 13 | 10 | 40 2/8 | 325 | 19 |
| ♦ *Teton County / Bruce K. McRae / Bruce K. McRae / 1986* | | | | | | | | | | | |
| 262 7/8 | 27 4/8 | 27 5/8 | 25 1/8 | 34 6/8 | 5 | 4 7/8 | 12 | 15 | 68 2/8 | * | * |
| ♦ *Teton County / Thomas R. Ford / Thomas R. Ford / 1984* | | | | | | | | | | | |

Photograph courtesy of Jeffrey A. Bechtel

Jeffrey A. Bechtel with the typical mule deer, score of 187-5/8 points, from his 1983 hunt in the Great Bear Wilderness Area of Montana. Great Bear lies on the Flathead National Forest and provides fine hunting.

**ALBERTA PROVINCE RECORD**
**TYPICAL MULE DEER**
**SCORE: 199-4/8**
Locality: Medicine Hat    Date: November 1981
Hunter: Duncan Baldie
Owner: D. Baldie & K.W. McKenzie

# ALBERTA

## TYPICAL MULE DEER

| Score | Length of Main Beam | | Inside Spread | Greatest Spread | Circumference at Smallest Place Between Burr and First Point | | Number of Points | | Total of Lengths Abnormal Points | All-Time Rank | Prov. Rank |
|---|---|---|---|---|---|---|---|---|---|---|---|
| | R | L | | | R | L | R | L | | | |
| ♦ Locality Killed / By Whom Killed / Owner / Date Killed | | | | | | | | | | | |

| 199 4/8 | 26 7/8 | 27 3/8 | 25 6/8 | 28 7/8 | 5 6/8 | 5 6/8 | 4 | 4 | | 187 | 1 |
|---|---|---|---|---|---|---|---|---|---|---|---|
| ♦ Medicine Hat / Duncan Baldie / D. Baldie & K.W. McKenzie / 1981 | | | | | | | | | | | |
| 198 6/8 | 23 4/8 | 22 2/8 | 21 6/8 | 26 3/8 | 5 1/8 | 5 2/8 | 5 | 5 | | 211 | 2 |
| ♦ Hines Creek / Charles Lundgard / Charles Lundgard / 1960 | | | | | | | | | | | |

**ALBERTA PROVINCE RECORD**
**WORLD'S RECORD**
**NON-TYPICAL MULE DEER**
**SCORE: 355-2/8**
Locality: Chip Lake    Date: November 1926
Hunter: Ed Broder

# ALBERTA

## NON-TYPICAL MULE DEER

| Score | Length of Main Beam R | Length of Main Beam L | Inside Spread | Greatest Spread | Circumference at Smallest Place Between Burr and First Point R | Circumference at Smallest Place Between Burr and First Point L | Number of Points R | Number of Points L | Total of Lengths Abnormal Points | All-Time Rank | Prov. Rank |
|---|---|---|---|---|---|---|---|---|---|---|---|
| ♦ *Locality Killed / By Whom Killed / Owner / Date Killed* | | | | | | | | | | | |
| 355 2/8 | 26 2/8 | 26 1/8 | 22 1/8 | 38 5/8 | 5 | 4 7/8 | 22 | 21 | 147 7/8 | 1 | 1 |
| ♦ *Chip Lake / Ed Broder / Ed Broder / 1926* | | | | | | | | | | | |
| 254 4/8 | 25 1/8 | 24 | 18 5/8 | 30 1/8 | 5 4/8 | 5 2/8 | 13 | 15 | 88 5/8 | 159 | 2 |
| ♦ *Maloy / Otto Schmalzbauer / Otto Schmalzbauer / 1930* | | | | | | | | | | | |
| 252 | 22 7/8 | 22 1/8 | 24 6/8 | 37 | 5 4/8 | 5 4/8 | 18 | 16 | 95 1/8 | 175 | 3 |
| ♦ *Grease Creek / Jack McCallum / J.H. Fry / PR 1940* | | | | | | | | | | | |
| 247 5/8 | 28 4/8 | 26 7/8 | 24 4/8 | 33 | 6 | 5 7/8 | 10 | 13 | 38 7/8 | 217 | 4 |
| ♦ *Waterton Park / Eric Westergreen / Eric Westergreen / 1941* | | | | | | | | | | | |
| 245 2/8 | 23 6/8 | 24 6/8 | 24 3/8 | 34 5/8 | 5 1/8 | 5 | 18 | 12 | 55 1/8 | 247 | 5 |
| ♦ *Lac Lariche / Julius Hagen / Olaf Hagen / 1945* | | | | | | | | | | | |
| 243 6/8 | 24 1/8 | 27 2/8 | 27 3/8 | 36 7/8 | 5 5/8 | 5 4/8 | 16 | 18 | 70 6/8 | 271 | 6 |
| ♦ *Slave Lake / R.W.H. Eben-Ebenau / R.W.H. Eben-Ebenau / 1930* | | | | | | | | | | | |
| 238 2/8 | 23 6/8 | 24 1/8 | 26 5/8 | 31 2/8 | 5 1/8 | 5 | 16 | 11 | 50 1/8 | 322 | 7 |
| ♦ *Walsh / Rick M. MacDonald / Rick M. MacDonald / 1987* | | | | | | | | | | | |

Photograph Courtesy of Buddy D. Baker

**BRITISH COLUMBIA PROVINCE RECORD**
**TYPICAL MULE DEER**
**SCORE: 199-5/8**
Locality: Princeton    Date: November 1979
Hunter: Buddy D. Baker

# BRITISH COLUMBIA

## TYPICAL MULE DEER

| Score | Length of Main Beam R | Length of Main Beam L | Inside Spread | Greatest Spread | Circumference at Smallest Place Between Burr and First Point R | Circumference at Smallest Place Between Burr and First Point L | Number of Points R | Number of Points L | Total of Lengths Abnormal Points | All-Time Rank | Prov. Rank |
|---|---|---|---|---|---|---|---|---|---|---|---|
| ♦ *Locality Killed / By Whom Killed / Owner / Date Killed* | | | | | | | | | | | |
| 199 5/8 | 27 5/8 | 26 | 21 5/8 | 25 3/8 | 5 5/8 | 5 6/8 | 5 | 5 | | 185 | 1 |
| ♦ *Princeton / Buddy D. Baker / Buddy D. Baker / 1979* | | | | | | | | | | | |
| 197 7/8 | 28 1/8 | 27 6/8 | 24 5/8 | 27 5/8 | 5 2/8 | 5 3/8 | 5 | 5 | | 247 | 2 |
| ♦ *Rossland / Robert Simm / Robert Simm / 1968* | | | | | | | | | | | |
| 197 5/8 | 28 6/8 | 27 4/8 | 23 1/8 | 27 4/8 | 5 1/8 | 5 1/8 | 5 | 5 | | 258 | 3 |
| ♦ *Kootenay River / Raymond Carry / Raymond Carry / 1982* | | | | | | | | | | | |
| 196 7/8 | 27 5/8 | 27 | 25 1/8 | 29 6/8 | 5 1/8 | 5 1/8 | 5 | 5 | | 296 | 4 |
| ♦ *Scherf Creek / Manuela Selby / Manuela Selby / 1984* | | | | | | | | | | | |
| 195 5/8 | 27 4/8 | 27 6/8 | 24 1/8 | 32 7/8 | 6 | 5 7/8 | 7 | 7 | 12 | 367 | 5 |
| ♦ *Slocan Valley / John Braun / John Braun / 1962* | | | | | | | | | | | |
| 195 4/8 | 26 2/8 | 26 4/8 | 24 2/8 | 29 2/8 | 5 3/8 | 5 2/8 | 5 | 5 | | 375 | 6 |
| ♦ *Princeton / Glen Stadler / Glen Stadler / 1958* | | | | | | | | | | | |
| 195 1/8 | 27 | 29 5/8 | 29 1/8 | 31 7/8 | 5 7/8 | 6 | 5 | 5 | | 397 | 7 |
| ♦ *Fruitvale / Allan Endersby / Allan Endersby / 1968* | | | | | | | | | | | |

**BRITISH COLUMBIA PROVINCE RECORD
NON-TYPICAL MULE DEER
SCORE: 265-3/8**
Locality: Tyaughton River    Date: September 1970
Hunter: Terry E. Crawford

# BRITISH COLUMBIA

## NON-TYPICAL MULE DEER

| Score | Length of Main Beam R | Length of Main Beam L | Inside Spread | Greatest Spread | Circumference at Smallest Place Between Burr and First Point R | Circumference at Smallest Place Between Burr and First Point L | Number of Points R | Number of Points L | Total of Lengths Abnormal Points | All-Time Rank | Prov. Rank |
|---|---|---|---|---|---|---|---|---|---|---|---|
| ♦ *Locality Killed / By Whom Killed / Owner / Date Killed* | | | | | | | | | | | |
| 265 3/8 | 25 6/8 | 25 1/8 | 21 5/8 | 29 4/8 | 5 3/8 | 5 3/8 | 13 | 14 | 73 4/8 | 79 | 1 |
| ♦ *Tyaughton River / Terry E. Crawford / Terry E. Crawford / 1970* | | | | | | | | | | | |
| 258 2/8 | 29 5/8 | 30 5/8 | 29 3/8 | 39 1/8 | 6 6/8 | 6 7/8 | 15 | 14 | 47 7/8 | 125 | 2 |
| ♦ *Rock Creek / George Whiting / B.C. Game Dept. / 1909* | | | | | | | | | | | |
| 244 5/8 | 26 | 25 | 18 6/8 | 28 6/8 | 5 5/8 | 5 4/8 | 15 | 20 | 63 7/8 | 254 | 3 |
| ♦ *Rossland / Victor Mattiazzi / Victor Mattiazzi / 1970* | | | | | | | | | | | |
| 241 3/8 | 19 | 24 6/8 | 20 | 31 6/8 | 6 2/8 | 6 4/8 | 12 | 15 | 63 7/8 | 300 | 4 |
| ♦ *Nakusp / Frank Vicen / Frank Vicen / 1967* | | | | | | | | | | | |
| 240 | 28 | 28 2/8 | 25 | 32 3/8 | 5 4/8 | 5 4/8 | 7 | 10 | 42 2/8 | 318 | 5 |
| ♦ *Kamloops / Ralph McLean / Ralph McLean / 1960* | | | | | | | | | | | |

Photograph Courtesy of Brett E. Seidle

**SASKATCHEWAN SECOND PLACE (TIE)**
**TYPICAL MULE DEER**
**SCORE: 197-5/8**
Locality: Beechy   Date: November 1983
Hunter: Brett E. Seidle

# SASKATCHEWAN

## TYPICAL MULE DEER

| Score | Length of Main Beam R | Length of Main Beam L | Inside Spread | Greatest Spread | Circumference at Smallest Place Between Burr and First Point R | Circumference at Smallest Place Between Burr and First Point L | Number of Points R | Number of Points L | Total of Lengths Abnormal Points | All-Time Rank | Prov. Rank |
|---|---|---|---|---|---|---|---|---|---|---|---|
| ♦ Locality Killed / By Whom Killed / Owner / Date Killed | | | | | | | | | | | |
| 199 2/8 | 27 1/8 | 25 4/8 | 26 | 30 1/8 | 5 | 5 2/8 | 7 | 5 | 5 4/8 | 196 | 1 |
| ♦ Beechy / Marvin Taylor / Marvin Taylor / 1961 | | | | | | | | | | | |
| 197 5/8 | 22 7/8 | 22 | 22 1/8 | 27 4/8 | 4 5/8 | 4 4/8 | 5 | 5 | | 258 | 2 |
| ♦ Major / Art Heintz / Art Heintz / 1961 | | | | | | | | | | | |
| 197 5/8 | 25 6/8 | 26 1/8 | 19 5/8 | 22 7/8 | 5 1/8 | 5 2/8 | 5 | 5 | | 258 | 2 |
| ♦ Beechy / Brett E. Seidle / Brett E. Seidle / 1983 | | | | | | | | | | | |
| 197 2/8 | 26 4/8 | 26 4/8 | 21 6/8 | 24 4/8 | 7 | 6 6/8 | 7 | 5 | 4 | 277 | 4 |
| ♦ Beechy / Pete Perrin / Pete Perrin / 1947 | | | | | | | | | | | |
| 195 2/8 | 26 4/8 | 25 5/8 | 26 4/8 | 32 4/8 | 4 2/8 | 4 2/8 | 5 | 5 | | 389 | 5 |
| ♦ Antelope Lake / Doug Westergaard / Doug Westergaard / 1977 | | | | | | | | | | | |

**SASKATCHEWAN PROVINCE RECORD**
**NON-TYPICAL MULE DEER**
**SCORE: 282-6/8**
Locality: Cabri    Date: 1962
Hunter: Robert Comba
Owner: Don Schaufler

# SASKATCHEWAN

## NON-TYPICAL MULE DEER

| Score | Length of Main Beam R | L | Inside Spread | Great-est Spread | Circumference at Smallest Place Between Burr and First Point R | L | Number of Points R | L | Total of Lengths Abnor-mal Points | All-Time Rank | Prov. Rank |
|---|---|---|---|---|---|---|---|---|---|---|---|
| Locality Killed / By Whom Killed / Owner / Date Killed | | | | | | | | | | | |
| 282 6/8 | 24 4/8 | 24 2/8 | 25 4/8 | 35 5/8 | 5 4/8 | 5 2/8 | 14 | 16 | 96 | 28 | 1 |
| ◆ Cabri / Robert Comba / Don Schaufler / 1962 | | | | | | | | | | | |
| 282 2/8 | 25 3/8 | 25 6/8 | 24 | 31 5/8 | 7 | 6 2/8 | 17 | 13 | 71 2/8 | 30 | 2 |
| ◆ Sasktchewan / Herman Cox / Herman Cox / 1947 | | | | | | | | | | | |
| 280 2/8 | 25 7/8 | 24 4/8 | 24 2/8 | 34 7/8 | 6 | 6 | 10 | 15 | 88 4/8 | 32 | 3 |
| ◆ Otthon / Unknown / Don Schaufler / 1940 | | | | | | | | | | | |
| 275 6/8 | 25 4/8 | 26 3/8 | 19 2/8 | 31 | 5 | 5 2/8 | 20 | 16 | 82 | 43 | 4 |
| ◆ Dahlton / Jim Hewitt / Jim Hewitt / 1932 | | | | | | | | | | | |
| 268 5/8 | 27 | 25 1/8 | 25 1/8 | 36 | 5 | 5 4/8 | 14 | 16 | 88 6/8 | 64 | 5 |
| ◆ Leader / Cocks Brothers / Richard Jensen / 1954 | | | | | | | | | | | |
| 256 4/8 | 24 | 24 5/8 | 25 2/8 | 34 2/8 | 6 | 6 1/8 | 12 | 11 | 57 7/8 | 145 | 6 |
| ◆ Portreeve / Mike Spies / Mike Spies / 1947 | | | | | | | | | | | |
| 253 4/8 | 25 6/8 | 26 5/8 | 30 2/8 | 34 6/8 | 4 6/8 | 4 6/8 | 11 | 11 | 58 5/8 | 162 | 7 |
| ◆ East End / Henry Leroy / Henry Leroy / 1960 | | | | | | | | | | | |
| 248 | 23 3/8 | 22 4/8 | 23 2/8 | 33 1/8 | 5 6/8 | 5 6/8 | 12 | 14 | 57 6/8 | 210 | 8 |
| ◆ Val Marie / J. Milton Brown / J. Milton Brown / 1958 | | | | | | | | | | | |
| 247 7/8 | 21 2/8 | 21 6/8 | 24 6/8 | 36 5/8 | 5 4/8 | 5 7/8 | 9 | 10 | 61 5/8 | 213 | 9 |
| ◆ Cabri / Enos Mitchell, Jr. / Enos Mitchell, Jr. / 1960 | | | | | | | | | | | |
| 242 3/8 | 23 1/8 | 22 3/8 | 17 3/8 | 29 2/8 | 4 7/8 | 5 | 12 | 12 | 61 4/8 | 287 | 10 |
| ◆ Arborfield / Joseph Fournier / Joseph Fournier / 1930 | | | | | | | | | | | |
| 242 1/8 | 20 7/8 | 23 2/8 | 17 4/8 | 31 1/8 | 6 | 5 7/8 | 12 | 11 | 77 1/8 | 290 | 11 |
| ◆ Cabri / Gordon Millward / Gordon Millward / 1960 | | | | | | | | | | | |
| 268 1/8 | 27 4/8 | 27 7/8 | 30 3/8 | 38 3/8 | 5 2/8 | 5 5/8 | 14 | 14 | 68 4/8 | * | * |
| ◆ Elbow / Allan J. Selzler / Allan J. Selzler / 1986 | | | | | | | | | | | |

Photograph by Wm. H. Nesbitt

**MEXICO RECORD**
**TYPICAL MULE DEER**
**SCORE: 204-3/8**
Locality: Sonora    Date: December 1986
Hunter: David V. Collis

# MEXICO

## TYPICAL MULE DEER

| Score | Length of Main Beam R | Length of Main Beam L | Inside Spread | Great-est Spread | Circumference at Smallest Place Between Burr and First Point R | Circumference at Smallest Place Between Burr and First Point L | Number of Points R | Number of Points L | Total of Lengths Abnor-mal Points | All-Time Rank | Mex. Rank |
|---|---|---|---|---|---|---|---|---|---|---|---|
| | | | | | ◆ Locality Killed / By Whom Killed / Owner / Date Killed | | | | | | |
| 204 3/8 | 29 2/8 | 30 1/8 | 35 | 35 5/8 | 4 4/8 | 4 5/8 | 5 | 5 | | 60 | 1 |
| | ◆ Sonora / David V. Collis / David V. Collis / 1986 | | | | | | | | | | |
| 200 7/8 | 28 7/8 | 29 | 36 5/8 | 38 6/8 | 5 4/8 | 5 5/8 | 7 | 5 | 5 3/8 | 140 | 2 |
| | ◆ Sonora / Toby J. Johnson / Toby J. Johnson / 1986 | | | | | | | | | | |
| 198 2/8 | 25 6/8 | 25 5/8 | 24 3/8 | 32 5/8 | 5 1/8 | 5 | 5 | 6 | 3 1/8 | 229 | 3 |
| | ◆ Sonora / Heinz G. Holdorf / Heinz G. Holdorf / 1966 | | | | | | | | | | |
| 197 | 25 4/8 | 25 6/8 | 25 | 29 | 5 1/8 | 5 2/8 | 6 | 6 | | 288 | 4 |
| | ◆ Sonora / J.G. Cigarroa, Sr. / J.G. Cigarroa, Sr. / 1957 | | | | | | | | | | |
| 189 6/8 | 23 5/8 | 24 2/8 | 27 6/8 | 29 6/8 | 4 7/8 | 4 6/8 | 5 | 5 | | 422 | 5 |
| | ◆ Sonora / Joseph J. Luterbach / Joseph J. Luterbach / 1986 | | | | | | | | | | |

TOP 10 COLUMBIA BLACKTAIL LISTINGS INDEX

TOP 10 SITKA BLACKTAIL LISTINGS INDEX

# Tabulations of Recorded Columbia and Sitka Blacktail Deer

The trophy data shown on the following pages is taken from score charts in the Records Archives of the Boone and Crockett Club. A comparison of all-time rankings of this book with those of the last all-time records book (*Records of North American Big Game*, 9th Ed., 1988) will show some significant differences. This is generally caused by two factors: the addition of trophies accepted during the 20th Awards entry period (1986-1988) and elimination of the "double penalty" for excessive inside spread. The rankings shown in this book are official and supercede those of the all-time records and other publications.

Columbia and Sitka blacktails are subspecies of the common mule deer, with smaller racks and body size. Found in the coastal areas of the pacific states, geographic boundaries describe the areas from which trophies may be entered. (See the 9th Ed. all-time records and/or *Measuring and Scoring N.A. Big Game Trophies* for the detailed boundary descriptions.)

The scores and rank shown are final, except for trophies shown with an asterisk. The asterisk identifies entry scores subject to final certification by an Awards Panel of Judges. The asterisk can be removed (except in the case of a potential World's Record) by the submission of two additional, independent scorings by Official Measurers of the Boone and Crockett Club. The Records Committee of the Club will review the three scorings available (original plus two additional) and determine which, if any, will be accepted in lieu of the Judges Panel measurement. When the score has been accepted as final by the Records Committee, the asterisk will be removed in future editions of the all-time records book and other publications. In the case of a potential World's Record, the trophy *must* come before a Judges Panel at the end of an entry period. Only a Judges Panel can certify a World's Record and finalize its score. Asterisked trophies are shown at the end of their category, without rank.

Photograph by J.J. McBride

**CALIFORNIA STATE RECORD**
**COLUMBIA BLACKTAIL DEER**
**SCORE: 166-2/8**
Locality: Glenn Co.    Date: September 1949
Hunter: Peter Gerbo
Owner: Loaned to B&C National Collection by Dennis P. Garcia

# CALIFORNIA

## COLUMBIA BLACKTAIL DEER

| Score | Length of Main Beam R | Length of Main Beam L | Inside Spread | Greatest Spread | Circumference at Smallest Place Between Burr and First Point R | Circumference at Smallest Place Between Burr and First Point L | Number of Points R | Number of Points L | Total of Lengths Abnormal Points | All-Time Rank | State Rank |
|---|---|---|---|---|---|---|---|---|---|---|---|
| | ◆ Locality Killed / By Whom Killed / Owner / Date Killed | | | | | | | | | | |
| 166 2/8 | 23 2/8 | 24 3/8 | 26 5/8 | 30 5/8 | 5 4/8 | 5 1/8 | 6 | 6 | 8 1/8 | 6 | 1 |
| | ◆ Glenn County / Peter Gerbo / Loaned to B&C Natl. Collection / 1949 by Dennis P. Garcia | | | | | | | | | | |
| 163 1/8 | 23 3/8 | 21 5/8 | 20 4/8 | 23 | 5 | 4 7/8 | 7 | 6 | 3 5/8 | 10 | 2 |
| | ◆ Siskiyou County / Frank Barago / Frank Barago / 1945 | | | | | | | | | | |
| 162 3/8 | 22 | 22 1/8 | 18 1/8 | 20 7/8 | 4 4/8 | 4 4/8 | 5 | 5 | | 13 | 3 |
| | ◆ Trinity County / Sidney A. Nystrom / Sidney A. Nystrom / 1961 | | | | | | | | | | |
| 162 2/8 | 24 5/8 | 25 1/8 | 19 2/8 | 22 5/8 | 4 2/8 | 4 2/8 | 5 | 5 | | 14 | 4 |
| | ◆ Glenn County / Roger L. Spencer / Roger L. Spencer / 1956 | | | | | | | | | | |
| 160 4/8 | 23 5/8 | 24 3/8 | 21 | 23 4/8 | 4 7/8 | 4 7/8 | 5 | 6 | 2 | 17 | 5 |
| | ◆ Siskiyou County / John L. Masters / John L. Masters / 1967 | | | | | | | | | | |
| 160 3/8 | 23 1/8 | 23 5/8 | 26 5/8 | 30 | 4 | 4 | 6 | 5 | 2 | 18 | 6 |
| | ◆ Trinity County / A.H. Hilbert / Jack T. Brusatori / 1929 | | | | | | | | | | |
| 160 1/8 | 25 1/8 | 24 7/8 | 24 7/8 | 25 5/8 | 5 | 5 5/8 | 5 | 4 | | 19 | 7 |
| | ◆ Trinity County / Lorio Verzasconi / Lorio Verzasconi / 1946 | | | | | | | | | | |
| 159 7/8 | 22 2/8 | 21 7/8 | 16 3/8 | 20 4/8 | 4 | 4 | 5 | 5 | | 20 | 8 |
| | ◆ Siskiyou County / John C. Ley / E.R. Cummins / 1937 | | | | | | | | | | |
| 159 7/8 | 22 5/8 | 22 3/8 | 21 7/8 | 23 4/8 | 4 5/8 | 4 4/8 | 5 | 5 | | 20 | 8 |
| | ◆ Siskiyou County / Francis M. Sullivan / Francis M. Sullivan / 1951 | | | | | | | | | | |
| 159 4/8 | 24 4/8 | 23 6/8 | 14 7/8 | 17 | 4 5/8 | 4 4/8 | 6 | 6 | 2 7/8 | 24 | 10 |
| | ◆ Mendocino County / Russ McLennan / Russ McLennan / 1984 | | | | | | | | | | |
| 159 1/8 | 21 5/8 | 22 1/8 | 19 1/8 | 23 5/8 | 4 6/8 | 4 6/8 | 5 | 5 | | 25 | 11 |
| | ◆ Trinity County / A.H. Hilbert / A.H. Hilbert / 1939 | | | | | | | | | | |
| 158 4/8 | 24 | 24 4/8 | 22 5/8 | 24 5/8 | 4 5/8 | 4 5/8 | 6 | 6 | 4 5/8 | 27 | 12 |
| | ◆ Trinity County / David Phillips / David Phillips / 1974 | | | | | | | | | | |
| 158 | 21 7/8 | 21 7/8 | 18 2/8 | 20 6/8 | 4 4/8 | 4 4/8 | 5 | 5 | | 30 | 13 |
| | ◆ Trinity County / Charles A. Strickland / Charles A. Strickland / 1984 | | | | | | | | | | |

# CALIFORNIA COLUMBIA BLACKTAIL DEER *(continued)*

| Score | Length of Main Beam R | L | Inside Spread | Greatest Spread | Circumference at Smallest Place Between Burr and First Point R | L | Number of Points R | L | Total of Lengths Abnormal Points | All-Time Rank | State Rank |
|---|---|---|---|---|---|---|---|---|---|---|---|
| | | | | | | | | | | | |
| 157 5/8 | 22 6/8 | 23 3/8 | 21 5/8 | 25 4/8 | 4 2/8 | 4 3/8 | 5 | 5 | | 32 | 14 |
| ♦ Shasta County / Richard L. Sobrato / Richard L. Sobrato / 1969 | | | | | | | | | | | |
| 157 | 24 7/8 | 26 1/8 | 24 1/8 | 28 6/8 | 5 | 5 1/8 | 5 | 7 | 10 5/8 | 34 | 15 |
| ♦ Santa Clara County / Brud Eade / Brud Eade / 1961 | | | | | | | | | | | |
| 155 2/8 | 21 5/8 | 21 6/8 | 23 1/8 | 25 1/8 | 3 3/8 | 3 4/8 | 5 | 5 | | 41 | 16 |
| ♦ Trinity County / Fred Heider / Fred Heider / 1927 | | | | | | | | | | | |
| 155 2/8 | 22 1/8 | 22 7/8 | 19 2/8 | 23 6/8 | 5 3/8 | 4 7/8 | 5 | 5 | | 41 | 16 |
| ♦ Mendocino County / Gary Land / Gary Land / 1972 | | | | | | | | | | | |
| 155 1/8 | 21 | 21 6/8 | 18 5/8 | 22 7/8 | 4 3/8 | 4 3/8 | 4 | 4 | | 45 | 18 |
| ♦ Shasta County / Vance Corrigan / Vance Corrigan / 1956 | | | | | | | | | | | |
| 154 6/8 | 20 4/8 | 20 3/8 | 20 4/8 | 23 6/8 | 4 5/8 | 4 5/8 | 4 | 4 | | 46 | 19 |
| ♦ Mendocino County / W.A. McAllister / W.A. McAllister / 1968 | | | | | | | | | | | |
| 154 5/8 | 24 | 22 7/8 | 23 3/8 | 25 1/8 | 4 3/8 | 4 4/8 | 5 | 5 | | 48 | 20 |
| ♦ Humboldt County / Phillip Brown / Phillip Brown / 1962 | | | | | | | | | | | |
| 154 5/8 | 24 7/8 | 24 3/8 | 21 | 24 4/8 | 4 7/8 | 4 6/8 | 6 | 7 | 4 5/8 | 48 | 20 |
| ♦ Siskiyou County / Darrell R. Jones / Darrell R. Jones / 1984 | | | | | | | | | | | |
| 154 1/8 | 21 6/8 | 22 2/8 | 18 6/8 | 24 1/8 | 4 6/8 | 4 7/8 | 6 | 7 | 4 1/8 | 50 | 22 |
| ♦ Glenn County / Mitchell A. Thorson / Mitchell A. Thorson / 1969 | | | | | | | | | | | |
| 154 | 26 4/8 | 25 7/8 | 28 6/8 | 35 3/8 | 4 4/8 | 4 6/8 | 6 | 6 | 9 6/8 | 52 | 23 |
| ♦ Trinity County / A.H. Hilbert / A.H. Hilbert / 1930 | | | | | | | | | | | |
| 153 3/8 | 21 2/8 | 21 5/8 | 17 4/8 | 21 6/8 | 5 | 5 | 6 | 5 | 4 3/8 | 56 | 24 |
| ♦ Tehama County / James L. Carr / James L. Carr / 1979 | | | | | | | | | | | |
| 153 | 22 6/8 | 23 6/8 | 14 6/8 | 16 5/8 | 4 3/8 | 4 5/8 | 6 | 5 | 1 4/8 | 59 | 25 |
| ♦ Siskiyou County / John Carmichael / J.A. Brose / 1969 | | | | | | | | | | | |
| 152 5/8 | 22 1/8 | 22 | 19 5/8 | 22 7/8 | 4 | 4 3/8 | 5 | 5 | | 60 | 26 |
| ♦ Mendocino County / Harold D. Schneider / H.D. & M.J. Schneider / 1979 | | | | | | | | | | | |
| 152 4/8 | 23 | 23 | 20 | 22 2/8 | 4 | 4 | 6 | 7 | 4 | 61 | 27 |
| ♦ Tehama County / Don Strickler / Don Strickler / 1979 | | | | | | | | | | | |
| 152 1/8 | 22 4/8 | 21 4/8 | 17 7/8 | 20 3/8 | 4 2/8 | 4 1/8 | 5 | 5 | | 62 | 28 |
| ♦ Trinity County / Robert V. Strickland / Robert V. Strickland / 1966 | | | | | | | | | | | |
| 152 | 23 3/8 | 22 7/8 | 21 6/8 | 23 2/8 | 4 4/8 | 4 4/8 | 5 | 5 | | 64 | 29 |
| ♦ Yolo County / Herman Darneille / E.L. Gallup / 1943 | | | | | | | | | | | |
| 151 5/8 | 22 1/8 | 21 7/8 | 22 5/8 | 24 2/8 | 4 6/8 | 4 6/8 | 5 | 5 | | 68 | 30 |
| ♦ Siskiyou County / Jim A. Turnbow / Jim A. Turnbow / 1973 | | | | | | | | | | | |

*♦ Locality Killed / By Whom Killed / Owner / Date Killed*

| Score | Length of Main Beam R | Length of Main Beam L | Inside Spread | Greatest Spread | Circumference at Smallest Place Between Burr and First Point R | Circumference at Smallest Place Between Burr and First Point L | Number of Points R | Number of Points L | Total of Lengths Abnormal Points | All-Time Rank | State Rank |
|---|---|---|---|---|---|---|---|---|---|---|---|
| ♦ *Locality Killed / By Whom Killed / Owner / Date Killed* | | | | | | | | | | | |
| 151 | 20 ⅛ | 21 | 19 2/8 | 23 2/8 | 4 2/8 | 4 ⅛ | 5 | 5 | | 72 | 31 |
| ♦ *Humboldt County / Elgin T. Gates / Elgin T. Gates / 1952* | | | | | | | | | | | |
| 150 6/8 | 22 | 21 4/8 | 17 | 21 | 4 2/8 | 4 2/8 | 5 | 5 | | 76 | 32 |
| ♦ *Siskiyou County / Raymond Whittaker / Raymond Whittaker / 1978* | | | | | | | | | | | |
| 150 4/8 | 24 ⅛ | 24 2/8 | 19 ⅝ | 21 6/8 | 5 ⅛ | 5 | 6 | 6 | 2 ⅞ | 78 | 33 |
| ♦ *Trinity County / E.L. Brightenstine / E.L. Brightenstine / 1978* | | | | | | | | | | | |
| 150 ⅛ | 22 4/8 | 22 | 16 ⅛ | 20 ⅛ | 4 ⅛ | 4 ⅛ | 5 | 5 | | 79 | 34 |
| ♦ *Napa County / Robert G. Wiley / Robert G. Wiley / 1965* | | | | | | | | | | | |
| 150 ⅛ | 21 | 21 | 20 ⅛ | 22 ⅞ | 3 ⅞ | 3 ⅞ | 5 | 5 | | 79 | 34 |
| ♦ *Trinity County / Thomas L. Hough / Thomas L. Hough / 1969* | | | | | | | | | | | |
| 150 | 24 | 25 ⅛ | 24 | 26 | 4 ⅝ | 4 4/8 | 4 | 4 | | 83 | 36 |
| ♦ *Napa County / W.C. Lambert / W.C. Lambert / 1957* | | | | | | | | | | | |
| 150 | 20 ⅞ | 20 2/8 | 20 | 22 6/8 | 5 ⅜ | 5 ⅜ | 4 | 4 | | 83 | 36 |
| ♦ *Lake County / Bruce Strickler / Bruce Strickler / 1970* | | | | | | | | | | | |
| 150 | 20 4/8 | 21 ⅞ | 16 6/8 | 19 | 4 2/8 | 4 2/8 | 5 | 5 | | 83 | 36 |
| ♦ *Tehama County / Marion F. Foster / Barbara J. Foster / 1971* | | | | | | | | | | | |
| 149 6/8 | 22 ⅞ | 22 | 18 ⅞ | 24 4/8 | 5 | 5 | 5 | 6 | 1 ⅞ | 88 | 39 |
| ♦ *Siskiyou County / Emit C. Jones / Emit C. Jones / 1961* | | | | | | | | | | | |
| 149 ⅝ | 20 | 21 ⅜ | 17 ⅞ | 22 2/8 | 4 4/8 | 4 4/8 | 5 | 5 | | 89 | 40 |
| ♦ *Humboldt County / Robert C. Stephens / Robert C. Stephens / 1961* | | | | | | | | | | | |
| 149 4/8 | 22 ⅝ | 21 | 20 6/8 | 23 2/8 | 5 ⅛ | 5 2/8 | 5 | 5 | | 91 | 41 |
| ♦ *Glenn County / George Stewart, Jr. / George Stewart, Jr. / 1957* | | | | | | | | | | | |
| 149 ⅜ | 22 ⅜ | 21 2/8 | 20 ⅜ | 23 6/8 | 5 2/8 | 5 4/8 | 5 | 5 | | 92 | 42 |
| ♦ *Trinity County / Lyle L. Johnson / Lyle L. Johnson / 1979* | | | | | | | | | | | |
| 149 2/8 | 24 ⅜ | 24 ⅜ | 17 6/8 | 20 ⅞ | 5 4/8 | 5 4/8 | 8 | 8 | 20 6/8 | 93 | 43 |
| ♦ *Trinity County / Lauren A. Johnson / Lauren A. Johnson / 1964* | | | | | | | | | | | |
| 148 ⅞ | 22 ⅛ | 21 ⅜ | 18 | 21 4/8 | 4 ⅞ | 4 ⅞ | 6 | 5 | 1 ⅛ | 97 | 44 |
| ♦ *Humboldt County / F. Joe Parker / F. Joe Parker / 1946* | | | | | | | | | | | |
| 148 4/8 | 23 2/8 | 22 ⅞ | 20 6/8 | 25 ⅜ | 4 ⅜ | 4 ⅝ | 5 | 5 | | 99 | 45 |
| ♦ *Mendocino County / N.D. Windbigler / N.D. Windbigler / 1969* | | | | | | | | | | | |
| 148 2/8 | 24 | 24 4/8 | 23 4/8 | 26 | 6 2/8 | 5 6/8 | 6 | 6 | 4 2/8 | 104 | 46 |
| ♦ *Shasta County / Jerry W. Sander / Jerry W. Sander / 1977* | | | | | | | | | | | |
| 147 ⅞ | 22 | 22 ⅜ | 18 ⅝ | | 4 ⅛ | 4 2/8 | 5 | 5 | | 106 | 47 |
| ♦ *Glenn County / Emmet T. Frye / Emmet T. Frye / 1937* | | | | | | | | | | | |

| Score | Length of Main Beam R | L | Inside Spread | Greatest Spread | Circumference at Smallest Place Between Burr and First Point R | L | Number of Points R | L | Total of Lengths Abnormal Points | All-Time Rank | State Rank |
|---|---|---|---|---|---|---|---|---|---|---|---|
| | ◆ *Locality Killed  /  By Whom Killed  /  Owner  /  Date Killed* | | | | | | | | | | |
| 147 7/8 | 20 6/8 | 20 7/8 | 21 6/8 | 23 | 5 | 4 7/8 | 5 | 5 | | 106 | 47 |
| | ◆ *Trinity County  /  Chauncy Willburn  /  Chauncy Willburn  /  1955* | | | | | | | | | | |
| 147 7/8 | 22 1/8 | 22 2/8 | 18 5/8 | 21 3/8 | 4 2/8 | 4 3/8 | 6 | 6 | 4 4/8 | 106 | 47 |
| | ◆ *Humboldt County  /  Melvin H. Kadle  /  Melvin H. Kadle  /  1979* | | | | | | | | | | |
| 147 6/8 | 19 7/8 | 21 7/8 | 22 1/8 | 25 | 4 6/8 | 4 7/8 | 6 | 5 | 2 3/8 | 109 | 50 |
| | ◆ *Siskiyou County  /  James C. Elliott  /  James C. Elliott  /  1974* | | | | | | | | | | |
| 147 5/8 | 23 | 23 6/8 | 19 5/8 | 22 7/8 | 4 4/8 | 4 3/8 | 5 | 4 | | 110 | 51 |
| | ◆ *Santa Clara County  /  Maitland Armstrong  /  Maitland Armstrong  /  1944* | | | | | | | | | | |
| 147 5/8 | 22 3/8 | 22 7/8 | 22 3/8 | 25 3/8 | 4 5/8 | 4 5/8 | 4 | 4 | | 110 | 51 |
| | ◆ *Mendocino County  /  Richard Sterling  /  Richard Sterling  /  1986* | | | | | | | | | | |
| 147 1/8 | 21 2/8 | 21 | 16 7/8 | 19 2/8 | 4 3/8 | 4 3/8 | 5 | 6 | 1 6/8 | 113 | 53 |
| | ◆ *Trinity County  /  Craig L. Brown  /  Craig & Joy Brown  /  1980* | | | | | | | | | | |
| 147 | 18 | 18 2/8 | 17 | 19 2/8 | 4 3/8 | 4 2/8 | 5 | 5 | | 114 | 54 |
| | ◆ *Siskiyou County  /  Ray Whittaker  /  Ray Whittaker  /  1966* | | | | | | | | | | |
| 146 6/8 | 20 | 20 4/8 | 18 4/8 | 22 | 4 3/8 | 4 3/8 | 5 | 5 | | 117 | 55 |
| | ◆ *Siskiyou County  /  Richard Silva  /  Richard Silva  /  1958* | | | | | | | | | | |
| 146 4/8 | 21 2/8 | 21 2/8 | 17 2/8 | 19 1/8 | 4 6/8 | 4 7/8 | 5 | 5 | | 120 | 56 |
| | ◆ *Glenn County  /  L.E. Germeshausen  /  L.E. Germeshausen  /  1983* | | | | | | | | | | |
| 146 3/8 | 23 4/8 | 23 6/8 | 24 6/8 | 26 3/8 | 4 5/8 | 4 5/8 | 5 | 5 | 1 1/8 | 122 | 57 |
| | ◆ *Trinity County  /  Carroll E. Dow  /  Carroll E. Dow  /  1962* | | | | | | | | | | |
| 146 2/8 | 21 6/8 | 22 3/8 | 13 6/8 | 15 4/8 | 5 6/8 | 5 6/8 | 5 | 5 | | 123 | 58 |
| | ◆ *Shasta County  /  William H. Taylor  /  William H. Taylor  /  1971* | | | | | | | | | | |
| 146 1/8 | 23 1/8 | 23 5/8 | 19 1/8 | 21 2/8 | 4 5/8 | 4 | 4 | 4 | | 125 | 59 |
| | ◆ *Trinity County  /  Kenneth M. Brown  /  Kenneth M. Brown  /  1972* | | | | | | | | | | |
| 145 7/8 | 23 4/8 | 23 3/8 | 22 | 27 2/8 | 5 3/8 | 5 4/8 | 6 | 8 | 12 5/8 | 127 | 60 |
| | ◆ *Lake County  /  Floyd Goodrich  /  Mrs. William Olson  /  1926* | | | | | | | | | | |
| 145 7/8 | 22 | 23 5/8 | 16 3/8 | 19 7/8 | 4 5/8 | 4 7/8 | 5 | 5 | | 127 | 60 |
| | ◆ *Napa County  /  C.H.N. Dailey  /  Tony Stoer  /  1948* | | | | | | | | | | |
| 145 7/8 | 22 6/8 | 22 6/8 | 21 7/8 | 27 3/8 | 4 3/8 | 4 5/8 | 5 | 5 | | 127 | 60 |
| | ◆ *Shasta County  /  Gary J. Miller  /  Gary J. Miller  /  1968* | | | | | | | | | | |
| 145 5/8 | 22 4/8 | 23 | 18 7/8 | 20 5/8 | 4 1/8 | 4 1/8 | 6 | 5 | 1 6/8 | 133 | 63 |
| | ◆ *Humboldt County  /  Joe Dickerson  /  Jay Grunert  /  1962* | | | | | | | | | | |
| 145 5/8 | 21 2/8 | 21 1/8 | 19 5/8 | 21 1/8 | 3 7/8 | 4 | 5 | 5 | | 133 | 63 |
| | ◆ *Siskiyou County  /  Wallace D. Barlow  /  Wallace D. Barlow  /  1985* | | | | | | | | | | |

| Score | Length of Main Beam R | L | Inside Spread | Greatest Spread | Circumference at Smallest Place Between Burr and First Point R | L | Number of Points R | L | Total of Lengths Abnormal Points | All-Time Rank | State Rank |
|---|---|---|---|---|---|---|---|---|---|---|---|
| | ♦ *Locality Killed  /  By Whom Killed  /  Owner  /  Date Killed* | | | | | | | | | | |
| 145 3/8 | 22 3/8 | 21 | 23 4/8 | 26 1/8 | 4 5/8 | 4 6/8 | 5 | 5 | | 137 | 65 |
| | ♦ *Mendocino County  /  Paul M. Holleman II  /  Paul M. Holleman II  /  1976* | | | | | | | | | | |
| 145 2/8 | 22 4/8 | 22 5/8 | 21 | 26 | 5 3/8 | 5 1/8 | 7 | 9 | 15 2/8 | 138 | 66 |
| | ♦ *Tehama County  /  Clint Heiber  /  Clint Heiber  /  1979* | | | | | | | | | | |
| 145 1/8 | 23 5/8 | 23 4/8 | 23 3/8 | 24 6/8 | 5 1/8 | 5 2/8 | 5 | 5 | | 143 | 67 |
| | ♦ *Tehama County  /  Lamar G. Hanson  /  Lamar G. Hanson  /  1972* | | | | | | | | | | |
| 145 | 22 2/8 | 21 4/8 | 21 2/8 | 24 4/8 | 5 1/8 | 5 1/8 | 7 | 5 | 6 4/8 | 145 | 68 |
| | ♦ *Mendocino County  /  Ralph I. Sibley  /  Ralph I. Sibley  /  1986* | | | | | | | | | | |
| 144 6/8 | 22 2/8 | 22 4/8 | 22 4/8 | 26 5/8 | 4 4/8 | 4 6/8 | 5 | 5 | | 149 | 69 |
| | ♦ *Mendocino County  /  Richard Vannelli  /  Richard Vannelli  /  1970* | | | | | | | | | | |
| 144 4/8 | 21 4/8 | 21 3/8 | 19 4/8 | 21 5/8 | 4 3/8 | 4 2/8 | 5 | 5 | | 154 | 70 |
| | ♦ *Shasta County  /  Ernie Young  /  Chet Young  /  1953* | | | | | | | | | | |
| 144 3/8 | 22 1/8 | 23 3/8 | 21 3/8 | 23 3/8 | 5 | 5 2/8 | 5 | 4 | | 158 | 71 |
| | ♦ *Santa Clara County  /  Maitland Armstrong  /  Maitland Armstrong  /  1946* | | | | | | | | | | |
| 144 3/8 | 21 | 20 7/8 | 16 5/8 | 18 2/8 | 4 7/8 | 4 5/8 | 5 | 5 | | 158 | 71 |
| | ♦ *Humboldt County  /  Gerald Wescott  /  Gerald Wescott  /  1980* | | | | | | | | | | |
| 144 2/8 | 21 | 22 4/8 | 20 4/8 | 24 4/8 | 4 4/8 | 4 4/8 | 5 | 5 | | 160 | 73 |
| | ♦ *Mendocino County  /  Frank Kester  /  Frank Kester  /  1981* | | | | | | | | | | |
| 143 7/8 | 20 5/8 | 19 5/8 | 20 3/8 | 23 | 5 | 5 1/8 | 5 | 5 | | 167 | 74 |
| | ♦ *Humboldt County  /  Lois C. Miller  /  Lois C. Miller  /  1986* | | | | | | | | | | |
| 143 6/8 | 20 5/8 | 20 2/8 | 19 7/8 | 21 3/8 | 5 2/8 | 5 2/8 | 6 | 6 | 2 1/8 | 170 | 75 |
| | ♦ *Tehama County  /  Clint Heiber  /  Clint Heiber  /  1978* | | | | | | | | | | |
| 143 6/8 | 19 5/8 | 19 4/8 | 15 2/8 | 19 5/8 | 4 7/8 | 4 6/8 | 5 | 6 | 2 | 170 | 75 |
| | ♦ *Mendocino County  /  Mark Ciancio  /  Mark Ciancio  /  1986* | | | | | | | | | | |
| 143 5/8 | 20 4/8 | 20 4/8 | 18 5/8 | 22 1/8 | 4 4/8 | 4 4/8 | 4 | 4 | | 174 | 77 |
| | ♦ *Siskiyou County  /  Emit C. Jones  /  Emit C. Jones  /  1960* | | | | | | | | | | |
| 143 5/8 | 20 5/8 | 19 3/8 | 18 5/8 | 22 7/8 | 4 1/8 | 4 2/8 | 5 | 5 | | 174 | 77 |
| | ♦ *Trinity County  /  Kenneth L. Cogle, Jr.  /  Kenneth L. Cogle, Jr.  /  1985* | | | | | | | | | | |
| 143 4/8 | 21 | 20 4/8 | 17 | 19 4/8 | 4 6/8 | 4 6/8 | 5 | 5 | | 177 | 79 |
| | ♦ *Trinity County  /  Barry Griffin  /  Barry Griffin  /  1983* | | | | | | | | | | |
| 143 2/8 | 22 3/8 | 22 6/8 | 21 4/8 | 23 3/8 | 4 2/8 | 4 2/8 | 5 | 5 | | 182 | 80 |
| | ♦ *Lake County  /  Mario Sereni, Jr.  /  Mario Sereni, Jr.  /  1965* | | | | | | | | | | |
| 143 2/8 | 19 5/8 | 19 4/8 | 17 2/8 | 19 7/8 | 4 | 4 | 5 | 5 | | 182 | 80 |
| | ♦ *Humboldt County  /  Jack Stedman  /  Jack Stedman  /  1965* | | | | | | | | | | |

| Score | Length of Main Beam R | L | Inside Spread | Greatest Spread | Circumference at Smallest Place Between Burr and First Point R | L | Number of Points R | L | Total of Lengths Abnormal Points | All-Time Rank | State Rank |
|---|---|---|---|---|---|---|---|---|---|---|---|
| 143 2/8 | 26 | 26 | 25 | 30 | 4 6/8 | 4 6/8 | 5 | 6 | 9 4/8 | 182 | 80 |
| ◆ *Mendocino County / George W. Rogers / George W. Rogers / 1977* | | | | | | | | | | | |
| 143 1/8 | 22 | 22 1/8 | 18 1/8 | 19 5/8 | 4 1/8 | 4 | 5 | 5 | | 187 | 83 |
| ◆ *Humboldt County / Mitchell A. Thorson / Mitchell A. Thorson / 1965* | | | | | | | | | | | |
| 142 5/8 | 20 2/8 | 20 | 16 5/8 | 22 4/8 | 4 1/8 | 4 | 5 | 5 | | 193 | 84 |
| ◆ *Santa Clara County / Picked Up / Ray & Neal Haera / PR 1966* | | | | | | | | | | | |
| 142 5/8 | 22 5/8 | 22 6/8 | 19 7/8 | 22 6/8 | 4 2/8 | 4 2/8 | 5 | 5 | | 193 | 84 |
| ◆ *Santa Clara County / Picked Up / Russel Rasmussen / PR 1966* | | | | | | | | | | | |
| 142 5/8 | 21 4/8 | 20 3/8 | 19 7/8 | 22 2/8 | 4 4/8 | 4 3/8 | 4 | 4 | | 193 | 84 |
| ◆ *Trinity County / Larry Brown / Larry Brown / 1979* | | | | | | | | | | | |
| 142 5/8 | 23 1/8 | 22 1/8 | 20 1/8 | 24 | 4 6/8 | 4 1/8 | 7 | 6 | 7 | 193 | 84 |
| ◆ *Tehama County / Kenneth R. Hall / Kenneth R. Hall / 1979* | | | | | | | | | | | |
| 142 4/8 | 22 2/8 | 22 6/8 | 13 3/8 | 15 3/8 | 4 6/8 | 4 6/8 | 4 | 5 | 1 3/8 | 199 | 88 |
| ◆ *Trinity County / Jace Comfort / Jace Comfort / 1965* | | | | | | | | | | | |
| 142 3/8 | 20 6/8 | 20 7/8 | 17 3/8 | 22 | 4 3/8 | 4 5/8 | 5 | 5 | | 203 | 89 |
| ◆ *Laytonville / Byron J. Rowland, Jr. / Byron J. Rowland, Jr. / 1964* | | | | | | | | | | | |
| 142 3/8 | 23 | 22 | 19 3/8 | 21 4/8 | 4 | 4 | 5 | 4 | | 203 | 89 |
| ◆ *Humboldt County / Darol L. Damm / Darol L. Damm / 1976* | | | | | | | | | | | |
| 142 2/8 | 23 4/8 | 23 2/8 | 17 | 20 1/8 | 4 2/8 | 4 1/8 | 6 | 5 | 4 4/8 | 205 | 91 |
| ◆ *Mendocino County / James A. Shelton / James A. Shelton / 1944* | | | | | | | | | | | |
| 142 1/8 | 21 3/8 | 22 3/8 | 19 7/8 | 22 6/8 | 5 1/8 | 5 1/8 | 5 | 4 | | 207 | 92 |
| ◆ *Shasta County / Richard R. Lowell / Richard R. Lowell / 1953* | | | | | | | | | | | |
| 141 7/8 | 21 4/8 | 21 2/8 | 17 7/8 | 20 6/8 | 4 1/8 | 5 | 5 | 5 | | 214 | 93 |
| ◆ *Trinity County / Pedro H. Henrich / Pedro H. Henrich / 1977* | | | | | | | | | | | |
| 141 5/8 | 19 7/8 | 19 6/8 | 20 3/8 | 25 1/8 | 4 | 4 2/8 | 5 | 5 | | 220 | 94 |
| ◆ *Trinity County / A.H. Hilbert / A.H. Hilbert / PR 1955* | | | | | | | | | | | |
| 141 4/8 | 21 2/8 | 21 1/8 | 16 2/8 | 18 6/8 | 4 2/8 | 4 2/8 | 5 | 5 | | 222 | 95 |
| ◆ *Mendocino County / Greg Rocha / Greg Rocha / 1985* | | | | | | | | | | | |
| 141 4/8 | 20 7/8 | 20 4/8 | 20 | 22 3/8 | 4 1/8 | 4 4/8 | 5 | 5 | | 222 | 95 |
| ◆ *Del Norte County / Les Johnson / Les Johnson / 1986* | | | | | | | | | | | |
| 141 3/8 | 22 1/8 | 21 5/8 | 18 7/8 | 22 | 4 7/8 | 4 5/8 | 5 | 4 | | 226 | 97 |
| ◆ *Trinity County / Larry Brown / Larry Brown / 1980* | | | | | | | | | | | |
| 141 | 21 3/8 | 21 1/8 | 17 | 20 3/8 | 3 7/8 | 4 1/8 | 5 | 5 | | 232 | 98 |
| ◆ *Humboldt County / Allen Pierce, Jr. / Allen Pierce, Jr. / 1959* | | | | | | | | | | | |

| Score | Length of Main Beam R | Length of Main Beam L | Inside Spread | Greatest Spread | Circumference at Smallest Place Between Burr and First Point R | Circumference at Smallest Place Between Burr and First Point L | Number of Points R | Number of Points L | Total of Lengths Abnormal Points | All-Time Rank | State Rank |
|---|---|---|---|---|---|---|---|---|---|---|---|
| ♦ *Locality Killed / By Whom Killed / Owner / Date Killed* | | | | | | | | | | | |
| 141 | 21 | 20 2/8 | 19 4/8 | 25 5/8 | 4 4/8 | 4 | 5 | 4 | | 232 | 98 |
| ♦ *Mendocino County / Richard Vannelli / Richard Vannelli / 1970* | | | | | | | | | | | |
| 141 | 23 | 24 4/8 | 22 | 24 | 5 4/8 | 5 4/8 | 7 | 6 | 8 4/8 | 232 | 98 |
| ♦ *Mendocino County / Gerald W. Whitmire / Gerald W. Whitmire / 1976* | | | | | | | | | | | |
| 140 7/8 | 21 1/8 | 20 1/8 | 21 1/8 | 24 4/8 | 4 3/8 | 4 4/8 | 5 | 5 | | 235 | 101 |
| ♦ *Shasta County / Dave Swenson / Dave Swenson / 1968* | | | | | | | | | | | |
| 140 7/8 | 23 3/8 | 22 | 16 5/8 | 18 2/8 | 3 7/8 | 4 | 5 | 5 | | 235 | 101 |
| ♦ *Mendocino County / Douglas W. Lim / Douglas W. Lim / 1981* | | | | | | | | | | | |
| 140 6/8 | 23 4/8 | 23 | 18 6/8 | 20 5/8 | 4 6/8 | 5 1/8 | 5 | 4 | 1 4/8 | 238 | 103 |
| ♦ *Mendocino County / Robert Lynch / Robert Lynch / 1971* | | | | | | | | | | | |
| 140 6/8 | 23 | 22 4/8 | 20 | 22 | 5 4/8 | 5 4/8 | 5 | 5 | | 238 | 103 |
| ♦ *Mendocino County / Jerry D. Smith / Jerry D. Smith / 1978* | | | | | | | | | | | |
| 140 5/8 | 23 | 21 7/8 | 18 3/8 | 20 2/8 | 4 6/8 | 4 5/8 | 5 | 5 | | 241 | 105 |
| ♦ *Shasta County / Luther Clements / R.H. Bernhardy / 1944* | | | | | | | | | | | |
| 140 4/8 | 19 4/8 | 20 | 17 2/8 | 21 2/8 | 4 4/8 | 4 4/8 | 5 | 5 | | 243 | 106 |
| ♦ *Trinity County / Loran G. August / Larry Brown / 1980* | | | | | | | | | | | |
| 140 4/8 | 21 1/8 | 21 3/8 | 14 2/8 | 17 1/8 | 4 1/8 | 4 1/8 | 5 | 5 | | 243 | 106 |
| ♦ *Mendocino County / Jay M. Gates III / Jay M. Gates III / 1986* | | | | | | | | | | | |
| 140 3/8 | 20 1/8 | 20 5/8 | 16 5/8 | 19 2/8 | 3 7/8 | 4 3/8 | 4 | 5 | | 246 | 108 |
| ♦ *Humboldt County / George S. Johnson / Roy F. Johnson / 1934* | | | | | | | | | | | |
| 140 3/8 | 22 | 21 | 17 7/8 | 21 2/8 | 4 | 4 | 5 | 5 | | 246 | 108 |
| ♦ *Siskiyou County / Rodney Irwin / Rodney Irwin / 1966* | | | | | | | | | | | |
| 140 2/8 | 21 4/8 | 21 4/8 | 19 6/8 | 21 4/8 | 3 7/8 | 3 7/8 | 5 | 5 | | 248 | 110 |
| ♦ *Mendocino County / Earl E. Hamlow, Jr. / Earl E. Hamlow, Jr. / 1977* | | | | | | | | | | | |
| 140 2/8 | 22 | 21 4/8 | 23 4/8 | 26 | 4 3/8 | 4 3/8 | 4 | 5 | 3 | 248 | 110 |
| ♦ *Trinity County / Charles E. Davy / Charles E. Davy / 1983* | | | | | | | | | | | |
| 140 1/8 | 21 2/8 | 21 5/8 | 15 6/8 | 18 1/8 | 4 2/8 | 4 2/8 | 5 | 7 | 2 7/8 | 251 | 112 |
| ♦ *Mendocino County / Clarence W. Nelson / Clarence W. Nelson / 1948* | | | | | | | | | | | |
| 140 1/8 | 20 4/8 | 19 4/8 | 16 3/8 | 20 2/8 | 4 3/8 | 4 2/8 | 4 | 4 | | 251 | 112 |
| ♦ *Santa Clara County / Dick Sullivan / Dick Sullivan / 1977* | | | | | | | | | | | |
| 140 1/8 | 21 1/8 | 20 2/8 | 16 3/8 | 18 1/8 | 3 7/8 | 4 | 4 | 4 | | 251 | 112 |
| ♦ *Siskiyou County / Rickford M. Fisher / Rickford M. Fisher / 1986* | | | | | | | | | | | |
| 140 1/8 | 21 6/8 | 21 | 17 1/8 | 19 2/8 | 4 | 4 4/8 | 5 | 6 | 1 2/8 | 251 | 112 |
| ♦ *Trinity County / Wayne Sorensen / C.W. Sorensen / 1986* | | | | | | | | | | | |

| Score | Length of Main Beam R | Length of Main Beam L | Inside Spread | Greatest Spread | Circumference at Smallest Place Between Burr and First Point R | Circumference at Smallest Place Between Burr and First Point L | Number of Points R | Number of Points L | Total of Lengths Abnormal Points | All-Time Rank | State Rank |
|---|---|---|---|---|---|---|---|---|---|---|---|
| ♦ *Locality Killed / By Whom Killed / Owner / Date Killed* | | | | | | | | | | | |
| 140 | 20 2/8 | 20 2/8 | 16 | 22 4/8 | 4 7/8 | 4 6/8 | 7 | 5 | 4 2/8 | 258 | 116 |
| ♦ *Mendocino County / Roy Bergstrom / Roy Bergstrom / 1966* | | | | | | | | | | | |
| 140 | 22 4/8 | 22 2/8 | 18 | 20 6/8 | 5 5/8 | 5 2/8 | 5 | 5 | | 258 | 116 |
| ♦ *Mendocino County / Nick Deffterios / Nick Deffterios / 1970* | | | | | | | | | | | |
| 140 | 22 | 21 3/8 | 17 6/8 | 21 2/8 | 4 1/8 | 4 1/8 | 5 | 5 | | 258 | 116 |
| ♦ *Humboldt County / Carl A. Anderson / Carl A. Anderson / 1980* | | | | | | | | | | | |
| 140 | 21 5/8 | 22 1/8 | 19 | 22 1/8 | 3 7/8 | 4 2/8 | 4 | 5 | | 258 | 116 |
| ♦ *Trinity County / William J. Olson / William J. Olson / 1981* | | | | | | | | | | | |
| 139 7/8 | 19 | 18 6/8 | 15 5/8 | 19 | 4 | 4 | 4 | 5 | | 263 | 120 |
| ♦ *Siskiyou County / Roy Eastlick / Roy Eastlick / 1954* | | | | | | | | | | | |
| 139 7/8 | 22 1/8 | 20 7/8 | 21 3/8 | 24 2/8 | 5 1/8 | 5 | 4 | 5 | 1 2/8 | 263 | 120 |
| ♦ *Trinity County / Craig L. Brown / Craig & Joy Brown / 1981* | | | | | | | | | | | |
| 139 6/8 | 21 5/8 | 22 4/8 | 16 | 18 1/8 | 4 1/8 | 4 | 5 | 5 | | 266 | 122 |
| ♦ *Shasta County / Warren Hunter / Warren Hunter / 1964* | | | | | | | | | | | |
| 139 3/8 | 19 4/8 | 19 5/8 | 20 6/8 | 22 4/8 | 4 2/8 | 4 2/8 | 6 | 5 | 1 | 274 | 123 |
| ♦ *Mendocino County / Walter R. Schubert / Walter R. Schubert / 1952* | | | | | | | | | | | |
| 139 3/8 | 24 5/8 | 23 3/8 | 21 5/8 | 23 7/8 | 4 7/8 | 4 7/8 | 5 | 5 | 2 6/8 | 274 | 123 |
| ♦ *Trinity County / Andy Burgess / Andy Burgess / 1964* | | | | | | | | | | | |
| 139 3/8 | 21 4/8 | 21 5/8 | 22 5/8 | 25 1/8 | 4 3/8 | 4 1/8 | 5 | 5 | | 274 | 123 |
| ♦ *Siskiyou County / Loren L. Lutz / Loren L. Lutz / 1964* | | | | | | | | | | | |
| 139 2/8 | 21 3/8 | 21 4/8 | 20 1/8 | 22 1/8 | 4 1/8 | 4 1/8 | 5 | 4 | 1 3/8 | 280 | 126 |
| ♦ *Humboldt County / Jeff Bryant / Jeff Bryant / 1964* | | | | | | | | | | | |
| 139 2/8 | 22 5/8 | 21 1/8 | 18 6/8 | 22 7/8 | 3 3/8 | 3 5/8 | 4 | 6 | 3 6/8 | 280 | 126 |
| ♦ *Trinity County / Gary L. Mayberry / Gary L. Mayberry / 1968* | | | | | | | | | | | |
| 139 2/8 | 21 | 21 | 16 7/8 | 20 7/8 | 3 7/8 | 3 7/8 | 5 | 6 | 3 7/8 | 280 | 126 |
| ♦ *Trinity County / Terry H. Walker / Terry H. Walker / 1986* | | | | | | | | | | | |
| 139 1/8 | 22 | 21 2/8 | 18 5/8 | 20 2/8 | 4 2/8 | 4 2/8 | 5 | 5 | | 284 | 129 |
| ♦ *Humboldt County / George E. Watson / George E. Watson / 1933* | | | | | | | | | | | |
| 139 1/8 | 22 1/8 | 22 | 17 5/8 | 20 2/8 | 4 | 5 6/8 | 4 | 5 | | 284 | 129 |
| ♦ *Mendocino County / John Winn, Jr. / John Winn, Jr. / 1972* | | | | | | | | | | | |
| 138 7/8 | 21 | 22 2/8 | 20 5/8 | 22 3/8 | 4 5/8 | 4 2/8 | 4 | 4 | | 291 | 131 |
| ♦ *Siskiyou County / Darrell Nowdesha / Darrell Nowdesha / 1961* | | | | | | | | | | | |
| 138 7/8 | 19 1/8 | 20 5/8 | 15 3/8 | 18 | 5 | 4 7/8 | 6 | 5 | 2 2/8 | 291 | 131 |
| ♦ *Trinity County / William O. Louderback / William O. Louderback / 1963* | | | | | | | | | | | |

| Score | Length of Main Beam | | Inside Spread | Greatest Spread | Circumference at Smallest Place Between Burr and First Point | | Number of Points | | Total of Lengths Abnormal Points | All-Time Rank | State Rank |
|---|---|---|---|---|---|---|---|---|---|---|---|
| | R | L | | | R | L | R | L | | | |
| ◆ Locality Killed / By Whom Killed / Owner / Date Killed | | | | | | | | | | | |
| 138 6/8 | 21 3/8 | 20 4/8 | 16 | 18 5/8 | 4 | 4 1/8 | 5 | 5 | | 296 | 133 |
| ◆ Humboldt County / Larry Bowermaster / Larry Bowermaster / 1964 | | | | | | | | | | | |
| 138 6/8 | 22 2/8 | 21 1/8 | 22 2/8 | 24 2/8 | 4 1/8 | 4 | 5 | 5 | | 296 | 133 |
| ◆ Mendocino County / Gordon O. Hanson / Gordon O. Hanson / 1988 | | | | | | | | | | | |
| 138 4/8 | 22 4/8 | 22 7/8 | 18 6/8 | 20 3/8 | 4 | 4 | 5 | 4 | | 302 | 135 |
| ◆ Mendocino County / Jess Jones / Jess Jones / 1950 | | | | | | | | | | | |
| 138 4/8 | 21 1/8 | 20 | 18 2/8 | 21 1/8 | 4 3/8 | 4 | 5 | 5 | | 302 | 135 |
| ◆ Siskiyou County / Bob Courts / Bob Courts / 1965 | | | | | | | | | | | |
| 138 4/8 | 19 4/8 | 19 4/8 | 17 2/8 | 20 2/8 | 4 | 4 | 5 | 6 | 1 2/8 | 302 | 135 |
| ◆ Siskiyou County / John Carmichael / John Carmichael / 1969 | | | | | | | | | | | |
| 138 3/8 | 22 4/8 | 22 2/8 | 18 | 21 4/8 | 4 4/8 | 4 1/8 | 5 | 5 | 11 1/8 | 305 | 138 |
| ◆ Humboldt County / Garry Hughes / Garry Hughes / 1968 | | | | | | | | | | | |
| 138 2/8 | 21 3/8 | 21 3/8 | 15 6/8 | 17 3/8 | 4 | 3 7/8 | 5 | 5 | | 308 | 139 |
| ◆ Tehama County / Robert L. Armanasco / Robert L. Armanasco / 1968 | | | | | | | | | | | |
| 138 2/8 | 21 5/8 | 22 | 17 6/8 | 19 2/8 | 3 6/8 | 3 6/8 | 5 | 5 | | 308 | 139 |
| ◆ Trinity County / Thomas A. Pettigrew, Jr. / Thomas A. Pettigrew, Jr. / 1972 | | | | | | | | | | | |
| 138 2/8 | 18 | 18 | 14 4/8 | 17 4/8 | 4 4/8 | 4 1/8 | 5 | 5 | | 308 | 139 |
| ◆ Mendocino County / Kenzia L. Drake / Kenzia L. Drake / 1985 | | | | | | | | | | | |
| 138 | 22 3/8 | 21 7/8 | 21 1/8 | 22 6/8 | 4 7/8 | 5 | 5 | 6 | 1 3/8 | 315 | 142 |
| ◆ Mendocino County / Brian K. Isaac / Brian K. Isaac / 1985 | | | | | | | | | | | |
| 137 7/8 | 20 4/8 | 19 4/8 | 18 6/8 | 23 4/8 | 4 | 4 2/8 | 6 | 5 | 1 1/8 | 318 | 143 |
| ◆ Shasta County / Paul G. Carter / Paul G. Carter / 1964 | | | | | | | | | | | |
| 137 7/8 | 18 4/8 | 17 5/8 | 17 3/8 | 19 6/8 | 4 | 4 | 5 | 5 | | 318 | 143 |
| ◆ Trinity County / Picked Up / North Coast Tax. / 1965 | | | | | | | | | | | |
| 137 7/8 | 18 | 18 5/8 | 18 5/8 | 26 1/8 | 5 | 4 5/8 | 4 | 4 | | 318 | 143 |
| ◆ Santa Clara County / F.L. Johnston, Jr. / F.L. Johnston, Jr. / 1967 | | | | | | | | | | | |
| 137 6/8 | 20 2/8 | 20 7/8 | 19 6/8 | 21 3/8 | 3 6/8 | 3 7/8 | 4 | 5 | | 323 | 146 |
| ◆ Trinity County / Kevin Clair / Kevin Clair / 1986 | | | | | | | | | | | |
| 137 5/8 | 20 4/8 | 20 3/8 | 19 5/8 | 23 2/8 | 4 4/8 | 4 5/8 | 5 | 5 | | 324 | 147 |
| ◆ Mendocino County / P.R. Borton / John R. Borton / 1965 | | | | | | | | | | | |
| 137 4/8 | 19 3/8 | 19 | 17 | 18 4/8 | 4 1/8 | 4 1/8 | 5 | 5 | | 325 | 148 |
| ◆ Trinity County / Philip Grunert / Philip Grunert / 1967 | | | | | | | | | | | |
| 137 4/8 | 21 1/8 | 21 1/8 | 19 | 22 1/8 | 4 1/8 | 4 3/8 | 5 | 5 | | 325 | 148 |
| ◆ Trinity County / Picked Up / Craig & Joy Brown / 1982 | | | | | | | | | | | |

| Score | Length of Main Beam R | L | Inside Spread | Greatest Spread | Circumference at Smallest Place Between Burr and First Point R | L | Number of Points R | L | Total of Lengths Abnormal Points | All-Time Rank | State Rank |
|---|---|---|---|---|---|---|---|---|---|---|---|
| | | | | | *Locality Killed / By Whom Killed / Owner / Date Killed* | | | | | | |
| 137 1/8 | 20 | 20 5/8 | 23 3/8 | 28 | 4 3/8 | 4 3/8 | 5 | 6 | 1 4/8 | 330 | 150 |
| ◆ *Shasta County / Jack Floyd / Jack Floyd / 1957* | | | | | | | | | | | |
| 137 1/8 | 23 | 22 4/8 | 22 7/8 | 24 3/8 | 5 | 4 6/8 | 5 | 4 | | 330 | 150 |
| ◆ *Tehama County / Clint Heiber / Clint Heiber / 1977* | | | | | | | | | | | |
| 137 | 20 4/8 | 21 | 21 6/8 | 24 | 3 7/8 | 3 6/8 | 5 | 5 | | 334 | 152 |
| ◆ *Siskiyou County / Shirley Eastlick / Shirley Eastlick / 1962* | | | | | | | | | | | |
| 136 6/8 | 21 6/8 | 23 | 18 2/8 | 20 2/8 | 4 7/8 | 4 6/8 | 4 | 4 | | 338 | 153 |
| ◆ *Shasta County / Vance Corrigan / Vance Corrigan / 1957* | | | | | | | | | | | |
| 136 4/8 | 20 3/8 | 20 1/8 | 18 | 20 | 4 4/8 | 4 4/8 | 5 | 5 | | 345 | 154 |
| ◆ *Ukiah / Charles Tollini / Charles Tollini / 1960* | | | | | | | | | | | |
| 136 2/8 | 20 6/8 | 20 4/8 | 20 2/8 | 21 7/8 | 3 6/8 | 4 1/8 | 4 | 5 | | 349 | 155 |
| ◆ *Covelo / David G. Cox / David G. Cox / 1967* | | | | | | | | | | | |
| 136 2/8 | 21 6/8 | 22 | 21 4/8 | 22 6/8 | 5 | 4 7/8 | 5 | 5 | | 349 | 155 |
| ◆ *Siskiyou County / Wayne G. Rose / Wayne G. Rose / 1977* | | | | | | | | | | | |
| 136 | 21 6/8 | 23 | 19 | 23 | 5 1/8 | 5 1/8 | 6 | 6 | 9 6/8 | 354 | 157 |
| ◆ *Santa Clara County / Mrs. Maitland / Mrs. Maitland / 1956* | | | | | | | | | | | |
| | | | Armstrong | | Armstrong | | | | | | |
| 136 | 21 4/8 | 21 | 17 | 19 6/8 | 4 4/8 | 4 3/8 | 5 | 5 | | 354 | 157 |
| ◆ *Mendocino Natl. For. / Ed Q. Garayalde / Ed Q. Garayalde / 1966* | | | | | | | | | | | |
| 136 | 21 4/8 | 21 | 19 2/8 | 21 1/8 | 4 6/8 | 4 7/8 | 4 | 5 | | 354 | 157 |
| ◆ *Tehama County / Robert L. Armanasco / Robert L. Armanasco / 1968* | | | | | | | | | | | |
| 136 | 23 1/8 | 23 | 21 6/8 | 23 6/8 | 4 7/8 | 4 6/8 | 3 | 4 | | 354 | 157 |
| ◆ *San Mateo County / Dan Caughey, Sr. / Dan Caughey, Sr. / 1973* | | | | | | | | | | | |
| 136 | 20 4/8 | 19 2/8 | 19 | 22 3/8 | 4 1/8 | 4 1/8 | 6 | 6 | 8 2/8 | 354 | 157 |
| ◆ *Trinity County / Richard G. Shelton / Richard G. Shelton / 1973* | | | | | | | | | | | |
| 136 | 20 4/8 | 19 6/8 | 19 2/8 | 24 2/8 | 4 | 4 | 5 | 5 | | 354 | 157 |
| ◆ *Trinity County / John P. Morton / John P. Morton / 1987* | | | | | | | | | | | |
| 135 7/8 | 19 2/8 | 19 3/8 | 16 1/8 | 18 4/8 | 4 2/8 | 4 2/8 | 4 | 4 | | 360 | 163 |
| ◆ *Tehama County / John A. Crockett / John A. Crockett / 1982* | | | | | | | | | | | |
| 135 6/8 | 20 2/8 | 20 1/8 | 19 4/8 | 21 6/8 | 3 4/8 | 3 3/8 | 4 | 4 | | 364 | 164 |
| ◆ *Trinity County / Roy J. Renner / Roy J. Renner / 1965* | | | | | | | | | | | |
| 135 2/8 | 19 6/8 | 20 | 15 | 17 | 3 4/8 | 3 3/8 | 4 | 4 | | 373 | 165 |
| ◆ *Trinity County / Andy Burgess / Andy Burgess / 1959* | | | | | | | | | | | |

| Score | Length of Main Beam R | Length of Main Beam L | Inside Spread | Greatest Spread | Circumference at Smallest Place Between Burr and First Point R | Circumference at Smallest Place Between Burr and First Point L | Number of Points R | Number of Points L | Total of Lengths Abnormal Points | All-Time Rank | State Rank |
|---|---|---|---|---|---|---|---|---|---|---|---|
| ♦ *Locality Killed / By Whom Killed / Owner / Date Killed* | | | | | | | | | | | |
| 135 2/8 | 19 1/8 | 19 4/8 | 13 2/8 | 16 6/8 | 3 4/8 | 3 4/8 | 4 | 4 | | 373 | 165 |
| ♦ *Humboldt County / Chris A. Umbertus / Chris A. Umbertus / 1981* | | | | | | | | | | | |
| 135 | 19 | 19 5/8 | 15 4/8 | 19 6/8 | 4 1/8 | 4 2/8 | 5 | 5 | | 376 | 167 |
| ♦ *Humboldt County / Edward F. Burgess / Edward F. Burgess / 1965* | | | | | | | | | | | |
| 135 | 18 6/8 | 18 6/8 | 15 6/8 | 17 4/8 | 4 3/8 | 4 2/8 | 5 | 5 | | 376 | 167 |
| ♦ *Trinity County / Andrew M. Felt / Andrew M. Felt / 1986* | | | | | | | | | | | |
| 134 7/8 | 18 5/8 | 18 6/8 | 20 2/8 | 24 5/8 | 4 5/8 | 4 4/8 | 9 | 9 | 11 3/8 | 380 | 169 |
| ♦ *Mendocino County / O.E. Schubert / Walter R. Schubert / 1917* | | | | | | | | | | | |
| 134 7/8 | 19 6/8 | 20 5/8 | 14 5/8 | 18 | 4 1/8 | 4 1/8 | 5 | 5 | | 380 | 169 |
| ♦ *Mendocino County / Jesse P. Foster, Jr. / Jesse P. Foster, Jr. / 1964* | | | | | | | | | | | |
| 134 7/8 | 22 3/8 | 22 2/8 | 18 3/8 | 21 5/8 | 4 | 4 2/8 | 4 | 5 | | 380 | 169 |
| ♦ *Tehama County / Mario Sereni, Jr. / Mario Sereni, Jr. / 1964* | | | | | | | | | | | |
| 134 7/8 | 21 1/8 | 21 5/8 | 14 4/8 | 17 | 4 1/8 | 4 2/8 | 5 | 6 | 3 5/8 | 380 | 169 |
| ♦ *San Bernadino County / James Tacke / James Tacke / 1966* | | | | | | | | | | | |
| 134 6/8 | 19 4/8 | 20 | 16 3/8 | 19 7/8 | 4 4/8 | 4 4/8 | 5 | 6 | 4 7/8 | 385 | 173 |
| ♦ *Trinity County / Donald E. Stevens / Donald E. Stevens / 1979* | | | | | | | | | | | |
| 134 5/8 | 20 4/8 | 20 3/8 | 15 5/8 | 18 6/8 | 4 5/8 | 4 6/8 | 5 | 5 | | 388 | 174 |
| ♦ *Siskiyou County / Roy Eastlick / Roy Eastlick / 1965* | | | | | | | | | | | |
| 134 4/8 | 21 1/8 | 21 2/8 | 20 2/8 | 22 1/8 | 4 1/8 | 4 3/8 | 7 | 6 | 9 2/8 | 389 | 175 |
| ♦ *Trinity County / William M. Longhurst / William M. Longhurst / 1951* | | | | | | | | | | | |
| 134 4/8 | 19 4/8 | 20 | 17 | 19 | 4 4/8 | 4 2/8 | 5 | 5 | | 389 | 175 |
| ♦ *Humboldt County / J.A. Phelps / J.A. Phelps / 1966* | | | | | | | | | | | |
| 134 4/8 | 22 | 21 4/8 | 18 4/8 | 21 | 5 2/8 | 5 1/8 | 5 | 4 | | 389 | 175 |
| ♦ *Sonoma County / Richard O'Farrell / Richard O'Farrell / 1984* | | | | | | | | | | | |
| 134 3/8 | 22 5/8 | 21 2/8 | 22 3/8 | 24 3/8 | 4 7/8 | 4 7/8 | 5 | 4 | | 395 | 178 |
| ♦ *Tehama County / Bob C. Haase / Bob C. Haase / 1987* | | | | | | | | | | | |
| 134 2/8 | 19 4/8 | 21 | 16 | 18 3/8 | 4 | 4 3/8 | 4 | 4 | | 399 | 179 |
| ♦ *Humboldt County / G.L. Dorris / G.L. Dorris / 1973* | | | | | | | | | | | |
| 134 2/8 | 24 1/8 | 23 6/8 | 22 4/8 | 26 6/8 | 4 3/8 | 4 4/8 | 4 | 4 | | 399 | 179 |
| ♦ *Colusa County / Gregory R. Bonetti / Gregory R. Bonetti / 1983* | | | | | | | | | | | |
| 134 2/8 | 19 3/8 | 19 6/8 | 20 2/8 | 22 | 4 7/8 | 4 6/8 | 6 | 5 | 1 6/8 | 399 | 179 |
| ♦ *Mendocino County / Sebastian Carrasco / Sebastian Carrasco / 1986* | | | | | | | | | | | |

| Score | Length of Main Beam R | L | Inside Spread | Greatest Spread | Circumference at Smallest Place Between Burr and First Point R | L | Number of Points R | L | Total of Lengths Abnormal Points | All-Time Rank | State Rank |
|---|---|---|---|---|---|---|---|---|---|---|---|
| | | | | *Locality Killed / By Whom Killed / Owner / Date Killed* | | | | | | | |
| 134 1/8 | 19 5/8 | 20 | 16 5/8 | 19 4/8 | 4 1/8 | 4 4/8 | 5 | 5 | | 404 | 182 |
| ♦ *Mendocino County / Danny Pardini / Danny Pardini / 1976* | | | | | | | | | | | |
| 134 1/8 | 18 2/8 | 18 2/8 | 14 7/8 | 17 2/8 | 4 | 4 | 6 | 5 | 1 2/8 | 404 | 182 |
| ♦ *Trinity County / David Deininger / David Deininger / 1980* | | | | | | | | | | | |
| 134 | 19 6/8 | 19 2/8 | 16 2/8 | 18 1/8 | 3 6/8 | 3 4/8 | 7 | 5 | 3 | 408 | 184 |
| ♦ *Siskiyou County / Alicia Whittaker / Alicia Whittaker / 1970* | | | | | | | | | | | |
| 133 7/8 | 20 4/8 | 21 3/8 | 13 5/8 | 16 5/8 | 3 6/8 | 3 5/8 | 5 | 5 | | 409 | 185 |
| ♦ *Siskiyou County / William E. Turner / William E. Turner / 1982* | | | | | | | | | | | |
| 133 6/8 | 21 2/8 | 21 5/8 | 17 2/8 | 21 3/8 | 4 3/8 | 4 3/8 | 5 | 4 | | 410 | 186 |
| ♦ *Mendocino County / Marvin DeAngelis / Marvin DeAngelis / 1978* | | | | | | | | | | | |
| 133 6/8 | 21 2/8 | 21 1/8 | 16 | 17 6/8 | 3 7/8 | 4 | 5 | 5 | | 410 | 186 |
| ♦ *Mendocino County / Terence K. Prechter / Terence K. Prechter / 1986* | | | | | | | | | | | |
| 133 4/8 | 21 | 22 4/8 | 17 4/8 | 20 4/8 | 4 6/8 | 5 | 6 | 5 | 5 | 417 | 188 |
| ♦ *Trinity County / Barry Griffin / Barry Griffin / 1976* | | | | | | | | | | | |
| 133 4/8 | 22 | 20 4/8 | 20 4/8 | 24 4/8 | 4 6/8 | 4 4/8 | 5 | 6 | 1 4/8 | 417 | 188 |
| ♦ *Trinity County / George M. Moxon / George M. Moxon / 1977* | | | | | | | | | | | |
| 133 2/8 | 19 1/8 | 18 5/8 | 16 | 21 7/8 | 3 2/8 | 3 2/8 | 5 | 5 | | 427 | 190 |
| ♦ *Trinity County / Kirk Finch / Kirk Finch / 1975* | | | | | | | | | | | |
| 133 2/8 | 20 2/8 | 20 7/8 | 17 | 19 2/8 | 4 2/8 | 4 2/8 | 5 | 5 | | 427 | 190 |
| ♦ *Trinity County / Ralph L. Perry / Ralph L. Perry / 1980* | | | | | | | | | | | |
| 133 1/8 | 22 7/8 | 22 | 21 1/8 | 23 3/8 | 4 5/8 | 5 | 5 | 5 | | 433 | 192 |
| ♦ *Trinity County / Hugh A. Dow / Hugh A. Dow / 1969* | | | | | | | | | | | |
| 133 | 20 4/8 | 20 4/8 | 19 4/8 | 21 6/8 | 4 4/8 | 5 | 4 | 4 | | 437 | 193 |
| ♦ *Napa County / Fred C. Framsted / Fred C. Framsted / 1966* | | | | | | | | | | | |
| 132 7/8 | 21 6/8 | 23 3/8 | 19 4/8 | 22 | 4 5/8 | 4 4/8 | 6 | 5 | 1 3/8 | 440 | 194 |
| ♦ *Tehama County / Joe McBrayer / Joe McBrayer / 1981* | | | | | | | | | | | |
| 132 7/8 | 20 6/8 | 21 4/8 | 19 1/8 | 21 1/8 | 4 2/8 | 4 3/8 | 5 | 5 | | 440 | 194 |
| ♦ *Humboldt County / Dennis R. Lake / Dennis R. Lake / 1988* | | | | | | | | | | | |
| 132 6/8 | 19 1/8 | 17 6/8 | 16 4/8 | 18 | 3 6/8 | 3 7/8 | 5 | 5 | | 444 | 196 |
| ♦ *Tehama County / Daniel E. Osborne / Daniel E. Osborne / 1956* | | | | | | | | | | | |
| 132 6/8 | 19 5/8 | 21 | 18 6/8 | 19 5/8 | 4 4/8 | 4 4/8 | 5 | 5 | | 444 | 196 |
| ♦ *Mendocino County / Mason Geisinger / Mason Geisinger / 1967* | | | | | | | | | | | |

| Score | Length of Main Beam R | L | Inside Spread | Greatest Spread | Circumference at Smallest Place Between Burr and First Point R | L | Number of Points R | L | Total of Lengths Abnormal Points | All-Time Rank | State Rank |
|---|---|---|---|---|---|---|---|---|---|---|---|
| | *Locality Killed / By Whom Killed / Owner / Date Killed* | | | | | | | | | | |
| 132 6/8 | 22 | 22 6/8 | 21 6/8 | 23 1/8 | 4 4/8 | 4 6/8 | 5 | 4 | 2 | 444 | 196 |
| | *Mendocino County / Jay M. Gates III / Jay M. Gates III / 1984* | | | | | | | | | | |
| 132 6/8 | 20 5/8 | 21 5/8 | 17 6/8 | 20 1/8 | 4 4/8 | 4 4/8 | 5 | 5 | | 444 | 196 |
| | *Siskiyou County / Paul J. Bruno / Paul J. Bruno / 1985* | | | | | | | | | | |
| 132 3/8 | 22 2/8 | 22 | 19 | 21 | 5 1/8 | 4 5/8 | 5 | 4 | 1 1/8 | 453 | 200 |
| | *Trinity County / David L. Matley / David L. Matley / 1981* | | | | | | | | | | |
| 132 3/8 | 18 7/8 | 19 7/8 | 18 1/8 | 22 7/8 | 4 | 4 1/8 | 5 | 5 | | 453 | 200 |
| | *Siskiyou County / Lawrence F. Weckerle / Lawrence F. Weckerle / 1982* | | | | | | | | | | |
| 132 2/8 | 19 5/8 | 18 7/8 | 18 2/8 | 24 7/8 | 4 5/8 | 4 1/8 | 5 | 4 | | 458 | 202 |
| | *Mendocino County / P.R. Borton / William R. Borton / 1971* | | | | | | | | | | |
| 132 2/8 | 21 3/8 | 19 3/8 | 14 6/8 | 17 2/8 | 4 6/8 | 4 1/8 | 5 | 4 | | 458 | 202 |
| | *Humboldt County / Guy Hooper / Guy Hooper / 1977* | | | | | | | | | | |
| 132 2/8 | 20 | 20 | 16 4/8 | 18 4/8 | 4 1/8 | 4 2/8 | 5 | 5 | | 458 | 202 |
| | *Mendocino County / Richard L. Moore / Richard L. Moore / 1987* | | | | | | | | | | |
| 132 1/8 | 20 6/8 | 20 4/8 | 15 1/8 | 17 1/8 | 5 2/8 | 5 1/8 | 4 | 4 | | 463 | 205 |
| | *Trinity County / R.C. Kauffman / R.C. Kauffman / 1936* | | | | | | | | | | |
| 132 1/8 | 20 6/8 | 19 6/8 | 19 1/8 | 22 1/8 | 3 2/8 | 3 2/8 | 4 | 4 | | 463 | 205 |
| | *Mendocino County / Fred E. Borton II / Matthew E. Borton / 1971* | | | | | | | | | | |
| 132 1/8 | 20 | 19 4/8 | 18 1/8 | 21 1/8 | 4 | 4 | 5 | 5 | | 463 | 205 |
| | *Trinity County / Ronald L. Schneider / Ronald L. Schneider / 1979* | | | | | | | | | | |
| 131 6/8 | 19 1/8 | 19 3/8 | 14 | 16 3/8 | 4 | 3 7/8 | 5 | 5 | | 467 | 208 |
| | *Siskiyou County / Sid E. Ziegler / Sid E. Ziegler / 1957* | | | | | | | | | | |
| 131 6/8 | 21 | 19 4/8 | 18 | 20 3/8 | 5 | 5 | 5 | 5 | | 467 | 208 |
| | *Trinity County / Carter B. Dow / Carter B. Dow / 1961* | | | | | | | | | | |
| 131 6/8 | 19 1/8 | 18 5/8 | 14 4/8 | 17 3/8 | 4 2/8 | 4 2/8 | 5 | 5 | | 467 | 208 |
| | *Humboldt County / Larry Wilson / Larry Wilson / 1978* | | | | | | | | | | |
| 131 6/8 | 18 5/8 | 19 3/8 | 13 6/8 | 15 4/8 | 5 1/8 | 4 6/8 | 6 | 5 | 2 4/8 | 467 | 208 |
| | *Trinity County / Melvin M. Clair / Melvin M. Clair / 1979* | | | | | | | | | | |
| 131 6/8 | 20 2/8 | 20 | 18 2/8 | 21 7/8 | 3 6/8 | 4 | 5 | 5 | | 467 | 208 |
| | *Trinity County / Kenneth L. Cogle, Jr. / Kenneth L. Cogle, Jr. / 1981* | | | | | | | | | | |
| 131 4/8 | 19 6/8 | 19 1/8 | 17 2/8 | 21 | 3 6/8 | 3 6/8 | 5 | 6 | 3 4/8 | 474 | 213 |
| | *Mendocino County / James J. McBride / James J. McBride / 1982* | | | | | | | | | | |

| Score | Length of Main Beam R | Length of Main Beam L | Inside Spread | Greatest Spread | Circumference at Smallest Place Between Burr and First Point R | Circumference at Smallest Place Between Burr and First Point L | Number of Points R | Number of Points L | Total of Lengths Abnormal Points | All-Time Rank | State Rank |
|---|---|---|---|---|---|---|---|---|---|---|---|
| | ◆ *Locality Killed / By Whom Killed / Owner / Date Killed* | | | | | | | | | | |
| 131 2/8 | 19 6/8 | 19 6/8 | 17 4/8 | 19 6/8 | 4 | 3 7/8 | 5 | 5 | | 481 | 214 |
| | ◆ *Trinity County / L. Irvin Barnhart / L. Irvin Barnhart / 1986* | | | | | | | | | | |
| 131 | 18 4/8 | 17 4/8 | 15 6/8 | 20 4/8 | 3 7/8 | 4 | 5 | 5 | | 485 | 215 |
| | ◆ *Siskiyou County / George Quigley / George Quigley / 1971* | | | | | | | | | | |
| 131 | 18 2/8 | 18 4/8 | 18 4/8 | 21 | 4 2/8 | 4 2/8 | 5 | 5 | | 485 | 215 |
| | ◆ *Siskiyou County / Raymond Whittaker / Raymond Whittaker / 1981* | | | | | | | | | | |
| 130 7/8 | 20 7/8 | 20 4/8 | 16 5/8 | 19 4/8 | 3 7/8 | 3 7/8 | 5 | 5 | | 489 | 217 |
| | ◆ *Tehama County / James D. Fiske / James D. Fiske / 1956* | | | | | | | | | | |
| 130 6/8 | 21 6/8 | 21 4/8 | 19 4/8 | 21 2/8 | 4 | 4 2/8 | 8 | 6 | 10 2/8 | 490 | 218 |
| | ◆ *Siskiyou County / Larry E. Richey / Larry E. Richey / 1956* | | | | | | | | | | |
| 130 6/8 | 20 5/8 | 19 | 19 | 21 2/8 | 4 3/8 | 4 | 5 | 4 | | 490 | 218 |
| | ◆ *Mendocino County / Tom Enberg / Tom Enberg / 1970* | | | | | | | | | | |
| 130 5/8 | 18 | 20 | 17 1/8 | 19 | 5 | 5 | 6 | 6 | 3 4/8 | 495 | 220 |
| | ◆ *Lake County / Bernard Domries / Bernard Domries / 1940* | | | | | | | | | | |
| 130 5/8 | 24 2/8 | 23 3/8 | 23 2/8 | 25 | 4 3/8 | 4 4/8 | 4 | 5 | 1 1/8 | 495 | 220 |
| | ◆ *Siskiyou County / Vernon Sutherlin / Vernon Sutherlin / 1961* | | | | | | | | | | |
| 130 4/8 | 21 6/8 | 21 7/8 | 18 6/8 | 18 6/8 | 5 2/8 | 4 2/8 | 5 | 3 | | 498 | 222 |
| | ◆ *Mendocino County / Mitchell A. Thorson / Mitchell A. Thorson / 1969* | | | | | | | | | | |
| 130 4/8 | 19 | 19 5/8 | 15 4/8 | 19 3/8 | 4 2/8 | 4 2/8 | 4 | 4 | | 498 | 222 |
| | ◆ *Santa Cruz County / William J. McGrath / William J. McGrath / 1982* | | | | | | | | | | |
| 130 4/8 | 22 5/8 | 22 1/8 | 21 1/8 | 22 6/8 | 4 2/8 | 4 1/8 | 4 | 5 | 1 1/8 | 498 | 222 |
| | ◆ *Trinity County / Wayne Erickson / Wayne Erickson / 1985* | | | | | | | | | | |
| 130 3/8 | 20 | 20 | 16 3/8 | 18 4/8 | 4 | 4 | 5 | 5 | | 504 | 225 |
| | ◆ *Siskiyou County / John Carmichael / John Carmichael / 1970* | | | | | | | | | | |
| 130 1/8 | 20 3/8 | 20 1/8 | 20 1/8 | 21 5/8 | 4 2/8 | 4 5/8 | 4 | 4 | | 507 | 226 |
| | ◆ *San Mateo County / Dan Caughey III / Dan Caughey III / 1988* | | | | | | | | | | |
| 130 | 22 1/8 | 22 2/8 | 15 6/8 | 17 7/8 | 3 5/8 | 3 5/8 | 5 | 3 | | 509 | 227 |
| | ◆ *Trinity County / Terry H. Walker / Terry H. Walker / 1979* | | | | | | | | | | |
| 129 | 20 | 17 5/8 | 14 4/8 | 17 6/8 | 3 7/8 | 4 7/8 | 4 | 5 | | 511 | 228 |
| | ◆ *Humboldt County / Stephen Walker / Stephen Walker / 1961* | | | | | | | | | | |
| 125 5/8 | 18 2/8 | 19 5/8 | 22 5/8 | 23 5/8 | 3 6/8 | 3 5/8 | 4 | 4 | | 517 | 229 |
| | ◆ *Humboldt County / Lodewijk J. Wurfbain / Lodewijk J. Wurfbain / 1986* | | | | | | | | | | |

| Score | Length of Main Beam R | L | Inside Spread | Greatest Spread | Circumference at Smallest Place Between Burr and First Point R | L | Number of Points R | L | Total of Lengths Abnormal Points | All-Time Rank | State Rank |
|---|---|---|---|---|---|---|---|---|---|---|---|
| | | | | | | | | | | | |
| 122 6/8 | 21 7/8 | 19 6/8 | 16 | 17 3/8 | 4 4/8 | 4 4/8 | 4 | 5 | | 522 | 230 |
| ♦ *San Mateo County / Daniel R. Caughey, Jr. / Daniel R. Caughey, Jr. / 1964* | | | | | | | | | | | |
| 122 3/8 | 19 4/8 | 21 | 16 1/8 | 18 6/8 | 4 3/8 | 4 1/8 | 4 | 4 | | 524 | 231 |
| ♦ *San Mateo County / Daniel R. Caughey, Jr. / Daniel R. Caughey, Jr. / 1986* | | | | | | | | | | | |
| 122 2/8 | 19 | 20 | 15 4/8 | 18 | 4 4/8 | 4 1/8 | 5 | 5 | | 526 | 232 |
| ♦ *Humboldt County / Don L. Corley / Don L. Corley / 1982* | | | | | | | | | | | |
| 122 2/8 | 19 | 18 5/8 | 17 | 19 6/8 | 4 2/8 | 5 | 5 | 4 | | 526 | 232 |
| ♦ *Sonoma County / Richard O'Farrell / Richard O'Farrell / 1983* | | | | | | | | | | | |
| 122 1/8 | 20 2/8 | 19 6/8 | 17 7/8 | 20 | 4 | 4 | 4 | 4 | | 530 | 234 |
| ♦ *Trinity County / Terry H. Walker / Terry H. Walker / 1976* | | | | | | | | | | | |
| 121 | 18 6/8 | 18 6/8 | 18 6/8 | 20 7/8 | 4 | 4 | 4 | 4 | | 531 | 235 |
| ♦ *San Mateo County / Daniel R. Caughey, Jr. / Daniel R. Caughey, Jr. / 1971* | | | | | | | | | | | |
| 152 5/8 | 23 6/8 | 22 7/8 | 18 5/8 | 19 4/8 | 5 | 5 3/8 | 5 | 4 | 1 2/8 | * | * |
| ♦ *Trinity County / Larry Brown / Larry Brown / 1979* | | | | | | | | | | | |

**OREGON STATE RECORD
COLUMBIA BLACKTAIL DEER
SCORE: 170-6/8**
Locality: Elk City    Date: 1962
Hunter: Clark D. Griffith

# OREGON

## COLUMBIA BLACKTAIL DEER

| Score | Length of Main Beam | | Inside Spread | Greatest Spread | Circumference at Smallest Place Between Burr and First Point | | Number of Points | | Total of Lengths Abnormal Points | All-Time Rank | State Rank |
|---|---|---|---|---|---|---|---|---|---|---|---|
| | R | L | | | R | L | R | L | | | |
| ♦ Locality Killed / By Whom Killed / Owner / Date Killed | | | | | | | | | | | |
| 170 6/8 | 23 1/8 | 24 | 21 4/8 | 25 3/8 | 5 3/8 | 5 4/8 | 5 | 5 | | 2 | 1 |
| ♦ Elk City / Clark D. Griffith / Clark D. Griffith / 1962 | | | | | | | | | | | |
| 170 1/8 | 23 | 22 6/8 | 19 5/8 | 24 1/8 | 5 | 4 6/8 | 5 | 5 | | 3 | 2 |
| ♦ Linn County / Woodrow W. Gibbs / Woodrow W. Gibbs / 1963 | | | | | | | | | | | |
| 167 4/8 | 24 3/8 | 24 3/8 | 19 4/8 | 26 | 4 7/8 | 5 | 5 | 6 | 1 2/8 | 5 | 3 |
| ♦ Marion County / Robert L. Brown / Robert L. Brown / 1980 | | | | | | | | | | | |
| 165 4/8 | 23 6/8 | 24 5/8 | 21 6/8 | 24 1/8 | 5 1/8 | 5 1/8 | 4 | 4 | | 7 | 4 |
| ♦ Yamhill County / Jim McKinley / Jim McKinley / 1971 | | | | | | | | | | | |
| 163 7/8 | 21 7/8 | 21 7/8 | 19 5/8 | 25 6/8 | 4 4/8 | 4 4/8 | 5 | 5 | | 9 | 5 |
| ♦ Lincoln County / Picked Up / Bruce & Scott Wales / 1987 | | | | | | | | | | | |
| 163 1/8 | 21 3/8 | 22 5/8 | 19 1/8 | | 5 1/8 | 5 | 5 | 5 | | 10 | 6 |
| ♦ Eugene / Russell Thomas / Russell Thomas / 1964 | | | | | | | | | | | |
| 160 7/8 | 23 3/8 | 23 3/8 | 19 3/8 | 24 6/8 | 4 6/8 | 4 5/8 | 6 | 5 | 5 6/8 | 15 | 7 |
| ♦ Jackson County / G. Scott Jennings / G. Scott Jennings / 1972 | | | | | | | | | | | |
| 160 5/8 | 20 5/8 | 21 4/8 | 16 5/8 | 23 1/8 | 4 5/8 | 4 5/8 | 4 | 4 | | 16 | 8 |
| ♦ Camas Valley / Bernard L. Den / Bernard L. Den / 1958 | | | | | | | | | | | |
| 159 6/8 | 25 5/8 | 24 4/8 | 22 4/8 | 26 7/8 | 4 6/8 | 4 4/8 | 6 | 6 | 3 4/8 | 22 | 9 |
| ♦ Jackson County / Frank Chapman / Frank Chapman / 1965 | | | | | | | | | | | |
| 159 6/8 | 24 3/8 | 24 1/8 | 16 1/8 | 18 5/8 | 4 5/8 | 4 6/8 | 5 | 8 | 3 5/8 | 22 | 9 |
| ♦ Jackson County / Douglas L. Milburn / Douglas L. Milburn / 1985 | | | | | | | | | | | |
| 158 6/8 | 22 | 22 1/8 | 17 4/8 | 19 | 4 3/8 | 4 4/8 | 5 | 5 | | 26 | 11 |
| ♦ Marion County / Bradley M. Brenden / Bradley M. Brenden / 1973 | | | | | | | | | | | |
| 158 2/8 | 22 4/8 | 23 7/8 | 19 6/8 | 22 1/8 | 4 6/8 | 4 6/8 | 5 | 5 | | 28 | 12 |
| ♦ Josephine County / James E. Brierley / James E. Brierley / 1983 | | | | | | | | | | | |
| 158 | 22 7/8 | 23 3/8 | 18 4/8 | 20 3/8 | 4 6/8 | 4 6/8 | 5 | 5 | | 30 | 13 |
| ♦ Camas Valley / Frank Kinnan / Frank Kinnan / 1968 | | | | | | | | | | | |

## OREGON COLUMBIA BLACKTAIL DEER *(continued)*

| Score | Length of Main Beam R | L | Inside Spread | Greatest Spread | Circumference at Smallest Place Between Burr and First Point R | L | Number of Points R | L | Total of Lengths Abnormal Points | All-Time Rank | State Rank |
|---|---|---|---|---|---|---|---|---|---|---|---|
| | *Locality Killed / By Whom Killed / Owner / Date Killed* | | | | | | | | | | |
| 157 4/8 | 21 1/8 | 19 4/8 | 17 1/8 | 23 1/8 | 4 1/8 | 5 | 5 | 5 | | 33 | 14 |
| *Yamhill County / Henry Davenport / Henry Davenport / 1932* | | | | | | | | | | | |
| 156 4/8 | 19 6/8 | 19 7/8 | 16 6/8 | 22 7/8 | 4 3/8 | 4 2/8 | 5 | 6 | 3 4/8 | 36 | 15 |
| *Lincoln County / Bruce G. Wales / Bruce G. Wales / 1985* | | | | | | | | | | | |
| 156 1/8 | 22 2/8 | 22 | 20 2/8 | 24 3/8 | 4 4/8 | 4 4/8 | 5 | 6 | 3 7/8 | 38 | 16 |
| *Lincoln County / Robert G. Biron / Robert G. Biron / 1963* | | | | | | | | | | | |
| 156 | 25 | 23 2/8 | 21 | 23 1/8 | 4 4/8 | 4 4/8 | 6 | 5 | 1 | 39 | 17 |
| *Polk County / Wayne Bond / Wayne Bond / 1965* | | | | | | | | | | | |
| 155 2/8 | 22 3/8 | 23 1/8 | 20 6/8 | 25 2/8 | 5 3/8 | 5 | 4 | 5 | | 41 | 18 |
| *Jackson County / L.M. Morgan & L. Miller / Lewis M. Morgan / 1971* | | | | | | | | | | | |
| 154 1/8 | 20 4/8 | 20 4/8 | 18 1/8 | 20 3/8 | 4 4/8 | 4 4/8 | 5 | 5 | | 50 | 19 |
| *Lane County / Eldon Lundy / Eldon Lundy / 1943* | | | | | | | | | | | |
| 154 | 24 4/8 | 24 3/8 | 19 5/8 | 21 6/8 | 4 1/8 | 4 4/8 | 5 | 5 | 1 1/8 | 52 | 20 |
| *Josephine County / Wayne H. Breeze / Wayne H. Breeze / 1986* | | | | | | | | | | | |
| 153 4/8 | 21 3/8 | 20 7/8 | 17 6/8 | 22 3/8 | 4 6/8 | 4 7/8 | 5 | 5 | | 55 | 21 |
| *Linn County / Greg L. Anderson / Greg L. Anderson / 1983* | | | | | | | | | | | |
| 153 3/8 | 21 5/8 | 20 5/8 | 19 1/8 | 23 5/8 | 5 2/8 | 5 2/8 | 6 | 7 | 6 | 56 | 22 |
| *Columbia County / J.H. Roberts / Oreg. Dept. Fish & Wildl. / 1946* | | | | | | | | | | | |
| 153 1/8 | 22 4/8 | 22 | 19 7/8 | 21 5/8 | 5 1/8 | 5 2/8 | 6 | 6 | 4 2/8 | 58 | 23 |
| *Canton Creek / Marell Abeene / Marell Abeene / 1967* | | | | | | | | | | | |
| 152 | 20 6/8 | 21 7/8 | 15 2/8 | 20 | 4 6/8 | 4 7/8 | 6 | 6 | 6 | 64 | 24 |
| *Clackamas County / Larry W. Peterson / Larry W. Peterson / 1980* | | | | | | | | | | | |
| 151 7/8 | 25 | 24 3/8 | 20 3/8 | 23 | 4 3/8 | 4 5/8 | 5 | 5 | | 66 | 25 |
| *Jackson County / David Ellefson / David Ellefson / 1972* | | | | | | | | | | | |
| 151 6/8 | 22 2/8 | 22 4/8 | 17 4/8 | 20 4/8 | 5 4/8 | 5 1/8 | 6 | 5 | 1 6/8 | 67 | 26 |
| *Glide / William Cellers / William Cellers / 1947* | | | | | | | | | | | |
| 151 4/8 | 20 3/8 | 19 1/8 | 16 4/8 | 18 4/8 | 4 5/8 | 4 7/8 | 5 | 5 | | 69 | 27 |
| *Marion County / John Davenport / John Davenport / 1958* | | | | | | | | | | | |
| 151 3/8 | 23 1/8 | 22 6/8 | 19 4/8 | 22 3/8 | 5 | 5 | 5 | 6 | 1 3/8 | 70 | 28 |
| *Josephine County / E.L. McKie & S.E. McKie / Ernie L. McKie / 1977* | | | | | | | | | | | |
| 151 1/8 | 21 5/8 | 21 5/8 | 16 1/8 | 19 | 4 | 4 | 4 | 4 | | 71 | 29 |
| *Josephine County / Jim Wineteer / Jim Wineteer / 1980* | | | | | | | | | | | |
| 150 7/8 | 21 7/8 | 22 | 19 5/8 | 23 | 4 4/8 | 4 5/8 | 5 | 5 | | 75 | 30 |
| *Jackson County / Darrell Leek / Darrell Leek / 1974* | | | | | | | | | | | |

| Score | Length of Main Beam R | Length of Main Beam L | Inside Spread | Greatest Spread | Circumference at Smallest Place Between Burr and First Point R | Circumference at Smallest Place Between Burr and First Point L | Number of Points R | Number of Points L | Total of Lengths Abnormal Points | All-Time Rank | State Rank |
|---|---|---|---|---|---|---|---|---|---|---|---|
| ♦ *Locality Killed / By Whom Killed / Owner / Date Killed* | | | | | | | | | | | |
| 150 5/8 | 21 4/8 | 20 7/8 | 16 5/8 | 19 6/8 | 5 4/8 | 5 6/8 | 5 | 5 | | 77 | 31 |
| ♦ *Yamhill County / Russell W. Byers / Russell W. Byers / 1961* | | | | | | | | | | | |
| 150 1/8 | 22 7/8 | 23 1/8 | 19 3/8 | 21 7/8 | 4 6/8 | 4 7/8 | 5 | 6 | 2 2/8 | 79 | 32 |
| ♦ *Clackamas County / E. Clint Kuntz / E. Clint Kuntz / 1981* | | | | | | | | | | | |
| 150 | 20 5/8 | 21 5/8 | 16 6/8 | 20 4/8 | 5 | 4 7/8 | 5 | 5 | | 83 | 33 |
| ♦ *Douglas County / Norman Burnett / Norman Burnett / 1967* | | | | | | | | | | | |
| 149 5/8 | 22 7/8 | 22 4/8 | 17 1/8 | 19 1/8 | 4 3/8 | 4 5/8 | 5 | 5 | | 89 | 34 |
| ♦ *Clackamas County / Ray W. Bunnell / Ray W. Bunnell / 1970* | | | | | | | | | | | |
| 149 2/8 | 20 2/8 | 20 3/8 | 14 6/8 | 16 5/8 | 4 2/8 | 4 | 5 | 5 | | 93 | 35 |
| ♦ *Clackamas County / Lance V. Bentz / Lance V. Bentz / 1980* | | | | | | | | | | | |
| 149 2/8 | 21 6/8 | 22 6/8 | 19 4/8 | 22 3/8 | 4 4/8 | 4 2/8 | 5 | 5 | | 93 | 35 |
| ♦ *Lane County / Richard C. MacKenzie / Richard C. MacKenzie / 1983* | | | | | | | | | | | |
| 148 6/8 | 24 5/8 | 24 2/8 | 20 2/8 | 22 6/8 | 5 | 5 1/8 | 5 | 5 | 1 | 98 | 37 |
| ♦ *Tillamook County / Fred Dick / Fred Dick / 1948* | | | | | | | | | | | |
| 148 4/8 | 21 6/8 | 22 5/8 | 15 6/8 | 17 7/8 | 5 3/8 | 5 6/8 | 5 | 5 | | 99 | 38 |
| ♦ *Linn County / Marlin D. Brinkley / Marlin D. Brinkley / 1982* | | | | | | | | | | | |
| 148 3/8 | 21 2/8 | 21 | 19 5/8 | 21 4/8 | 4 3/8 | 4 2/8 | 5 | 5 | | 102 | 39 |
| ♦ *Douglas County / Unknown / Bud Jackson / 1929* | | | | | | | | | | | |
| 148 3/8 | 21 7/8 | 21 1/8 | 18 6/8 | 24 6/8 | 4 2/8 | 4 1/8 | 5 | 10 | 6 1/8 | 102 | 39 |
| ♦ *Marion County / Mike Fenimore / Mike Fenimore / 1961* | | | | | | | | | | | |
| 148 1/8 | 23 4/8 | 22 4/8 | 15 5/8 | 17 7/8 | 5 1/8 | 5 1/8 | 6 | 5 | 2 | 105 | 41 |
| ♦ *Clackamas County / Steven C. Oaks / Steven C. Oaks / 1986* | | | | | | | | | | | |
| 147 2/8 | 22 6/8 | 23 4/8 | 19 6/8 | 22 4/8 | 4 2/8 | 4 3/8 | 4 | 5 | | 112 | 42 |
| ♦ *Jackson County / Mike Taylor / Mike Taylor / 1969* | | | | | | | | | | | |
| 146 6/8 | 21 4/8 | 21 5/8 | 18 4/8 | 22 6/8 | 4 7/8 | 5 | 6 | 5 | 1 | 117 | 43 |
| ♦ *Camas Valley / Adam J. Hipp / Adam J. Hipp / 1961* | | | | | | | | | | | |
| 146 5/8 | 21 6/8 | 21 | 16 3/8 | 18 4/8 | 4 3/8 | 4 3/8 | 5 | 5 | | 119 | 44 |
| ♦ *Coos County / Pete Serafin / Pete Serafin / 1968* | | | | | | | | | | | |
| 146 2/8 | 20 7/8 | 21 4/8 | 14 2/8 | 17 4/8 | 4 4/8 | 4 4/8 | 5 | 5 | | 123 | 45 |
| ♦ *Douglas County / Bernard H. Schum / Bernard H. Schum / 1966* | | | | | | | | | | | |
| 146 | 20 2/8 | 20 7/8 | 15 2/8 | 19 5/8 | 5 | 5 | 5 | 5 | | 126 | 46 |
| ♦ *Little Fall Creek / Gene B. Johnson / Gene B. Johnson / 1963* | | | | | | | | | | | |
| 145 7/8 | 24 5/8 | 22 4/8 | 19 | 20 5/8 | 5 5/8 | 5 6/8 | 6 | 5 | 2 1/8 | 127 | 47 |
| ♦ *Linn County / Harold Tonkin / C. Vernon Humble / 1954* | | | | | | | | | | | |

| Score | Length of Main Beam R | L | Inside Spread | Greatest Spread | Circumference at Smallest Place Between Burr and First Point R | L | Number of Points R | L | Total of Lengths Abnormal Points | All-Time Rank | State Rank |
|---|---|---|---|---|---|---|---|---|---|---|---|
| | ◆ *Locality Killed / By Whom Killed / Owner / Date Killed* | | | | | | | | | | |
| 145 4/8 | 20 1/8 | 20 4/8 | 14 2/8 | 17 | 4 2/8 | 4 1/8 | 6 | 5 | 1 1/8 | 135 | 48 |
| | ◆ *Jackson County / Gary D. Kaiser / Gary D. Kaiser / 1967* | | | | | | | | | | |
| 145 4/8 | 21 1/8 | 20 | 16 2/8 | 18 5/8 | 4 7/8 | 4 7/8 | 5 | 5 | | 135 | 48 |
| | ◆ *Douglas County / Daniel J. Fisher / Daniel J. Fisher / 1973* | | | | | | | | | | |
| 145 2/8 | 22 4/8 | 21 2/8 | 16 2/8 | 18 | 4 4/8 | 4 7/8 | 5 | 5 | | 138 | 50 |
| | ◆ *Jackson County / Bill Hays / Bill Hays / 1968* | | | | | | | | | | |
| 145 2/8 | 20 2/8 | 21 | 16 4/8 | 18 6/8 | 5 4/8 | 5 2/8 | 5 | 5 | | 138 | 50 |
| | ◆ *Marion County / James J. Edgell / James J. Edgell / 1979* | | | | | | | | | | |
| 145 2/8 | 23 | 23 6/8 | 22 7/8 | 24 4/8 | 4 3/8 | 4 4/8 | 6 | 5 | 3 3/8 | 138 | 50 |
| | ◆ *Josephine County / Jim Breeze / Jim Breeze / 1986* | | | | | | | | | | |
| 145 1/8 | 19 6/8 | 19 5/8 | 15 1/8 | 17 1/8 | 4 6/8 | 4 5/8 | 5 | 5 | | 143 | 53 |
| | ◆ *Lane County / Boyd Iverson / Boyd Iverson / 1982* | | | | | | | | | | |
| 145 | 19 2/8 | 19 2/8 | 19 2/8 | 21 7/8 | 4 5/8 | 4 4/8 | 5 | 5 | | 145 | 54 |
| | ◆ *Douglas County / Larry E. Waller / Larry E. Waller / 1980* | | | | | | | | | | |
| 144 7/8 | 20 6/8 | 20 4/8 | 13 3/8 | 16 3/8 | 4 | 4 1/8 | 5 | 5 | | 147 | 55 |
| | ◆ *Clatsop County / Pravomil Raichl / Pravomil Raichl / 1959* | | | | | | | | | | |
| 144 7/8 | 22 1/8 | 23 1/8 | 22 7/8 | 26 4/8 | 4 1/8 | 4 1/8 | 5 | 5 | | 147 | 55 |
| | ◆ *Lane County / Clair R. Thomas / Clair R. Thomas / 1959* | | | | | | | | | | |
| 144 6/8 | 21 3/8 | 22 4/8 | 19 5/8 | 24 2/8 | 6 | 6 | 5 | 4 | 2 7/8 | 149 | 57 |
| | ◆ *Lincoln County / William D. Harmon / Merle W. Emmert / 1976* | | | | | | | | | | |
| 144 5/8 | 22 6/8 | 22 4/8 | 21 5/8 | 23 5/8 | 4 4/8 | 4 4/8 | 5 | 5 | | 153 | 58 |
| | ◆ *Josephine County / Jerry C. Sparlin / Jerry C. Sparlin / 1963* | | | | | | | | | | |
| 144 4/8 | 21 6/8 | 21 5/8 | 16 2/8 | 18 4/8 | 4 2/8 | 4 3/8 | 5 | 5 | | 154 | 59 |
| | ◆ *Clackamas County / John R. Vollmer, Jr. / John R. Vollmer, Jr. / 1960* | | | | | | | | | | |
| 144 4/8 | 21 2/8 | 20 5/8 | 17 2/8 | 20 5/8 | 4 2/8 | 4 2/8 | 5 | 5 | | 154 | 59 |
| | ◆ *Powers / Ray A. Davis / Ray A. Davis / 1968* | | | | | | | | | | |
| 144 2/8 | 20 3/8 | 21 6/8 | 17 2/8 | 19 | 4 4/8 | 4 5/8 | 5 | 5 | | 160 | 61 |
| | ◆ *Jackson County / Warren Pestka / Warren Pestka / 1974* | | | | | | | | | | |
| 144 2/8 | 20 2/8 | 19 6/8 | 20 3/8 | 26 2/8 | 3 5/8 | 3 5/8 | 6 | 5 | 4 | 160 | 61 |
| | ◆ *Josephine County / Clinton Moore / Clinton Moore / 1975* | | | | | | | | | | |
| 144 2/8 | 21 6/8 | 21 3/8 | 15 6/8 | 18 4/8 | 4 6/8 | 4 6/8 | 6 | 5 | 1 | 160 | 61 |
| | ◆ *Marion County / Arthur L. Schmidt / Arthur L. Schmidt / 1978* | | | | | | | | | | |
| 144 1/8 | 21 7/8 | 21 3/8 | 17 7/8 | 19 5/8 | 4 5/8 | 4 4/8 | 5 | 5 | | 164 | 64 |
| | ◆ *Siskiyou Natl. For. / Dennis E. Bourn / Dennis E. Bourn / 1971* | | | | | | | | | | |

| Score | Length of Main Beam R | L | Inside Spread | Greatest Spread | Circumference at Smallest Place Between Burr and First Point R | L | Number of Points R | L | Total of Lengths Abnormal Points | All-Time Rank | State Rank |
|---|---|---|---|---|---|---|---|---|---|---|---|
| 144 | 21 2/8 | 21 5/8 | 17 | 20 3/8 | 4 7/8 | 5 1/8 | 5 | 5 | | 165 | 65 |
| ♦ Linn County / Ed A. Taylor / Ed A. Taylor / 1981 | | | | | | | | | | | |
| 143 7/8 | 21 7/8 | 23 | 20 6/8 | 23 2/8 | 5 | 4 5/8 | 6 | 6 | 3 1/8 | 167 | 66 |
| ♦ Linn County / Clarence Howe / Clarence Howe / 1941 | | | | | | | | | | | |
| 143 7/8 | 23 4/8 | 22 7/8 | 21 3/8 | 24 | 5 | 4 6/8 | 5 | 5 | | 167 | 66 |
| ♦ Clackamas County / Richard G. Mathis / Richard G. Mathis / 1965 | | | | | | | | | | | |
| 143 4/8 | 22 | 23 | 16 4/8 | 18 4/8 | 3 7/8 | 4 | 5 | 5 | | 177 | 68 |
| ♦ Josephine County / Virgil Welch / Virgil Welch / 1983 | | | | | | | | | | | |
| 143 2/8 | 21 6/8 | 21 5/8 | 19 | 21 | 4 3/8 | 4 5/8 | 5 | 5 | | 182 | 69 |
| ♦ Linn County / Basil C. Bradbury / Basil C. Bradbury / 1960 | | | | | | | | | | | |
| 143 1/8 | 21 4/8 | 20 7/8 | 17 3/8 | 20 3/8 | 4 4/8 | 4 4/8 | 6 | 5 | 1 2/8 | 187 | 70 |
| ♦ Benton County / A.C. Nelson / A.C. Nelson / 1957 | | | | | | | | | | | |
| 142 7/8 | 20 1/8 | 22 | 16 3/8 | 19 1/8 | 4 | 4 | 4 | 4 | | 189 | 71 |
| ♦ Clackamas County / Larry Tracy / Larry Tracy / 1965 | | | | | | | | | | | |
| 142 6/8 | 21 2/8 | 21 7/8 | 19 4/8 | 22 | 4 6/8 | 5 | 5 | 4 | | 190 | 72 |
| ♦ Linn County / R. Reid & D. Liles / R. Reid & D. Liles / 1982 | | | | | | | | | | | |
| 142 6/8 | 23 2/8 | 22 | 17 2/8 | 20 | 3 7/8 | 4 | 4 | 4 | | 190 | 72 |
| ♦ Linn County / Kenneth W. Wegner / Kenneth W. Wegner / 1982 | | | | | | | | | | | |
| 142 6/8 | 20 4/8 | 20 1/8 | 20 7/8 | 23 5/8 | 4 4/8 | 3 7/8 | 5 | 4 | | 190 | 72 |
| ♦ Josephine County / Reginald P. Breeze / Reginald P. Breeze / 1986 | | | | | | | | | | | |
| 142 5/8 | 22 | 22 3/8 | 17 1/8 | 19 1/8 | 4 2/8 | 4 1/8 | 5 | 5 | | 193 | 75 |
| ♦ Marion County / Robert E. Bochsler / Robert E. Bochsler / 1950 | | | | | | | | | | | |
| 142 5/8 | 19 6/8 | 19 4/8 | 17 7/8 | 19 5/8 | 4 6/8 | 4 6/8 | 5 | 5 | | 193 | 75 |
| ♦ Jackson County / Leonard B. Sequeira / Nancy Sequeira / 1959 | | | | | | | | | | | |
| 142 4/8 | 21 6/8 | 22 | 16 6/8 | 21 5/8 | 4 3/8 | 4 3/8 | 6 | 5 | 2 3/8 | 199 | 77 |
| ♦ Clackamas County / Henry A. Charriere / Henry A. Charriere / 1970 | | | | | | | | | | | |
| 142 4/8 | 22 4/8 | 22 7/8 | 21 | 24.9 | 4 3/8 | 3 7/8 | 4 | 3 | | 199 | 77 |
| ♦ Jackson County / Donald G. Spence / Donald G. Spence / 1980 | | | | | | | | | | | |
| 142 2/8 | 20 7/8 | 20 4/8 | 16 2/8 | 18 1/8 | 4 3/8 | 4 6/8 | 5 | 5 | | 205 | 79 |
| ♦ Jackson County / Eileen F. Damone / Eileen F. Damone / 1976 | | | | | | | | | | | |
| 142 | 24 | 23 5/8 | 16 7/8 | 20 4/8 | 5 1/8 | 5 6/8 | 8 | 5 | 11 1/8 | 208 | 80 |
| ♦ Marion County / Hugh W. Gardner / Hugh W. Gardner / 1966 | | | | | | | | | | | |
| 141 6/8 | 21 3/8 | 21 3/8 | 19 2/8 | 21 7/8 | 4 4/8 | 4 4/8 | 5 | 5 | | 216 | 81 |
| ♦ Lane County / Jerry Shepard / Jerry Shepard / 1954 | | | | | | | | | | | |

| Score | Length of Main Beam R | L | Inside Spread | Greatest Spread | Circumference at Smallest Place Between Burr and First Point R | L | Number of Points R | L | Total of Lengths Abnormal Points | All-Time Rank | State Rank |
|---|---|---|---|---|---|---|---|---|---|---|---|
| | ◆ *Locality Killed / By Whom Killed / Owner / Date Killed* | | | | | | | | | | |
| 141 6/8 | 20 2/8 | 20 7/8 | 18 2/8 | 20 6/8 | 4 5/8 | 4 4/8 | 5 | 5 | | 216 | 81 |
| | ◆ *Linn County / Eugene L. Wilson / Eugene L. Wilson / 1982* | | | | | | | | | | |
| 141 2/8 | 21 4/8 | 20 6/8 | 18 2/8 | 21 4/8 | 4 3/8 | 4 2/8 | 5 | 5 | | 228 | 83 |
| | ◆ *Marion County / Arthur L. Schmidt / Arthur L. Schmidt / 1986* | | | | | | | | | | |
| 141 1/8 | 23 3/8 | 23 2/8 | 17 5/8 | 19 6/8 | 4 2/8 | 4 4/8 | 6 | 6 | 2 2/8 | 230 | 84 |
| | ◆ *Jackson County / Harold R. Embury / Harold R. Embury / 1985* | | | | | | | | | | |
| 140 7/8 | 23 7/8 | 23 7/8 | 18 6/8 | 23 | 5 | 5 | 10 | 8 | 20 3/8 | 235 | 85 |
| | ◆ *Polk County / Gale A. Draper / Gale A. Draper / 1984* | | | | | | | | | | |
| 140 4/8 | 21 1/8 | 20 7/8 | 18 2/8 | 20 1/8 | 4 7/8 | 4 6/8 | 6 | 5 | 4 4/8 | 243 | 86 |
| | ◆ *Yamhill County / Richard Watts / Richard Watts / 1981* | | | | | | | | | | |
| 140 1/8 | 20 7/8 | 22 1/8 | 16 5/8 | 19 2/8 | 4 3/8 | 4 3/8 | 5 | 5 | | 251 | 87 |
| | ◆ *Lincoln County / Darrel R. Grishaber / Darrel R. Grishaber / 1984* | | | | | | | | | | |
| 140 | 21 | 20 1/8 | 17 | 23 4/8 | 5 | 4 6/8 | 6 | 8 | 9 2/8 | 258 | 88 |
| | ◆ *Polk County / Harold E. Stepp / Harold E. Stepp / 1970* | | | | | | | | | | |
| 139 7/8 | 20 7/8 | 20 1/8 | 18 7/8 | 21 1/8 | 5 2/8 | 5 | 5 | 5 | | 263 | 89 |
| | ◆ *Jackson County / Dale E. Hoskins / Dale E. Hoskins / 1946* | | | | | | | | | | |
| 139 6/8 | 20 6/8 | 19 6/8 | 18 1/8 | 20 7/8 | 4 4/8 | 4 2/8 | 5 | 6 | 4 1/8 | 266 | 90 |
| | ◆ *Josephine County / Richard H. Caswell / Richard H. Caswell / 1969* | | | | | | | | | | |
| 139 4/8 | 21 7/8 | 21 5/8 | 20 4/8 | 23 | 4 1/8 | 4 2/8 | 5 | 5 | | 270 | 91 |
| | ◆ *Lane County / Gene Tinker / Gene Tinker / 1955* | | | | | | | | | | |
| 139 4/8 | 21 7/8 | 21 1/8 | 17 2/8 | 20 | 3 4/8 | 3 4/8 | 7 | 5 | 2 6/8 | 270 | 91 |
| | ◆ *Jackson County / Arthur A. Ekerson / Arthur A. Ekerson / 1966* | | | | | | | | | | |
| 139 4/8 | 20 7/8 | 22 3/8 | 19 4/8 | 29 6/8 | 4 7/8 | 4 5/8 | 6 | 7 | 6 4/8 | 270 | 91 |
| | ◆ *Jackson County / Everett B. Music, Jr. / Everett B. Music, Jr. / 1985* | | | | | | | | | | |
| 139 3/8 | 21 4/8 | 21 1/8 | 17 7/8 | 19 3/8 | 4 3/8 | 4 4/8 | 5 | 5 | | 274 | 94 |
| | ◆ *Monmouth / Roy W. Miller / Roy W. Miller / 1967* | | | | | | | | | | |
| 139 3/8 | 20 7/8 | 20 6/8 | 19 5/8 | 21 6/8 | 4 6/8 | 4 5/8 | 5 | 5 | | 274 | 94 |
| | ◆ *Marion County / Richard A. Hart / Richard A. Hart / 1982* | | | | | | | | | | |
| 139 2/8 | 21 7/8 | 23 3/8 | 17 1/8 | 20 4/8 | 5 1/8 | 4 3/8 | 7 | 4 | 7 1/8 | 280 | 96 |
| | ◆ *Josephine County / David L. Teasley / David L. Teasley / 1986* | | | | | | | | | | |
| 139 1/8 | 21 7/8 | 21 7/8 | 18 5/8 | 21 | 3 7/8 | 4 1/8 | 4 | 5 | | 284 | 97 |
| | ◆ *Florence / Edwin C. Stevens / Warner Pinkney / 1928* | | | | | | | | | | |
| 139 | 19 3/8 | 19 3/8 | 18 2/8 | 20 5/8 | 4 1/8 | 4 | 5 | 5 | | 287 | 98 |
| | ◆ *Douglas County / Richard Wigle / Richard Wigle / 1968* | | | | | | | | | | |

| Score | Length of Main Beam R | L | Inside Spread | Greatest Spread | Circumference at Smallest Place Between Burr and First Point R | L | Number of Points R | L | Total of Lengths Abnormal Points | All-Time Rank | State Rank |
|---|---|---|---|---|---|---|---|---|---|---|---|
| | *Locality Killed / By Whom Killed / Owner / Date Killed* | | | | | | | | | | |
| 139 | 21 2/8 | 21 3/8 | 16 4/8 | 19 3/8 | 3 7/8 | 3 7/8 | 5 | 5 | | 287 | 98 |
| ♦ *Marion County / Gene Collier / Gene Collier / 1983* | | | | | | | | | | | |
| 138 7/8 | 23 7/8 | 24 2/8 | 18 4/8 | | 4 4/8 | 4 4/8 | 5 | 5 | 5 5/8 | 291 | 100 |
| ♦ *Tiller / Ronald Elliott / Ronald Elliott / 1963* | | | | | | | | | | | |
| 138 7/8 | 20 4/8 | 20 5/8 | 16 5/8 | 19 | 4 2/8 | 4 2/8 | 5 | 5 | | 291 | 100 |
| ♦ *Tillamook County / Henry Naegeli / Henry Naegeli / 1970* | | | | | | | | | | | |
| 138 5/8 | 21 | 21 | 15 5/8 | 17 7/8 | 5 2/8 | 5 | 5 | 5 | | 301 | 102 |
| ♦ *Clatsop County / Russell L. Hemphill / Russell L. Hemphill / 1972* | | | | | | | | | | | |
| 138 3/8 | 22 5/8 | 22 | 20 5/8 | 23 | 4 7/8 | 4 5/8 | 5 | 5 | | 305 | 103 |
| ♦ *Clackamas County / J.B. Mitts / Wes Mitts / 1896* | | | | | | | | | | | |
| 138 2/8 | 18 6/8 | 18 6/8 | 15 6/8 | 19 7/8 | 4 1/8 | 4 3/8 | 5 | 5 | | 308 | 104 |
| ♦ *Marion County / Gene Collier / Gene Collier / 1974* | | | | | | | | | | | |
| 138 2/8 | 21 1/8 | 21 2/8 | 17 4/8 | 19 4/8 | 5 | 5 1/8 | 5 | 4 | | 308 | 104 |
| ♦ *Linn County / Douglas J. Morehead / Douglas J. Morehead / 1984* | | | | | | | | | | | |
| 138 1/8 | 18 5/8 | 20 3/8 | 17 1/4 | 19 3/8 | 4 2/8 | 4 3/8 | 5 | 5 | | 314 | 106 |
| ♦ *Columbia County / Virginia L. Brown / Steve Crossley / 1981* | | | | | | | | | | | |
| 138 | 19 6/8 | 19 6/8 | 16 7/8 | 19 5/8 | 4 6/8 | 4 5/8 | 5 | 6 | 1 7/8 | 315 | 107 |
| ♦ *Douglas County / Will H. Brown / Will H. Brown / 1948* | | | | | | | | | | | |
| 138 | 19 3/8 | 20 1/8 | 15 | 18 | 4 1/8 | 4 2/8 | 5 | 5 | | 315 | 107 |
| ♦ *Marion County / Frank C. Bersin / Frank C. Bersin / 1977* | | | | | | | | | | | |
| 137 7/8 | 20 4/8 | 20 3/8 | 17 | 20 4/8 | 4 4/8 | 4 5/8 | 5 | 6 | 2 1/8 | 318 | 109 |
| ♦ *Yamhill County / Wallace Hill / Wallace Hill / 1963* | | | | | | | | | | | |
| 137 2/8 | 19 3/8 | 20 7/8 | 18 | 20 7/8 | 4 2/8 | 4 1/8 | 5 | 5 | | 328 | 110 |
| ♦ *Douglas County / Bernard L. Den / Bernard L. Den / 1934* | | | | | | | | | | | |
| 137 2/8 | 19 6/8 | 20 | 15 | 18 3/8 | 4 3/8 | 4 1/8 | 5 | 5 | | 328 | 110 |
| ♦ *Douglas County / Francis R. Young / Francis R. Young / 1972* | | | | | | | | | | | |
| 137 1/8 | 21 3/8 | 19 2/8 | 15 7/8 | 21 | 4 2/8 | 4 2/8 | 5 | 5 | | 330 | 112 |
| ♦ *Douglas County / Peter Serafin / Peter Serafin / 1932* | | | | | | | | | | | |
| 137 1/8 | 20 4/8 | 20 1/8 | 15 5/8 | 19 7/8 | 4 5/8 | 4 6/8 | 5 | 5 | | 330 | 112 |
| ♦ *Tillamook County / Iola M. Pfaff / Iola M. Pfaff / 1940* | | | | | | | | | | | |
| 137 | 20 | 19 5/8 | 15 6/8 | 17 7/8 | 4 6/8 | 4 6/8 | 5 | 5 | | 334 | 114 |
| ♦ *Polk County / Ralph Cooper / Ralph Cooper / 1978* | | | | | | | | | | | |
| 136 5/8 | 21 5/8 | 22 1/8 | 19 5/8 | 22 4/8 | 4 5/8 | 4 6/8 | 5 | 5 | | 342 | 115 |
| ♦ *Tillamook County / J.A. Aaron / J.A. Aaron / 1943* | | | | | | | | | | | |

| Score | Length of Main Beam R | L | Inside Spread | Greatest Spread | Circumference at Smallest Place Between Burr and First Point R | L | Number of Points R | L | Total of Lengths Abnormal Points | All-Time Rank | State Rank |
|---|---|---|---|---|---|---|---|---|---|---|---|
| | | | | *Locality Killed / By Whom Killed / Owner / Date Killed* | | | | | | | |
| 136 5/8 | 21 6/8 | 21 6/8 | 15 7/8 | 17 5/8 | 4 1/8 | 4 | 5 | 5 | | 342 | 115 |
| ♦ Marion County / Ronald A. Bersin / Ronald A. Bersin / 1978 | | | | | | | | | | | |
| 136 3/8 | 20 2/8 | 20 1/8 | 19 1/8 | 20 7/8 | 4 | 4 1/8 | 4 | 5 | | 347 | 117 |
| ♦ Douglas County / Gerry F. Edwards / Gerry F. Edwards / 1971 | | | | | | | | | | | |
| 136 3/8 | 20 2/8 | 19 7/8 | 15 7/8 | 17 6/8 | 4 3/8 | 4 2/8 | 5 | 5 | | 347 | 117 |
| ♦ Tillamook County / Guy L. Thompson / Guy L. Thompson / 1983 | | | | | | | | | | | |
| 136 2/8 | 20 3/8 | 20 5/8 | 16 | 17 4/8 | 3 6/8 | 3 5/8 | 4 | 5 | 2 4/8 | 349 | 119 |
| ♦ Jackson County / Martin S. Durbin / Ellis A. Jones / 1921 | | | | | | | | | | | |
| 136 2/8 | 20 3/8 | 21 3/8 | 17 | 19 | 4 7/8 | 5 2/8 | 5 | 5 | | 349 | 119 |
| ♦ Yamhill County / Monty Dickey / Monty Dickey / 1967 | | | | | | | | | | | |
| 136 1/8 | 20 4/8 | 20 | 15 1/8 | 17 1/8 | 4 3/8 | 4 2/8 | 5 | 5 | | 353 | 121 |
| ♦ Jackson County / Nancy J. Eden / Nancy J. Eden / 1971 | | | | | | | | | | | |
| 135 7/8 | 22 1/8 | 22 2/8 | 17 3/8 | 19 | 4 4/8 | 4 4/8 | 4 | 3 | | 360 | 122 |
| ♦ Jackson County / Mrs. Ila B. Bethany / Mrs. Ila B. Bethany / 1972 | | | | | | | | | | | |
| 135 6/8 | 21 2/8 | 20 4/8 | 18 | 23 1/8 | 4 4/8 | 4 | 4 | 4 | | 364 | 123 |
| ♦ Linn County / Gene Collier / Gene Collier / 1966 | | | | | | | | | | | |
| 135 2/8 | 20 5/8 | 19 3/8 | 19 1/8 | 24 6/8 | 5 3/8 | 5 1/8 | 7 | 8 | 15 3/8 | 373 | 124 |
| ♦ Benton County / H.G. Slocum / H.G. Slocum / 1953 | | | | | | | | | | | |
| 135 | 19 1/8 | 19 4/8 | 15 4/8 | 19 3/8 | 4 3/8 | 4 3/8 | 5 | 5 | | 376 | 125 |
| ♦ Clackamas County / Ray W. Bunnell / Ray W. Bunnell / 1978 | | | | | | | | | | | |
| 134 7/8 | 21 2/8 | 21 4/8 | 16 1/8 | 17 | 3 4/8 | 3 6/8 | 4 | 4 | | 380 | 126 |
| ♦ Butte Falls / Bob Doan, Jr. / Bob Doan, Jr. / 1973 | | | | | | | | | | | |
| 134 3/8 | 21 3/8 | 21 6/8 | 19 5/8 | 21 3/8 | 4 2/8 | 4 2/8 | 5 | 5 | | 395 | 127 |
| ♦ Benton County / John E. Peterson / John E. Peterson / 1965 | | | | | | | | | | | |
| 134 2/8 | 20 3/8 | 19 6/8 | 16 4/8 | 18 6/8 | 4 2/8 | 4 3/8 | 5 | 5 | | 399 | 128 |
| ♦ Douglas County / John R. Hughey / John R. Hughey / 1965 | | | | | | | | | | | |
| 134 1/8 | 20 3/8 | 21 3/8 | 19 3/8 | 20 7/8 | 3 7/8 | 3 7/8 | 5 | 5 | | 404 | 129 |
| ♦ Coos County / Dan Woolley / Dan Woolley / 1971 | | | | | | | | | | | |
| 133 5/8 | 21 1/8 | 19 5/8 | 15 | 17 5/8 | 4 6/8 | 4 7/8 | 6 | 5 | 2 3/8 | 413 | 130 |
| ♦ Columbia County / Duane M. Bernard / Duane M. Bernard / 1952 | | | | | | | | | | | |
| 133 5/8 | 22 2/8 | 21 1/8 | 18 1/8 | 20 | 5 5/8 | 5 1/8 | 6 | 4 | 3 6/8 | 413 | 130 |
| ♦ Linn County / Richard L. Rounds / Richard L. Rounds / 1978 | | | | | | | | | | | |
| 133 5/8 | 19 | 19 5/8 | 15 7/8 | 20 5/8 | 4 1/8 | 4 2/8 | 5 | 6 | 1 2/8 | 413 | 130 |
| ♦ Clackamas County / Richard K. Hughes / Richard K. Hughes / 1981 | | | | | | | | | | | |

| Score | Length of Main Beam R | L | Inside Spread | Greatest Spread | Circumference at Smallest Place Between Burr and First Point R | L | Number of Points R | L | Total of Lengths Abnormal Points | All-Time Rank | State Rank |
|---|---|---|---|---|---|---|---|---|---|---|---|
| | ♦ *Locality Killed / By Whom Killed / Owner / Date Killed* | | | | | | | | | | |
| 133 5/8 | 18 6/8 | 18 1/8 | 13 1/8 | 16 2/8 | 4 2/8 | 4 3/8 | 5 | 5 | | 413 | 130 |
| | ♦ *Josephine County / Jack D. Chambers / Jack D. Chambers / 1985* | | | | | | | | | | |
| 133 4/8 | 20 4/8 | 19 6/8 | 15 2/8 | 17 2/8 | 5 6/8 | 4 4/8 | 5 | 5 | | 417 | 134 |
| | ♦ *Clackamas County / C.A. Pond / C.A. Pond / 1940* | | | | | | | | | | |
| 133 4/8 | 19 4/8 | 20 3/8 | 17 2/8 | 19 1/8 | 4 | 4 | 5 | 5 | | 417 | 134 |
| | ♦ *Coos County / Toby J. Johnson / Toby J. Johnson / 1981* | | | | | | | | | | |
| 133 4/8 | 18 7/8 | 19 3/8 | 18 | 20 4/8 | 3 7/8 | 4 | 6 | 6 | 7 | 417 | 134 |
| | ♦ *Josephine County / Randy L. Hansen / Randy L. Hansen / 1981* | | | | | | | | | | |
| 133 3/8 | 18 6/8 | 19 3/8 | 17 6/8 | 20 3/8 | 4 2/8 | 4 | 6 | 5 | 3 3/8 | 423 | 137 |
| | ♦ *Coos County / Frank Neal / Foster H. Thompson / 1924* | | | | | | | | | | |
| 133 3/8 | 19 3/8 | 19 6/8 | 18 5/8 | 20 6/8 | 4 | 3 7/8 | 5 | 5 | | 423 | 137 |
| | ♦ *Lane County / John D. Woodmark / John D. Woodmark / 1969* | | | | | | | | | | |
| 133 3/8 | 21 4/8 | 20 5/8 | 16 5/8 | 18 6/8 | 4 1/8 | 4 1/8 | 5 | 5 | | 423 | 137 |
| | ♦ *Marion County / Gene Collier / Gene Collier / 1984* | | | | | | | | | | |
| 133 2/8 | 20 | 19 7/8 | 14 6/8 | 17 4/8 | 4 1/8 | 4 2/8 | 5 | 5 | | 427 | 140 |
| | ♦ *Linn County / Leon Plueard / Leon Plueard / 1965* | | | | | | | | | | |
| 133 2/8 | 19 | 19 5/8 | 17 | 21 3/8 | 4 2/8 | 4 | 4 | 4 | | 427 | 140 |
| | ♦ *Clackamas County / Mary A. Schoenborn / Mary A. Schoenborn / 1971* | | | | | | | | | | |
| 133 1/8 | 23 2/8 | 23 | 20 3/8 | 26 1/8 | 3 7/8 | 4 6/8 | 4 | 5 | | 433 | 142 |
| | ♦ *Lane County / Picked Up / Wayne E. Everett / 1971* | | | | | | | | | | |
| 133 1/8 | 19 4/8 | 19 2/8 | 15 5/8 | 19 | 4 2/8 | 4 2/8 | 5 | 5 | | 433 | 142 |
| | ♦ *Josephine County / Michael J. Collins / Michael J. Collins / 1983* | | | | | | | | | | |
| 133 | 18 3/8 | 18 7/8 | 15 6/8 | 19 4/8 | 3 7/8 | 4 | 5 | 5 | | 437 | 144 |
| | ♦ *Lane County / Karl R. Rymer / Karl R. Rymer / 1969* | | | | | | | | | | |
| 132 7/8 | 18 4/8 | 19 4/8 | 18 1/8 | 20 2/8 | 4 7/8 | 4 6/8 | 5 | 5 | | 440 | 145 |
| | ♦ *Clackamas County / Kerry L. Schoenborn / Kerry L. Schoenborn / 1978* | | | | | | | | | | |
| 132 7/8 | 21 6/8 | 22 5/8 | 18 6/8 | 20 2/8 | 3 6/8 | 4 2/8 | 4 | 4 | 1 7/8 | 440 | 145 |
| | ♦ *Jackson County / Lorin C. Bosch / Lorin C. Bosch / 1986* | | | | | | | | | | |
| 132 6/8 | 21 4/8 | 20 3/8 | 15 2/8 | 17 2/8 | 4 | 4 | 4 | 5 | | 444 | 147 |
| | ♦ *Jackson County / Brad B. Brown / Brad B. Brown / 1985* | | | | | | | | | | |
| 132 4/8 | 19 5/8 | 20 7/8 | 16 2/8 | 18 5/8 | 4 2/8 | 4 4/8 | 5 | 5 | | 450 | 148 |
| | ♦ *Linn County / Gene Collier / Gene Collier / 1964* | | | | | | | | | | |
| 132 4/8 | 20 4/8 | 19 7/8 | 15 2/8 | 17 1/8 | 4 | 3 7/8 | 5 | 5 | | 450 | 148 |
| | ♦ *Clackamas County / Katherine M. Searls / Katherine M. Searls / 1982* | | | | | | | | | | |

| Score | Length of Main Beam R | L | Inside Spread | Greatest Spread | Circumference at Smallest Place Between Burr and First Point R | L | Number of Points R | L | Total of Lengths Abnormal Points | All-Time Rank | State Rank |
|---|---|---|---|---|---|---|---|---|---|---|---|
| | ♦ Locality Killed / By Whom Killed / Owner / Date Killed | | | | | | | | | | |
| 132 3/8 | 21 4/8 | 22 4/8 | 15 1/8 | 17 | 4 | 3 7/8 | 4 | 4 | 3 | 453 | 150 |
| | ♦ Tillamook County / Greg E. Myers / Greg E. Myers / 1977 | | | | | | | | | | |
| 132 2/8 | 21 6/8 | 21 1/8 | 12 4/8 | 14 7/8 | 5 2/8 | 4 6/8 | 4 | 4 | | 458 | 151 |
| | ♦ Douglas County / William McCaleb / William McCaleb / 1963 | | | | | | | | | | |
| 131 4/8 | 19 5/8 | 20 4/8 | 16 4/8 | 19 | 4 3/8 | 4 3/8 | 5 | 5 | | 474 | 152 |
| | ♦ Tillamook County / Ted Wolcott / Ted Wolcott / 1943 | | | | | | | | | | |
| 131 4/8 | 18 | 18 3/8 | 14 2/8 | 16 | 4 3/8 | 4 4/8 | 5 | 5 | | 474 | 152 |
| | ♦ Lane County / Helen Sanderlin / Helen Sanderlin / 1966 | | | | | | | | | | |
| 131 3/8 | 19 | 19 | 16 1/8 | 22 | 4 2/8 | 4 2/8 | 4 | 4 | | 479 | 154 |
| | ♦ Lincoln County / Bert Kessi / Bert Kessi / 1942 | | | | | | | | | | |
| 131 3/8 | 20 | 19 6/8 | 14 4/8 | 16 6/8 | 4 | 4 | 5 | 5 | 1 1/8 | 479 | 154 |
| | ♦ Linn County / Boyd Iverson / Boyd Iverson / 1985 | | | | | | | | | | |
| 131 2/8 | 24 4/8 | 24 | 19 7/8 | 22 4/8 | 4 1/8 | 4 2/8 | 5 | 4 | 1 3/8 | 481 | 156 |
| | ♦ Polk County / Ray Burtis / Ray Burtis / 1960 | | | | | | | | | | |
| 131 2/8 | 19 1/8 | 17 6/8 | 13 6/8 | 16 3/8 | 4 4/8 | 4 4/8 | 5 | 5 | | 481 | 156 |
| | ♦ Estacada / Roy Tracy / Lamont Rumgay / 1967 | | | | | | | | | | |
| 131 | 17 5/8 | 17 4/8 | 14 6/8 | 17 3/8 | 4 4/8 | 4 1/8 | 5 | 5 | | 485 | 158 |
| | ♦ Jackson County / Robert R. Maben / Robert R. Maben / 1963 | | | | | | | | | | |
| 130 6/8 | 22 | 22 | 16 6/8 | 18 7/8 | 4 4/8 | 4 4/8 | 5 | 5 | | 490 | 159 |
| | ♦ Linn County / Gene Collier / Gene Collier / 1967 | | | | | | | | | | |
| 130 6/8 | 19 4/8 | 20 4/8 | 16 2/8 | 24 2/8 | 4 2/8 | 4 2/8 | 5 | 6 | 3 6/8 | 490 | 159 |
| | ♦ Jackson County / Roy D. Hugie / Univ. of Mont. Mus. / 1983 | | | | | | | | | | |
| 130 6/8 | 19 4/8 | 19 3/8 | 14 4/8 | 17 1/8 | 4 1/8 | 4 3/8 | 5 | 5 | | 490 | 159 |
| | ♦ Yamhill County / Picked Up / John N. Washburn / 1984 | | | | | | | | | | |
| 130 5/8 | 19 7/8 | 20 5/8 | 14 5/8 | 16 4/8 | 4 | 4 3/8 | 5 | 5 | | 495 | 162 |
| | ♦ Josephine County / Raymond D. Dodge / Raymond D. Dodge / 1987 | | | | | | | | | | |
| 130 4/8 | 21 | 21 5/8 | 17 2/8 | 19 6/8 | 5 1/8 | 4 7/8 | 6 | 4 | 5 | 498 | 163 |
| | ♦ Multnomah County / Dennis R. Thorud / Dennis R. Thorud / 1985 | | | | | | | | | | |
| 130 2/8 | 20 4/8 | 20 | 16 4/8 | 18 6/8 | 4 4/8 | 4 5/8 | 5 | 5 | | 506 | 164 |
| | ♦ Clackamas County / Thomas A. Tremain / Thomas A. Tremain / 1976 | | | | | | | | | | |
| 128 5/8 | 18 6/8 | 18 4/8 | 13 7/8 | 15 5/8 | 4 | 4 2/8 | 4 | 5 | | 512 | 165 |
| | ♦ Lincoln County / Ken E. Bernet / Ken E. Bernet / 1986 | | | | | | | | | | |
| 127 1/8 | 21 | 21 1/8 | 20 1/8 | 22 3/8 | 4 2/8 | 4 3/8 | 4 | 5 | | 515 | 166 |
| | ♦ Marion County / John E. Williams / John E. Williams / 1974 | | | | | | | | | | |

| Score | Length of Main Beam R | Length of Main Beam L | Inside Spread | Greatest Spread | Circumference at Smallest Place Between Burr and First Point R | Circumference at Smallest Place Between Burr and First Point L | Number of Points R | Number of Points L | Total of Lengths Abnormal Points | All-Time Rank | State Rank |
|---|---|---|---|---|---|---|---|---|---|---|---|
| ♦ *Locality Killed / By Whom Killed / Owner / Date Killed* | | | | | | | | | | | |
| 126 3/8 | 20 7/8 | 16 4/8 | 17 3/8 | 19 | 4 | 4 4/8 | 4 | 4 | | 516 | 167 |
| ♦ *Columbia County / Charles Lindberg / Charles Lindberg / 1971* | | | | | | | | | | | |
| 125 5/8 | 21 3/8 | 20 7/8 | 16 1/8 | 17 6/8 | 3 6/8 | 3 1/8 | 4 | 5 | | 517 | 168 |
| ♦ *Marion County / Douglas G. Ellis / Douglas G. Ellis / 1984* | | | | | | | | | | | |
| 122 2/8 | 19 | 18 6/8 | 16 2/8 | 20 6/8 | 4 2/8 | 4 | 5 | 4 | | 526 | 169 |
| ♦ *Yamhill County / Picked Up / Mike McQuaw / 1980* | | | | | | | | | | | |
| 172 2/8 | 26 3/8 | 25 7/8 | 20 4/8 | 26 5/8 | 5 2/8 | 5 3/8 | 7 | 7 | 6 2/8 | * | * |
| ♦ *Marion County / B.G. Shurtleff / B.G. Shurtleff / 1969* | | | | | | | | | | | |
| 170 2/8 | 25 6/8 | 25 5/8 | 20 2/8 | 22 2/8 | 4 5/8 | 4 6/8 | 5 | 5 | | * | * |
| ♦ *Jackson County / Dennis R. King / King Tax. Studios / 1970* | | | | | | | | | | | |
| 162 6/8 | 24 1/8 | 25 4/8 | 18 4/8 | 24 2/8 | 5 4/8 | 5 4/8 | 7 | 8 | 8 6/8 | * | * |
| ♦ *Clackamas County / Curtis A. Lee / Steve Crossley / 1981* | | | | | | | | | | | |
| 162 2/8 | 23 6/8 | 22 4/8 | 21 | 24 | 5 2/8 | 5 2/8 | 5 | 5 | | * | * |
| ♦ *Jackson County / Mickey Geary / Mickey Geary / 1973* | | | | | | | | | | | |
| 161 2/8 | 24 | 23 3/8 | 19 2/8 | 22 6/8 | 4 5/8 | 4 5/8 | 5 | 5 | | * | * |
| ♦ *Clackamas County / Darrell Stewart / Darrell Stewart / 1977* | | | | | | | | | | | |

**WASHINGTON STATE RECORD**
**WORLD'S RECORD**
**COLUMBIA BLACKTAIL DEER**
**SCORE: 182-2/8**
Locality: Lewis Co.    Date: 1953
Hunter: Lester H. Miller

# WASHINGTON

## COLUMBIA BLACKTAIL DEER

| Score | Length of Main Beam R | L | Inside Spread | Greatest Spread | Circumference at Smallest Place Between Burr and First Point R | L | Number of Points R | L | Total of Lengths Abnormal Points | All-Time Rank | State Rank |
|---|---|---|---|---|---|---|---|---|---|---|---|
| 182 2/8 | 24 2/8 | 24 5/8 | 20 1/8 | 22 4/8 | 5 2/8 | 5 2/8 | 5 | 5 | | 1 | 1 |
| ◆ Lewis County / Lester H. Miller / Lester H. Miller / 1953 | | | | | | | | | | | |
| 169 3/8 | 23 2/8 | 22 1/8 | 18 3/8 | 22 1/8 | 5 1/8 | 6 1/8 | 6 | 6 | 6 | 4 | 2 |
| ◆ Lewis County / Larry V. Taylor / Thomas Gogan / 1941 | | | | | | | | | | | |
| 164 1/8 | 20 5/8 | 20 1/8 | 21 2/8 | 24 4/8 | 4 6/8 | 4 5/8 | 6 | 5 | 1 4/8 | 8 | 3 |
| ◆ Cowlitz County / Harold Melland / Harold Melland / 1962 | | | | | | | | | | | |
| 162 6/8 | 25 | 25 1/8 | 23 2/8 | 26 4/8 | 4 5/8 | 4 6/8 | 7 | 7 | 6 4/8 | 12 | 4 |
| ◆ Pierce County / Dick Allen / Craig Allen / 1952 | | | | | | | | | | | |
| 158 2/8 | 22 6/8 | 24 4/8 | 18 6/8 | 21 1/8 | 5 2/8 | 4 5/8 | 5 | 5 | | 28 | 5 |
| ◆ Lewis County / Keith A. Heldreth / Keith A. Heldreth / 1984 | | | | | | | | | | | |
| 156 6/8 | 22 2/8 | 21 3/8 | 20 2/8 | 24 2/8 | 4 5/8 | 4 4/8 | 5 | 5 | | 35 | 6 |
| ◆ Pierce County / Horst A. Vierthaler / Horst A. Vierthaler / 1963 | | | | | | | | | | | |
| 156 4/8 | 22 4/8 | 21 6/8 | 17 | 21 2/8 | 3 5/8 | 3 6/8 | 5 | 5 | | 36 | 7 |
| ◆ King County / Byron Gusa / Byron Gusa / 1980 | | | | | | | | | | | |
| 155 7/8 | 23 1/8 | 23 7/8 | 16 2/8 | 19 2/8 | 4 6/8 | 4 7/8 | 5 | 6 | 3 1/8 | 40 | 8 |
| ◆ Pierce County / J. Bennett & F. Duell / J. Bennett & F. Duell / 1983 | | | | | | | | | | | |
| 155 2/8 | 21 7/8 | 20 2/8 | 17 6/8 | 20 4/8 | 4 2/8 | 4 2/8 | 5 | 5 | | 41 | 9 |
| ◆ King County / Horst A. Vierthaler / Horst A. Vierthaler / 1960 | | | | | | | | | | | |
| 154 6/8 | 22 4/8 | 23 4/8 | 18 | 20 5/8 | 4 5/8 | 4 6/8 | 5 | 6 | 4 2/8 | 46 | 10 |
| ◆ Cowlitz County / Bud Whittle / Bud Whittle / 1957 | | | | | | | | | | | |
| 151 | 20 4/8 | 21 6/8 | 17 2/8 | 24 6/8 | 4 6/8 | 4 6/8 | 6 | 6 | 5 6/8 | 72 | 11 |
| ◆ Lewis County / Norman Henspeter / Norman Henspeter / 1941 | | | | | | | | | | | |
| 151 | 23 2/8 | 24 | 17 4/8 | 20 2/8 | 5 3/8 | 5 3/8 | 7 | 6 | 13 6/8 | 72 | 11 |
| ◆ Lewis County / Harold Gossard / George V. Bagley / 1967 | | | | | | | | | | | |
| 150 1/8 | 20 3/8 | 21 | 14 1/8 | 17 | 5 2/8 | 5 2/8 | 5 | 5 | | 79 | 13 |
| ◆ Lewis County / Carroll H. Fenn / Carroll H. Fenn / 1959 | | | | | | | | | | | |

| Score | Length of Main Beam | | Inside Spread | Greatest Spread | Circumference at Smallest Place Between Burr and First Point | | Number of Points | | Total of Lengths Abnormal Points | All-Time Rank | State Rank |
|---|---|---|---|---|---|---|---|---|---|---|---|
| | R | L | | | R | L | R | L | | | |
| ♦ Locality Killed / By Whom Killed / Owner / Date Killed | | | | | | | | | | | |
| 150 | 22 5/8 | 22 7/8 | 19 4/8 | 24 | 5 6/8 | 5 5/8 | 5 | 5 | | 83 | 14 |
| ♦ King County / Roscoe Rainey / Roscoe Rainey / 1963 | | | | | | | | | | | |
| 149 1/8 | 21 4/8 | 22 7/8 | 16 1/8 | 18 1/8 | 5 | 4 7/8 | 5 | 5 | | 96 | 15 |
| ♦ Clallam County / Otis Dahman / E.A. Dahman / 1943 | | | | | | | | | | | |
| 148 4/8 | 22 5/8 | 22 1/8 | 16 5/8 | 18 2/8 | 4 4/8 | 4 4/8 | 6 | 5 | 1 1/8 | 99 | 16 |
| ♦ Skamania County / Alan D. Borroz / Alan D. Borroz / 1978 | | | | | | | | | | | |
| 147 | 20 | 20 4/8 | 21 4/8 | 24 | 5 | 5 | 5 | 5 | | 114 | 17 |
| ♦ King County / Robert B. Gracey / Robert B. Gracey / 1963 | | | | | | | | | | | |
| 146 7/8 | 22 4/8 | 22 2/8 | 15 1/8 | 17 6/8 | 5 3/8 | 5 3/8 | 5 | 5 | | 116 | 18 |
| ♦ Clallam County / Charles W. Lockhart / Charles W. Lockhart / 1946 | | | | | | | | | | | |
| 146 4/8 | 22 6/8 | 22 7/8 | 22 | 24 1/8 | 5 2/8 | 5 4/8 | 5 | 5 | | 120 | 19 |
| ♦ King County / Leo Klinkhammer / Leo Klinkhammer / 1961 | | | | | | | | | | | |
| 145 6/8 | 22 2/8 | 20 5/8 | 17 | 21 4/8 | 4 2/8 | 4 2/8 | 5 | 5 | | 131 | 20 |
| ♦ King County / Terry Flowers / Terry Flowers / 1959 | | | | | | | | | | | |
| 145 6/8 | 19 4/8 | 20 2/8 | 14 6/8 | 18 1/8 | 5 3/8 | 6 | 5 | 6 | 3 | 131 | 20 |
| ♦ Whatcom County / Dennis Miller / Dennis Miller / 1970 | | | | | | | | | | | |
| 144 6/8 | 20 | 20 4/8 | 19 4/8 | 24 4/8 | 3 4/8 | 3 4/8 | 5 | 4 | 3 | 149 | 22 |
| ♦ King County / R. Walter Williams / R. Walter Williams / 1956 | | | | | | | | | | | |
| 144 6/8 | 22 2/8 | 22 1/8 | 17 1/8 | 19 5/8 | 4 4/8 | 4 3/8 | 6 | 6 | 2 3/8 | 149 | 22 |
| ♦ Skamania County / Melvin D. Robertson / Melvin D. Robertson / 1983 | | | | | | | | | | | |
| 144 4/8 | 21 | 21 7/8 | 17 | 24 | 3 7/8 | 3 6/8 | 4 | 4 | | 154 | 24 |
| ♦ Snohomish County / Roy Shogren / Roy Shogren / 1979 | | | | | | | | | | | |
| 144 | 20 7/8 | 20 4/8 | 17 2/8 | 18 7/8 | 4 4/8 | 4 5/8 | 5 | 5 | | 165 | 25 |
| ♦ Skamania County / Wayne Crockford / Wayne Crockford / 1960 | | | | | | | | | | | |
| 143 6/8 | 20 1/8 | 20 2/8 | 16 1/8 | 18 7/8 | 5 | 5 | 5 | 5 | | 170 | 26 |
| ♦ Lewis County / Bill W. Latimer / Bill W. Latimer / 1974 | | | | | | | | | | | |
| 143 5/8 | 21 2/8 | 21 2/8 | 17 1/8 | 19 6/8 | 5 6/8 | 5 7/8 | 5 | 6 | 3 | 174 | 27 |
| ♦ Grays Harbor County / Eddie & Bob Dierick / Eddie & Bob Dierick / 1958 | | | | | | | | | | | |
| 143 4/8 | 21 4/8 | 22 5/8 | 16 2/8 | | 4 1/8 | 4 3/8 | 5 | 5 | | 177 | 28 |
| ♦ Clark County / A.W. Gerber / Earl Gerber / 1929 | | | | | | | | | | | |
| 143 4/8 | 21 4/8 | 21 1/8 | 21 1/8 | 23 2/8 | 4 4/8 | 4 4/8 | 5 | 4 | | 177 | 28 |
| ♦ Snoqualmie / Milton L. James / Milton L. James / 1964 | | | | | | | | | | | |
| 142 | 20 1/8 | 20 6/8 | 17 | 19 | 4 3/8 | 4 2/8 | 5 | 5 | | 208 | 30 |
| ♦ Cowlitz County / Harold C. Johnson / Harold C. Johnson / 1947 | | | | | | | | | | | |

| Score | Length of Main Beam R | L | Inside Spread | Greatest Spread | Circumference at Smallest Place Between Burr and First Point R | L | Number of Points R | L | Total of Lengths Abnormal Points | All-Time Rank | State Rank |
|---|---|---|---|---|---|---|---|---|---|---|---|
| 142 | 21 6/8 | 22 5/8 | 20 2/8 | 22 1/8 | 4 5/8 | 4 6/8 | 6 | 5 | 2 4/8 | 208 | 30 |
| ◆ Mt. Sheazer / Joseph B. Wilcox / Joseph B. Wilcox / 1953 | | | | | | | | | | | |
| 142 | 24 6/8 | 24 6/8 | 17 | 19 1/8 | 5 | 5 | 4 | 5 | 2 | 208 | 30 |
| ◆ Skamania County / Ted Howell / Ted Howell / 1968 | | | | | | | | | | | |
| 142 | 25 3/8 | 24 | 18 3/8 | 21 | 7 | 6 4/8 | 7 | 4 | 2 5/8 | 208 | 30 |
| ◆ Doty / Leslie A. Lusk / Leslie A. Lusk / 1973 | | | | | | | | | | | |
| 142 | 23 | 20 7/8 | 21 4/8 | 23 5/8 | 4 4/8 | 4 4/8 | 5 | 5 | | 208 | 30 |
| ◆ Skamania County / Herbert P. Roberts / Herbert P. Roberts / 1983 | | | | | | | | | | | |
| 141 7/8 | 20 7/8 | 21 3/8 | 18 1/8 | 22 | 5 5/8 | 5 5/8 | 4 | 4 | | 214 | 35 |
| ◆ Whatcom County / Kjell A. Thompson / Kjell A. Thompson / 1963 | | | | | | | | | | | |
| 141 6/8 | 22 7/8 | 22 2/8 | 17 5/8 | 19 4/8 | 4 5/8 | 4 6/8 | 6 | 7 | 3 3/8 | 216 | 36 |
| ◆ Pierce County / Joseph Kominski / Joseph Kominski / 1954 | | | | | | | | | | | |
| 141 6/8 | 19 7/8 | 19 3/8 | 16 4/8 | 18 7/8 | 4 7/8 | 4 7/8 | 5 | 5 | | 216 | 36 |
| ◆ Hobart / Donald R. Heinle / Donald R. Heinle / 1958 | | | | | | | | | | | |
| 141 5/8 | 23 | 22 5/8 | 15 7/8 | 18 4/8 | 5 2/8 | 4 7/8 | 5 | 5 | | 220 | 38 |
| ◆ Skamania County / E. Gerald Tikka / E. Gerald Tikka / 1987 | | | | | | | | | | | |
| 141 4/8 | 20 2/8 | 20 6/8 | 17 6/8 | 19 5/8 | 4 7/8 | 5 | 5 | 5 | | 222 | 39 |
| ◆ Morton / Ralph W. Cournyer / Ralph W. Cournyer / 1962 | | | | | | | | | | | |
| 141 4/8 | 22 | 22 5/8 | 15 4/8 | 17 6/8 | 5 2/8 | 5 1/8 | 5 | 5 | | 222 | 39 |
| ◆ Pierce County / Ron Dick / Ron Dick / 1965 | | | | | | | | | | | |
| 141 2/8 | 25 6/8 | 25 3/8 | 21 5/8 | 24 7/8 | 5 4/8 | 5 6/8 | 6 | 6 | 3 3/8 | 228 | 41 |
| ◆ Pierce County / John Streepy, Sr. / John Streepy, Sr. / 1956 | | | | | | | | | | | |
| 141 1/8 | 22 2/8 | 22 4/8 | 17 7/8 | 19 7/8 | 4 6/8 | 4 6/8 | 5 | 5 | | 230 | 42 |
| ◆ Pierce County / Jerry E. Burke / Jerry E. Burke / 1980 | | | | | | | | | | | |
| 140 6/8 | 17 6/8 | 18 5/8 | 17 2/8 | 20 6/8 | 4 5/8 | 4 4/8 | 5 | 6 | 2 2/8 | 238 | 43 |
| ◆ Lewis County / Nick Nilson / Nick Nilson / 1944 | | | | | | | | | | | |
| 140 5/8 | 21 | 21 | 18 6/8 | 21 1/8 | 4 6/8 | 4 6/8 | 6 | 5 | 4 5/8 | 241 | 44 |
| ◆ Glacier / John J.A. Weatherby / John J.A. Weatherby / 1965 | | | | | | | | | | | |
| 140 2/8 | 20 4/8 | 21 3/8 | 16 2/8 | 18 2/8 | 4 7/8 | 4 5/8 | 5 | 5 | | 248 | 45 |
| ◆ Lewis County / Randy J. Brossard / Randy J. Brossard / 1978 | | | | | | | | | | | |
| 140 1/8 | 23 7/8 | 22 7/8 | 18 1/8 | 19 6/8 | 5 | 4 4/8 | 6 | 6 | 8 | 251 | 46 |
| ◆ Lewis County / George Nichols / George Nichols / 1964 | | | | | | | | | | | |
| 140 1/8 | 19 | 19 6/8 | 16 5/8 | 19 4/8 | 4 5/8 | 4 6/8 | 5 | 5 | | 251 | 46 |
| ◆ Snohomish County / Kenneth A. Peterson / Kenneth A. Peterson / 1985 | | | | | | | | | | | |

| Score | Length of Main Beam R | L | Inside Spread | Greatest Spread | Circumference at Smallest Place Between Burr and First Point R | L | Number of Points R | L | Total of Lengths Abnormal Points | All-Time Rank | State Rank |
|---|---|---|---|---|---|---|---|---|---|---|---|
| 139 6/8 | 21 1/8 | 21 3/8 | 18 6/8 | 20 7/8 | 5 | 4 6/8 | 5 | 5 | | 266 | 48 |
| ♦ Thurston County / Eric Anderson / Eric Anderson / 1937 | | | | | | | | | | | |
| 139 5/8 | 21 2/8 | 21 2/8 | 14 4/8 | 16 1/8 | 4 2/8 | 4 2/8 | 6 | 5 | 1 3/8 | 269 | 49 |
| ♦ Cowlitz County / David A. Martin / David A. Martin / 1962 | | | | | | | | | | | |
| 139 4/8 | 22 2/8 | 21 5/8 | 16 | 18 3/8 | 4 6/8 | 4 6/8 | 4 | 5 | | 270 | 50 |
| ♦ Lewis County / Kevin Pointer / Kevin Pointer / 1972 | | | | | | | | | | | |
| 139 3/8 | 20 1/8 | 20 2/8 | 15 5/8 | 19 | 4 2/8 | 4 1/8 | 5 | 5 | | 274 | 51 |
| ♦ Whatcom County / Kim S. Scott / Kim S. Scott / 1959 | | | | | | | | | | | |
| 139 | 21 1/8 | 22 3/8 | 16 2/8 | 19 6/8 | 4 5/8 | 4 5/8 | 5 | 5 | | 287 | 52 |
| ♦ Jefferson County / Picked Up / Aubrey F. Taylor / 1947 | | | | | | | | | | | |
| 139 | 20 | 20 5/8 | 16 4/8 | 18 4/8 | 4 6/8 | 4 4/8 | 5 | 5 | | 287 | 52 |
| ♦ Lewis County / Mike Cournyer / Mike Cournyer / 1964 | | | | | | | | | | | |
| 138 7/8 | 19 7/8 | 19 7/8 | 15 7/8 | 18 6/8 | 4 4/8 | 4 4/8 | 5 | 5 | | 291 | 54 |
| ♦ Pacific County / Russell Case / Russell Case / 1956 | | | | | | | | | | | |
| 138 6/8 | 20 2/8 | 21 3/8 | 15 5/8 | 17 3/8 | 5 1/8 | 5 2/8 | 6 | 7 | 3 5/8 | 296 | 55 |
| ♦ Snohomish County / Walter J. Kau / Walter J. Kau / 1950 | | | | | | | | | | | |
| 138 6/8 | 23 3/8 | 23 | 15 6/8 | 17 6/8 | 4 4/8 | 4 5/8 | 5 | 6 | 1 | 296 | 55 |
| ♦ Pierce County / James Latimer / James Latimer / 1962 | | | | | | | | | | | |
| 138 3/8 | 23 7/8 | 22 4/8 | 16 3/8 | 18 2/8 | 5 3/8 | 5 4/8 | 5 | 6 | 8 | 305 | 57 |
| ♦ Pierce County / George W. Halcott / George W. Halcott / 1966 | | | | | | | | | | | |
| 138 2/8 | 19 4/8 | 21 | 16 2/8 | 19 2/8 | 5 2/8 | 4 4/8 | 5 | 5 | | 308 | 58 |
| ♦ Snohomish County / James McCarthy / James McCarthy / 1961 | | | | | | | | | | | |
| 137 | 24 | 23 6/8 | 21 2/8 | 23 4/8 | 4 3/8 | 4 3/8 | 4 | 5 | | 334 | 59 |
| ♦ King County / Douglas F. Dammarell / Douglas F. Dammarell / 1974 | | | | | | | | | | | |
| 136 7/8 | 21 3/8 | 20 7/8 | 17 5/8 | 20 5/8 | 4 2/8 | 4 4/8 | 4 | 5 | | 337 | 60 |
| ♦ Lewis County / Allen J. Roehrick / Allen J. Roehrick / 1968 | | | | | | | | | | | |
| 136 6/8 | 21 3/8 | 21 | 14 | 16 3/8 | 5 2/8 | 5 2/8 | 5 | 5 | | 338 | 61 |
| ♦ King County / Ed Lochus / George B. Johnson / 1930 | | | | | | | | | | | |
| 136 6/8 | 19 3/8 | 20 | 14 3/8 | 16 3/8 | 4 5/8 | 5 | 6 | 6 | 2 7/8 | 338 | 61 |
| ♦ Lewis County / Mark G. Frohmader / Mark G. Frohmader / 1969 | | | | | | | | | | | |
| 136 6/8 | 20 5/8 | 21 1/8 | 16 | 17 6/8 | 4 1/8 | 4 1/8 | 5 | 5 | | 338 | 61 |
| ♦ Pierce County / Patrick M. Blackwell / Patrick M. Blackwell / 1971 | | | | | | | | | | | |
| 136 5/8 | 21 4/8 | 22 3/8 | 19 | 21 | 5 6/8 | 5 2/8 | 5 | 4 | 1 1/8 | 342 | 64 |
| ♦ Arlington / Ernest J. Kaesther / Ernest J. Kaesther / 1959 | | | | | | | | | | | |

| Score | Length of Main Beam R | Length of Main Beam L | Inside Spread | Greatest Spread | Circumference at Smallest Place Between Burr and First Point R | Circumference at Smallest Place Between Burr and First Point L | Number of Points R | Number of Points L | Total of Lengths Abnormal Points | All-Time Rank | State Rank |
|---|---|---|---|---|---|---|---|---|---|---|---|
| ♦ *Locality Killed / By Whom Killed / Owner / Date Killed* | | | | | | | | | | | |
| 136 4/8 | 23 4/8 | 22 1/8 | 18 2/8 | 20 1/8 | 4 6/8 | 4 6/8 | 5 | 5 | | 345 | 65 |
| ♦ *Lewis County / Larry F. Smith / Larry F. Smith / 1964* | | | | | | | | | | | |
| 135 7/8 | 20 3/8 | 21 1/8 | 16 7/8 | 19 3/8 | 5 | 5 | 5 | 5 | | 360 | 66 |
| ♦ *Snohomish County / Edmund L. Hurst / Edmund L. Hurst / 1984* | | | | | | | | | | | |
| 135 6/8 | 20 5/8 | 19 7/8 | 15 | 19 3/8 | 5 4/8 | 5 4/8 | 5 | 6 | 1 2/8 | 364 | 67 |
| ♦ *Whatcom County / Jack R. Teeter / Jack R. Teeter / 1969* | | | | | | | | | | | |
| 135 6/8 | 20 | 20 2/8 | 17 2/8 | 19 2/8 | 4 6/8 | 4 6/8 | 5 | 5 | | 364 | 67 |
| ♦ *Cowlitz County / William R. Gottfryd / William R. Gottfryd / 1986* | | | | | | | | | | | |
| 135 5/8 | 19 6/8 | 19 3/8 | 17 5/8 | 20 6/8 | 4 3/8 | 4 1/8 | 4 | 4 | | 369 | 69 |
| ♦ *Clallam County / Gary L. Smith / Gary L. Smith / 1956* | | | | | | | | | | | |
| 135 5/8 | 22 4/8 | 23 2/8 | 20 1/8 | 22 2/8 | 4 4/8 | 4 3/8 | 4 | 4 | | 369 | 69 |
| ♦ *Pierce County / Mark A. Dye / Mark A. Dye / 1987* | | | | | | | | | | | |
| 135 4/8 | 20 4/8 | 20 1/8 | 16 6/8 | 18 4/8 | 3 6/8 | 3 7/8 | 5 | 5 | | 371 | 71 |
| ♦ *Lewis County / Oren Layton / Oren Layton / 1977* | | | | | | | | | | | |
| 135 3/8 | 21 5/8 | 21 2/8 | 17 6/8 | 22 | 4 6/8 | 4 5/8 | 6 | 6 | 3 7/8 | 372 | 72 |
| ♦ *Clark County / Francis E. Gillette / Francis E. Gillette / 1934* | | | | | | | | | | | |
| 135 | 20 | 19 7/8 | 16 2/8 | 19 7/8 | 4 1/8 | 4 1/8 | 5 | 5 | | 376 | 73 |
| ♦ *Whatcom County / Dennis R. Beebe / Dennis R. Beebe / 1981* | | | | | | | | | | | |
| 134 6/8 | 22 4/8 | 22 6/8 | 16 | 18 6/8 | 5 1/8 | 5 1/8 | 5 | 6 | 3 6/8 | 385 | 74 |
| ♦ *Thurston County / George W. Sharrow / George W. Sharrow / 1946* | | | | | | | | | | | |
| 134 6/8 | 21 5/8 | 23 2/8 | 19 2/8 | 20 6/8 | 4 3/8 | 4 2/8 | 5 | 5 | | 385 | 74 |
| ♦ *Cowlitz County / Kenneth D. Nicholson / Kenneth D. Nicholson / 1970* | | | | | | | | | | | |
| 134 4/8 | 22 2/8 | 23 2/8 | 18 2/8 | 20 4/8 | 4 5/8 | 4 6/8 | 4 | 4 | | 389 | 76 |
| ♦ *Thurston County / Joseph Kominski / Joseph Kominski / 1955* | | | | | | | | | | | |
| 134 4/8 | 21 6/8 | 22 5/8 | 13 | 16 5/8 | 4 3/8 | 4 4/8 | 6 | 6 | 2 2/8 | 389 | 76 |
| ♦ *Lewis County / Douglas G. McArthur / Douglas G. McArthur / 1967* | | | | | | | | | | | |
| 134 4/8 | 26 | 27 1/8 | 20 2/8 | 22 3/8 | 4 7/8 | 4 6/8 | 5 | 4 | | 389 | 76 |
| ♦ *Lewis County / Daniel E. Longmire / Daniel E. Longmire / 1974* | | | | | | | | | | | |
| 134 3/8 | 18 | 15 | 17 7/8 | 20 6/8 | 4 6/8 | 4 2/8 | 6 | 5 | 1 2/8 | 395 | 79 |
| ♦ *Lewis County / Melvin B. Henle / Melvin B. Henle / 1973* | | | | | | | | | | | |
| 134 2/8 | 21 7/8 | 22 1/8 | 16 | 18 5/8 | 4 4/8 | 4 4/8 | 4 | 5 | | 399 | 80 |
| ♦ *Pierce County / James B. August / James B. August / 1971* | | | | | | | | | | | |
| 134 1/8 | 20 4/8 | 20 4/8 | 14 5/8 | 18 | 4 2/8 | 4 2/8 | 5 | 5 | | 404 | 81 |
| ♦ *King County / Greg E. Connell / Greg E. Connell / 1979* | | | | | | | | | | | |

| Score | Length of Main Beam R | L | Inside Spread | Greatest Spread | Circumference at Smallest Place Between Burr and First Point R | L | Number of Points R | L | Total of Lengths Abnormal Points | All-Time Rank | State Rank |
|---|---|---|---|---|---|---|---|---|---|---|---|
| | ◆ Locality Killed / By Whom Killed / Owner / Date Killed | | | | | | | | | | |
| 133 6/8 | 20 6/8 | 21 5/8 | 18 1/8 | 21 3/8 | 4 7/8 | 5 3/8 | 6 | 6 | 3 3/8 | 410 | 82 |
| | ◆ Pierce County / K.S. Sheets / K.S. Sheets / 1966 | | | | | | | | | | |
| 133 4/8 | 21 3/8 | 20 2/8 | 13 6/8 | 16 2/8 | 4 7/8 | 5 | 5 | 5 | | 417 | 83 |
| | ◆ Clallam County / Tony M. Rickel / Tony M. Rickel / 1987 | | | | | | | | | | |
| 133 3/8 | 20 7/8 | 21 7/8 | 12 1/8 | 15 | 4 4/8 | 4 6/8 | 5 | 5 | | 423 | 84 |
| | ◆ Clallam County / Glen W. Gooding / Glen W. Gooding / 1957 | | | | | | | | | | |
| 133 2/8 | 21 1/8 | 21 1/8 | 13 6/8 | 15 7/8 | 4 6/8 | 4 5/8 | 5 | 5 | | 427 | 85 |
| | ◆ Skagit County / L.A. Willoughby / L.A. Willoughby / 1951 | | | | | | | | | | |
| 133 2/8 | 20 5/8 | 20 4/8 | 14 6/8 | 16 5/8 | 4 5/8 | 4 6/8 | 5 | 5 | | 427 | 85 |
| | ◆ Pierce County / Lowell Apple / Lowell Apple / 1968 | | | | | | | | | | |
| 133 | 22 4/8 | 23 3/8 | 20 6/8 | 23 4/8 | 5 6/8 | 4 6/8 | 9 | 4 | 7 1/8 | 437 | 87 |
| | ◆ Lewis County / George Sevey / George Sevey / 1941 | | | | | | | | | | |
| 132 5/8 | 20 4/8 | 20 1/8 | 17 7/8 | 20 | 4 7/8 | 4 7/8 | 6 | 5 | 2 1/8 | 449 | 88 |
| | ◆ Mason County / Brian L. Martin / Brian L. Martin / 1984 | | | | | | | | | | |
| 132 4/8 | 19 | 18 2/8 | 14 | 17 | 4 7/8 | 4 7/8 | 4 | 4 | | 450 | 89 |
| | ◆ Lewis County / Robert L. Peck / Robert L. Peck / 1964 | | | | | | | | | | |
| 132 3/8 | 19 6/8 | 19 | 15 5/8 | 18 5/8 | 5 2/8 | 5 1/8 | 5 | 5 | | 453 | 90 |
| | ◆ Cowlitz County / James H. Wilson / James H. Wilson / 1959 | | | | | | | | | | |
| 132 3/8 | 21 2/8 | 21 5/8 | 16 3/8 | 20 1/8 | 4 | 4 | 5 | 5 | | 453 | 90 |
| | ◆ Grays Harbor County / Jack A. Allen / Jack A. Allen / 1963 | | | | | | | | | | |
| 132 2/8 | 20 3/8 | 20 2/8 | 16 2/8 | 18 3/8 | 5 1/8 | 5 | 5 | 4 | | 458 | 92 |
| | ◆ Island County / Bert Klineburger / Bert Klineburger / 1969 | | | | | | | | | | |
| 132 1/8 | 21 1/8 | 20 4/8 | 13 1/8 | 14 7/8 | 4 3/8 | 4 5/8 | 5 | 5 | | 463 | 93 |
| | ◆ Lewis County / George W. Rodrick III / George W. Rodrick III / 1980 | | | | | | | | | | |
| 131 5/8 | 19 1/8 | 19 6/8 | 14 7/8 | 17 1/8 | 4 6/8 | 4 6/8 | 5 | 5 | | 472 | 94 |
| | ◆ Whatcom County / C.H. Head / C.H. Head / 1972 | | | | | | | | | | |
| 131 5/8 | 22 | 21 6/8 | 17 1/8 | 19 3/8 | 4 2/8 | 4 2/8 | 4 | 5 | | 472 | 94 |
| | ◆ Pierce County / Lyle O. Brateng / Lyle O. Brateng / 1984 | | | | | | | | | | |
| 131 4/8 | 18 4/8 | 18 6/8 | 16 2/8 | 19 4/8 | 5 7/8 | 5 1/8 | 5 | 6 | 1 | 474 | 96 |
| | ◆ Lewis County / Ron N. Nilson / Ron N. Nilson / 1963 | | | | | | | | | | |
| 131 4/8 | 18 2/8 | 17 4/8 | 14 4/8 | 18 2/8 | 4 6/8 | 5 | 5 | 5 | | 474 | 96 |
| | ◆ Snohomish County / Philip C. Thompson / Philip C. Thompson / 1986 | | | | | | | | | | |
| 131 2/8 | 21 1/8 | 20 7/8 | 13 5/8 | 16 2/8 | 4 6/8 | 4 6/8 | 7 | 6 | 5 1/8 | 481 | 98 |
| | ◆ Skamania County / Thomas E. Krebs / Thomas E. Krebs / 1977 | | | | | | | | | | |

| Score | Length of Main Beam R | L | Inside Spread | Greatest Spread | Circumference at Smallest Place Between Burr and First Point R | L | Number of Points R | L | Total of Lengths Abnormal Points | All-Time Rank | State Rank |
|---|---|---|---|---|---|---|---|---|---|---|---|
| | | | | | *Locality Killed / By Whom Killed / Owner / Date Killed* | | | | | | |
| 31 | 21 6/8 | 20 5/8 | 15 2/8 | 18 5/8 | 4 5/8 | 4 4/8 | 5 | 5 | | 485 | 99 |
| | *King County / J.A. Ryezek / George B. Johnson / 1935* | | | | | | | | | | |
| 30 4/8 | 21 | 20 6/8 | 17 3/8 | 19 2/8 | 4 6/8 | 4 6/8 | 6 | 5 | 1 5/8 | 498 | 100 |
| | *Pierce County / Don Argo / Don Argo / 1950* | | | | | | | | | | |
| 30 4/8 | 20 4/8 | 20 2/8 | 12 4/8 | 14 2/8 | 4 3/8 | 4 3/8 | 5 | 5 | | 498 | 100 |
| | *Cowlitz County / Michael A. Demery / Steven J. Hellem / 1978* | | | | | | | | | | |
| 30 3/8 | 19 1/8 | 18 3/8 | 15 3/8 | 20 4/8 | 4 2/8 | 4 2/8 | 5 | 5 | | 504 | 102 |
| | *Mt. Jupiter / Jack Dustin / Jack Dustin / 1946* | | | | | | | | | | |
| 30 1/8 | 19 2/8 | 19 5/8 | 17 1/8 | 22 2/8 | 4 7/8 | 5 1/8 | 5 | 6 | 1 2/8 | 507 | 103 |
| | *Thurston County / Gano S. Hayes / Gano S. Hayes / 1985* | | | | | | | | | | |
| 30 | 17 2/8 | 17 2/8 | 16 | 19 | 4 3/8 | 4 2/8 | 5 | 5 | | 509 | 104 |
| | *Cowlitz County / Harold E. Koenig / Harold E. Koenig / 1949* | | | | | | | | | | |
| 28 2/8 | 20 4/8 | 20 2/8 | 14 6/8 | 17 3/8 | 4 1/8 | 4 2/8 | 5 | 5 | | 513 | 105 |
| | *Clallam County / James W. Fatherson / James W. Fatherson / 1983* | | | | | | | | | | |
| 27 5/8 | 20 3/8 | 21 | 19 6/8 | 22 1/8 | 5 1/8 | 5 2/8 | 6 | 7 | 6 5/8 | 514 | 106 |
| | *Clallam County / Harry E. Reed, Jr. / Harry E. Reed, Jr. / 1977* | | | | | | | | | | |
| 23 5/8 | 21 3/8 | 21 6/8 | 18 1/8 | 21 4/8 | 3 6/8 | 3 5/8 | 3 | 3 | | 519 | 107 |
| | *King County / Gene D. Collecchi / Gene D. Collecchi / 1987* | | | | | | | | | | |
| 23 3/8 | 20 5/8 | 21 | 18 5/8 | 22 | 4 4/8 | 4 3/8 | 7 | 8 | 20 1/8 | 520 | 108 |
| | *Lewis County / Unknown / Robert E. Shirer / PR 1960* | | | | | | | | | | |
| 23 1/8 | 22 1/8 | 21 2/8 | 18 3/8 | 21 4/8 | 4 3/8 | 4 2/8 | 5 | 4 | 1 2/8 | 521 | 109 |
| | *Pierce County / Robert J. Keeley / Robert J. Keeley / 1968* | | | | | | | | | | |
| 22 6/8 | 19 6/8 | 20 1/8 | 14 4/8 | 17 1/8 | 3 6/8 | 3 6/8 | 4 | 5 | | 522 | 110 |
| | *Jefferson County / Ralph E. Wean / Ralph E. Wean / 1987* | | | | | | | | | | |
| 22 3/8 | 18 | 16 6/8 | 14 1/8 | 16 7/8 | 5 | 4 6/8 | 5 | 5 | | 524 | 111 |
| | *Pierce County / Guy A. Hanson / Guy A. Hanson / 1984* | | | | | | | | | | |
| 22 2/8 | 22 | 21 5/8 | 16 4/8 | 18 1/8 | 4 1/8 | 4 1/8 | 4 | 4 | | 526 | 112 |
| | *King County / Russell L. McKinnon / Russell L. McKinnon / 1987* | | | | | | | | | | |

**BRITISH COLUMBIA PROVINCE RECORD**
**COLUMBIA BLACKTAIL DEER**
**SCORE: 153-7/8**
Locality: Cultus Lake    Date: September 1983
Hunter: Steven R. Rupp

# BRITISH COLUMBIA
## COLUMBIA BLACKTAIL DEER

| Score | Length of Main Beam R | L | Inside Spread | Greatest Spread | Circumference at Smallest Place Between Burr and First Point R | L | Number of Points R | L | Total of Lengths Abnormal Points | All-Time Rank | Prov. Rank |
|---|---|---|---|---|---|---|---|---|---|---|---|
| | ◆ Locality Killed / By Whom Killed / Owner / Date Killed | | | | | | | | | | |
| 153 7/8 | 21 4/8 | 21 6/8 | 18 1/8 | 22 | 4 2/8 | 4 2/8 | 5 | 5 | | 54 | 1 |
| | ◆ Cultus Lake / Steven R. Rupp / Steven R. Rupp / 1983 | | | | | | | | | | |
| 152 1/8 | 20 4/8 | 21 1/8 | 17 4/8 | 23 1/8 | 5 5/8 | 5 7/8 | 7 | 6 | 8 3/8 | 62 | 2 |
| | ◆ Pemberton / Jim Decker / Jim Decker / 1968 | | | | | | | | | | |
| 145 2/8 | 22 5/8 | 17 5/8 | 17 2/8 | 20 6/8 | 4 | 4 | 4 | 4 | | 138 | 3 |
| | ◆ Lake Harrison / Lloyd L. Ward, Jr. / Lloyd L. Ward, Jr. / 1947 | | | | | | | | | | |
| 143 6/8 | 19 3/8 | 20 2/8 | 16 | 18 2/8 | 4 6/8 | 4 7/8 | 5 | 5 | | 170 | 4 |
| | ◆ Squamish / B. Miller / B. Miller / 1962 | | | | | | | | | | |
| 143 3/8 | 20 | 20 1/8 | 15 3/8 | 17 1/8 | 4 7/8 | 4 7/8 | 5 | 5 | | 181 | 5 |
| | ◆ Chehalis River / Clair A. Howard / Clair A. Howard / 1971 | | | | | | | | | | |
| 143 2/8 | 20 6/8 | 19 6/8 | 19 | 23 | 4 7/8 | 6 2/8 | 7 | 6 | 7 2/8 | 182 | 6 |
| | ◆ Jones Lake / James Haslam / James Haslam / 1967 | | | | | | | | | | |
| 142 4/8 | 18 3/8 | 18 3/8 | 15 | 20 2/8 | 4 5/8 | 4 6/8 | 5 | 5 | | 199 | 7 |
| | ◆ Chilliwack / Frank Rosenauer / Frank Rosenauer / 1967 | | | | | | | | | | |
| 141 3/8 | 19 6/8 | 19 7/8 | 17 6/8 | 22 5/8 | 4 7/8 | 4 6/8 | 7 | 6 | 4 3/8 | 226 | 8 |
| | ◆ Harrison Lake / D. Harrison / D. Harrison / 1963 | | | | | | | | | | |
| 138 6/8 | 20 2/8 | 21 3/8 | 15 4/8 | 18 5/8 | 4 5/8 | 4 5/8 | 5 | 5 | | 296 | 9 |
| | ◆ Chipmunk Creek / Larri H. Woodrow / Larri H. Woodrow / 1987 | | | | | | | | | | |
| 137 7/8 | 20 5/8 | 20 5/8 | 16 6/8 | 20 2/8 | 4 5/8 | 4 6/8 | 6 | 5 | 2 3/8 | 318 | 10 |
| | ◆ Vancouver Island / Gordie Simpson / Gordie Simpson / 1966 | | | | | | | | | | |
| 137 3/8 | 23 6/8 | 23 6/8 | 17 3/8 | 19 3/8 | 4 1/8 | 4 2/8 | 4 | 4 | | 327 | 11 |
| | ◆ Vancouver Island / Herb Klein / Herb Klein / 1964 | | | | | | | | | | |
| 135 7/8 | 18 5/8 | 19 1/8 | 15 7/8 | 18 6/8 | 4 2/8 | 4 2/8 | 5 | 5 | | 360 | 12 |
| | ◆ Langley / Charles R. Yeomans / James G. Hill / 1959 | | | | | | | | | | |

| Score | Length of Main Beam R | Length of Main Beam L | Inside Spread | Greatest Spread | Circumference at Smallest Place Between Burr and First Point R | Circumference at Smallest Place Between Burr and First Point L | Number of Points R | Number of Points L | Total of Lengths Abnormal Points | All-Time Rank | Prov. Rank |
|---|---|---|---|---|---|---|---|---|---|---|---|
| | ◆ *Locality Killed / By Whom Killed / Owner / Date Killed* | | | | | | | | | | |
| 135 ⁶⁄₈ | 21 ⅛ | 21 ⅛ | 18 ²⁄₈ | 20 ⅞ | 4 ⅞ | 4 ⅞ | 5 | 5 | | 364 | 13 |
| | ◆ *Powell River / Paddy Price / Duncan Formby / 1939* | | | | | | | | | | |
| 134 ³⁄₈ | 21 ³⁄₈ | 21 ²⁄₈ | 19 ⅞ | 22 ³⁄₈ | 4 ⅝ | 4 ⅞ | 5 | 5 | | 395 | 14 |
| | ◆ *Toba Inlet / L. Mitchell / Peters Sport Shop / 1962* | | | | | | | | | | |
| 133 ⅛ | 18 ²⁄₈ | 18 ⅝ | 13 ⅝ | 16 ³⁄₈ | 4 ²⁄₈ | 4 ⅛ | 5 | 5 | | 433 | 15 |
| | ◆ *Langley / Frank Jackson / Brooke Whitelaw / 1935* | | | | | | | | | | |

Photograph courtesy of John P. Morton

John P. Morton with a very symmetrical Columbia blacktail deer from California. This buck scores 136 points final score and was taken in the Trinity Alps Wilderness Area of Northern California in 1987.

Photograph by Wm. H. Nesbitt

**ALASKA STATE RECORD**
**WORLD'S RECORD**
**SITKA BLACKTAIL DEER**
**SCORE: 128**
Locality: Kodiak Island    Date: 1985
Hunter: Unknown
Owner: Craig Allen

# ALASKA

## SITKA BLACKTAIL DEER

| Score ♦ Locality Killed / By Whom Killed / Owner / Date Killed | Length of Main Beam R | L | Inside Spread | Greatest Spread | Circumference at Smallest Place Between Burr and First Point R | L | Number of Points R | L | Total of Lengths Abnormal Points | All-Time Rank | State Rank |
|---|---|---|---|---|---|---|---|---|---|---|---|
| 28 | 19 6/8 | 19 | 19 4/8 | 21 3/8 | 4 7/8 | 4 7/8 | 5 | 5 | | 1 | 1 |
| ♦ Kodiak Island / Unknown / Craig Allen / 1985 | | | | | | | | | | | |
| 26 3/8 | 18 5/8 | 19 4/8 | 14 5/8 | 16 5/8 | 4 | 4 1/8 | 5 | 5 | | 2 | 2 |
| ♦ Sunny Hay Mt. / Harry R. Horner / Harry R. Horner / 1987 | | | | | | | | | | | |
| 26 2/8 | 19 6/8 | 20 3/8 | 16 3/8 | 18 4/8 | 4 5/8 | 4 4/8 | 5 | 6 | 3 5/8 | 3 | 3 |
| ♦ Control Lake / William B. Steele, Jr. / William B. Steele, Jr. / 1987 | | | | | | | | | | | |
| 25 7/8 | 17 7/8 | 18 6/8 | 13 5/8 | 16 1/8 | 4 | 4 | 4 | 4 | | 4 | 4 |
| ♦ Tenakee Inlet / Donald E. Thompson / Donald E. Thompson / 1964 | | | | | | | | | | | |
| 24 2/8 | 19 1/8 | 18 2/8 | 14 4/8 | 16 6/8 | 4 3/8 | 4 | 5 | 5 | | 5 | 5 |
| ♦ Exchange Cove / Daniel J. Leo / Daniel J. Leo / 1986 | | | | | | | | | | | |
| 23 4/8 | 21 4/8 | 20 3/8 | 17 6/8 | 19 7/8 | 3 6/8 | 3 6/8 | 4 | 4 | | 6 | 6 |
| ♦ Uganik Bay / Donna D. Braendel / Donna D. Braendel / 1983 | | | | | | | | | | | |
| 23 2/8 | 18 4/8 | 18 3/8 | 14 4/8 | 16 | 4 3/8 | 4 1/8 | 5 | 5 | | 7 | 7 |
| ♦ Prince of Wales Island / Kenneth W. Twitchell / Kenneth W. Twitchell / 1987 | | | | | | | | | | | |
| 20 4/8 | 18 4/8 | 16 1/8 | 14 6/8 | 17 5/8 | 3 7/8 | 4 1/8 | 5 | 5 | | 8 | 8 |
| ♦ Cleveland Pen. / Dennis E. Northrup / Dennis E. Northrup / 1986 | | | | | | | | | | | |
| 20 1/8 | 17 6/8 | 17 6/8 | 16 3/8 | 18 7/8 | 4 5/8 | 4 4/8 | 5 | 5 | | 9 | 9 |
| ♦ Halibut Bay / James W. Bickman / James W. Bickman / 1987 | | | | | | | | | | | |
| 18 5/8 | 17 | 16 6/8 | 15 1/8 | 17 5/8 | 3 7/8 | 3 7/8 | 5 | 5 | | 10 | 10 |
| ♦ Uganik Lake / Larry D. Leuenberger / Larry D. Leuenberger / 1985 | | | | | | | | | | | |
| 17 4/8 | 17 | 16 6/8 | 15 2/8 | 16 7/8 | 3 7/8 | 3 7/8 | 5 | 5 | | 11 | 11 |
| ♦ Shrubby Island / Alfred Oglend / Alfred Oglend / 1986 | | | | | | | | | | | |
| 17 1/8 | 16 4/8 | 16 4/8 | 13 1/8 | 15 6/8 | 4 1/8 | 4 2/8 | 5 | 6 | 2 2/8 | 12 | 12 |
| ♦ Baird Peak / William C. Dunham / William C. Dunham / 1984 | | | | | | | | | | | |
| 16 | 17 2/8 | 16 5/8 | 16 | 18 5/8 | 4 1/8 | 3 6/8 | 5 | 5 | | 13 | 13 |
| ♦ Kiliuda Bay / Timothy Tittle / Timothy Tittle / 1984 | | | | | | | | | | | |

| Score | Length of Main Beam R | L | Inside Spread | Greatest Spread | Circumference at Smallest Place Between Burr and First Point R | L | Number of Points R | L | Total of Lengths Abnormal Points | All-Time Rank | State Rank |
|---|---|---|---|---|---|---|---|---|---|---|---|
| | ◆ *Locality Killed / By Whom Killed / Owner / Date Killed* | | | | | | | | | | |
| 114 7/8 | 15 7/8 | 16 1/8 | 14 3/8 | 16 4/8 | 3 7/8 | 4 | 5 | 6 | 1 4/8 | 14 | 14 |
| | ◆ *Control Lake / Timothy C. Winsenberg / Timothy C. Winsenberg / 1985* | | | | | | | | | | |
| 114 7/8 | 17 7/8 | 19 1/8 | 17 5/8 | 19 3/8 | 4 2/8 | 4 | 5 | 5 | | 14 | 14 |
| | ◆ *Dall Island / Picked Up / Lynn W. Merrill / 1987* | | | | | | | | | | |
| 114 | 15 7/8 | 16 | 13 6/8 | 17 3/8 | 4 | 3 7/8 | 5 | 5 | | 16 | 16 |
| | ◆ *Olga Bay / Frank E. Entsminger / Frank E. Entsminger / 1986* | | | | | | | | | | |
| 113 6/8 | 17 5/8 | 19 1/8 | 16 2/8 | 18 5/8 | 3 2/8 | 3 2/8 | 4 | 4 | | 17 | 17 |
| | ◆ *Long Island / Picked Up / Allan C. Merrill / 1987* | | | | | | | | | | |
| 113 4/8 | 18 4/8 | 18 1/8 | 15 4/8 | 19 | 3 5/8 | 3 4/8 | 4 | 4 | | 18 | 18 |
| | ◆ *Viekoda Bay / Edward R. Hajdys / Edward R. Hajdys / 1980* | | | | | | | | | | |
| 113 1/8 | 17 5/8 | 18 7/8 | 16 1/8 | 17 6/8 | 3 6/8 | 3 7/8 | 5 | 5 | | 19 | 19 |
| | ◆ *Wadding Cove / Kurt W. Kuehl / Kurt W. Kuehl / 1984* | | | | | | | | | | |
| 112 3/8 | 18 2/8 | 17 7/8 | 17 5/8 | 19 4/8 | 3 5/8 | 4 | 7 | 6 | 4 4/8 | 20 | 20 |
| | ◆ *Alder Creek / Richard L. Reeves / Richard L. Reeves / 1988* | | | | | | | | | | |
| 112 2/8 | 19 | 19 2/8 | 16 4/8 | 18 2/8 | 4 3/8 | 4 2/8 | 4 | 4 | | 21 | 21 |
| | ◆ *Olga Bay / John D. Frost / John D. Frost / 1987* | | | | | | | | | | |
| 112 1/8 | 17 | 16 2/8 | 15 5/8 | 18 | 4 1/8 | 4 | 5 | 5 | | 22 | 22 |
| | ◆ *Alitak Bay / Dale J. Bunnage / Dale J. Bunnage / 1988* | | | | | | | | | | |
| 111 7/8 | 18 5/8 | 18 6/8 | 15 5/8 | 18 | 4 2/8 | 4 1/8 | 4 | 5 | | 23 | 23 |
| | ◆ *Uganik Bay / Jeff A. Buffum / Jeff A. Buffum / 1987* | | | | | | | | | | |
| 111 3/8 | 18 | 17 6/8 | 16 3/8 | 18 4/8 | 4 | 3 7/8 | 5 | 5 | | 24 | 24 |
| | ◆ *Spiridon Lake / David H. Raskey / David H. Raskey / 1986* | | | | | | | | | | |
| 111 | 16 3/8 | 16 5/8 | 14 2/8 | 16 7/8 | 3 6/8 | 3 7/8 | 5 | 5 | | 25 | 25 |
| | ◆ *Karluk Lake / Ted H. Spraker / Ted H. Spraker / 1983* | | | | | | | | | | |
| 110 3/8 | 16 5/8 | 17 | 13 7/8 | 16 2/8 | 3 3/8 | 3 4/8 | 5 | 5 | | 26 | 26 |
| | ◆ *Hidden Basin / Don J. Edwards / Don J. Edwards / 1987* | | | | | | | | | | |
| 110 1/8 | 19 | 18 6/8 | 15 4/8 | 17 4/8 | 3 7/8 | 4 | 6 | 6 | 6 7/8 | 27 | 27 |
| | ◆ *Outlet Cape / Henry T. Hamelin / Henry T. Hamelin / 1981* | | | | | | | | | | |
| 109 6/8 | 17 7/8 | 17 3/8 | 14 4/8 | 16 4/8 | 4 3/8 | 4 4/8 | 5 | 5 | | 28 | 28 |
| | ◆ *Cleveland Pen. / Dennis E. Northrup / Dennis E. Northrup / 1983* | | | | | | | | | | |
| 109 5/8 | 17 1/8 | 17 | 15 1/8 | 17 1/8 | 3 5/8 | 3 3/8 | 5 | 5 | | 29 | 29 |
| | ◆ *Terror Bay / Christopher L. Linford / Christopher L. Linford / 1987* | | | | | | | | | | |
| 109 4/8 | 19 | 17 7/8 | 17 2/8 | 19 1/8 | 3 6/8 | 3 7/8 | 4 | 4 | | 30 | 30 |
| | ◆ *Uganik Bay / Harvey D. Harms / Harvey D. Harms / 1982* | | | | | | | | | | |

| Score | Length of Main Beam R | L | Inside Spread | Greatest Spread | Circumference at Smallest Place Between Burr and First Point R | L | Number of Points R | L | Total of Lengths Abnormal Points | All-Time Rank | State Rank |
|---|---|---|---|---|---|---|---|---|---|---|---|
| 109 2/8 | 18 2/8 | 18 2/8 | 15 2/8 | 17 | 4 | 4 | 4 | 4 | | 31 | 31 |
| ♦ Olga Bay / David G. Kelleyhouse / David G. Kelleyhouse / 1987 | | | | | | | | | | | |
| 109 1/8 | 18 4/8 | 18 7/8 | 14 7/8 | 16 5/8 | 3 7/8 | 3 7/8 | 5 | 5 | | 32 | 32 |
| ♦ Kupreanof Pen. / John B. Murray / John B. Murray / 1982 | | | | | | | | | | | |
| 109 1/8 | 18 3/8 | 18 | 16 7/8 | 19 | 4 | 3 6/8 | 5 | 5 | | 32 | 32 |
| ♦ Ugak Bay / Donald H. Tetzlaff / Donald H. Tetzlaff / 1984 | | | | | | | | | | | |
| 109 | 17 4/8 | 16 5/8 | 16 4/8 | 19 7/8 | 4 | 4 | 5 | 5 | | 34 | 34 |
| ♦ Uganik Bay / Karl G. Braendel / Karl G. Braendel / 1982 | | | | | | | | | | | |
| 109 | 17 | 17 4/8 | 15 2/8 | 17 3/8 | 4 | 4 | 5 | 5 | | 34 | 34 |
| ♦ Kodiak Island / D. Roger Liebner / D. Roger Liebner / 1983 | | | | | | | | | | | |
| 109 | 17 7/8 | 18 | 15 | 17 1/8 | 4 1/8 | 4 | 5 | 5 | | 34 | 34 |
| ♦ Dall Island / Sharla L. Merrill / Sharla L. Merrill / 1985 | | | | | | | | | | | |
| 109 | 15 5/8 | 16 | 15 6/8 | 18 4/8 | 3 6/8 | 3 5/8 | 5 | 5 | | 34 | 34 |
| ♦ Terror Bay / John R. Odom III / John R. Odom III / 1985 | | | | | | | | | | | |
| 108 6/8 | 17 2/8 | 17 3/8 | 15 4/8 | 17 4/8 | 3 4/8 | 3 6/8 | 5 | 5 | | 38 | 38 |
| ♦ Barling Bay / Guy C. Powell / Guy C. Powell / 1984 | | | | | | | | | | | |
| 108 4/8 | 19 3/8 | 19 6/8 | 15 | 16 4/8 | 4 | 4 | 4 | 4 | | 39 | 39 |
| ♦ Cleveland Pen. / Dennis E. Northrup / Dennis E. Northrup / 1985 | | | | | | | | | | | |
| 108 2/8 | 18 7/8 | 19 2/8 | 15 7/8 | 17 1/8 | 4 4/8 | 4 7/8 | 7 | 5 | 8 3/8 | 40 | 40 |
| ♦ Whale Passage / Howard W. Honsey / Howard W. Honsey / 1985 | | | | | | | | | | | |
| 108 | 16 6/8 | 17 3/8 | 14 4/8 | 16 4/8 | 3 6/8 | 3 6/8 | 5 | 5 | | 41 | 41 |
| ♦ Kizhuyak Bay / Gene D. Carter / Gene D. Carter / 1987 | | | | | | | | | | | |
| 107 2/8 | 17 | 17 1/8 | 16 | 17 7/8 | 3 7/8 | 4 | 4 | 5 | | 42 | 42 |
| ♦ Uganik Bay / Robert C. Jones / Robert C. Jones / 1987 | | | | | | | | | | | |
| 107 | 17 | 17 | 16 6/8 | 18 | 3 6/8 | 4 | 5 | 5 | | 43 | 43 |
| ♦ Kodiak Island / Andrew G. Johnson / Andrew G. Johnson / 1986 | | | | | | | | | | | |
| 104 4/8 | 16 6/8 | 15 5/8 | 15 4/8 | 17 2/8 | 3 5/8 | 3 4/8 | 5 | 4 | 1 | 44 | 44 |
| ♦ Malina Bay / Thomas A. Ray / Thomas A. Ray / 1981 | | | | | | | | | | | |
| 104 2/8 | 15 4/8 | 15 4/8 | 15 4/8 | 17 4/8 | 4 | 3 7/8 | 5 | 5 | | 45 | 45 |
| ♦ Uganik Bay / John A. Miller / John A. Miller / 1984 | | | | | | | | | | | |
| 104 | 17 3/8 | 17 2/8 | 15 6/8 | 17 4/8 | 3 3/8 | 3 5/8 | 5 | 5 | | 46 | 46 |
| ♦ Kodiak Island / Robert C. Jones / Robert C. Jones / 1987 | | | | | | | | | | | |
| 103 | 17 1/8 | 17 6/8 | 17 6/8 | 19 4/8 | 3 7/8 | 3 5/8 | 4 | 4 | | 47 | 47 |
| ♦ Viekoda Bay / Forrest E. Weiant / Forrest E. Weiant / 1984 | | | | | | | | | | | |

| Score | Length of Main Beam R | L | Inside Spread | Greatest Spread | Circumference at Smallest Place Between Burr and First Point R | L | Number of Points R | L | Total of Lengths Abnormal Points | All-Time Rank | State Rank |
|---|---|---|---|---|---|---|---|---|---|---|---|
| | | | | | | | | | | | |
| *Locality Killed / By Whom Killed / Owner / Date Killed* | | | | | | | | | | | |
| 102 6/8 | 17 | 16 7/8 | 15 4/8 | 20 2/8 | 3 5/8 | 3 6/8 | 4 | 4 | | 48 | 48 |
| ◆ *Browns Lagoon / Charles R. Price / Charles R. Price / 1986* | | | | | | | | | | | |
| 102 3/8 | 17 6/8 | 16 2/8 | 14 5/8 | 17 | 3 6/8 | 3 4/8 | 5 | 5 | | 49 | 49 |
| ◆ *Uyak Bay / Toby J. Johnson / Toby J. Johnson / 1987* | | | | | | | | | | | |
| 102 2/8 | 16 | 16 1/8 | 15 4/8 | 18 7/8 | 3 4/8 | 3 4/8 | 6 | 5 | 3 | 50 | 50 |
| ◆ *Kodiak Island / John H. Saunby / John H. Saunby / 1983* | | | | | | | | | | | |
| 101 6/8 | 18 | 17 3/8 | 15 | 17 4/8 | 3 5/8 | 3 5/8 | 5 | 4 | | 51 | 51 |
| ◆ *Karluk Lake / Randy S. Shumate / Randy S. Shumate / 1988* | | | | | | | | | | | |
| 100 1/8 | 16 3/8 | 16 5/8 | 13 5/8 | 15 6/8 | 4 | 4 3/8 | 4 | 4 | | 52 | 52 |
| ◆ *Viekoda Bay / Forrest E. Weiant / Forrest E. Weiant / 1985* | | | | | | | | | | | |
| 131 5/8 | 19 2/8 | 20 5/8 | 16 5/8 | 19 1/8 | 5 | 4 5/8 | 7 | 6 | 8 2/8 | * | * |
| ◆ *Luck Lake / Picked Up / Ronald L. Sowards / 1982* | | | | | | | | | | | |
| 120 3/8 | 17 5/8 | 17 4/8 | 15 7/8 | 18 4/8 | 4 4/8 | 4 3/8 | 5 | 5 | | * | * |
| ◆ *Boulder Bay / Ronald D. Swingle / Ronald D. Swingle / 1983* | | | | | | | | | | | |
| 119 5/8 | 18 7/8 | 19 6/8 | 14 7/8 | 16 7/8 | 3 6/8 | 4 2/8 | 4 | 5 | | * | * |
| ◆ *Coffman Cove / Gary R. Dilley / Gary R. Dilley / 1987* | | | | | | | | | | | |
| 118 3/8 | 17 5/8 | 19 2/8 | 17 3/8 | 19 4/8 | 4 1/8 | 4 2/8 | 5 | 5 | | * | * |
| ◆ *Uganik Lake / Robert D. Gilliland / Robert D. Gilliland / 1983* | | | | | | | | | | | |
| 118 1/8 | 16 7/8 | 17 2/8 | 14 1/8 | 16 1/8 | 4 | 4 2/8 | 5 | 5 | | * | * |
| ◆ *Long Island / Daniel G. Bowden / Daniel G. Bowden / 1981* | | | | | | | | | | | |
| 112 7/8 | 17 | 18 | 15 1/8 | 17 5/8 | 3 6/8 | 3 6/8 | 5 | 5 | | * | * |
| ◆ *Kodiak Island / Gene Coughlin / Gene Coughlin / 1984* | | | | | | | | | | | |
| 112 4/8 | 17 6/8 | 17 3/8 | 16 | 18 1/8 | 3 7/8 | 4 1/8 | 5 | 5 | | * | * |
| ◆ *Prince of Wales Island / William H. Welton / William H. Welton / 1988* | | | | | | | | | | | |
| 112 2/8 | 17 5/8 | 17 4/8 | 16 4/8 | 18 6/8 | 4 1/8 | 3 7/8 | 5 | 5 | | * | * |
| ◆ *Uganik Lake / George W. Gozelski / George W. Gozelski / 1983* | | | | | | | | | | | |
| 111 3/8 | 18 | 17 5/8 | 15 5/8 | 18 7/8 | 4 | 4 1/8 | 5 | 4 | | * | * |
| ◆ *Uyak Bay / Charlie W. Hastings / Charlie W. Hastings / 1986* | | | | | | | | | | | |
| 110 5/8 | 19 1/8 | 18 2/8 | 15 5/8 | 17 4/8 | 3 6/8 | 3 7/8 | 4 | 5 | | * | * |
| ◆ *Afognak Island / Dale W. Grove / Dale W. Grove / 1987* | | | | | | | | | | | |
| 109 2/8 | 16 | 17 6/8 | 15 2/8 | 18 4/8 | 3 6/8 | 3 5/8 | 6 | 5 | 1 | * | * |
| ◆ *Uyak Bay / Bradley A. Pope / Bradley A. Pope / 1986* | | | | | | | | | | | |

Photograph courtesy of Allan C. Merrill

Sharla L. Merrill was hunting with her father when she took this Sitka blacktail deer in 1985 on Dall Island in southeastern Alaska. She was just nine years old at the time she took this trophy that scores 109 points.

This book was:

Compiled with able assistance of:
    Eugene C. Harter 3rd
    Carol A. Palmerino
    Margaret E. Sefchick

Book design and layout by:
    Wm. H. Nesbitt

Typesetting by systems designed by:
    Wm. H. Nesbitt

Printed and bound by:
    Haddon Craftsmen
    Scranton, PA

---